Interrogating Popular Culture

Interrogating Popular Culture: Key Questions offers an accessible introduction to the study of popular culture, both historical and contemporary. Beginning with the assumption that cultural systems are dynamic, contradictory, and hard to pin down, Stacy Takacs explores the field through a survey of important questions, addressing:

- *Definitions:* What is popular culture? How has it developed over time? What functions does it serve?

- *Method:* What is a proper object of study? How should we analyze and interpret popular texts and practices?

- *Influence:* How does popular culture relate to social power and control?

- *Identity and disposition:* How do we relate to popular culture? How does it move and connect us?

- *Environment:* How does popular culture shape the ways we think, feel, and act in the world?

Illustrated with a wide variety of case studies, covering everything from medieval spectacle to reality TV, sports fandom, and Youtube, *Interrogating Popular Culture* gives students a theoretically rich analytical toolkit for understanding the complex relationship between popular culture, identity, and society.

Stacy Takacs is Associate Professor and Director of American Studies at Oklahoma State University. She is also the author of *Terrorism TV: Popular Entertainment in Post-9/11 America*.

D0074235

Interrogating Popular Culture

Key Questions

Stacy Takacs

Routledge
Taylor & Francis Group

NEW YORK AND LONDON

First published 2015
by Routledge
711 Third Avenue, New York, NY 10017

and by Routledge
2 Park Square, Milton Park, Abingdon, Oxon OX14 4RN

Routledge is an imprint of the Taylor & Francis Group, an informa business

Library of Congress Cataloging-in-Publication Data

Takacs, Stacy.
  Interrogating popular culture : key questions / Stacy Takacs.
    pages cm
  Includes bibliographical references and index.
 1. Popular culture—Study and teaching. 2. Culture—Study and
teaching. 3. Mass media—Study and teaching. I. Title.
  HM623.T335 2015
  306.07—dc23
  2014010938

ISBN: 978-0-415-84118-4 (hbk)
ISBN: 978-0-415-84119-1 (pbk)
ISBN: 978-0-203-76658-3 (ebk)

Typeset in Stone Serif
by Apex CoVantage, LLC

Printed and bound in the United States of America by
Edwards Brothers Malloy on sustainably sourced paper

For Betsy, always

CONTENTS

LIST OF FIGURES

PREFACE

This text is designed to introduce students to the study of popular culture. It begins from the assumption that cultural systems are dynamic and contradictory, rather than static and coherent. They do not stand still long enough for us to say anything definitive about them. Thus, instead of attempting a comprehensive survey of the field—a nearly impossible task—this book takes a more interrogative approach. It is organized around a series of questions that scholars in a variety of disciplines have brought to the study of popular culture. The questions are broad and provide an opportunity to survey a range of possible theoretical and methodological responses. They include questions of *definition* (What is popular culture? How has it developed over time? What functions does it serve?), of *method* (What is the proper object of study? How should we analyze and interpret popular texts and practices?), of *influence* (How does popular culture relate to social power and control?), of *identity and disposition* (How do we relate to popular culture? How does it move and connect us?), and of *environment* (How does popular culture shape the ways we think, feel, and act in the world?)

I chose this approach for several reasons. One, it models the process-oriented, reflexive reasoning strategies identified with "critical thinking." Critical thinking is less about acquiring information than learning to ask good questions, weigh the merits of the resulting answers, and make a case for one's beliefs based on the evidence. The chapters in this book are designed to model such thinking-in-action. Two, the emphasis on questions, rather than answers, is a tacit reminder that the meanings, uses, and pleasures of popular culture are always context-specific. If sense is being made, it is being made in a particular way, as a response to particular circumstances, which ought to be investigated. By starting with questions, we avoid imposing our assumptions and biases on these encounters. Finally, the interrogative design lends the text a certain modularity, which invites students and instructors to supplement and remix the contents as they see fit. Drawing lessons from popular culture itself, I have tried to provide multiple points of entry into the subject matter and to encourage methodological experimentation, critique, and play. I want users to value the text and spread its insights in new directions through their own analytical practices. Thus, I have tried to make its design as **producerly** (i.e., open to appropriation) as possible.

While the text surveys a range of approaches to popular culture, it favors a cultural studies approach, which emphasizes the tension between the social institutions who produce cultural resources and the people who use them. It will assume there are agents on both ends of these processes, and that these agents have agendas they wish to articulate in and through their cultural practices. It will treat popular culture as a vital resource for the creation of social meanings, identities, and affiliations, and it will foreground the instances of power, resistance, and negotiation that take place through the creation, appropriation, and use of cultural forms. In short, it will view popular culture as an essential part of the structure of complex societies, and it will pay as much attention to these social relations as it does to the meanings and pleasures of the forms themselves. At the end of the journey, students should possess a set of theoretical and methodological tools they can use to conduct their own situated investigations of, and interventions into, the field of popular culture.

ACKNOWLEDGMENTS

I thank the editors at Routledge who helped bring this book to fruition, particularly Erica Wetter and Simon Jacobs. The comments from the anonymous reviewers were invaluable in shaping the final text and enhancing several of the arguments, so I also extend my gratitude to them. I want to thank Alison Bechdel (of *Dykes to Watch Out For*) and Maki Nora (of the online comic Sc.I.eN.Ce; http://sci-ence.org/on-playing-well-with-others/) for permission to reprint their wonderful comics. Kudos, as well, to Andrew Slack and Paul DeGeorge at the Harry Potter Alliance for their good works and for allowing me to grab a few frames from their cheeky web series "Harry Potter and the Dark Lord Waldemart" (2006).

Tony Harkins, Emily Satterwhite, and the audience who participated in the roundtable on "Teaching Introductory Popular Culture" at the 2013 Popular Culture Association Conference helped me clarify a number of things regarding the content and organization of this text. Oklahoma State University provided various forms of support for the development of this book, including a much-appreciated sabbatical. I would like to thank my colleagues in the American Studies Program, the Gender and Women's Studies Program, and the Departments of English and History for their long-term support. Special recognition goes to Lu Bailey, Laura Belmonte, Carol Mason, and Carol Moder for emotional support; Nicole Lupardus for research support; and John Kinder and David Gray, who vetted many of the chapters in this book and provided invaluable commentary. This book is much better for having been touched by all of you.

CHAPTER 1

What Is Popular Culture?

If you were to look up the word "culture" in the dictionary, you would be confronted with a variety of conflicting meanings. Used as a verb, the term refers to a process of growth or development. Microbiologists use it to refer to the growth of a substance in a catalytic medium. Thus, an epidemiologist might "culture" (grow) a sample of bacteria taken from a hospital patient to determine the cause of an ailment. Agronomists (scientists who study crop production) might use the word as a synonym for "cultivation," the growing of plants for food and fuel. Beginning in the eighteenth century, social theorists applied the term to the growth or development of the human mind, but, in doing so, they slightly shifted the meaning and function of the term. Culture became less the *process* of "cultivation" than the set of tools necessary to achieve it or the state of having achieved it. In other words, culture went from being used as a verb to being used as a noun or an adjective. Thus we arrive at definitions like this:

> *Culture:* **1a.** the arts and other manifestations of human intellectual achievement regarded collectively (*a city lacking in culture*). **b.** a refined understanding of this; intellectual development (*a person of culture*). **2.** the customs, civilization, and achievements of a particular time or people.[1]

In the nineteenth century, to be "cultured" meant to be familiar with "the best that has been thought and said." This is the message of British scholar Matthew Arnold's famous work *Culture and Anarchy* (1869), whose title suggests one of the presumed uses of cultural knowledge—to ameliorate social conflict by providing a shared set of meanings and ideals. For Arnold, culture could *prevent* anarchy, and he believed that enculturation, the intellectual project to spread cultural knowledge, was a sacred duty of the already cultivated. "[Culture] seeks to do away with classes," he said, "to make the best that has been thought and known in the world current everywhere; to make all men live in an atmosphere of sweetness and light, where they may use ideas . . . freely—nourished and not bound by them." To Arnold, "the men of culture are the true apostles of equality" because they provide the lower classes with the tools (cultural knowledge) to achieve a higher quality of life (though not necessarily a higher standard of living).[2]

Needless to say, "equality" for Arnold meant training people to enjoy the things that he and his social ilk already liked. It was less a democratic project than a paternalistic one that imagined "the people" as children in need of intellectual, emotional, and moral guidance. Arnold's culture was an **elite culture** fashioned in opposition to "the people," whose spirit and energy were thought to derive from nature and, thus, to require the exercise of social control. This identification of culture with a narrow slice of social experience—the "high" arts and intellectual pursuits of (mostly) European nation-states—came under increasing scrutiny in the late nineteenth century for being value-laden and unnecessarily restrictive. The first blow to this definition of culture was struck by newly empowered social groups—the working classes, women, and peoples of color—who sought to contest the political status quo and their exclusion from the benefits of so-called civilization. These groups created their own cultural formations to challenge the depiction of themselves as embodiments of "nature" and "anarchy." New songs, newspapers, protest rituals, and other social customs gave voice to the identities and allegiances of these groups and expressed (sometimes eloquently, sometimes vulgarly) their opposition to elite culture and the power it defended.[3] The existence of these groups and their cultural formations mandated a reconsideration of the meaning of culture, for, clearly, cultural forms and practices were being used for a social project, but not exactly the project Arnold had in mind.

The new academic discipline of anthropology (established in the late nineteenth century) also played a role in expanding the definition of culture. Anthropologists working with so-called primitive societies in Africa and the Americas offered evidence that these societies were not devoid of culture or civilization. It was true that they ate different foods, spoke different languages, and worshipped different gods, but they had highly elaborated social systems, and these were held together by shared texts, symbols, rituals, and practices. While accepting the Arnoldian notion that culture serves a socializing function, anthropologists rejected the value-laden assumption that one type of culture was better than another. Instead, they embraced a conception of culture as "that complex whole which includes knowledge, belief, art, morals, law, custom, and any other capabilities and habits acquired by man as a member of society."[4]

While this anthropological definition of culture as "a whole way of life"[5] has increasingly displaced the model of culture as the "best that has been known and thought," debates still rage over the meaning and importance of culture in modern societies. Older notions of culture as tradition and the high arts persist, for example, in conservative calls to revive courses in "Western Civilization" or the "Great Books" in the United States and Europe.[6] Citizenship tests assess the cultural knowledge of the foreign-born before admitting them fully into the national public, and, even then, expressions of cultural difference, like wearing a veil in the US, may lead some to suspect a citizen's "true" allegiance. Yet, even as culture is used to police the boundaries of identity, capitalism makes such boundaries increasingly blurry. The promise of profit has encouraged people the world over to transform their cultural traditions into commodities that can be bought and sold on the internet, making the idea of a fixed, homogenous, or "pure" culture feel more and more absurd in practice.

Still, we cling to the notion of culture as an explanatory tool. Today we speak of a "culture of poverty," "corporate culture," "youth culture," "American culture," "Latino culture," "virtual culture," and so on. What these uses share is a sense that culture—whatever objects or practices it may consist of—serves a social function: it identifies and locates one as a member of a group. As **cultural studies** scholar John Fiske puts it, "[culture is] the active process of generating and circulating meanings and pleasures within a social system."[7]

This definition contains two key insights worth developing further. First, it identifies culture as a process we participate in, rather than a static body of knowledge we possess (or fail to possess). The objective of cultural study is not to identify and transmit "the best that has been known and thought," but to assess how and why particular types of thoughts and actions occur as they do in a given society. How does a society arrange the world in a certain way and then explain that arrangement to itself and others? What meanings and pleasures are shared among the members of that group? Which are contested? How do these contests help identify the boundaries, or limits, of community? The focus of analysis is less on *what* is known, than on *how* it is known. The second insight is that culture is collective by definition; it is a *shared* system of meanings and pleasures (or pains). Indeed, *culture is constitutive of society.* We require shared systems of meaning—cultural systems—to communicate with one another and negotiate the distribution of social resources. We cannot know or understand the world without these systems of meaning. Language, for example, is a cultural system that enables us to understand and convey our needs and desires to each other. We literally cannot know the world except through language, and differences in language may construct different views of the same world.

For example, Hmong societies refer to "epilepsy" as *qaug dab peg,* which translates roughly as "the spirit catches you and you fall down." The difference here is not just the difference between scientific explanation and superstition, knowledge and belief. It entails a different perspective on the status and treatment of afflicted individuals. Western doctors tend to treat the symptoms apart from the emotional and psychic health of the subject. Because Hmong healers view illness as a spiritual issue, they treat the body, soul, and life circumstances of both the individual and her family. What has caused the individual's soul to flee or to be stolen? How might the family arrange things around the individual so that it doesn't happen again? Epilepsy involves much more than a broken synapse or chemical imbalance for the Hmong. Moreover, the different language entails a different perspective on the capabilities of the individual. Hmong do not view epilepsy as a "disease" or a "handicap" but as a "gift." Epileptics are endowed with the ability to cross between the spiritual and physical realms, and they are often assigned high social standing (often as shamans, or healers) because of this talent. Thus, linguistic differences embody cultural differences, which, in turn, create different experiences of the world.[8] And, lest we think the Western way is better because it is based on science, note that the valuation of science over belief is itself an act of world-shaping. It is a cultural belief that entails certain social priorities and arrangements of resources. In the US we devote billions of dollars to scientific research, but very little to religious research. We take our ailments to doctors, rather than priests. These are choices, and, as such, they may be made differently, but different choices would lead to a fundamentally different sort of society. Thus, culture constructs, or constitutes, society.

To summarize, "[culture is] the active process of generating and circulating meanings and pleasures within a social system." Every social system requires a system of meanings and values (i.e., culture) to guide its members and help them communicate with one another. In a familiar phrase, culture acts as "the glue that holds societies together." This does not mean its only function is to build consensus, however. As we will see, culture is a terrain of struggle. As a process, it is never fixed or completed; the terms, beliefs, values, and assumptions that guide a society are always subject to negotiation and renegotiation, and a lot of the power struggles in our societies are cultural struggles.

WHAT IS POPULAR CULTURE?

This text is concerned with **popular culture**, a subset of culture whose boundaries are difficult to identify because they are fashioned in practice. As you might expect, there is some debate about how best to define this term, as well. Some theorists define popular culture based on a numerical calculation of popularity. Historian Lawrence Levine, for example, argues that popular culture is simply "culture that is popular; culture that is widely accessible and widely accessed; widely disseminated and widely viewed or heard or read."[9] This definition is simple and elegant to look at, but, in practice, it raises a number of questions. For one, how are we to distinguish between popular culture and culture proper according to this definition? For instance, language is widely accessible and widely accessed; does that make it a part of popular culture? Second, exactly how should we measure popularity? Should it refer to materials taken up by thousands, millions, tens of millions of people? Should the count begin and end with a work's initial appearance, or should we consider its lifetime popularity? Would a novel like James Joyce's *Ulysses* (1918), a very difficult text that requires specialized knowledge and training to decipher, suddenly qualify as "popular" because millions of university students have been forced to read it for literature class? And, if *Ulysses* qualifies, what is the difference between high, or elite, culture and popular culture? Likewise, would a US television program canceled after only two episodes qualify as popular just because the structure of the US TV industry ensures four million people will watch even the worst program options? What is the threshold of popularity? In the end, this definition fails to provide a workable set of criteria for distinguishing popular culture.

Another important strand of cultural theory suggests that popular culture is distinguished by its modes of production (commercial and industrial) and transmission (second-hand, over distances).[10] This body of theory, which we will call **critical theory,** often refers to popular culture as **mass culture** because it is mass-produced for commercial profit by centralized **cultural industries**. We will discuss this brand of theory in greater depth in Chapter 5, when we take up questions of power, but for now I want to emphasize two key assumptions underlying the theory. First, mass culture critics tend to assume that the mode of cultural production is the most important element of any study of popular culture, and thus they tend to ignore questions of reception and use. When they do discuss reception, they often do so in a deterministic fashion. For example, they might argue that the mass-produced Barbie doll carries with it a standardized image of femininity, which it then transmits to Barbie users. At best, mass culture theorists imagine Barbie-players to be passive recipients of messages embedded in the doll by its corporate maker (Mattel); at worst, Barbie-players are assumed to be dupes who irrationally embrace their own oppression. Either way the assumption is that standardized commodities lead inevitably to standardized uses and the standardization of human beings.

The assumption that production determines consumption carries with it second assumption about the relative quality of the cultural texts and practices under scrutiny. In a famous essay called "A Theory of Mass Culture" (1957), American cultural critic Dwight Macdonald argued that mass culture "really [was]n't culture at all" because it lacked any touch of originality.[11] Even bad art expresses the idiosyncratic "feelings, ideas, tastes, and visions" of a creator, he complained. Cultural industries, by contrast, rely on templates, molds, and formulas for their ideas and cater to the whims of the audience, rather than the artist. The result is not an expression of creativity or thought, but another widget cranked out by machine. Mass culture is not just different, according to Macdonald; it is deficient and dangerous. It dulls the mind and enslaves the populace; it turns men into masses, drones who not only lack individuality or agency but are all the happier for it.[12] Macdonald and other mass culture theorists also take pains to distinguish between mass culture and **folk culture**, which they view as an organic expression of a community that exists apart from the ruling powers (state or corporate). "Folk art grew mainly from below," Macdonald explains, and was "shaped by the people to fit their own needs." Mass culture, on the other hand, "is fabricated by technicians hired by businessmen" whose only interest is profit.[13] Unlike folk culture, which expresses the needs and desires of a people, mass culture expresses nothing but the profit motive that drives capitalism, or so these types of critics suggest.

Mass culture theorists certainly have a point when they note that cultural industries have an inordinate amount of power to create and circulate meanings in contemporary societies. They are not wrong to draw attention to the work of seriality and repetition in capitalist modes of cultural production (see Chapter 6), and they are right that the results can often be mind-numbing. Just think of the latest 1970s TV-show-turned-movie or the latest iteration in the *Transformers* film franchise, and you can see what they mean. They are also right to assert that folk production differs in form and function from this type of large-scale, industrial production. The problems arise in the application of the theory to actual cultural forms. Mass culture theory proclaims that culture is homogenizing and manipulative. Because of the circumstances of its production, it can never express the interests and desires of people. Thus, this theory cannot explain why some mass cultural texts fail to find an audience while others thrive. It cannot explain why people respond to some texts and ignore others. Finally, it cannot explain what drives cultural workers to join "the business." Are writers of popular fiction, directors of movies, or celebrity performers really just in it for the money? If they were, wouldn't it be easier to make a living in a more stable occupation? Moreover, what of the amateur producers who make and post cultural texts on blogs, fan fiction websites, and YouTube for free? Can the theory of mass culture explain Web 2.0? Surely popular agency—choice, desire, expression—has something to do with all of this, and mass culture theory simply makes no allowance for "the people" within the systems it describes.

This leads to a third way of understanding popular culture: as the expression of people's interests, choices, and activities. This method, called cultural studies, holds that people are active agents in the production of cultural meanings and pleasures and that they use the raw materials provided by the cultural industries to enact their agency. The "popular" of popular culture, in this case, refers to "people" (members of the populace) and the work they do to transform the cultural resources available in society into meaningful expressions of localized desire. For example, rather than focusing on the standardized form of the Barbie doll and arguing that it projects a standardized notion of femininity, cultural studies theorists might examine the ways people actually play with or use Barbie. Filmmaker Susan Stern takes this approach in her documentary *Barbie Nation* (1998), and the result is a fascinating glimpse at the ways people of different ages, genders, ethnicities, and sexual preferences have used the doll to negotiate their everyday lives. Two young girls use Barbie to help imagine adult gender roles; a gay man whose lover died of AIDS uses Barbie as therapy to help him overcome depression; a young woman uses Barbie as an art object to make political statements about body image and eating disorders in the US; still others use Barbie to remember their happy (or, rather, relatively happier) childhoods. In each case, culture is not embodied in the commodity (the Barbie doll), but in the things people do with the commodity. Barbie play becomes a means to interpret, evade, and/or reconstruct the world around the player.

Popular culture in this sense refers to *the ways people "make do" with what the reigning cultural industries and institutions provide*.[14] Most theorists who take this approach are less interested in the ways we are coopted into the reigning social order via our use of cultural commodities (a process called **incorporation**), than in how we take these commodities and use them in new and creative ways (a process called **excorporation**). They focus less on how we are duped or pacified through our consumption of cultural commodities and more on the ways we express ourselves through these commodities. Indeed, for Fiske and others, "mass culture" is a contradiction in terms because culture does not inhere in objects or texts, but in the practices people use to make sense of those objects and texts. Until a cultural commodity is taken up and put to use, there *is* no meaning and thus no culture.[15]

While cultural studies scholars sometimes lapse into an uncritical celebration of popular agency—forgetting that not every use of cultural forms is progressive, meaningful, or healthy—the approach does have some important merits. First, it can help us move beyond the debate over aesthetic value, which says that elite culture is the only one worthy of study. For cultural studies scholars, what distinguishes elite cultural forms from popular ones is not their quality but their accessibility. They do not view popular forms as degraded or deficient; they view them as usable. Yes, they say, Bollywood movies or American TV programs are obvious, clichéd, spectacular, ephemeral, and repetitive; that they don't measure up to the best classical literary or theatrical works is a given. But, this does not mean the texts are worthless or completely derivative. Each iteration of a musical is not the same as every other, and the differences in the application of the formula open up different sets of meanings and possibilities for user engagement. It is these potentialities and how they are activated that are of interest to cultural studies theorists, not just the aesthetic qualities of the work.

The cultural studies approach also understands that the walls once separating elite from mass from folk culture have come tumbling down in today's complex societies. Not only is elite culture highly commodified and subject to the same forms of reproduction and dissemination as mass cultural forms, but there are very few social spaces left for an authentic folk culture to develop. Culture is no longer produced in an autonomous fashion by either "artists" or "the folk"; both artistic and folk productions are inevitably entangled with the centralized, corporatized, and commercialized forms of mass cultural production, and both now come to users second-hand, mediated by institutions and economic value chains. For example, folk works created by self-taught artists are now regularly included in art museums and can be easily purchased at souvenir stands or on the internet. Likewise, formally trained artists now often use elements of everyday life to make aesthetic and political statements, which are then re-inserted into everyday life via posters, T-Shirts, coasters, and even printed toilet paper. Andy Warhol, to cite a well-known example, made Campbell's soup cans into art and played with the logics of seriality, ephemerality, and stardom that characterize mass cultural forms (consider his serial portraits of famous figures like Mao Zedong, Marilyn Monroe, and Elvis). He made art user-friendly and showed how objects of everyday life could be employed to produce new and profound meanings. By erasing the boundaries between high and low, elite, mass, and folk cultures, his "Pop Art" provoked people to ask where these categories came from in the first place. Thus, the meaning of Warhol's work is not contained in its content but in the ways it interacts with and helps explain everyday life.

Like Warhol's work, cultural studies approaches acknowledge that the boundaries separating elite, mass, and folk cultures have always been artificial and somewhat irrelevant. People frequently traverse these boundaries in their search for meanings and pleasures, and electronic and digital media have only made such travel easier. For instance, a trip to see the film *O Brother, Where Art Thou* (2000), a mass cultural text, might inspire me to read Homer's *Odyssey* (800 B.C.E.), the work upon which the story is based and a work of "high culture," or to track down original recordings of the bluegrass tunes ("folk culture") featured on the film's soundtrack. Thanks to the internet and various recording and reproduction technologies, I can do this all in one day and from one location. That my access to most of these texts will come second hand and at a price hardly negates their utility or defines their value. Reproductions may lack the "aura" of original works of art or folk culture, and the meanings individuals make of them may change with the context, but the works themselves do not suddenly lose the capacity to provoke meanings and pleasures. Those who would argue that mass culture threatens to replace the high and folk arts with degraded trash are needlessly concerned. We could as easily argue that mass culture has kept art and folk culture alive by making their texts and performances more widely accessible and available for popular use.

Given these practical considerations, the relevant question is not "which branch of culture does a work belong to?" It is: "how is the work used by institutions and individuals to order social relations?" A definition of popular culture that focuses on the uses, rather than the origins, of various texts, artifacts, and performances allows us to treat works from across the cultural and historical spectrum. It also focuses our attention on the practices of authorization and interpretation, power and pleasure, that create categories like "high," "low," "mass," and "folk." In other words, we can recognize these categories as *effects* of particular battles over meaning and value. The investigation of such battles ought to be the real aim of studying popular culture. How do cultural practices engender debates that, in turn, shape social relations and priorities?

WHO ARE THE PEOPLE OF POPULAR CULTURE?

We will rely largely on the cultural studies approach in this text. Before we can get on with the discussion, however, two important questions remain to be addressed. First, how does popular culture differ from regular culture, or, rather, what is the value of retaining the adjective "popular" given the collapse of the categorical boundaries discussed above? The quick answer is that the designation "popular" reminds us of our focus—people and their practices of creation, interpretation, and agency. The term embodies a distinct orientation to cultural study, one which emphasizes people's power to create and discriminate, to make choices about whether and how to use the expressive resources available in their societies. Nothing about this theoretical orientation precludes the study of "high" cultural forms or institutions, but, in practice, most studies of "popular culture" are really studies of the ways that mass cultural texts, objects, and performances are created, circulated, and received by individuals in their everyday lives. They emphasize the transformation of mass artifacts into meaningful expressions of personal identity and social belonging. Thus, the term "popular culture" remains important because most scholars still recognize and use it in a specific way: to refer to studies that focus on the **popular arts** (cultural forms designed for a mass audience and intended to be appreciated by ordinary people) and the **micropolitics of everyday life** (The small-scale power relations that operate in and through our day-to-day interactions).

The second key question is: who are "the people" of popular culture? How should we identify, locate, and study their activities? Are "the people" those who occupy the mainstream of society (as in "The American People"), or are they those who differ from the majority (so-called **subcultures**)? Are they identifiable by a particular social category, class, or political position, or can anyone from any fraction of society form part of "the people"? Cultural studies work has traditionally focused "on . . . disempowered or marginalized [groups] within a dominant culture and the ways struggles for power are conducted through representation[al systems]."[16] Most cultural studies scholars also acknowledge, however, that "the people" are hard to locate or pin down. The term does not refer to a pre-existing social group (women, blacks, gays, seniors, etc.) or political position (left, right, or center); rather, it refers to a "felt collectivity" produced, in part, through the engagement with cultural forms, social rituals, and opposing forces.[17] Formations of the people cannot be identified in advance of their encounter with culture, for culture constitutes identities and social allegiances, just as it constitutes our sense of the world. How we make sense of the particular social facts we encounter in our daily lives determines who we think we are, what we think we stand for, and who we think we ought to stand with or against. Thus, one of the goals of studying popular culture is to identify and track popular formations in motion. Where, when, and how does a "felt collectivity" (a people, or popular formation) emerge, and why? What can this popular formation and its activities tell us about the social forces at work in a specific context? The goal is not to understand a **text** or even a reader's use of it, but to understand how the interaction between texts and readers embodies social relations. What can this interaction tell us about how a given society is being organized and policed? What can it tell us about how people experience and deal with the forces that surround them?

So, how do we determine who "the people" are, and what they want, if they are so elusive? One place to look is where the people gather—at texts or phenomena that attract a lot of people (bringing us back to Levine's definition of popular culture). Another place to look is in the realm of **discourse**. Discourse refers to the social application of language, or how it is used in institutional and social settings to organize and delimit knowledge about the world. The term presumes that language and representation are never neutral or descriptive systems; rather, they are prescriptive and regulatory. They define what can and cannot be said in a particular context about a particular topic. As philosopher Judith Butler puts it, they define "the limits of acceptable speech."[18] Fiske describes discourse as "applied power" because discourses are often wielded as weapons, or means of control, in our societies. So, for example, in the US, debates about violence in the media are conducted through a shared discourse that assumes, among other things, that representations of violence are always bad and that some people (kids, the mentally ill, etc.) are incapable of discriminating between representational violence and the real thing. **Moral panics** of this sort tend to argue for the elimination, or censorship, of violent imagery by painting these groups or their representatives (the Columbine shooters, for example) as a threat to "normal society." This is no neutral use of language; it is one intended to control social groups by controlling the definition of what's normal or desirable. It is an exercise in power. What does discourse have to do with finding "the people"? Well, you can bet that wherever you find official or institutional discourses obsessing over a subject, you will also find a popular formation rankling authority.

In sum, the meaning of "the people" shifts according to the situation, but you can usually begin your inquiry at the site where "widespread consumption" crosses with "widespread critical disapproval," for that is where people will be fighting over the meanings and values that guide social relations.[19] This is another way of saying that the meaning of "the people" emerges out of tensions between self-definition (**identity**) and social definition (**subjectivity**). To identify who "the people" of popular culture are and try to figure out what they are doing and why, we need to pay close attention to the historical, social, and institutional contexts within which or against which they operate. In particular, we need to ask how texts, objects, and performances are being used as avenues of **articulation.** This word has a special usage in cultural studies based on its double meaning in English. On the one hand, "to articulate" means to speak or express one's thoughts; on the other, it means to connect two objects at a flexible joint, as in an articulated bus or an articulated skeleton. Articulation theory, thus, asks how cultural forms are being used both to *express meanings* and to *forge relationships* between people and things that might otherwise be unconnected. The connections—whether they be between people, objects, or ideas—are always political in that they are calculated to achieve some social effect. So, for example, conservatives in the US frequently connect (articulate) homosexuality to bestiality so as to code the former as "unnatural." If there is no "natural" basis for homosexual attraction, then there is no need to accommodate its practices within the law. But, because each articulation is flexible (i.e., temporary), the politics of articulation can work the other way, as well. Thus, gays have taken the once-derogatory word "queer" and re-articulated it as an expression of pride and defiance. They have forged a new linkage between the term and the social subjects it describes. As these examples illustrate, articulation is highly context-specific and highly unstable. Linkages can be forged quickly and melted down just as rapidly. So, we have to keep our eyes on the social field within which popular utterances are being made if we are to grasp their meanings and effects. For practitioners of a cultural studies approach, *one cannot study popular culture in the absence of social context.*

CASE STUDY: CLUB CULTURES

Sociologist Sarah Thornton's work on British club cultures in the 1980s provides an excellent illustration of how to analyze popular culture in its social contexts.[20] The inspiration for the study came from her own familiarity with clubbing in London, but the clubs also embodied those two ingredients of popularity discussed above: they were places where a lot of people gathered regularly, and they experienced a high degree of official disapproval. She begins by detailing the cultural practices of "clubbers"—how they gather, what they listen to, where and how they listen to it, what paraphernalia (from costumes and records to drugs) they use to heighten the experience, and why they claim to do what they do. She emphasizes the importance of shared tastes (in music and fashion) to their collective identity and discusses the way they use micro media, like word of mouth, flyers, and zines, to orchestrate their gatherings. The text is full of rich descriptions of club practices including the arts of DJ-ing and remixing, the use of music videos to substitute for live performance, and the role of dance and drugs in producing a **carnivalesque** release from social norms and expectations.

These practices produce a temporary coalition of individuals, which often melts away the next day, next week, or next season. Thus, club cultures are the quintessential example of how fluid the boundaries of a popular formation can be. Social categories like race or class have little bearing on the shape of club communities (though age is a prime determinant of inclusion). People from all walks of life are welcome as long as they are young, embody the proper aesthetic, and perceive themselves as opposed to the "mainstream." Local and niche media help individuals "find" the club crowd, but **taste** and **discourse** are what hold these groups together. The term " taste" refers to more than just an individual's personal preferences. Taste is socially constructed and differs from situation to situation, group to group. We learn to classify and judge in the same way we learn language, and, as with language, we learn to "code switch" depending on the context and the people we are with. The classifications and hierarchies that make up "taste" serve a very real social function: they help us understand our place in a given situation and anticipate the likely outcomes of decisions we make in that situation. When we worry about what to wear on a date, for example, we are less worried about our personal sense of comfort than about what our clothes will say to those we meet. We want to give the "right" impression. Though club cultures pretend to be free form and non-judgmental, they are full of implicit rules of proper decorum. They have their own sense of "what is authentic and legitimate in popular culture," and adherence to these unwritten rules of "hipness" is mandatory for inclusion in the group.[21] Often this is quite literal, as, for example, when doorkeepers at trendy clubs review the gathered crowds and determine whose style and personality best fits the "internal image" of the club.[22] If you do not pass the "style test," you cannot gain entry into the world of the clubbers.

More metaphorically, those who fail to live up to the standards of taste and authenticity are subject to ridicule, and this ridicule comprises a shared discourse that firmly establishes the limits of club identity. For example, the "mainstream" is often identified with pop music and places where "Sharon and Tracy dance around their handbags."[23] The names, Sharon and Tracy, represent working-class aspirants to the good life. Such individuals are seen as staid, unhip, and undiscriminating in their tastes; they are only at the club for the booze and the boys, not the music. The handbag they carry is a symbol of adulthood and work, "of the social and financial shackles of the housewife"; it is "definitely not a sartorial sign of youth culture," which generally eschews work and all things sober and serious.[24] Many clubbers interviewed by Thornton used such figures (Sharons, Tracys, or later, in the 1990s, "Acid Teds") to explain the difference between the hip and the unhip, the true club culture and the false (coopted) one. Whether these were fair or accurate descriptions of the practices of actual working-class girls and boys was irrelevant; what mattered was the role such characters played in defining a shared vision of "the mainstream." The discourse about Sharons and Tracys helped define what clubbers *were* by identifying what they *were not*. Thus, clubbers were held together as much by their shared hierarchies and classifications (their discourse) as they were by their shared love of a certain kind of music and fashion (their tastes).

Many cultural studies scholars have described subcultures as grassroots social movements crafted in opposition to mainstream institutions and power structures and, thus, as inherently progressive. As the above discussion indicates, Thornton takes a much more complicated view. She notes that clubbers rely on cultural industries for their music (which is recorded, rather than live), for information about reigning fashion trends, and for their sense of "felt collectivity." Thus, they live in a symbiotic relationship with the mainstream; they do not exist apart from it. Moreover, their practices express the reigning ideologies of their time. As Thornton puts it, "the youth of my research were . . . 'Thatcher's children'. Well versed in the virtues of [capitalist] competition, their cultural heroes came in the form of radical young entrepreneurs, starting up clubs and record labels, rather than the politicians and poets of yesterday."[25] Like all forms of popular culture, club cultures embody a complex dance of incorporation and excorporation, power and liberation. Thornton's study attends to these contradictions. Rather than taking the opposition between the mainstream and the underground at face value, she traces how these terms have been produced and articulated to each other in the practices of the clubbers and through media framing.

Thornton is careful to note that "the media" are not one, big monolith. The word "media" is actually the plural of "medium," and we need to keep that plurality in mind when we study media operations in practice. There are different levels of mediation—micromedia (person-to-person communications), niche media (industrial magazines and other texts that cater to a subculture), and mass media (broadcast communications, like TV, that cater to large, indiscriminate audiences)—and each operates differently in different contexts. In the case of club culture, each of these media contributed to the formation and framing of the subculture, but they did so in different ways. Micromedia advertised upcoming gatherings and ensured clubbers could find one another. Though produced within and by members of the subculture, they were not completely independent from, or resistant to, the corporate forms of mediation, for they frequently recycled and amplified information gleaned from more "mainstream" sources. Niche media, meanwhile, did more than just incorporate, or coopt, the subculture for commerce. Industry magazines helped construct a shared identity by itemizing, categorizing, valorizing, and labeling those features of cultural practice that defined the tastes of the group. They wrote the subculture's history, compared its formations to other sounds or styles, advertised upcoming events, and explained what was "hip" at any given moment. In short, they gave shape to the cultural formation so that it might endure. Finally, the mass media played a highly contradictory role in the production of club culture. On the one hand, mainstream music programs, like *Top of the Pops* (a sort of *American Bandstand* for British audiences), incorporated aspects of the musical tastes and styles of the subculture and broadcast them to "the mainstream." On the other hand, news coverage used the activities of the clubbers to foment a moral panic, or hyped-up controversy, about the dangers of youth delinquency and drug use. The simultaneous celebration and condemnation of youth culture demonstrates how internally fragmented the "mainstream media" really is. In effect, there is no "mainstream media"; there are only ways of speaking of mainstream media. Thus, we should be skeptical whenever we hear words like "the media" or "the mainstream" and always ask: Who is using these words, why, and to what effect? What subtleties are being glossed over when we accept this terminology?

Thornton's other major insight with regard to the media relates to the work of "moral panics" in articulating youth cultures to rebellion. Traditionally, cultural studies scholars have assumed that youth were victims of this process of stigmatization, but Thornton's work shows that clubbers actively embraced, even contributed to, the media hype surrounding their practices. They imagined themselves as inhabiting an "underground" social space, beneath the mainstream and beyond its understanding. Thus, they reveled in behaviors designed to shock and counter official morality. Instead of work, they engaged in play; instead of sobriety, they embraced drug-induced "ecstasy" (also the name of their drug of choice); instead of valuing personal property, they reveled in the artistry of the DJ and the re-mix. In all these ways, clubbers defined their identity through opposition to a set of dominant social norms, which they identified as "the mainstream."

Because they viewed themselves as outré, clubbers actively embraced the negative exposure provided by mainstream media outlets. In their own media, they worked to disarticulate the discourse of moral panic from its mainstream connotations and rearticulate it as a badge of honor. Both club zines and music industry magazines "tracked the tabloids' every move, reproduced whole front pages, re-printed and analysed their copy and decried the misrepresentations" as "media hysteria." Clubbers, and the industries that catered to them, recognized that media condemnation would help "baptize [their] transgression"; it could turn "difference into defiance, lifestyle into social upheaval, leisure into revolt."[26] In short, it could provide a negative pole against which to forge a felt collectivity. Without such negative coverage, the subculture's coherence may have suffered and slackened over time. Negative press coverage both kept the subculture alive in the public mind and legitimated their claims to be an oppositional, or "dangerous," social force. Of course, it also generated a lot of money for the niche media producers who engineered much of the reverse hype. As Thornton notes, "the hysterical reports of the popular press" amount to "priceless PR" for niche producers.[27] A detailed analysis of the hype shows that moral panics involving youth cultures are not just attempts to quash youth rebellion; they are also frequently a means of crafting subcultural identity and marketing goods to those groups.

In all, Thornton's study demonstrates that "popular culture in industrial societies is contradictory to its core."[28] Both the "mainstream" and the "subculture" are fluid collectivities organized around temporary alliances and interests. Clubbers use the mainstream media when it suits them and disdain them when it doesn't. The cultural industries, likewise, profit from the subculture but also from the critique of the subculture, depending on the context. To truly understand club cultures, then, we must look at more than just the cultural texts and practices of the clubbers. Knowing the music, fashion, and dance tastes only gets one so far; knowing how clubbers turn mainstream cultural articles to popular uses is also limited; knowing how all of these factors interact within a field of pre-structured social relations—that's the real goal! Thornton's primary questions are: How is personal identity being articulated to available social roles or positions? How do people express their agency in this process, and what are the limits of this agency?

CONCLUSION

A key lesson of Thornton's text is that there is no pure resistance to the social order, no authenticate space outside of its reach. Popular culture exists in the cracks of the culture proper; it is about mining the resources provided by cultural industries and official institutions for popular use. It involves turning the culture, accenting its expression, articulating it to new voices, identities, and projects. It is a sphere of constant struggle: the struggle to speak, shape, and reshape existing discourses, and to recover lost histories and voices. One has to be realistic about the political value of such work. Not every expression of popular culture is necessarily progressive or something to be celebrated. Club cultures, for example, operated according to their own logics of exclusion, many of which overlapped with and reproduced existing assumptions about the proper place of women, gays, and peoples of color in society. The use of "Sharons and Tracy's" to embody the "unhip" mainstream impacted the ability of women and working-class youth to attain positions as club organizers, promoters, and DJs within the subculture. Straight, white, middle-class men made up the majority of those at the top of the club hierarchy, just as they did in the "mainstream" of British society at the time.

So, while subcultures often articulate critiques of the dominant culture, this is not always or automatically the case. Scholars of popular culture need to examine the interplay of dominant and popular forces as they manifest themselves in the specific social and cultural contexts. If popular culture is not always progressive, it *can* always tell us something about the shape of our societies—where and how the lines of force intersect and why. Ultimately, the aim of studying popular culture is not to identify (with) resistance (a common critique of the cultural studies approach), but to understand ourselves, our world, and our social relations better. If such knowledge can empower us to better our personal situations or press for positive social change, that's a happy (and much to be hoped for) side-effect.

Chapter 2 extends these discussions by examining the tensions between processes of cultural authorization and popular interpretation in different historical periods. It draws connections between postmodern cultural practices and those of earlier ages, including classical Rome, medieval Europe, and modern America and Egypt. While most cultural studies scholars define popular culture strictly as a modern phenomenon, we will define it more broadly and examine the ways ordinary people, across the ages, have interpreted and made use of the cultural resources their societies provided.

SUMMARY

- Culture is the active process of generating and circulating meanings and pleasures within a social system. It helps identify us as members of a group and provides us with a shared vocabulary through which to communicate with one another.

- By shaping our perspectives, cultural systems actively construct social relations. They make some ideas and attitudes more available than others and create tensions between those within the group and those outside.

- This text takes a cultural studies approach to popular culture, which means it focuses on questions of social agency: how do people interpret, use, and value the cultural resources available to them?

- Cultural studies scholars emphasize the importance of context (historical, social, and institutional) in determining the significance of cultural activities.

- Cultural studies scholars are particularly interested in issues of articulation—in other words, how cultural forms are used to *express meanings* and *forge relationships*.

NOTES

1 "Culture," in *The Concise Oxford English Dictionary*, ed. Catherine Soanes and Angus Stevenson (New York: Oxford University Press, 2008).
2 Matthew Arnold, *Culture and Anarchy* (New York: Cambridge University Press, 1990), 70.

3 See, for example: E.P. Thompson, *The Making of the English Working Class* (New York: Vintage, 1966); W.E.B. Du Bois, *Black Reconstruction in America, 1860–1880* (New York: Free Press, 1999); Lawrence Levine, *Black Culture and Black Consciousness: Afro-American Folk Thought from Slavery to Freedom* (New York: Oxford University Press, 2007); Katherine H. Adams and Michael L. Keene, *Alice Paul and the American Suffrage Campaign* (Urbana: University of Illinois Press, 2007).

4 Edward B. Tylor, *Primitive Culture: Researches into the Development of Mythology, Philosophy, Religion, Language, Art, and Custom,* vol. 1 (London: John Murray, 1903), 1.

5 Raymond Williams, *Culture and Society, 1780–1950* (New York: Columbia University Press, 1983), 325.

6 See, for example, Allan Bloom, *Closing of the American Mind: How Higher Education Has Failed Democracy and Impoverished the Souls of Today's Students* (New York: Simon & Schuster, 2012). For a counter-argument, see Lawrence Levine, *The Opening of the American Mind* (Ypsilanti, MI: Beacon Press, 1997).

7 John Fiske, *Understanding Popular Culture* (New York: Routledge, 2011), 19.

8 For the complications these different worldviews may create, see Anne Fadiman, *The Sprit Catches You and You Fall Down* (New York: Farrar, Straus and Giroux, 1998).

9 Lawrence Levine, "The Folklore of Industrial Society: Popular Culture and Its Audiences," *American Historical Review* 97 (Dec. 1992), 1373.

10 See, for example, Theodor W. Adorno and Max Horkheimer, *Dialectic of Enlightenment* (New York: Continuum, 1997); Dwight Macdonald, "Masscult & Midcult," in *Against the Grain* (New York: Da Capo Press, 1962).

11 Macdonald, "Masscult & Midcult," 3–4.

12 Ibid., 11.

13 Ibid., 14.

14 Michel de Certeau, *The Practice of Everyday Life* (Chicago: University of Chicago Press, 1988); Fiske, *Understanding Popular Culture.*

15 Fiske, *Understanding Popular Culture,* 37.

16 Carla Freccero, *Popular Culture: An Introduction* (New York: New York University Press, 1999), 14.

17 Fiske, *Understanding Popular Culture,* 20.

18 Judith Butler, *Excitable Speech: A Politics of the Performative* (New York: Routledge, 1997), 77.

19 Fiske, *Understanding Popular Culture,* 85.

20 Sarah Thornton, *Club Cultures: Music, Media, and Subcultural Capital* (Middletown, CT: Wesleyan University Press, 1996).

21 Thornton, *Club Cultures,* 3.

22 Ibid., 115.

23 Ibid., 99.

24 Ibid., 101.

25 Ibid., 208.

26 Ibid., 129.

27 Ibid., 136.

28 Fiske, *Understanding Popular Culture,* 19.

REFERENCES

Adams, Katherine H., and Michael L. Keene. *Alice Paul and the American Suffrage Campaign*. Urbana: University of Illinois Press, 2007.

Adorno, Theodor W., and Max Horkheimer. *Dialectic of Enlightenment*. New York: Continuum, 1997.

Arnold, Matthew. *Culture and Anarchy*. New York: Cambridge University Press, 1990.

Bloom, Allan. *Closing of the American Mind: How Higher Education Has Failed Democracy and Impoverished the Souls of Today's Students*. New York: Simon & Schuster, 2012.

Butler, Judith. *Excitable Speech: A Politics of the Performative*. New York: Routledge, 1997.

Certeau, Michel de. *The Practice of Everyday Life*. Chicago: University of Chicago Press, 1988.

"Culture." In *The Concise Oxford English Dictionary,* edited by Catherine Soanes and Angus Stevenson. New York: Oxford University Press, 2008.

Du Bois, W.E.B. *Black Reconstruction in America, 1860–1880*. New York: Free Press, 1999.

Fadiman, Anne. *The Sprit Catches You and You Fall Down*. New York: Farrar, Straus and Giroux, 1998.

Fiske, John. *Understanding Popular Culture*. New York: Routledge, 2011.

Freccero, Carla. *Popular Culture: An Introduction*. New York: New York University Press, 1999.

Levine, Lawrence. *Black Culture and Black Consciousness: Afro-American Folk Thought from Slavery to Freedom*. New York: Oxford University Press, 2007.

———. "The Folklore of Industrial Society: Popular Culture and Its Audiences." *American Historical Review* 97 (Dec. 1992): 1369–1399.

———. *The Opening of the American Mind*. Ypsilanti, MI: Beacon Press, 1997.

Macdonald, Dwight. "Masscult & Midcult." In *Against the Grain,* 3–75. New York: Da Capo Press, 1962.

Thompson, E.P. *The Making of the English Working Class*. New York: Vintage, 1966.

Thornton, Sarah. *Club Cultures: Music, Media, and Subcultural Capital*. Middletown, CT: Wesleyan University Press, 1996.

Tylor, Edward B. *Primitive Culture: Researches into the Development of Mythology, Philosophy, Religion, Language, Art, and Custom*. vol. 1. London: John Murray, 1903.

Williams, Raymond. *Culture and Society, 1780–1950*. New York: Columbia University Press, 1983.

CHAPTER 2

Is Popular Culture Modern?

Cultural studies scholars are often accused of treating popular culture as if it were only a modern or contemporary phenomenon, born of the growth of capitalist markets and Big Business. Indeed, as cultural studies scholar John Storey admits, most definitions of popular culture within the field have shared "[an] insistence that whatever else popular culture might be, it is definitely a culture that only emerged following industrialization and urbanization."[1] Before that period, according to this theory, there was a common culture, which everyone in society more or less participated in, and there were distinct spheres of culture defined by **class** position. Language and various religious and political rituals were held in common, but other aspects of culture were defined by one's location in the class hierarchy. Elite culture was produced and consumed by the dominant classes and was distinguished by its refinement while folk culture was produced and consumed largely by rural people and was designed to be more functional than artistic or expressive. Truly "popular" culture only emerges, according to this argument, when industrialization throws masses of working people together in the city and makes it worthwhile, economically speaking, to cater to their tastes. This story of cultural development, with its emphasis on **capitalism** and class conflict, shows the influence of Marxist theory on cultural studies, and it has proven very useful for examining modern forms of mass-produced culture (see, for example, the analysis of the cultural industries in Chapter 6 of this book). Yet, as with any form of authoritative discourse, we should ask: What does this way of defining popular culture leave out or exclude? How does it limit the ways we think about and study popular culture?

Historians have long complained that this way of defining popular culture is needlessly narrow. By confusing popular culture with industrially produced mass culture, it has hampered the study of pre-modern cultural practices that might be considered popular according to a broader definition. If, instead of focusing on the mode of production, we focus on the work people do to transform the available resources into meaningful expressions of interest, then there would be no reason to deny the existence of popular culture in the pre-modern era. Popular formations may emerge in, around, and in response to a variety of cultural institutions and authorities, not just industrialized entertainment industries. While the mode of production matters, it cannot explain questions of popular investment. Issues of **status** and **cultural authorization** may prove more decisive in explaining the decisions people make about what to take an interest in. Status is related to one's class, or socioeconomic category, but is not reducible to income or wealth. It refers to the patterns of consumption or lifestyle choices that mark an individual as belonging to a particular "tribe" (in the loosest sense of that term). A focus on status means asking questions like: What type of clothing, food, religion, and entertainment (among other things) does a person consume? Who does that affiliate him or her with and how? Cultural authorization refers to the way prestige or legitimacy get attached to certain cultural practices and detached from others. The key questions here would be: Who has the power to authorize culture in a particular context and who does not? Which cultural practices receive the approval of the reigning social institutions and authorities and which do not? And, how do people respond to or intervene in these processes?

These sorts of questions get around the trap of having to define popular culture by form, function, or mode of production and direct our attention to the sites of distribution and interpretation where formations of the people emerge. They also enable us to account for different types and modalities of popularity. As historian Parker Holt explains, "rock and TV, Elvis memorial china and pigeon-fancying, are all popular in quite different ways and to quite different groups. This is because they are created as Other by differing authorities."[2] Instead of focusing on how many people participate in or consume a cultural form, then, we can focus on the processes of authorization and **othering** that mark some aspects of culture as more worthy (hence official) than others.

This chapter provides an overview of popular culture in historical perspective. As such, it offers a fairly conventional survey of popular forms in the pre-modern, modern, and post-modern eras, but it also insists that the boundaries between these periods are relatively porous. To ground the chapter, I will focus on three common aspects of popular forms—the **vernacular,** the carnivalesque, and the **spectacular**—and trace the persistence of these dynamics across the ages. I hope that by identifying the continuities that define popular culture across these periods, we can shift our attention from the practices of periodization to questions of authorization and experience. That is, instead of asking what forms of popular culture are unique to each age, we might ask more interesting questions like: Why did some forms become dominant in a particular period while others were marginalized? What forces have influenced what we remember, and what we forget, about the past? Finally, how and why have these power struggles played out differently in different periods?

THE SPECTACULAR NATURE OF PRE-MODERN LIFE

The fist stop on our tour of popular cultures past is the pre-modern era. For our purposes, the pre-modern era refers to any period after the birth of written language and before the era of modernity, which is defined by the rise of capitalist market relations, industrial manufacturing, and the nation-state as the anchor of government. While, of course, there are vast differences between Egyptian civilization, the civilizations of classical Greece and Rome, and the societies of medieval Europe, none of these pre-modern peoples possessed a fully developed capitalist system, and they all organized their cultural practices around similar things: religion, social hierarchy, and militarism. Most pre-modern societies were divided between an elite fraction of rulers and the masses of the ruled, and the approved cultural rituals were often designed to mediate the tensions between these factions. Approved rituals not only affirmed the social order; they allowed the masses to blow off steam on the theory that a controlled dose of anarchy could alleviate the angst that might otherwise build to a revolution.

Roman imperial spectacles (the Roman empire lasted roughly from B.C.E. 50 to 476 C.E.) offer a good example of this safety-valve theory of popular culture. The term spectacle comes from the Latin *spectaculum* ("a show"), which is itself a variation on *spectare* ("to view, or watch"). A spectacle, then, is a visually striking performance or show. While we often remember Rome as the source of democracy and the Enlightenment—a place where philosophers roamed the streets preaching to the populace and the arts of drama and poetry were born—it could also be a nasty, cruel, and inhumane place to live (as the 2005 HBO series *Rome* all-too-gleefully depicts). The Romans regularly staged elaborate feasts, pageants, and sporting competitions to distract the populace, making their society the original "society of the spectacle" (a phrase used by French Marxists in the 1960s to denigrate consumer culture). The phrase "bread and circuses" (*panem et circenses*) comes from these practices and has been used for centuries to dismiss popular culture as escapist fare that diverts attention from political and social problems. In Rome, however, the pageantry was not set apart from political or social life; it was thoroughly integrated into it.

The state orchestrated a variety of public games (called *ludi*) to commemorate various religious holidays. According to historian Richard Beacham, these amounted to between fifty and seventy-five performances a year, depending on how late in the empire it was and how many special celebrations were also held (to commemorate military victories or dedicate a temple, for example). "The provision of the various state games and their management was the responsibility of elected magistrates" called *aediles*, and it was virtually a requirement of political advancement that nobles serve, at some point, as *aedile* and provide games (Suzanne Collins uses these Roman precedents to construct her dystopian vision of "Panem's" Capitol in *The Hunger Games*). By the time of the late republic, these state-sponsored games were being supplemented by a number of private ceremonies, contests, and pageants, staged by nobles eager to increase their status in society. As historian Alexander Yakobson explains, "the Roman nobles . . . perhaps more than any other social elite in history, were dependent on popular elections for the very definition of their relative status in society."[3] To get (re)elected to the Senate, a noble had to display his family's wealth, power, and prestige by throwing lavish feasts and festivals for the people. Over time, the spectacles became more and more elaborate, as nobles tried to outdo each other and win a fickle public's favor. The levels of sensationalism, sensuousness, and violence increased in a self-perpetuating cycle that would be easily recognizable to modern critics. Indeed, by the late imperial period, Roman critics were themselves lamenting what Beacham calls the "theatricalization of culture" and its attendant problems: "an increased emphasis on image over essence, style over substance, fantasy over reality, and emotional gesture over reasoned analysis or discourse."[4] Thousands of years later, Marxist theorists would use similar sentiments to structure their critique of modernity and the "society of the spectacle."[5]

And, what did Roman spectacles look like? Again, a lot like contemporary amusements. Theatrical performances of various sorts—dramatic, comedic, mimetic—were a staple of the official holidays, but critics complained of a drift away from serious drama and toward comedy and mime, as the public's tastes assumed greater importance. Comedies featured political satire and slapstick humor targeted toward the social elite, but the mimes were, by far, the more scandalous entertainment because they lacked the ritual trappings of Greek and Roman theater. Beacham describes mime as a form of "unscripted and virtually plotless entertainment . . . presented without masks and includ[ing] female performers." Performers lampooned everyday mores, ridiculed important personalities, and reveled in sensationalism (including spectacular events like shipwrecks and kidnappings). It "was noted for its obscenity and license (including female nudity)" and bawdy humor.[6] The lack of masks and scripts made the humor more pointed and more dangerous. Without the traditional theatrical rituals, it could be hard to put the genie of merriment back in the social bottle.

In addition to theatrical spectacles, common forms of Roman entertainment included animal displays, staged hunts, and gladiatorial shows. *Aediles* struggled to outdo each other in terms of the content and scope of such performances, incorporating exotic African and Asian animals, sometimes by the hundreds, and pitting slaves and gladiators against each other and/or against the wild beasts. The winner would often end his day standing atop a pile of human and animal corpses, much to the delight of the audience. As in modern professional sports, Roman gladiators were highly skilled athletes, trained in commercial academies of the martial arts, and paid, often handsomely, for their services. Successful gladiators were often worshipped as heroes, and their battles became the stuff of popular myth and legend. One can imagine that gossip about gladiators was also a frequent form of social discourse and a convenient way to break the ice at parties.

Finally, there were the many funereal, triumphal, and occasional processions, or parades, that converged on the Roman circuses (open spaces for social congregation). Designed to celebrate great lives, great deeds, or greatness period, these parades consisted of thousands of participants, days-long celebrations, and much feasting and debauchery. Again, the frequency and familiarity of the pageants created opportunities for professionalization, and nobles who wanted to stage a classy processional were well-advised to hire professional female mourners and actors to stage their funeral songs and oratories.

While most of these amusements were traditional, in the sense that they were ritualistic and tied to religious holidays, they were all marked by lavish production values and a calculated appeal to the senses. Again, they were not that different from modern-day amusements, and the same complaints about escalating sex, violence, and extravagance were launched by many Roman critics. For example, the Roman poet Horace (B.C.E. 65–8) lamented the fact that theatrical performances had become occasions for indulging in the "vain delights" of comedy and spectacle. He was alarmed by the degree to which "the more cultured sections of the audience could be overwhelmed by the 'stupid and ill-educated' rabble that greatly outnumbered them."[7] The natural philosopher Pliny (23–79 C.E.) also believed the theatricalization of Roman life was undermining the morals of the public and blamed politicians for indulging the baser instincts of the populace in order to get elected.[8] Yet, this raises the question of who was leading whom. While these amusements were clearly authorized and staged by social elites, the way they were consumed by the people was not susceptible to elite control. Roman nobles could never be certain that their performances would satisfy the public, and so they escalated the level of sensationalism in pursuit of popular favor. Many a noble was driven to the poor house as a result of these political calculations. In hindsight, it seems the strategy of "bread and circuses" may have backfired. Instead of controlling the masses, it helped control and direct the behaviors of the elite. The power to authorize culture lay not with the nobles or officials, but with the masses, whose tastes (real or imagined) became the driving force in Roman politics.

The beginning of the medieval period, or Middle Ages, is usually dated to the fall of the Western Roman Empire at the end of the fifth century when the urban populations fled to the countryside to escape various invaders. We do not know much about the popular culture of the early medieval period, but by 1000 C.E. a feudal system had been established in many parts of Europe, providing the stability necessary for better historical records to be kept. As a way of life, **feudalism** centered on the formation of small villages whose citizens owed rent and labor to the nobles who controlled the property; they, in turn, owed their allegiance and military service to a set of overlords. Throughout the Middle Ages, cultural life continued to center on the pillars of religion, hierarchy, and militarism, but agricultural cycles also began to factor into the timing of cultural events. Church rituals and religious manuscripts formed the center of cultural life, but at the margins there began to emerge a robust popular culture full of heroic legends, superstitions, oral stories, ballads, broadsheets, and folk remedies. Crusades and pilgrimages even created a new literary genre—travel writing. The lurid and exoticized nature of this literature—which featured tales of cannibals, sea monsters, and human-animal hybrids—made it ripe for popular interest, and, though access to such texts was restricted by low literacy rates, the tales were shared orally and known broadly.[9]

As in classical Rome, public authorities in the Middle Ages sanctioned a variety of rituals that would allow for the temporary suspension of everyday social norms. Carnivals, fairs, mumming, and May Day celebrations were all marked by laughter

FIGURE 2.01   *"Illustrations of Monstrous Humans," Sebastian Münster,* Cosmographia *(1544). An example of medieval travel literature. Courtesy of Wikimedia Commons.*

and excess, bad taste, bad language, and bad behavior. Often they involved modes of disguise and the literal over-turning of the social order, as those with power masqueraded as the powerless and vice versa.[10] During Carnival, for example, lower-class participants would dress up as their social betters and imitate their manner-isms, thereby mocking the pretensions of the upper classes and providing a check on their authority. Mumming, too, involved dressing in disguise (often as the oppo-site gender), visiting one's neighbors, and attempting to deceive them for as long as possible. Later clerics described it as "the occasion of much uncleanness and debauchery, and directly opposite to the word of God" in that it allowed women to dress as men, but medieval officials saw no problem with the ritual.[11]

As these examples illustrate, ritual and tradition should not be equated with tedium, decency, or even social harmony. Pre-modern amusements more than occasionally promoted drinking, gambling, riots, and licentious behavior. They were as raunchy and violent as anything our postmodern societies might throw up. For example, bear-baiting, cock-throwing (throwing darts at male chickens), dog-fighting, bull-running, and bare-knuckle boxing were staple entertainments in medieval Europe. Historians J.M. Golby and A.W. Purdue offer the following description of sports competition in the pre-modern English countryside:

> Football was to be found almost everywhere but the requirement that some
> sort of ball be kicked, run with or thrown was the only common denominator

in what was in the modern sense hardly a sport at all. At Derby there could be as many as 1,000 a side playing in the annual Shrove Tuesday [or Mardi Gras] match, while in many towns holiday games could have the whole town as the playing area. Indeed, many football matches appear to have been more like battles than sport; on the Borders [near Scotland] they appear to have had . . . a close connection to actual warfare in that it was sometimes under cover of football matches that [Scottish] reivers were called together for raids [on English towns].[12]

As this example shows, many popular entertainments were staged in honor of the holy days, like Easter, yet the behaviors of the participants were anything but righteous. Even May Day festivals, which, by the Middle Ages, had become Catholic rituals devoted to the worship of Mary (the mother of Jesus), entailed drinking and a ceremonial tryst in the woods the night before.[13]

Critics of modern life sometimes romanticize pre-modern agrarian life in Europe, depicting the manorial estate as a stable community governed by a **moral economy** of mutual support that set limits on exploitation. Yet, it should be clear by now that such societies were just as conflicted and structured by money and power relations as capitalist ones. They may have placed greater emphasis on custom and tradition than modern societies do, and their amusements may have been more attuned to the rhythms of religious celebration, military campaigning, and agricultural labor. Nevertheless, popular amusements in these societies were not that different in form, substance, or function from modern amusements. They still provided opportunities to investigate and affirm social status, and they still functioned as occasions where elite social authorities and everyday folk collided both literally and metaphorically.

MODERNITY AND THE CARNIVALESQUE

By most accounts, modernity represents a major break from the past because it embodied a radical shift in the mode of production and productive relations. Feudalism, a way of life centered on the control of land and agricultural labor, gave way to capitalism, or a way of life organized around the control of industry, the production of goods for market, and the exchange of labor for wages. Secularism, rationalism, and the nation-state system of governance accompanied this transformation of productive relations, and altogether these changes represent a major departure in the organization and administration of popular life. While small-scale capitalist industries and markets began emerging in the sixteenth century, capitalism did not become the dominant economic system until the nineteenth century when new technologies (steam engines, electricity, light bulbs, etc.) made it possible to produce and sell goods in mass quantities. This Industrial Revolution changed far more than the way goods were made (by machine instead of hand); it increased income and wages for workers and capitalists alike; it drove peasants into the cities in search of factory jobs; it strained urban resources and created a need for welfare assistance, environmental legislation, building codes, and other forms of government regulation. Most importantly for our purposes, it democratized access to leisure time and leisure pursuits.

Labor struggles in the late nineteenth and early twentieth centuries earned workers higher wages and shorter working hours, and, for the first time in history, masses of ordinary folk had the time and money to indulge in the sort of leisure pursuits once reserved for the wealthy. A new amusement industry emerged to help satisfy the demand for popular entertainment. These new amusements were largely unrelated to the pillars of medieval society: the church, the military, and the political hierarchy. Instead, they were secular and commercial. Virtually anyone with the price of admission could indulge in the new amusements, which were also provided year-round and (often) around the clock. Commercialization, or for-profit production, gave rise to "show businessmen" who had a powerful incentive to target as broad an audience as possible. Together, industrialization (the introduction of manufacturing jobs and factory work), urbanization (the migration of populations to the city in search of work), and commercialization made it possible for amusements to become truly public. The rigid class segregation that used to characterize leisure pursuits—with the elite consuming exclusive content and the masses partaking of commonly available diversions—gave way to a new leisure economy premised on inclusion. As historian David Nasaw puts it, public amusement spaces "belonged to no particular social group" and were "respectable" enough to appeal broadly, across lines of class, ethnicity, gender, and (less often) race.[14]

The new amusements were not just democratically available to everyone; they were also democratic and democratizing in terms of their content. Much of the entertainment was structured around variety, with different types of acts pitched to different audience segments. For example, vaudeville shows included acrobats and horse ropers, comic skits and dramatic readings, popular ballads and operatic arias—literally something for everyone. The amusements were also easy to access, both physically and mentally. They rarely required a huge commitment of time, energy, money, or thought to enjoy. Much of the trade was of a casual "drop-in" quality and cost between five and twenty-five cents, which compared favorably to the one or two dollar admission fees charged at the more exclusive urban theaters. Amusement parlors, to cite just one example, featured a variety of different electronic amusements, from "peep show" machines (boxes where one could view short film clips) to phonographs, bubblegum dispensers, and X-ray machines, each of which cost from a penny to a nickel and could be consumed in a matter of seconds. The parlors were located near business districts to make it easy for workers and shoppers to sample the entertainments and then carry on with their usual activities.[15]

Modern methods of advertising, including the touting of stars and celebrity attractions, enabled showmen like P.T. Barnum and B.F. Keith to draw a crowd and keep it coming back. Barnum was particularly adept at the new marketing strategies and became so good at generating hype that "bunkum" (claptrap or nonsense) became a nickname for him (after satirist George Thompson lampooned Barnum in the 1856 pamphlet *The Autobiography of Petite Bunkum: The Great Yankee Showman*). Barnum orchestrated a series of hoaxes and cons to lure people into his New York–based American Museum, including the "Feejee Mermaid," a creature with the head of a monkey and the tail of a fish; "General Tom Thumb," a child-midget (in the parlance of the day) advertised as a full-grown man (and taught to smoke and drink at the age of 5 to prove it!); and the "What Is It," a black man who was advertised as Darwin's "missing link." "I don't believe in duping the public," Barnum said, "but I believe in first attracting and then pleasing them." The hoaxes were designed to get people through the door, but once inside the Museum, the other amusements more than satisfied.[16]

Nasaw argues that the democratic structure and accessibility of these amusements also had a democratizing effect on the populations who consumed them. That is, public amusements helped assimilate diverse social groups into a national public. They did this by throwing people together (sometimes literally) and giving them a set of shared reference points. Of the American context, Nasaw says: "Everywhere else—at home, in their neighborhoods and at work—[urban dwellers] straddled the social divisions of class and ethnicity. Only in the playgrounds furnished by the show businessmen could they submerge themselves in a corporate body, an 'American' public, that transcended these divisions."[17]

The one exception to this rule, of course, was African Americans who were over-represented on the new stages and screens—in minstrel shows, vaudeville acts, "coon" songs, and early films like "Nigger in a Woodpile" (1904), which worked through gross forms of stereotyping—but under-represented in the audiences. Indeed, the presentation of black caricature on stage, screen, and in sound enabled many previously marginalized ethnic minorities to claim whiteness by virtue of their difference from the blacks so lampooned. This was particularly true for Irish and Jewish performers who wore blackface on stage, but made sure the publicity photos always included a shot of them in dress attire with their "real" faces exposed. The effect was to make their ethnic bodies "look white" by comparison to the black mask. Many theaters also banned or segregated black patrons, thereby achieving the same effect for the general audience. Admittance to the venue signaled your acceptance into the white American mainstream. Although blacks would not be openly accepted in public venues until the 1950s, they did partake of popular amusements in a segregated fashion and even created their own popular amusements. Black-owned and -operated clubs, speakeasies, theaters, and film companies sprang up in the early 1910s and 1920s to cater to black (and sometimes mixed) audiences, while phonographs and radios enabled mainstream popular music and theater to be consumed in the safety of the private home. Even these designated "outcasts" thus shared in much of the common culture produced by the emerging entertainment industries.[18]

Lest we think this "melting pot" effect was restricted to America, other scholars have charted similar processes in England, Germany, France, and even Egypt.[19]

Ziad Fahmy reports, for example, that mass-produced entertainments of the early twentieth century helped forge a new national identity for Egyptians previously segregated by class, location (urban v. rural), and religion. "Hundreds of new periodicals and books were published; new theatrical plays and thousands of new songs were performed to increasingly larger and more politically discerning [i.e. urbane] audiences." Egypt had a fully developed recording industry by 1904, and "by the 1910s . . . mass-scale manufacturing of phonographs and discs made [recordings] cheaper and more accessible to a greater number of Egyptians." Colloquial songs quickly become national hits, spreading the local Cairene dialect of Arabic throughout the country and making it the de facto spoken language for the nation. Other new amusements, like films and vaudeville shows, trickled out of the urban centers of Cairo and Alexandria and into the countryside, where they "contribut[ed] to the formation of an increasingly homogeneous Egyptian national culture."[20] Here, as elsewhere, modern popular amusements helped to overcome differences in history, dialect, and experience and forge an imagined national community of identity and belonging.

If modern amusements allowed the masses to share some common experiences, however, they hardly produced social homogenization or harmony. For one thing, the wealth of leisure options available to the masses ensured a certain amount of competition between them for consumer attention. Instead of a unitary culture, there was a "decentered culture" predicated on conflict and the discourse of "choice."[21] Consumers cobbled together different assemblages of cultural experience from the range of available options and actively used their newfound rights to choose to invent new traditions and try on new identities. American historian Kathy Peiss has documented, for example, the way working-class shop girls in New York studied fashion trends and dressed to impress as a means of accruing status among their peers and breaking away from their families. Using consumer goods and their powers of discrimination, they were able to contest patriarchal authority and fashion a new identity as "modern women."[22] Far from promoting homogenization and the reproduction of traditions, then, modern commercial culture enabled new articulations of identity, status, and belonging, and they gave many people the means to achieve greater social mobility.

Another reason modern amusements failed to produce homogenization was because commercial amusements inspired a lot of social controversy and conflict. Many of these amusements centered on novelty, sensationalism, and hedonistic excess. They worked like medieval carnivals, but without the strong relation to social hierarchy and tradition. Thus, cultural authorities and middle-class reformers worried about their effects on the health and morality of the masses. They viewed public amusements as a threat to social order and worked to close them down or police their contents. The movies, which were invented in 1895 and popularized through the cheap nickelodeon theaters that sprang up throughout the first decade of the twentieth century, frequently came under attack for promoting licentiousness. The arguments were twofold. Some reformers worried that the dark, crowded theaters were physically and morally dangerous. They predicted that the overcrowd-ing, poor ventilation, and lack of fire exits in most nickel theaters would eventually lead to a pandemic or tragedy of mass proportions. More than that, though, they worried that the overcrowding and darkness would breed moral depravity. They took it as axiomatic that "contiguity led to aggression, loss of control, and social decline," and they were especially concerned that young boys and girls would suffer molestation in the darkened spaces.[23]

The second objection to the movies involved the content of the films them-selves. Jane Addams, the famous Chicago reformer and operator of the Hull House community center, described the films as "vice deliberately disguised as pleasure."[24] She and other reformers worried, in particular, about the impact of the crime films and other sensationalistic fare on the minds and morals of the city's youth, work-ing classes, and immigrants. These "childlike populations" were said to lack the intellectual, educational, and cultural savvy to distinguish between fact and fiction, and reformers feared they would "learn from viewing [commercial films] not only that crime paid but also that it paid handsomely and required much less toil than labor in factory, mine or mill."[25] In New York, Boston, and other cities, reformers tried to push through censorship laws, and, when that failed, they used health and safety codes to close down many of the nickelodeons by the 1920s. The effect was to deprive working class and immigrant populations of access to neighborhood theaters, making it infinitely harder for them to view these "dangerous" movies.[26]

The sense that "commercialized recreation means dissipation" also drove efforts to censor behavior in the new dancehalls and amusements parks. These were pub-lic spaces designed precisely to offer visitors a temporary escape from reality and the strict decorum it required. In the dancehalls, for example, young boys and girls could escape the oversight of their parents and indulge in a new form of sexual play known as "dating." In the words of New York social reporter, Julian Street, dancehalls created "a social mixture such as was never before dreamed of in this country [the US]—a hodge-podge of people in which respectable young married and unmarried women, and even debutantes, dance, not only under the same roof, but in the same room with women of the town." While he went on to celebrate this phenomenon with the French political slogan *"Liberté—Egalité—Fraternité"* (Liberty—Equality—Brotherhood), other observers were not so sure about the value of collapsing once-firm class distinctions.[27] Upper- and middle-class parents were horrified to discover that "their children were gyrating and embracing on the dance floor with the same abandon as the denizens of 'tenderloin' dives" and immediately banned dances like the "Fox Trot" and "Grizzly Bear." Enlisting the aid of high society dance instructors, like George and Irene Castle, they instituted new rules of decorum for social dancing: "Do not wiggle the shoulders. Do not shake the hips. Do not twist the body. Do not flounce the elbows. . . . Avoid low, fantastic, and acrobatic dips."[28]

Amusement parks, too, were designed as fantasy spaces where special rules obtained. The elaborate archways that marked the entrances of these parks signaled one's admission into a safe space of hedonistic revelry. Advertisements and press releases reassured visitors that "representatives of the rowdy element [would] not be tolerated" even as the attractions themselves promoted rowdiness. Indeed, Nasaw and historian John Kasson both argue that one of the functions of these parks was to transmute the dangers of modern life into harmless thrills. Disaster exhibits, for example, reenacted real natural disasters (earthquakes, fires, and floods) in a safe and spectacular way while mechanized amusements like the roller-coasters and Ferris wheels mimicked (in exaggerated proportions) the dizzying sensations of real-life streetcars and railway trains. Such rides not only helped acclimate the urban populations to the new conditions of modern life ("after such a ride, the worst twists of the New York elevated Railroad could hold no terror," as Kasson puts it), they provided many opportunities for individuals to come together.[29] Rides like The Tickler (a swirling barrel ride) or The Human Roulette Wheel (which used centrifugal force to fling people together around a spinning circle) broke down barriers by literally throwing people together. Other rides, like the ubiquitous Tunnels of Love gave young couples a chance to snuggle in the dark. Some attractions very deliberately announced their break from the rules of ordinary social decorum. For example, Steeplechase Park, the largest and longest-lasting of the Coney Island amusement parks, featured a booth with imitation china, which visitors were invited to break. "If you can't break up your own home," its posters announced, "break up ours!"

HUMAN ROULETTE WHEEL, NEW STEEPLECHASE PARK

FIGURE 2.02   *The Human Roulette Wheel at Steeple Chase Park, Coney Island, NY. Courtesy of the Library of Congress, Prints & Photograph Division.*

As Kasson argues, these amusement parks represented a "world turned upside down." Like earlier forms of carnival, they "tested and transformed accustomed social roles and values." Coney Island, in particular, attracted people *because* it mocked the established social order: "Against the values of thrift, sobriety, industry, and ambition, [Coney Island] encouraged extravagance, gaiety, abandon, revelry. [It] signaled the rise of a new mass culture no longer deferential to genteel tastes and values." In short, it helped to "[institutionalize] the carnival spirit for a culture that lacked the carnival tradition."[30]

Not everyone was happy about this development, however. Coney Island, and the new mass culture in general, "raised profound questions . . . about the nature of crowds, the ultimate influence of this new breed of amusement, and the future of . . . culture in an urban-industrial age."[31] Genteel defenders of tradition saw the sensual excess of Coney and other amusement complexes as morally depraved and dangerous. Well-known New York arts critic James Gibbons Huneker argued that a trip to Coney encouraged a type of abandonment akin to lunacy or morphine addiction. He compared it the Roman Saturnalia (a feast of drunkenness and debauchery held in honor of the god Saturn) and argued that "once en masse . . . humanity sheds its civilization and becomes half child, half savage."[32] In short, he feared the temporary license afforded by these public amusements would produce a permanent form of barbarous imbecility. Progressive reformers not surprisingly found the pleasures afforded by commercial amusements to be inferior to those provided by more wholesome forms of organized play. Whereas sports and games stimulated intellectual and physical development and promoted a healthy self-discipline, reformers argued, commercialized amusements did the opposite. To try to combat the influence of entertainment industries, reformers started their own "play movement," which targeted immigrant and working-class youth and featured gymnastic drills, calisthenics, and organized forms of sport undertaken in the fresh air and under the careful supervision of adults. Yet, such regimented play never really caught on with the youngsters, perhaps because they sensed the real goal of the reformers, which was to recapture their lost authority over the lives and tastes of the masses.

Most critiques of the commercial amusements failed to grant the populace the wit to distinguish between a temporary respite and a permanent state of affairs. Critics underestimated both the ability of the masses to make informed decisions about their own pleasure and the capacity of mass cultural amusements to provide something more than empty hedonism. As Kasson concludes, however, it would be a mistake to assume that the commercialization of public amusements in the modern era had no negative effects on the culture. As an "institutionalized bacchanal," Coney Island and other commercial amusements "offered 'fun' in a managed celebration for commercial ends." Its amusements were engineered "to keep customers in the role of active consumers."[33] The pleasures induced by these commodified experiences were instantaneously experienced and instantaneously used up. They could not fulfill a person's long-term need for dignity and mutual support in the face of a harsh existence.

Moreover, commercialized amusements often mimicked and reinforced the routines of modern industrial life. They used mass production methods to crank out more and better distractions and attuned modern subjects to life in a mechanized environment. Far from providing an escape from work, then, public amusements may have produced a tighter integration of work and leisure, and, by helping to refresh and distract modern workers, they may have made it easier to control them. The new amusements may have freed the masses from the stifling moral dictums of genteel culture, but only to subject them to a new form social control—the demands of capitalist production and consumption. Did the carnivalesque tendencies of the new mass culture only serve, in the end, to reconcile the public to the inequities of modern capitalist society?

THE VERNACULAR IN A POSTMODERN AGE

By the 1920s, the commercialized public amusements discussed by Nasaw and Kasson had ushered in a new culture of consumption, which indexed social status and identity to the freedom to buy. As Kasson observes, "mass production, mass distribution, and installment buying allowed people of moderate means to acquire products similar to those of the rich, from automobiles to electric ranges and toasters."[34] For much of the twentieth century, Fordist methods of mass production—named after Henry Ford, creator of the assembly line—ensured that a steady stream of consumer goods would be available to the masses, who would have the means to afford them by virtue of their jobs in the new factories. By the 1970s, however, this mass production / mass consumption model had reached a crisis. The costs of labor had become too high (or so the corporations said) and the output too standardized to thrive in an increasingly competitive global market. Many firms began downsizing and automating their labor forces, and they moved from the Fordist model of production, based on the large-scale manufacture of standardized goods for a mass market, to a Post-Fordist model, premised on the small-scale, flexible production of goods tailored to the tastes of different consumer niches. To many, these new productive relations signaled the end of the modern era and the beginning of a post-modern one.[35]

Cultural studies scholar Chris Barker defines **post-modernity** as "an historical period after modernity marked by the centrality of consumption in a post-industrial context."[36] By "post-industrial" he means an economy predicated less on the manufacture of material goods (things you can touch) than on the provision of immaterial goods like information and service (which you can't touch). In layman's terms, this means factory jobs have given way to jobs in the information, entertainment, and service sectors in most locations. Of course, this transition happened at different times in different places and has not happened yet in developing countries like Bangladesh, Indonesia, and Vietnam where the bulk of the world's consumer goods—from T-shirts to cellphones—are now manufactured. But even in these "developing" regions, consumerism has become an accepted part of everyday life. Thanks to **globalization** (about which see Chapter 9), citizens the world over are now addressed primarily as consumers, and the common culture is a consumer culture in which everything is available for a price. What you choose to buy—from products to ideas to political candidates—and what you are willing to pay become the key ways you denote your identity and status relative to others in a post-modern society.

The cultural milieu of post-modern society features an exaggerated emphasis on visuality, sensationalism, spectacle, and novelty. "It is a world of constantly shifting forms and arrangements" that respects no boundaries with regard to high versus low, us versus them, authentic versus inauthentic. As a cultural style it is "marked by **intertextuality**, irony, pastiche, genre blurring and *bricolage*," which is a fancy was of saying post-modern forms emphasize fragmentation, recombination, and openness to interpretation.[37] Think about television shows like *The Simpson's* (Fox, 1989–) or *The Sopranos* (HBO, 1999–2007), both of which have been global hits with large popular followings. The former is intertextual, irreverent, and parodic; it liberally mixes different media, genres, stars, and celebrities, from Shakespeare and Alfred Hitchcock to *Tom & Jerry* cartoons, into a cultural hodgepodge that invites viewers to play along. It also lampoons contemporary American social institutions and debates to the delight of both American and foreign audiences. *The Sopranos,* on the other hand, combined the violent crime genre with soap opera to interrogate the personal and professional impact of the move from an industrial to a post-industrial economy. Much of the action centers on Tony Soprano's attempts to maintain control over his crime empire in the face of small-scale entrepreneurs with a different management style (one not predicated on machismo and the application of force).

Both shows critique the rise of consumer culture and the impact it has had on our conceptions of identity, community, and social responsibility. Tony's most legitimate enterprise is his garbage business—a service industry devoted to the removal of consumer detritus. His identity is connected with his brand of car (a Cadillac Escalade), his love of classic rock, and his penchant for classic crime films like *Public Enemy* (1931). The more unstable he becomes psychologically, the more he turns to consumer goods, especially Hollywood films, to shore up his identity. Meanwhile, Homer Simpson is an omnivore whose insatiable appetites—for food, for beer, and for distraction—cause regular turmoil for his family and his neighbors. In *The Simpsons Movie* (2007), for example, Homer's inability to pass up free donuts leads him to poison Lake Springfield, setting off a chain of events that nearly spells the death of the town and its inhabitants. The series' producers regularly associate Homer with pigs and piggishness (in the film he adopts a pig), and he is constantly chastised for neglecting his responsibilities, especially to his family, in his pursuit of instant gratification. He is stupid, lazy, impulsive, and irrational, and he is that way, we are led to believe, because of the culture in which he is immersed, a culture that prioritizes consumption over production, pleasure over duty.

The Simpsons and *The Sopranos* both raise important questions about the influence of consumer discourses in the post-modern era. Namely, what happens

FIGURE 2.03 *Promos from* The Sopranos *(1999–2007) and* The Simpsons *(Fox, 1989–).*
The Simpsons *is suffused with intertextual references and in-jokes, such as this reference
to* The Sopranos.

to interpersonal relationships when people begin to think of their identities as "brands" to be managed? What is lost when humans use commodities—the giving and receiving of store-bought cards and gifts, for example—to cement their social relationships? Can we be truly satisfied when all of our identities and interactions are commodified in this way? What sort of life is this? That *The Simpsons* and *The Sopranos* are products of the cultural industries suggests that even our criticisms must be commodified in order to register. Yet, their existence also testifies to an inherent multiplicity within contemporary commercial culture. Whereas modern culture had a certain centripetal force, pulling different consumers together around shared experiences of standardized entertainment, post-modern culture is radically decentered. Instead of targeting "the great, unwashed masses," cultural texts and experiences are now designed with certain niche consumers in mind.

The Sopranos, for example, airs on the premium cable network HBO, which means viewers must pay to watch it. Such exclusivity enables the producers to tailor the show to a well-heeled, well-educated, and culturally well-endowed clientele. The masses may follow along in the show's wake if they desire, and more's the better if they do, but the show is not *aimed* at them and does not have to aim at them. In place of standardized products and a centralized cultural dominant, we get multiple, competing cultural experiences, which requires consumers to pick and choose what they will attend to. Those with greater financial and cultural capital obviously have more options and are freer to choose than other groups. Under these conditions, as Jim Collins notes, "the 'dominant' as a monolithic category [of culture] disappears, but domination only intensifies as the sites of conflict multiply . . . [and new] hierarchies proliferate."[38]

That aspects of post-modern life produce greater fragmentation, differentiation, division, and confusion cannot be denied. Yet, the existence of these forces does not necessarily dictate our response to them. We might just as easily take such fragmentation as an incitement to come together, to socialize more deliberately and with greater care. The emergence of new communications media has opened a whole new world of opportunities for people to meet, create, and connect with distant others. Later chapters will take up the impact of these changes on our patterns of communication, identity formation, and mental stimulation, but here I want to discuss the role of new media in the development of what Jean Burgess calls "vernacular creativity." The term "vernacular" refers to the localized idioms, customs, or practices of a people and has often been used exclusively to talk about pre-modern societies and "folk" cultures. Burgess defines it as "the ordinary practices of creativity that are already embedded in everyday life."[39] She refers to examples like family photography, scrapbooking, collecting, and other hobbies, which exist relatively independently of both the art world and the cultural industries, but draw on codes and skills acquired through a lifetime of exposure to those realms.

While vernacular creativity of this sort has persisted across the ages, it had been a more dominant source of amusement before the advent of mass-produced culture. Today, however, digital media and the internet are revitalizing interest in vernacular creativity by giving people the means and opportunity to record, remix, and share their work. While such activities hardly constitute an authentic folk culture ("authenticity" being a relative concept and "the folk" being a romanticized fantasy), they do knit people together and empower them to express themselves in new ways. Burgess points to things like the digital story-telling initiative, which trains people to create and share short video narratives about their experiences; Etsy, the handy-crafters online exchange; or Flickr, where people share and tag photos they have taken, as examples of the way vernacular creativity can inspire new forms of civic engagement. Her study of the Brisbanites group on Flickr, for example, shows how one man's personal photos of Brisbane, Australia, taken forty years ago, inspired a collective project to document and archive the changes in the cityscape over that span. Younger members were inspired by the photos to go out and snap matching shots of the same locations. The original poster then edited the photos together so that old and new appeared side-by-side, marking the passage of time and its effects on Brisbane. Together, members discussed the changes and learned more about the by-gone history of their city. "So there on a microscopic level," Burgess concludes, "you have vernacular creativity, remediation, social networking, and civic engagement threaded back and forth and adding up to something much more than just sharing photos."[40]

The genealogy craze might also be cited as a form of vernacular creativity dedicated to forging connections between individuals and historical periods. Genealogy involves the study of one's family history, and a bevy of new social apps and websites have sprung up to aid people seeking to trace their family trees. Some of these, like Ancestry.com, are commercial enterprises designed primarily to make a profit, but others, like The US GenWeb Project, are volunteer endeavors created to counter the commercialization of genealogy. In addition to the larger projects, there are hundreds of amateur blogs providing advice on the subject, sharing links and personal stories of research triumph and catastrophes. A list of such blogs can be found on the Geneablogs Facebook group, which exists to help amateur bloggers keep their genealogy blogs active. According to the market research firm Global Industry Analysts, "there are more than eighty million professional and amateur genealogists around the world," and the industry is projected to generate $4.83 billion by 2018.[41] It is safe to say genealogy is not just for Mormons and old people any more. It has become a global craze and inspired many a personal adventure in cross-cultural exchange.

According to *Esquire* editor A.J. Jacobs, the world of genealogy is currently undergoing a revolution related to the development of collaborative, Wikipedia-style websites and data-mining apps, which allow individuals to map the connections between their family trees and those of hundreds of their fellow genealogy buffs (WikiTree, WeRelate, and Geni are a few of these sites). He himself has merged his family tree dozens of times resulting in the discovery of nearly seventy-five million family members, including American actress Gwyneth Paltrow and German philosopher Karl Marx (more on him in Chapter 5). Jacobs has begun contacting some of his new "cousins" to invite them to a global family reunion, and many of them are actually responding (though no word yet from Gwyneth Paltrow). Professional genealogists scoff at such sites and worry about the validity of the evidence for the ancestral connections allegedly mapped, but amateur users seem to be driven by the sport of it (i.e., ancestor-hunting) and the romantic notion that all of these trees will eventually build to one giant megatree representing the Family of Man. Jacobs and others hope that such a megatree "might just make the world a kinder place" since we tend to put our family's well-being above all else.[42]

Such a sentiment expresses perfectly the utopian element at the heart of contemporary vernacular creativity. These amateur practices are not likely to lead to a career in the arts or the cultural industries. They may not even make any money on Etsy. Still, they provide ordinary people with a chance to express themselves and receive acknowledgement—however positive or negative—from a larger society. They also expand our sense of what counts as culture to include a range of activities previously dismissed as amateur, weird, or unworthy. Whatever else they do, those personalized portraits of "You with Jesus Christ," which sell on Etsy.com for $95, show that professionals have no monopoly on the codes of artistic practice. The subjects are posed like a professional studio portrait, and the technique is, at least, competent. All that seems to distinguish the portraits from more professional works of art is the subject matter and tone (specifically, the earnestness of the representation), and, if this is true, then our cultural hierarchies boil down to subjective matters of taste.

Professional artists and critics might find these Jesus portraits vulgar, pedestrian, and overly sentimental, but plenty of Christians do not. Moreover, there is no guarantee that the people who purchase these portraits do so with the same earnest intentions as the creator. It is perfectly possible to embrace these objects with a sense of irony—as comedienne April Winchell did with her "Regretsy" website and book[43]—or to view them as a commentary on the literal-mindedness of many contemporary Christians ("why do they feel the need to affirm their personal relationship with Jesus Christ by making it manifest?"). While it's easy to laugh at some of the stuff that appears on Etsy, the multiplicity of the site itself achieves the same ends as much professional post-modern art: it deconstructs our taste hierarchies, challenges the processes of authorization that produce "art," and reminds us that the power of a work is not inherent to it but derives from the uses to which the object is put.

What shows like *The Simpsons* and *The Sopranos* have in common with the vernacular practices of creativity described above is an acknowledgment of the multiplicity and openness of contemporary culture. As Dutch sociologist Giselinde Kuipers says of *The Simpsons*, "[its] brand of humor plays on the particular cultural capital that comes with living in a highly mediated society: recognizing styles and references, but also being able to see through the media logic."[44] What she means is that a certain amount of media savvy is now a requirement for survival in postmodern society. It is no longer the exclusive possession of "professional" producers but a common practice engaged in by many people on an everyday basis. The new vernacular creativity testifies to the broad dissemination of these media and cultural literacies. Though some of these creative practices are more invested than others in "seeing through the media logic," they all manifest the expectation that people are no longer passive consumers of culture but active, engaged, and productive participants in it. Still, as we shift from a "read-only" culture to a "read-write" culture marked by processes of "redaction," "remixing," and "reconfigurability," how will this affect the relations between individuals and groups in society? Does the end of a single dominant or centralized culture spell the end of domination per se, or does it just multiply the sites of struggles? And if the latter holds true, how are popular forms implicated in these struggles? These are the sorts of questions that will occupy us in the remaining chapters.

CONCLUSION

What should you take away from a historical survey like this? First, you should think about the methods and questions used to organize the argument, for they are representative of the cultural studies approach to popular culture. For one thing, the overviews show a consistent focus on the interplay between material social forces, like the economic relations of production and the institutions that govern them, and our ways of thinking about, or living, those forces (i.e., our cultural responses to those forces and our attempts to reshape them through imaginative labor). For another, they underscore how competitive and conflict-ridden the attempts to define cultural norms and values can be. In each period, different institutions and authorities may have been responsible for determining what counts as culture, but the question of legitimacy—whose cultural practices will be made to count and whose will not—has been a consistent feature of all of the discussions. Cultural studies scholars are particularly interested in these questions of power and position, domination and marginalization.

At the very least you should come away from this chapter with a sense of how our working definition of popular culture—as the ways people "make do" with what the reigning cultural industries and institutions provide—enables a relatively expansive investigation of popular forms and practices. While it is true that many cultural studies texts (including much of this one) focus more on the contemporary era than on the past, this is a preference, not a requirement of the approach. In fact, you may apply the same sets of questions to any cultural context—old or new, past or present. I hope that by tracing the play of popular forms across time I have amply demonstrated the flexibility of the approach. The next chapter will extend these conversations about culture and material life—how we live our relations to the world we inherited—by looking at the various functions that popular culture serves in society. It will ask: How do people use cultural resources in their everyday lives? What needs, desires, or requirements are they trying to fulfill through their cultural engagements? What, in short, does culture do, and what do people do with it?

SUMMARY

- This chapter takes a historical view of popular culture and rejects the idea that popular culture is equivalent to modern mass culture.

- Specifically, it examines the pre-modern, modern, and post-modern eras and considers how issues of status and authority shaped the availability and popularity of cultural resources in each period.

- The chapter focuses on the spectacular, the carnivalesque, and the vernacular as these appear across the ages in order to challenge the notion that historical periods are radically discontinuous. In fact, there is much about Rome that is recognizable to contemporary citizens and much about contemporary life that may seem ancient or foreign.

- Rather than focusing on questions of periodization, we should ask: how did the people interact with, modify, and use the "official" modes of culture available to them? Popular culture is shaped, after all, in dialogue with "official" cultures.

NOTES

1 John Storey, *Cultural Theory and Popular Culture* (New York: Pearson/Prentice Hall, 2001), 13.
2 Holt N. Parker, "Toward a Definition of Popular Culture," *History and Theory* 50 (May 2011), 167.
3 Alexander Yakobson, "Petitio et Largitio: Popular Participation in the Centuriate Assembly of the Late Republic," *Journal of Roman Studies* 82 (1992), 50.
4 Richard C. Beacham, *Spectacle Entertainments of Early Imperial Rome* (New Haven, CT: Yale University Press, 1999), 44.
5 In his 1967 work *The Society of the Spectacle*, French critic Guy Debord complained that "in societies where modern conditions of production prevail, all of life presents itself as an immense accumulation of spectacles. Everything that was directly lived has moved away into a representation." Guy Debord, *Society of the Spectacle* (Detroit, MI: Black & Red Books, 1967), 1.
6 Beacham, *Spectacle Entertainments of Early Imperial Rome*, 9.
7 Ibid., 8.
8 Ibid., 33.
9 See, for example, John Mandeville, "The Travels of Sir John Mandeville," in *British Library Online Collection*, ed. British Library (London, 1356).
10 Mikhail Bahktin, *Rabelais and His World*, trans. Hélène Iswolsky (Bloomington: Indiana University Press, 1984), 10.
11 J.M. Golby and A.W. Purdue, *The Civilisation of the Crowd: Popular Culture in England, 1750–1900* (New York: Schocken Books, 1985), 50.
12 Ibid., 23.
13 Ibid., 50.

14 David Nasaw, *Going Out: The Rise and Fall of Public Amusements* (Cambridge, MA: Harvard University Press, 1993), 5. While I will use the US as the primary example in this section, many of the innovations discussed were arrived at simultaneously around the world and advertised through a new breed of trade publications like *Billboard* (1894), *Motion Picture World* (1907), and *The Vaudeville News* (1920).

15 Nasaw, *Going Out*, 126–127.

16 Davis S. Reynolds and Kimberly R. Gladman, eds., *Venus in Boston, and Other Tales of Nineteenth Century Life* (Amherst: University of Massachusetts Press, 2002), xxxii–xxxiii.

17 Nasaw, *Going Out*, 60.

18 Ibid., Chapter 5.

19 See, for example, Golby and Purdue, *The Civilisation of the Crowd*; Bernhard Rieger, *Technology and the Culture of Modernity in Britain and Germany, 1890–1945* (Cambridge: Cambridge University Press, 2005); John Springhall, *Youth, Popular Culture and Moral Panics: Penny Gaffs to Gangsta-Rap, 1830–1996* (New York: St. Martin's Press, 1998); Eugen Weber, *Peasants into Frenchmen: The Modernization of Rural France, 1870–1914* (Stanford, CA: Stanford University Press, 1976).

20 Ziad Fahmy, *Ordinary Egyptians: Creating the Modern National through Popular Culture* (Stanford, CA: Stanford University Press, 2011), 5, 4.

21 Jim Collins, *Uncommon Cultures: Popular Culture and Post-Modernism* (New York: Routledge, 1989), 7.

22 Kathy Peiss, *Cheap Amusements: Working Women and Leisure in Turn-of-the-Century New York* (Philadelphia: Temple University Press, 1986), especially Chapter 3.

23 Cited in Nasaw, 181. (The quotation is taken from Captain Nathan Davis's novel of the era *Beulah* [1904]).

24 Ibid., 169.

25 Ibid., 175.

26 Ibid., 181.

27 Ibid., 105

28 Ibid., 106.

29 John F. Kasson, *Amusing the Million: Coney Island at the Turn of the Century* (New York: Hill & Wang, 1978), 77.

30 Ibid., 50.

31 Ibid., 87.

32 Ibid., 96.

33 Ibid., 105–106.

34 Ibid., 107.

35 See, for example, David Harvey, *The Condition of Postmodernity* (Cambridge: Blackwell, 1990).

36 Chris Barker, *Cultural Studies: Theory and Practice*, 4th ed. (Thousand Oaks, CA: SAGE Publications Ltd, 2012), 507.

37 Raymond F. Betts, *A History of Popular Culture: More of Everything, Faster, and Brighter* (New York: Routledge, 2004), 5.

38 Collins, *Uncommon Cultures*, 25.

39 Jean Burgess, "'Vernacular Creativity': An Interview with Jean Burgess (Part One)," October 8, 2007, http://henryjenkins.org/2007/10/vernacular_creativity_an_inter.html#sthash.ZriqSlHz.dpuf (accessed February 16, 2014).

40 Ibid.

41 Mike Richman, "Technology, Word of Mouth Help Genealogy Hit the Mainstream," September 26, 2013, http://www.voanews.com/content/technology-and-word-of-mouth-help-genealogy-hit-mainstream/1757389.html (accessed February 17, 2016).

42 A.J. Jacobs, "Are You My Cousin?," January 31, 2014, http://www.nytimes.com/2014/02/01/opinion/sunday/are-you-my-cousin.html?_r=0 (accessed February 17, 2014).

43 April Winchell, *Regretsy: Where DIY Meets WTF* (New York: Villard, 2012).

44 Giselinde Kuipers, "Culture Reviews: Comment Dit-on 'Do'h!' En Français?," *Contexts*, Winter, 2008, http://contexts.org/articles/winter-2008/comment-dit-on-doh-en-francais/.

REFERENCES

Bahktin, Mikhail. *Rabelais and His World*. Translated by Hélène Iswolsky. Bloomington, IN: Indiana University Press, 1984.

Barker, Chris. *Cultural Studies: Theory and Practice*. 4th ed. Thousand Oaks, CA: SAGE Publications Ltd, 2012.

Beacham, Richard C. *Spectacle Entertainments of Early Imperial Rome*. New Haven, CT: Yale University Press, 1999.

Betts, Raymond F. *A History of Popular Culture: More of Everything, Faster, and Brighter*. New York: Routledge, 2004.

Burgess, Jean. "'Vernacular Creativity': An Interview with Jean Burgess (Part One)." October 8, 2007. http://henryjenkins.org/2007/10/vernacular_creativity_an_inter.html—sthash.ZriqSlHz.dpuf.

Collins, Jim. *Uncommon Cultures: Popular Culture and Post-Modernism*. New York: Routledge, 1989.

Debord, Guy. *Society of the Spectacle*. Detroit, MI: Black & Red Books, 1967.

Fahmy, Ziad. *Ordinary Egyptians: Creating the Modern National through Popular Culture*. Stanford, CA: Stanford University Press, 2011.

Golby, J.M., and A.W. Purdue. *The Civilisation of the Crowd: Popular Culture in England, 1750–1900*. New York: Schocken Books, 1985.

Harvey, David. *The Condition of Postmodernity*. Cambridge: Blackwell, 1990.

Jacobs, A.J. "Are You My Cousin?" January 31, 2014. *New York Times*. http://www.nytimes.com/2014/02/01/opinion/sunday/are-you-my-cousin.html?_r=0.

Kasson, John F. *Amusing the Million: Coney Island at the Turn of the Century*. New York: Hill & Wang, 1978.

Kuipers, Giselinde. "Culture Reviews: Comment Dit-on 'Do'h!' En Français?" *Contexts*, Winter, 2008, http://contexts.org/articles/winter-2008/comment-dit-on-doh-en-francais/.

Mandeville, John. "The Travels of Sir John Mandeville." In *British Library Online Collection*, edited by British Library. London, 1356.

Nasaw, David. *Going Out: The Rise and Fall of Public Amusements*. Cambridge, MA: Harvard University Press, 1993.

Parker, Holt N. "Toward a Definition of Popular Culture." *History and Theory* 50 (May 2011): 147–170.

Peiss, Kathy. *Cheap Amusements: Working Women and Leisure in Turn-of-the-Century New York*. Philadelphia: Temple University Press, 1986.

Reynolds, Davis S., and Kimberly R. Gladman, eds. *Venus in Boston, and Other Tales of Nineteenth Century Life*. Amherst: University of Massachusetts Press, 2002.

Richman, Mike. "Technology, Word of Mouth Help Genealogy Hit the Mainstream." September 26, 2013. http://www.voanews.com/content/technology-and-word-of-mouth-help-genealogy-hit-mainstream/1757389.html.

Rieger, Bernhard. *Technology and the Culture of Modernity in Britain and Germany, 1890–1945*. Cambridge: Cambridge University Press, 2005.

Springhall, John. *Youth, Popular Culture and Moral Panics: Penny Gaffs to Gangsta-Rap, 1830–1996*. New York: St. Martin's Press, 1998.

Storey, John. *Cultural Theory and Popular Culture*. New York: Pearson/Prentice Hall, 2001.

Weber, Eugen. *Peasants into Frenchmen: The Modernization of Rural France, 1870–1914*. Stanford, CA: Stanford University Press, 1976.

Winchell, April. *Regretsy: Where DIY Meets WTF*. New York: Villard, 2012.

Yakobson, Alexander. "Petitio et Largitio: Popular Participation in the Centuriate Assembly of the Late Republic." *Journal of Roman Studies* 82 (1992): 32–52.

CHAPTER 3

What Is the Function of Popular Culture?

In Chapter 1, I argued that the focus of popular culture study should be on people and their practices of creation, interpretation, and agency. Such a focus raises the following questions: What does popular culture do to and for the individuals who make up a society? What purposes might it serve for the institutions and actors who make it, and what purposes might it serve for those who consume it? How and why do people use cultural resources in their everyday lives? There is no simple answer to these questions except to say that popular culture serves a variety of functions for a variety of actors. Those who produce cultural resources often have a very different agenda than those who consume or repurpose those resources. Perhaps the only thing we can say with any assurance is that popular culture is about more than just making money or distracting the masses (though those are two of its many functions). It is also about more than empowering consumers or expressing resistance to the mainstream. Production and consumption, power and resistance, are increasingly intertwined in contemporary cultures (about which see Chapters 5 and 6), and a proper appreciation of the functions of popular culture must take a dialectical approach. It must ask how culture works on us even as we work through it to express our own needs and desires.

This chapter will introduce you to some of the major functions served by popular culture in contemporary societies. It will draw on a range of theories about the utility of culture in the lives of nations, institutions, and individuals, and it will emphasize the dynamic nature of cultural meanings and uses. For schematic purposes, I will address each use in a separate section, but you should think of them as intertwined sets of possibilities. Any cultural technology, artifact, or practice can take on a range of functions in a given context; uses, motives, and effects may vary from person to person, institution to institution, and situation to situation. Different people may discover different meanings and uses for the same cultural resource even when they have similar life experiences. Likewise, the same person may find different uses for a cultural resource at different times in their lives or at different times of the day. For example, many people watch TV differently in the morning than they do in the evening, and they often report watching more TV as they age or when they are sick. Thus, a range of factors might affect decisions about when, where, and how to interact with cultural resources, including issues of availability and access, time constraints, monetary constraints, and interpersonal dynamics.

You should think of these functions as an interactive menu of options, any number of which may be in play at the same time. The only way to determine which functions are relevant is to study the cultural artifact or practice in its social context.

So, what are the major functions popular culture might serve in society? While there are a number of ways individuals might engage with cultural resources, these can be grouped into four major functions:

1. Popular culture may express and reaffirm social values (Disseminate ideology)

2. It may enlighten and empower individuals (Raise consciousness)

3. It may help individuals cope with their existing conditions (Provide therapy)

4. It may provide pleasure on its own terms (Offer stimulation and distraction)

Again, you should think of these practices as dynamic and interactive, susceptible to combination and recombination depending on changing circumstances. To illustrate the functions, I will use discussions of television as a technology, an industry, and a cultural form, combined with ethnographic reports of how people actually engage with the medium in their everyday lives. Television clearly plays a role in disseminating and reinforcing the common sense assumptions of society, but it also provides a range of opportunities for people to evade, complicate, or challenge those assumptions and to satisfy alternative needs and desires.

POPULAR CULTURE AND THE AFFIRMATION OF SOCIAL VALUES

One of the central functions of popular culture is to *articulate and reaffirm traditional norms, values, and ideals*. In previous eras, when communities were more homogenous, shared rituals (feasts, dances, rites of passage, etc.) and religious practices ensured that the group's values would be articulated and passed on to future generations, but, in today's complex societies, such rituals and beliefs are harder to come by. What we share is an engagement with the media and popular arts. Thus, popular culture has taken on some of the responsibility in our societies for articulating and affirming shared beliefs. There is some irony here, however, as the very same media that now transmit our shared cultural references also helped destabilize our concepts of time, space, and tradition in the first place. "Instead of relating to the past through a shared sense of place or ancestry," as historian George Lipsitz puts it, "consumers of electronic mass media can experience a common heritage with people they have never seen; they can acquire memories of a past to which they have no geographic or biological connection."[1] Having freed "the folk" from the bonds of geography and heritage, mass media have helped construct what historian Benedict Anderson calls "imagined communities." The nation is one such community, comprised of members who may never meet face-to-face or see eye-to-eye. Nevertheless, they are made to feel a kinship with their fellow citizens, in part, because they share the same symbolic reference points and rituals. Popular culture plays a vital role in forging such communion. *It is a social aggregator* that brings people together and keeps them on the same wavelength.

Anderson has claimed that national coherence was initially guaranteed through shared practices of reading. The rise of the novel and the newspaper helped train individuals to appreciate the interconnectedness of disparate events and created an illusion of shared space and time. The newspaper rendered this sense of togetherness in graphic fashion by juxtaposing simultaneous events from near and far. It trained readers to appreciate their connection to a distant and diverse citizenry and to understand current events in relation to a shared past (as contained in previous issues). Radio and television enhanced the illusion of togetherness by seeming to address audiences directly. US president Franklin Roosevelt's famous "fireside chats" during the Great Depression are a good example. These intimate conversations helped relieve social tensions by providing listeners with a sense of connection to the seats of power.[2] More mundanely, national weather and farm reports have helped audiences grasp the geography of the nation and attuned them to the temporal rhythms of the state. These reports, and the ritualized consumption of them, helped make the nation "visible and tangible in the lives of its citizens."[3] They provided a kind of education in national identity.

Television added pictures to the liveness and immediacy of the radio for even more emotional punch. Live morning programs, like *Today* (NBC, 1952–) and *Good Morning America* (ABC, 1975–) in the US or *Nationwide* (BBC, 1969–1983) and *This Morning* (ITV, 1988–) in Great Britain, have long "manifested 'togetherness' by bringing the world to the viewer, filtered through an ersatz family of hosts and assistants."[4] These hosts address viewers directly, drawing them into the "national family" and making "family" and "nation" the privileged lenses through which to view the rest of the world. Thus, for example, foreign policy discussion might be referenced on *Today* but always in relation to how it will affect American families. A classic instance was George W. Bush's 2006 appearance on *Today* to justify the use of water-boarding as a tactic in the War on Terrorism. Instead of defending the effectiveness of the technique, he appealed to the viewers' sense of vulnerability and desire for security: "What this government has done is to take steps necessary to protect you and your family. . . . These are people that want to come and kill your family."[5] Such rhetoric erects a boundary between the domestic and the foreign and encourages people to view home and family life as the root of national security. It positions the nation as an extension of the family circle in order to make the benefits of national belonging palpable to people. Such discourse, however hyperbolic, gives people a reason to identify with the nation and a vested interest in its pursuits. It teaches them the meaning of national identity and belonging (even as it short-circuits public debate about the morality of water-boarding).

While media today seem more concerned with developing lifestyle enclaves than cementing national bonds, television and other media still *play a powerful role in defining reality*. As James Carey argues, reality is not "an eternal given, merely awaiting accurate representation"; it is a "scarce resource" that is "formed and sustained, repaired and transformed, worshipped and celebrated in the ordinary business of living." Popular culture plays a key role in these processes. The constructed nature of reality ensures that it is an object of social struggle, as competing groups work to make their particular ideas, values, and beliefs the "common sense" of the society. This is why Carey describes "the power to define, allocate and display" reality "the fundamental form of power" in society.[6] As film theorists Jean-Louis Comolli and Jean Narboni put it, reality is "nothing but an expression of the prevailing ideology" of a society.[7] An **ideology** is a socially conditioned way of looking at the world. For those who grew up within a society, its unique way of looking at the world may appear to be natural or unremarkable ("just the way things are"), but for those who stand outside the society, whether by choice or by force, the constructed nature of this worldview is easy to discern.

For example, President Bush's appeal to the family as the locus of security constructs the foreign as inherently dangerous. Americans might not think twice about this ideology, but people in other countries, especially Middle Eastern, Arab, or Muslim countries, would likely find it cause for alarm. *The Today Show*'s emphasis on a particular type of family—middle-class, heterosexual, nuclear—also might not register as strange if a viewer's own family approximates that ideal. If you are unmarried, childless, gay, or have an "unconventional" family, however, *Today*'s idea of the family might seem overly narrowly. You might recognize it as a particular *view* of the family. Do *Today*'s producers consciously embed such pro-family messages into the show to serve a political agenda? Probably not, but the effect of the constant flood of stories about middle-class, heterosexual, nuclear families is to normalize a reductive view of family life. Any other way of life comes to seem "abnormal" by comparison, and this selective framing of reality can have material consequences, sanctioning the rights of some at the expense of others. For instance, married, heterosexual couples with children get all kinds of perks in US society—tax credits, insurance allowances, inheritance rights, etc.—which singles, unmarried couples, and gay couples (married or unmarried) are routinely denied.

The selective framing of reality in popular culture may help reinforce the prevailing power relations in society. Indeed, this is arguably another of its central functions: *to stabilize and legitimate the status quo*. This may sound a little nefarious, but it need not be. It is simply an acknowledgment that culture helps "reinforce existing . . . attitudes and lifeways" in a society.[8] The values, beliefs, and traditions (the ideologies) that predominate in a society may do so for a reason—because they seem right and true to most members of the population. They embody a social consensus, and all societies need shared beliefs, values, and practices to communicate and operate. Popular culture is a key location for the expression of what the society values; *it is a site where individuals may be socialized into the norms of the group*.

For instance, detective series like *Law & Order* (NBC, 1990–2010) or *Prime Suspect* (ITV, 1991–1997, 2004, 2006) feature violent criminals preying upon weak citizens. The flawed but recognizably human detectives and legal defenders in these series struggle to apprehend and punish the criminals within the bounds of the law. These characters frequently serve as positive role models, showing viewers what ordinary people can achieve if they set their minds to it. Inspector Jane Tennison of *Prime Suspect,* in particular, became an icon of female empowerment in the 1990s for her perseverance in the face of institutionalized sexism. At a time when women's participation in male-dominated institutions, like the police, was still relatively circumscribed, Tennison offered an image of what such participation might look like. While she was hardly an unalloyed feminist heroine, her actions did encourage viewers to think in new ways about the social value of sexual equality. The characters on *Law & Order* likewise embody ideals of public service, dedication to duty, and tenacity that many viewers find appealing. By *providing role models,* then, popular culture can do a lot of social good; it can affirm cherished truths about social relations, but it can also put a human face on social change, so that developments might be more readily accepted. Such role models teach people how to get along and provide shared reference points for discussion, which can help clarify and further disseminate social values.

In addition to providing role models, *Law & Order, Prime Suspect,* and the like, transmit on-going lessons about the line between right and wrong, good and evil. Each episode is like a mini-morality play that teaches viewers about proper social conduct and identifies the consequences of bad behavior. Perhaps most importantly, such programs endorse the equation between law and order that is a central tenet of democratic societies. They say "law entails order, without law there is no order," thereby reminding citizens of the basis of their rights in the social contract. The essence of this contract, according to Jean-Jacques Rousseau, is the subordination of the will of the individual to the will of the collective: "Each individual surrenders all his rights to the community. Since each man surrenders his rights without reservation, all are equal. And because all are equal, it is to everyone's interest to make life pleasant for his fellows."[9] This contract is the basis of democratic association, and presumably most individuals in democratic societies identify with its values of liberty, equality, and government of, by, and for the people. The reiteration of these principles on television helps broadly disseminate and reaffirm the lessons at the heart of democratic life.

This is likely a good thing, but it is not a politically or ideologically neutral thing. Even ideologies we agree with must be recognized as partial and particular worldviews. There is no position outside of ideology from which to operate. Everything we do and say embodies a perspective on the world. Learning to attend to the assumptions embedded in these perspectives is an important part of learning to interpret popular culture. We must always ask whose interests are served by a given representation or practice, and whose are not? What is the depiction trying to say about the world and our place in it, and what are the possibilities and limitations of that perspective? Should it be or become common sense?

More often than not, popular representations are produced "by the mainstream about the mainstream for the mainstream, or, at least, by and for the mainstream, about others."[10] In commercialized cultural industries, the rationale for such a focus is obvious: the mainstream is the majority population; you are more likely to attract consumers to your cultural wares if you emphasize identities, experiences, and beliefs with which they are already familiar. Confirming the experience of the majority is a way to maximize popularity and profits. This bias toward the mainstream also results from the make-up of the workers in many of these industries. In the British and US film and TV industries, for example, the majority of behind-the-scenes talent (producers, directors, and writers) remains white, heterosexual, and male. While having a woman write about women does not guarantee a better presentation of "female experience," it does help with that all-important **agenda-setting** function—getting women's issues and perspectives on the cultural map. This is often a challenge, and the impediments to producing a more inclusive fictional reality are rationalized through appeals to demographics or to "natural" inclinations. Such rationalizations have political effects, however.

For example, Lena Dunham, executive producer and head writer of the HBO series *Girls* (2012–present), has justified her lily-white depiction of New York through personal psychology: "I really wrote the show from a gut-level place, and each character was a piece of me or based or someone close to me. And only later did I realize that it was four white girls. . . . I did write something that was super-specific to my experience, and I always want to avoid rendering an experience I can't speak to accurately." Yet, as Camille Debose has argued, there were many ways she might have incorporated a different perspective.[11] Making a film and TV show is necessarily a collaborative process, so she might have included a woman of

FIGURE 3.01 *The HBO series* Girls *(2012–) depicts a lily-white New York.*

color on her writing staff or as an episode director. She might have brought in consultants to address her personal blind spots, or she might have sought to extend her personal experience through experimentation. A sensitive and thoughtful writer should be able to render any human experience, given enough attention to detail and a commitment to shaping reality in more inclusive ways. Dunham simply dropped the ball.

The larger point is that she dropped the ball because she could. Her experience conformed with the mainstream so completely that writing about her "super-specific experience" was saleable. Black artists and writers in the US are presumed to speak to the experience of only about 10 percent of the population. A show focused on their "super-specific experience" would be a hard sell to the network executives and advertisers who fund TV production and distribution. This is perhaps why black, female writer-producer Shonda Rhimes's multicultural, omnisexual comedy-drama *Gray's Anatomy* (ABC, 2005–) still centers on the white, heterosexual couple of Drs. Meredith Gray (Ellen Pompeo) and Derek "McDreamy" Shepherd (Patrick Dempsey). There is a double-standard within the industry when it comes to writing about your "super-specific experience," and whites, even white women, have the privilege to pursue their "personal vision."

This example illustrates how even innocent intentions can be ideological and bear political effects. The intense focus on "mainstream experience" in the popular arts leaves little room for other experiences to emerge as "real" or legitimate. Historically, marginal social groups, like gays and lesbians, blacks or immigrants, have been either "symbolically annihilated" from the popular arts, or they have been rendered in the caricatured form of the stereotype. **Symbolic annihilation** refers to the absence of a group from the spectrum of representational discourse. Media scholar Larry Gross coined the term to speak of the stark absence of gays and lesbians on US television up to the 1980s.[12] It might also apply to the virtual absence of black Americans from US television programming from the mid-1950s, when high-profile shows like *Amos & Andy* (CBS, 1951–1953) and *The Nat King Cole Show* (NBC, 1956) were cancelled, to the late 1960s, when *Julia* (NBC, 1968–1971) dared to feature a black actress (Diahann Carroll) in a leading role. Even then, however, the sitcom refused to address race or the racial tensions sweeping the country in the late 1960s. In *Julia*'s fictional reality, race simply did not exist as a social problem. Whites and blacks were fully integrated and got along swimmingly.

While the visibility of minority populations on television has moderately improved since the days when three networks ruled the airwaves, studies show that racial and sexual minorities continue to be under-represented on US television. According to a Gay and Lesbian Alliance Against Defamation (GLAAD) study of the 2006–2007 network television season, for instance, gay and lesbian characters accounted for only 1.3 percent of recurring characters though 8–10 percent of the US population is gay. On the Fox network for the same season, 14 percent of the regular characters were non-white though non-whites comprise over 30 percent of the US population.[13] When you consider programs set in major US cities, the disparities become even more stark: *CSI Miami* (CBS, 2002–2012) contained only two recurring Latino characters despite being set in a county that is 57 percent Latino, and *CSI New York* (CBS, 2004–2013) had no recurring Latino characters in a setting that is more than 30 percent Latino.[14] While symbolic annihilation is not the same as real violence, it does lead to a partial and particular view of US society, which may feed back into and shape real social relations. By constructing this skewed image of reality, television helps legitimate prevailing assumptions about who is or is not an "American" and who is or is not worthy of the state's time, energy, and resources. Such images influence people's mindsets and can impact the distribution of power and resources, ensuring that the "mainstream" continues to receive the lion's share of the state's support.

Stereotyping is another way in which the position and authority of the "mainstream" is upheld in the face of challenges posed by other groups. A **stereotype** is a "simple, striking, easily grasped" image of a social group that, nevertheless, condenses a whole set of assumptions about that group's character, social position, or worth.[15] The "dumb blonde" is a stereotype, for example, but to understand the meaning of that image you have to understand that the "blonde" in question is a woman, that women in US society occupy a lower social status than men, and that part of what legitimates that status is the cultural association between women and emotion. The joke describes the way US society thinks of women—as beings incapable of rational thought. Thus, to describe a male as a "dumb blonde," or a "blonde" at all, simply does not make sense. A whole set of assumptions about the world is packed into that image of the "dumb blonde." This ability to condense information is one of the great advantages of stereotypes: they provide handy short cuts for representation. A writer can convey a lot of information in a brief amount of time by describing a character as a "swarthy Italian," a "drunken Irishman," or a "dumb blonde." The popular arts are riddled with such stereotypical characters whose responsibility is not to carry the story, but to add color and sensation to it.

The problem is that such representations are two-dimensional renderings that refer to actual social groups. In projecting them, television and other popular forms encourage people to mistake the "shown particular" for the "implied general."[16] They encourage viewers to see such figures as representatives of a whole group and its way of life. When only the white characters, or only the male characters, or only the straight characters, or only the middle-class characters achieve three-dimensional complexity, this has the effect of drawing distinctions between these groups and others. It makes some groups seem human while others come to seem like animals or objects, sub-humans not worthy of empathy or care. The same detective series that tout the virtues of democracy and the rule of law, for example, also disproportionately feature violent criminals who are peoples of color. The stereotypical association of violence and drug abuse with blacks and Latinos, coupled with the lack of any investigation of the criminal's psychology or situation, results in a two-dimensional image that furthers the illusion that peoples of color are "naturally" different, "naturally" violent, "naturally" indifferent to human life. By making the distinctions between social groups seem obvious and firm, stereotypes erect a bulwark against the incursions of "others" into the privileges of the "mainstream." As cultural critic Walter Lippmann once put it, stereotypes act as a "fortress of *our* tradition . . . behind [whose] defenses . . . *we* can continue to feel ourselves safe in the position *we* occupy."[17] But, who is this "we," and what would it feel like not to be included within that frame of reference? You can only understand the impact of stereotyping if you learn to bear such questions in mind.

To summarize this section, then, one of the central functions of popular culture is to express and reaffirm tradition. It does so by acting as a social aggregator, bringing people together around certain shared rituals and reference points (identities, stories, role models, genres, discourses, stereotypes). While the affirmation of tradition may have positive effects—giving individuals a basis for communication and validating certain social norms—it is no politically neutral or innocent gesture. It always involves constructing and disseminating a particular view of the world; thus, it always involves power and privilege. Popular culture does not reflect reality so much as it frames and shapes it. By focusing on some groups or experiences, the process of representation necessarily leaves others blurry or out of the frame. This framed reality may not be an accurate reflection of the world, but it does shape the way we think and act toward others in our everyday lives. Every construction of reality conveys implicit lessons about the way the world works or ought to work. By constructing images of reality, popular culture may reconstruct our actual social relations. We may begin to live these images *as if* they were real; we may act *as if* they are true.

POPULAR CULTURE AS CONSCIOUSNESS-RAISING

We have seen how a popular medium like television may convey lessons in citizenship, morality, foreign policy, and other subjects, thereby socializing viewers into the norms of their society. Culture doesn't *only* transmit ideology and affirm tradition, however. It can also expose individuals to new information about their world and even change their minds about things they think they believe. Cultural critic Gary Harmon calls this function *consciousness-raising,* and notes that there are many ways popular culture may achieve this aim: by conveying information, making complex ideas more accessible, providing role models for behavior (a la Jane Tennison), introducing new ideas, attitudes, or lifestyles, and projecting possible futures. The gist of this approach is to recognize that **relevance** is a criteria of great importance for users of popular culture. Individuals embrace works that help them learn about the world and their place in it. They like stories that help them think about the ethical, moral, and social dilemmas people face as individuals and groups. Industry executives understand this, which is why they inject "ripped from the headlines" stories into their fictions and justify their practices as a "public good."

Television, again, is an excellent example of these functions. It *provides information* directly through news and documentary programming and indirectly through scripted and unscripted entertainment. Viewers and industry executives alike have long touted TV's ability to "bring the world into the home" through its news and documentary formats. "Being able to turn on and glimpse other cultures and ways of life, makes the world seem so small and accessible," as one respondent to the British Film Institute's (BFI) survey of viewer behaviors put it. Another credited travel and nature programs for "add[ing] a lot to one's knowledge of the world over the years."[18] Such rhetoric echoes the industry's sense of itself as an engine of enlightenment and uplift. In 1948, for example, future NBC programming chief Pat Weaver hailed the medium's capacity to promote enlightened citizenship by enabling viewers to attend "every event of importance, [meet] every personality of importance in your world, . . . observe members of every group, racial, national, sectional, cultural, religious; [recognize] every city, every country, every river and mountain on sight; [have] full contact with the explanations of every mystery of physics, mechanics and the sciences; [sit] at the feet of the most brilliant teachers, and [be] exposed to the whole range of diversity of mankind's past, present, and the aspirations for mankind's future." Weaver was certain the medium would create "a generation of informed youngsters whose great point of difference from us will be that they accept diversity, individuality, differences in belief, custom, language, et cetera, as wholly natural and desirable."[19] We have to take such pronouncements with a grain of salt, of course, since Weaver is unlikely to discuss the downsides of commercial television when lobbying for more government investment and less government regulation. Still, it is true that television institutions, whether commercial or state-run, have had the resources to travel the globe and bring us stories about distance peoples, places, and events. And they have had various reasons for doing so, not the least of which has been the need to justify their own continued existence. Information provision is a major part of what they do (whether they do it well is another question).

TV's greatest impact on intellect and imagination may not come from its documentary programming, however. It may come from the medium's *ability to translate complex social realities into simple, human dramas*. Reality TV programs, for instance, have often been described in sociological terms as experiments in living. Shows like *Big Brother* (1999–) and *Survivor* (2000–), which are franchised and shown all over the world in local iterations, engage audiences both emotionally and intellectually by putting "real people" in contrived situations to see how they will react. People want to know what the limits of human endurance are and what happens when existing social rules are suspended: How do people adapt to new terrain? Which adaptive mechanisms work, and which are counter-productive or self-defeating? It's a learning game, as much as a soap opera. *Survivor* and *The Amazing Race* (another popular global format) have the added benefit of being set in "exotic" locales. Every episode invites viewers to imaginatively engage with distant places, different peoples, and difficult dilemmas that viewers might have no cause to encounter in their everyday lives. So-called docusoaps, like *Airport* (BBC, 1997–2005) or *Intervention* (A&E, 2005–present), give viewers a peak behind the scenes of other people's ordinary lives and traumas. We get to learn something of how an airport is run, and we can vicariously experience the strain that different forms of addiction can cause on people's lives. Such programs extend our experience of the world and encourage us to become more familiar with the complexities of the human psyche. They are not just forms of distraction; they are also opportunities for intellectual and emotional development.

Even fictional programs on TV may provide information and enlightenment about complex social issues. Indeed, one might argue they are the best formats for conveying information because they are also the most accessible and enjoyable. Most fictional programming filters political or social issues through a melodramatic frame, which means that it simplifies and personalizes what are really complex dilemmas. For example, the US political drama *The West Wing* (NBC, 1999–2006) offered viewers an inside glimpse of the US political system, tackling policy issues both mundane and world-shaking. How does the census work; how are polls conducted and interpreted; what formula is used to determine school financing; how should we handle gun control, capital punishment, and the battle against terrorists? The program tackled these and many other issues, but did so through the techniques of melodrama. Like a soap opera, the show was relationship- and dialogue-driven, but the dialogue centered less on interpersonal issues than on issues of public policy and citizenship. By getting us to care about the main characters, the program was also able to deliver an enormous amount of information about democratic politics. When Deputy Director of White House Communications Sam Seaborn (Rob Lowe) engages a conservative colleague in a debate about the Equal Rights Amendment, for example, viewers are not just reminded that such an amendment once existed. They are treated to a reading of its text and a lengthy recitation of the rights guaranteed to all persons under Fourteenth Amendment to the Constitution. When's the last time you heard the Constitution quoted on the news? *The West Wing* regularly regaled its viewers with references to world history, economic doctrine, national and international law, and political and moral philosophy, and they got away with it because the arguments were articulated by characters we knew and loved. It simplified and personalized complex issues, yes, but such personalization made the information accessible. We might say that, like a Trojan Horse, the entertainment trappings of the series allowed producers to sneak substantive data into the mix without it feeling either "preachy" or "teachy."

TV's penchant for melodrama also makes it a perfect instrument for *exploring human psychology and introducing new life skills*. Thus, for instance, working-class ethnic family sitcoms of the 1950s were used to teach Americans to become better consumers. Episodes of programs like *The Goldbergs* (CBS, 1949–1951; NBC 1952–1953; Dumont, 1954; syndication, 1955–1956), *Life with Luigi* (CBS, 1952) and *I Remember Momma* (CBS, 1949–1957) dramatized the conflict between traditional values of thrift and conservation and the new consumer ethos of hedonism. Their **plots** often centered on the purchase of consumer goods and provided lessons in how to buy on the installment plan. According to George Lipsitz, learning to consume was presented as a means of assimilation, the route to integration and full American citizenship: "Jeannie MacClennan [of *Hey Jeannie*] learns to 'be an American' by dressing fashionably and wearing the right makeup; Luigi Basco hopes to prove himself a worthy candidate for citizenship by opening a checking account and purchasing an insurance policy; Molly Goldberg overcomes her fears of installment and vows to live above her means, 'the American way.'"[20] What made such messages successful was precisely their personalization. The actors were charismatic, and their characters led lives that were recognizable and familiar to many Americans, even those who had already made the transition to the suburban middle class. Such programs used traditional characters and values to smooth the transition to a new economic and social system.

Soap operas, too, have long been used to convey lessons about the proper management of home and family relations. Not the least of these lessons was to use more soap (hygiene = health). During the Great Depression, however, radio soaps taught listeners much more valuable lessons about perseverance. As Lawrence Levine argues, "the soaps reminded their listeners incessantly that while people can and do win victories over adversity, adversity is an inherent part of life over which no one ultimately triumphs."[21] The strong female role models they provided taught viewers how to cope with their own difficult experiences and hard times. Because they elicit intense emotional involvement from their viewers, soaps have frequently been used to convey more practical life lessons, as well. In Egypt, for example, soaps like *Wa ma zala al-Nil yajri* (*And the Nile Flows On*, 1994) have been created specifically to provide information about literacy, hygiene, and family planning. Sponsored by the US Agency for International Development, *And the Nile Flows On* tackled taboo subjects like child marriage, marital rape, and contraception use. It criticized the landed classes for their exploitation of the poor and offered strong female role models to inspire rural women, in particular, to change their lives.[22] This was all shockingly new information for most Egyptian viewers. More recently, the United Nations (UN) has used a similar platform to teach Haitians about the proper use of antibiotics in the midst of a post-earthquake cholera epidemic.[23]

Even soaps not designed to deliver explicit social messages might teach subtly subversive ideas, though. Turkish soap operas are now popular throughout the Middle East. They feature steamy sexual innuendo and idealized images of romantic partnerships that are taboo in many of these societies. Clerics in Saudi Arabia, to cite just one example, have condemned soaps like *Noor* (2005–2007) for being "replete with evil, wickedness, moral collapse, and a war on the virtues." Yet, the soap was incredibly popular in that country, and female fans purportedly took its lessons about companionate marriage to heart, imploring their husbands to be more like the men on the show. While *Noor* is not likely to foment a feminist revolution, it did open a space for dialogue about traditional conceptions of gender, marriage, and family life in some Islamic societies.[24] In other words, Turkish soaps provided "tools to think with," *resources for talking through social dilemmas and rectifying personal problems.*

While many TV programs seek to simplify complex issues, some aspire to add more complexity and nuance to simplistic political debates. In the US, for example, terrorist dramas like *The Grid* (TNT, 2004) and *Sleeper Cell* (Showtime, 2005–2006) helped promote a more self-conscious and complex understanding of terrorism during the early days of the US War on Terrorism. Such shows were carefully designed to distinguish between Arabs, Muslims, and terrorists and featured Arab and Muslim heroes, whom viewers were encouraged to identify with. Indeed, *Sleeper Cell* was a veritable primer on Islam, teaching viewers the meaning of words like "jihad" and "Koran," while offering Muslim characters who were also American and European, white, black, Asian, and Arab. By sympathizing with the black Muslim FBI agent, Darwyn al-Sayeed (Michael Ealy), as he struggled to defuse the terrorist threat, viewers could begin to imaginatively understand the limitations of the then-dominant discourse on terrorism, particularly the "us versus them" rhetoric of the political authorities.

Science fiction programs like *Battlestar Galactica* (SyFy, 2003–2009) and *Jericho* (CBS, 2006–2008) likewise provided a space for moral reasoning by *projecting possible futures* and illustrating the consequences of situational thinking. Both featured post-apocalyptic scenarios about the end of the world, and both featured numerous references to the then-on-going War on Terrorism. Both explored the ramifications of the use of torture, for example, and both placed sympathetic characters under conditions of occupation not unlike those experienced by the peoples of Iraq. By aligning viewer sympathy with the occupied, rather than the occupiers, such programs challenged the US news media's framing of the Iraq War and asked Western viewers to consider what they might do under conditions of foreign oppression. By projecting a version of future history, the show inspired viewers, critics, and pundits to think more deeply about the political and military decisions being undertaken in their names. That the news channels had, by 2006, largely abdicated their responsibility to cover the war only made these imaginative spaces of debate more important.[25]

Such programs are testimony to the power of simple, human stories to bring political and social issues to life for viewers. Since its inception TV has served as "the place where and the means by which . . . most people [get] to know about most other people, and about publicly important events or issues."[26] It doesn't just socialize individuals into the norms of their society; it provides them information about other societies and models alternative ethical and political worlds. It can inspire and help explain social change even as it works to validate and conserve elements of tradition. It can introduce us to new things and make us more reflective about the things we think we already know. Paul Hirsch and Horace Newcomb have described TV as a **cultural forum** for precisely this reason. Television, they argue, is too chaotic and multiplicitous to convey just one ideological worldview. Instead, it offers a wealth of stories about the world, its history, its present, and its peoples, which it asks viewers to confront, test, and affirm or condemn. Ultimately, it is up to individuals to make sense of the resources TV offers, and this is precisely what makes TV "popular" culture. What can be said of TV can be said of popular culture as a whole: "It is at once an information aggregator, a filter, and a space for trying out, or 'working through,' social and cultural concerns."[27] This is the essence of its consciousness-raising function.

POPULAR CULTURE AS THERAPY

In addition to expressing ideology and raising consciousness, popular culture may also provide resources to help individuals cope with or "muddle through" their daily existence. It offers users tools and techniques for living and comforts them when life seems most difficult. It is no coincidence, for example, that networks like Nickelodeon and TVLand, which rely on heavy rotations of "classic" TV sitcoms, saw a spike in viewership in the days following the 9/11 terrorist attacks in the US. The classic sitcom's familiar format and characters enabled a form of escape from the grim realities of life in the aftermath. Re-runs of *I Love Lucy* and *Happy Days* didn't just allow people to evade the news or tune out their own noisy minds; its formulaic structure offered an experience of order and predictability that was badly needed at the time. It also afforded harried subjects an opportunity to laugh and feel ordinary again. Such re-runs offered reassurance and security to a populace shaken by a recent experience of vulnerability. Popular culture often serves therapeutic ends by training individuals to cope with their everyday lives, by offering comfort, by temporarily fulfilling people's wishes and desires, and by allowing them to release emotions and play with social taboos. Like many of the most successful physical and psychotherapies, cultural therapy is largely about helping people learn to live with conditions they cannot change. It is a means of accommodating oneself to reality, not necessarily escaping or over-throwing it.

As a form of therapy, popular culture can *give individuals tools and techniques with which to navigate the pitfalls of everyday existence.* Such pitfalls might include those emotional lows, frustrations, and tensions we experience with loved ones, with bosses and co-workers, with other commuters on our way to work, etc. When other people do not accommodate themselves to us, we must learn to adjust to them or risk our sanity. Culture can teach us techniques for doing so. Feminist scholar Tania Modleski has argued, for example, that US soap operas teach women how to be better nurturers and domestic laborers by training them to anticipate the unspoken needs of their family members and juggle competing demands in the home. The soap's frequent use of close-ups, coupled with its thematic emphasis on secrecy, encourages viewers to learn to read the faces of the characters and guess at their internal motivations. These skills can be transferred to the real world where they enable women to forestall domestic strife by anticipating and attending to the needs of their loved ones before those needs are even expressed. Soaps also use techniques like naming, verbal recapping, and flashbacks to accommodate distracted viewing and multitasking. In these ways, they habituate women to the rhythms and requirements of domestic labor.[28] More practically, soaps frequently facilitate a type of therapeutic talk, whereby viewers use the soap's characters and events to work through certain issues in their lives. Marie Gillespie's study of consumption of the Australian soap *Neighbours* in Britain, for example, showed that South Asian teenagers "'[drew] on the soap as a cultural resource in their everyday interactions.' . . . *Neighbours* gave young people and their families the opportunity to discuss changing gender roles in the family . . . and . . . fed into the teenagers' emotional learning about relationships."[29] The soap helped these girls cope with the social strictures around them by giving them behavioral models and tools to pry open some breathing space.

Popular culture can also help us cope with daily existence by *offering fantasy solutions to problems and frustrations that seem intractable.* In real life, for example, the lack of universal healthcare in the US feels like an intractable social problem. We have been fighting over it for years. While most Americans want more affordable healthcare, or, at least, access to more and better insurance, some worry about the costs of the new system and whether it adequately addresses holes in the current system (rural areas remain chronically understaffed, for example). This is a difficult political dilemma with no easy or simple solutions. On TV, however, medical dramas like *ER* (NBC, 1994–2009) and *Grey's Anatomy* (ABC, 2005–) offer us reassuring fantasies of enlightened, caring, and devoted professionals, who are willing go above and beyond the call of duty to ensure our good health. Faced with a broken medical system, these doctors find a way to work around the obstacles and provide top-notch medical care to all, even the poor and socially marginalized. This fantasy of the "super-doctor" soothes our natural anxieties about illness and death while compensating for, or covering over, the very real crises in our current medical system. Watching these shows, we can imagine for a moment that the system can be fixed. It is a comforting fantasy that helps us get on with our lives.

Many forms of popular culture are designed to *allow us to blow off steam or play with social taboos in a controlled way* so that we might more readily accept our usual position within the social order. Cultural theorist Mikhail Bahktin calls such forms carnivalesque for their similarity to medieval carnival rituals. As discussed in Chapter 2, carnivals were sanctioned occasions for the release of pent-up frustrations. According to Bahktin, "carnival celebrated temporary liberation from the prevailing truth and from the established order; it marked the suspension of all hierarchical rank, privileges, norms and prohibitions."[30] Carnival rituals encouraged people to flout the ordinary rules of social decorum, but only for a limited time. It is not a way of life, but a temporary departure from it. It provides a provisional release of tension so that individuals can resign themselves all the more easily to their ordinary fate. There are many forms of contemporary popular culture that exhibit features of the carnivalesque.

The Jerry Springer Show (1991–), for example, is a proudly trashy US talk show that revels in the outlandishness of its guests and topics. Recent topics have included "Lesbian Hot Tub Party," "I Had Sex With Your Mom," and "The Recession Made Me Cheat." Guests consist of a hodge-podge of the poorly educated, poorly paid, poorly dressed, and poorly fed—not the sort of folks who make it onto the rest of TV—and they are openly encouraged to curse, scream, and "throw down," or fight each other (indeed, "Past Guest Throw Down" is a regular feature). While critics "tsk, tsk" over the show's excessive language, grotesquerie, and violence, viewers understand it to be an exaggerated morality play whose purpose is to reaffirm the social order (the

FIGURE 3.02   The Jerry Springer Show *(1991–) is a syndicated US talk show that is proudly trashy and revels in excess.*

normal) by ridiculing those who fail to conform to it (the abnormal). As if to underscore the point, Springer, the former Mayor of Cincinnati, always ends the show with a moral lecture and the injunction to "take care of yourselves and each other." Hardly a genuine attempt to uplift the masses, such lectures work symbolically to acknowledge the end of the period of fantasy and play. They are the audience's cue to resume the disciplined routines temporarily suspended during the program. Like all carnivalesque reprieves, this one, too, must come to an end.

The Jerry Springer Show also demonstrates how popular culture can *help individuals express latent, repressed, or taboo urges, frustrations and desires.* The show's outrageous pugnacity provides a safe space for the indulgence of behaviors and feelings we ordinarily work to suppress. Many of us might feel the occasional urge to assault our parents, spouses, siblings, or bosses, for example, but we would never act on those urges in real life. Yet, *The Jerry Springer Show* regularly stages such fantasy scenarios, giving viewers an opportunity to watch others do what we ourselves would not. The heightened unreality of the show—its exaggerated mode of display and performance—makes the violation of taboo permissible and gives it a frisson of pleasure. The pleasure comes from the evasion of regular disciplinary strictures. For a brief moment we can indulge our wildest fantasies and liberate ourselves from the social roles and routines that ordinarily confine us. The indulgence is temporary and provisional, though. As cultural critic Frederic Jameson explains, it is a way of managing desire through a type "psychic compromise." Fantasy content may be expressed but only "within careful symbolic containment structures" designed to defuse it. What makes this all therapeutic is that it "gratifie[s] intolerable, unrealizable, properly imperishable desires only to the degree to which they can again be laid to rest."[31] In other words, popular forms permit a temporary flight from social discipline in order to make such discipline more bearable in the long run. They manage, rather than fully indulge, our fantasies.

The therapeutic functions of popular culture ultimately help people navigate the institutions and relationships that surround them. Popular culture can provide tools and techniques that allow people to assert greater control over their everyday lives, but they do so on a micro-scale. Soap operas may help women learn to deal more effectively with their family roles and relationships, for example, but they do not advocate the overthrow of the patriarchal family system. Wish-fulfilling fantasies of the "super doctor" may enable us to imagine a resolution to an intractable social problem, but how realistic are such fantasies? Can isolated heroic efforts really rescue us from our complex social dilemmas? These are therapeutic interventions because they are about learning to accommodate oneself to things one cannot change. While this might sound inherently conservative—preserving social relations that people find oppressive or intolerable—part of the "therapy" is also to give people resources for stealing back some control over their everyday lives. As Levine argues, popular culture can help people learn "to handle their frustrations, adversities and misadventures and cope with life."[32] It can sustain them when times are hard, empower them to think differently, and help them to change the things they have the power to change. It is never merely conservative; it can also be a rehearsal for change by allowing people to "[try] out values and beliefs permissible in art but forbidden in social life."[33] As ever, popular culture is contradictory and can have various effects on social relations.

POPULAR CULTURE AS PLEASURABLE DISTRACTION

As this chapter has shown, popular culture has a lot of productive uses, most of which encourage us to conform to or fit within the social order that surrounds us. Some of them allow us to indulge in fantasy play, but even this play is often productive play—it helps us cope with circumstances beyond our control. But popular culture also has some decidedly non-productive, chaotic, time-wasting, brain-dissolving uses that require consideration. As historian T.J. Jackson Lears notes, "[a] functionalist emphasis on 'use' cannot catch the idiosyncratic, 'useless' qualities of play" that often define popular culture.[34] These non-functional uses may go by the name of "hedonism" or "the pleasure principle" and are usually about thwarting order and rationality just for the sake of it. The **pleasure principle** is a psychoanalytic concept that describes the human compulsion to seek pleasure and avoid pain. This drive was characterized by Sigmund Freud as infantile and regressive, a trait indulged primarily by the young or immature. As we age, we learn to delay gratification of our needs and to deal with the pain and suffering this might cause in a constructive way. It is important to recognize, however, that these stages of human development are intellectual constructs. In reality, we don't leave "early" stages of development behind completely as we progress up the ladder to maturity. The pleasure principle may reemerge at any time; indeed, life is a constant struggle to suppress our infantile, id-based urges in favor of "responsible" action. Sometimes, we lose this struggle. Sometimes, we choose to lose. Popular culture may facilitate such a loss of self. It may be used *to gratify urges we know are immature, inappropriate, and irresponsible,* and such gratification needn't have a purpose. It can be a matter of pure indulgence.

The hedonistic or irresponsible quality of popular play has always been difficult for critics to grasp because they have been trained to prioritize meaning over meaninglessness. Thus, an influential early theory of play, that of Dutch historian Johann Huizinga, held that humans participated in games largely for their socializing effects. Because games have fixed rules that all players share, engagement in play is less a distraction from society than an instance of it. While Huizinga argues that play has two aspects—freedom *and* order, physical release *and* ego-enhancement—he prioritized the latter over the former. Most followers of his theories have likewise emphasized order and ego-enhancement over pure pleasure. Thus, for example, John Cawelti has applied Huizinga's theory of rule-bound play to formula texts, arguing that things like Western films are "games" whose pleasures derive from an appreciation of the rules, rather than their violation.[35] But, pleasure is not always about reaffirming order or the rules. Sometimes it is about deliberately flouting or changing the rules.

Cultural studies scholars John Fiske has come closest to appreciating the elements of pleasure at stake in playing with popular culture. When he discusses the carnivalesque, for example, he ignores the fact that carnival is a sanctioned social occurrence. He prefers to describe it as an instance of pure indulgence, a liberation from the social order per se. This violates the spirit of Bahktin's original argument, but I take Fiske's "error" to be a deliberate and provocative act. He is struggling to theorize the value of freedom and physical release as ends in themselves, to think about how play with popular culture can produce pleasure despite meaning. "We need a theory of pleasure that goes beyond meanings and ideology," he says. What he offers is a concept of pleasure located in the actions of users, but, unfortunately, he still thinks of these actions as primarily meaning-making. "[We need]," he says, "a theory of pleasure that centers on the power to make meanings rather than on the meanings that are made."[36]

Sometimes, however, meaning is not at stake in popular play. People may use popular culture precisely *to avoid thinking or making sense of the world*. Joke Hermes's research with magazine readers showed, for example, that most readers considered their use of magazines a casual form of escape. They did not value the content, so much as the time away from productive activity that the magazines afforded. More specifically, users valued the fact that the magazines could be easily picked up and put down. "I wanted to know how women's magazines became meaningful for readers," Hermes concluded, "[but] readers told me that magazines had hardly any meaning at all."[37] Indeed, the evasion of meaning and meaning-making was precisely the point of the exercise.

Television is often used in this fashion, as well. For many people it serves as a type of "electronic wallpaper," a pretty decoration that demands little attention. Leaving the TV on in the background may serve a therapeutic function—helping lonely individuals feel like they have company—but more often than not it serves as a deliberate source of distraction. Like a white noise machine, it prevents them from concentrating on any one thing too intensely or for too long. Many more people will use television as a metaphoric valium, helping them relax physically and mentally after a long day. TV, like magazines, is an easily accessible and generally undemanding medium (though, as we will see in Chapter 10, recent programming trends have complicated this assessment). Its programs tend to be formulaic and simple, and they often accommodate scattered attention by making each narrative "beat" brief (about two minutes), cuing our attention through music, repeating key information, and naming characters frequently. Not surprisingly then, the BFI survey of TV use found that fully 78 percent of viewers reported turning to TV, at least occasionally, because "they did not feel like doing anything else." What was on—the program, or meaningful unit—hardly mattered on these occasions.[38] One respondent captured the non-functionality of television use quite well when she described her preference for "daft" comedies: "I spend a lot of time in real life being serious/having pretty intense conversations with people and sometimes watching something daft can be a relief from that!" Actively embracing passivity in this way—declaring oneself a proud couch potato—can be a means of avoiding the need to "cope" with life. Such evasion may prove counter-productive, as, for example, when students prefer to watch TV or play video games rather than complete their homework, but the brief indulgence of infantile needs may be its own reward. In a society structured by the mandate to produce, there is an equally strong compulsion to resist that command and so passivity can become its own source of pleasure.

Many forms of popular culture are more about stimulation and energy than passivity, though. Flash mobs, where people arrange to meet and perform some act of calculated madness (dancing, singing, slouching like a zombie, etc.), seem a perfect example. True, these events are usually designed to engender community, not unlike other social rituals, but they are also about unleashing anarchy. They celebrate a self-organizing ethos that challenges the need for hierarchy and order. Flash mobs are attractive largely because they disrupt ordinary social relations. They are a form of indulgence that undermines business as usual, and this is what makes them pleasurable, over and above any friendships that might develop around the events.

Sports fandom is also more than occasionally like this—a pure expenditure of energy only tangentially related to team activities or communal life. Think about the mechanics of sports fandom: we may ditch work or drive long miles to attend a game; we may bust our budgets to pay for the tickets; we may use the team colors as body armor or war paint; we party (indulge our appetites) before, during, and after the games; and we are encouraged to scream, shout, and jump up and down along with thousands of other people. Our individual egos dissolve, as we melt into the madness of the crowd. While playing sports might inculcate a respect for rules, order, and discipline, then, sports fandom may work in the opposite direction. Energy, once stimulated, may burst the bonds of social propriety completely, resulting in full-blown chaos. The phenomenon of the sports riot testifies to the presence of the unleashed id, the pleasure principle at work. This is not to say that fandom always or inevitably works this way. More often than not, fans participate in a ritualized form of play, whose rules of decorum are designed to curtail wildness. When wildness does break out, however, it may represent a form of resistant pleasure that demands a different theory.

Film and television may likewise stimulate or excite carnal energies for no good reason except to indulge the id. Horror films, women's weepies, and pornography, for example, all aspire to produce a physical response in the viewer (goosebumps, tears, sexual excitation), which is why film scholar Linda Williams calls them "body genres." Many people use these genres for their intended purposes—to mobilize the body and bring it to a peak of excitation or collapse. Doing so cleanses the body of the pressure and weight of social convention. Such apparently retrograde popular forms—and all of these are very popular, especially pornography—thus *express and gratify a utopian desire for escape from mundane reality*. Critics of horror often chide viewers for embracing the violence of the form, but such a critique presupposes that viewers read the violence in a meaningful way, that they recognize or care about the films' misogyny, endorsement of torture, or other political messaging. Quite often, they don't. They just want to see blood and guts; they want the excess; they want to squirm; they want that physical sensation; they want to *know* they are alive, not think about what it *means* to be alive.

We will return to the issue of physical stimulation in Chapter 7, when we talk about affect and its role in culture. For now it is enough to recognize that, in a world defined by social rules and regulations, where work increasingly encroaches upon leisure time, and spaces for the indulgence of the self grow ever smaller, popular culture can serve as a form of release and renewal. We may gratify ourselves and our desires at the expense of others, but in a relatively harmless way since we are usually the only ones hurt by our profligacy. It is *our* time that is wasted, *our* needs that go unmet, *our* intellectual growth that is stunted, and *we* are the ones who will pay the piper eventually. Indeed, indulging the pleasure principle may be a way of asserting control over our lives—of staking a claim to time and the experience of gratification in a society that seeks to monopolize the former and define the latter.

How does such indulgence differ from cultural therapy? In its spirit, its intention, and its intensity. Indulgence involves a willful resistance to the social order and its pressures; it is not about learning to cope with that order but about changing the rules entirely. It seeks to open a new register of experience, one that is devalued or marginalized in "normal" life. That such hedonism may also be self-destructive or self-defeating is beside the point; self-destruction may be the only means we have of asserting control over our lives in certain circumstances. And, besides, most of us do not engage in such behavior regularly. It is an occasional use, a recreational form of narcotism, if you will.

CONCLUSION

This chapter has reviewed several possible functions that popular culture might serve for individuals and societies. It may produce communities by creating shared references and ideals; it may disseminate and enforce social norms and values; it may introduce individuals to new information and new ways of thinking; it may package complex information in accessible forms; it may provide people with resources for thinking through or coping with their everyday lives; and it may offer a chance to indulge pleasure and forget pain. By now, some of you have no doubt noticed that these "uses" sometimes work at cross-purposes. How can culture both affirm tradition and legitimate social change? How can it construct reality and allow for its evasion? How can it control users even as it enables them to resist or evade such control? What ultimately, is the politics of popular culture: is it about affirming power or enabling resistance? These are questions we will take up more fully in Chapter 5, but, first, we will take a brief interlude to deal with some questions of method.

My discussion of television has been extremely wide-ranging. To make my points, I have analyzed the content of specific programs and episodes, discussed the cultural logics of the medium as a whole (its emphasis on liveness and immediacy), referred to some of the economic constraints on the TV industry, drawn attention to the unique affordances of television as a technology, and asked about how people use TV in their everyday lives. Such an approach differs in important ways from traditional literary or film studies approaches to popular culture, which tend to rely almost exclusively on practices of textual analysis, or "close reading." The goal of close reading is to divine the meaning and value of the text by looking at how it is constructed. This is all well and good, except that texts are rarely the transparent repositories of meaning that textual analysts presume them to be. Every text contains many possible meanings, and our readings of them may be shaped by a variety of factors that lie outside the text proper. To account for meaning-making as a process, then, we need a more complicated approach, one that takes the text seriously but also examines the social and historical contexts that shape its production, distribution, and reception. Chapter 4 will trace some of the history of textual analysis and make a case for this more complicated approach.

SUMMARY

- Popular culture serves a variety of social functions, but most of these cluster into one of four categories:

  - *Popular culture may disseminate ideology.* It provides a set of shared reference points, constructs a normative view of the world, and helps make these norms feel like "common sense."

  - *Popular culture may raise popular consciousness.* Popular culture provides "tools to think with," resources for talking through social dilemmas and resolving personal problems.

  - *Popular culture may help individuals cope with their existing conditions.* As a form of therapy, it offers people comfort, allows them to fulfill their fondest wishes, and helps them release their emotions.

  - *Popular culture may provide pleasure and facilitate distraction.* Popular culture can be used to tune-out, resist, or refuse the ideological norms that hold the society together.

- These practices are dynamic, interactive, and changeable. The only way to know which uses are operative is to study popular culture in its social and historical contexts.

NOTES

1 George Lipsitz, *Time Passages: Collective Memory and American Popular Culture* (Minneapolis: University of Minnesota Press, 1990), 5.
2 Lawrence Levine, "The Folklore of Industrial Society: Popular Culture and Its Audiences," *American Historical Review* 97 (Dec. 1992), 1393–1394.

3 Orvar Lofgren, quoted in David Morley, "At Home with Television," in *Television after TV: Essays on a Medium in Transition*, eds. Lynn Spigel and Jan Olsson (Durham, NC: Duke University Press, 2004), 311.

4 Alan Nadal, *Television in Black-and-White American: Race and National Identity* (Lawrence: University Press of Kansas, 2005), 27.

5 "9/11 Five Years Later: President Bush One-on-One," *Today Show* (NBC), 2006.

6 James Carey, *Communication as Culture: Essays on Media and Society* (New York: Routledge, 1992), 86–87.

7 Jean-Luc Comolli and Paul Narboni, "Cinema/Ideology/Criticism," *Screen* 12 (Spring 1971), 30.

8 Gary Harmon, "On the Nature and Functions of Popular Culture," in *Popular Culture Theory and Methodology: A Basic Introduction*, eds. Harold E. Hinds, Jr., Marilyn F. Motz, and Angela M.S. Nelson (Madison: University of Wisconsin Press, 2006), 69.

9 Jean Jacques Rousseau, "The Social Contract," August 1997, 1763, http://www.fordham.edu/halsall/mod/rousseau-soccon.asp (accessed July 29, 2012).

10 Lawrence Gross, quoted in Jonathan Gray, *Television Entertainment* (New York: Routledge, 2008), 125.

11 Camille Debose, "How Lena Dunham Set Me Free," July 17, 2012, http://flowtv.org/2012/07/how-lena-dunham-set-me-free/ (accessed July 5, 2012).

12 Larry Gross, "Out of the Mainstream: Sexual Minorities and the Mass Media," in *Media and Cultural Studies*, eds. Douglas Kellner and Meenakshi Gigi Durham (Malden, MA: Blackwell Publishing, 2001), 405–423.

13 Gray, *Television Entertainment*, 109.

14 Alison Hoffman and Chon Noriega, "Looking for Latino Regulars on Primetime Television: The Fall 2004 Season," (UCLA Chicano Studies Research Center, 2004).

15 Richard Dyer, "The Role of Stereotypes," in *Media Studies: A Reader*, eds. Paul Marris and Sue Thornham (New York: New York University Press, 2000), 246–247.

16 Gray, *Television Entertainment*, 105.

17 Quoted in Dyer, "The Role of Stereotypes," 245.

18 Quoted in David Gauntlett and Annette Hill, *TV Living: Television, Culture and Everyday Life* (New York: Routledge, 1999), 115.

19 Both are quoted in J. Fred Macdonald, *One Nation under Television: The Rise and Decline of Network TV* (New York: Pantheon, 1990), 54.

20 Lipsitz, *Time Passages*, 69.

21 Levine, "The Folklore of Industrial Society: Popular Culture and Its Audiences," 1383.

22 Lila Abu Lughod, *Dramas of Nationhood: The Politics of TV in Egypt* (Chicago: University of Chicago Press, 2001).

23 Alessandra Stanley, "Where Cholera and the Good Life Rub Shoulders," July 11, 2012, *New York Times*, http://www.nytimes.com/2012/07/12/arts/television/in-haiti-tv-tries-to-educate-with-mixed-results.html?_r=2&nl=todaysheadlines&emc=edit_th_20120712 (accessed August 3, 2012).

24 Charles Kenny, "How TV Can Still Save the World," *Foreign Policy* (November 2009), 70–74.

25 Stacy Takacs, *Terrorism TV: Popular Entertainment in Post-9/11 America* (Lawrence: University of Kansas Press, 2012).

26 John Hartley, *Television Truths* (Malden, MA: Blackwell Publishing, 2008), 122.

27 John Ellis, *Seeing Things: Television in the Age of Uncertainty* (London: IB Tauris, 2000), 80.

28 Tania Modleski, "The Search for Tomorrow in Today's Soaps," in *Media Studies: A Reader*, eds. Paul Marris and Sue Thornham (New York: New York University Press, 2000); Tania Modleski, "Rhythms of Reception: Daytime Television and Women's Work," in *Regarding Television: Critical Approaches*, ed. Kaplan, E. Ann (Santa Barbara, CA: Praeger, 1983).

29 Quoted in Gauntlett and Hill, *TV Living*, 217.

30 Mikhail Bahktin, *Rabelais and His World*, trans. Hélène Iswolsky (Bloomington: Indiana University Press, 1984), 10.

31 Frederic Jameson, "Reification and Utopia in Mass Culture," *Social Text* 1, 1 (1979), 141.
32 Levine, "The Folklore of Industrial Society," 1383.
33 Lipsitz, *Time Passages,* 16
34 T.J. Jackson Lears, "Making Fun of Popular Culture," *American Historical Review* 97 (December 1992), 1419.
35 John Cawelti, "The Concept of Formula in the Study of Popular Literature," in *Popular Culture Theory and Methodology: A Basic Introduction,* eds. Harold E. Hinds, Jr., Marilyn F. Motz, and Angela M.S. Nelson (Madison, WI: University of Wisconsin Press, 2006).
36 John Fiske, *Television Culture* (New York: Routledge, 1987), 239.
37 Joke Hermes, *Reading Women's Magazines* (Cambridge: Polity Press, 1995), 143.
38 Gauntlett and Hill, *TV Living,* 113.

REFERENCES

Bahktin, Mikhail. *Rabelais and His World.* Translated by Hélène Iswolsky. Bloomington: Indiana University Press, 1984.

Carey, James. *Communication as Culture: Essays on Media and Society.* New York: Routledge, 1992.

Cawelti, John. "The Concept of Formula in the Study of Popular Literature." In *Popular Culture Theory and Methodology: A Basic Introduction,* edited by Harold E. Hinds, Jr., Marilyn F. Motz, and Angela M.S. Nelson, 183–191. Madison: University of Wisconsin Press, 2006.

Comolli, Jean-Luc, and Paul Narboni. "Cinema/Ideology/Criticism," *Screen* 12 (Spring 1971): 39–48.

Debose, Camille. "How Lena Dunham Set Me Free." July 17, 2012. http://flowtv.org/2012/07/how-lena-dunham-set-me-free/.

Dyer, Richard. "The Role of Sterotypes." In *Media Studies: A Reader,* edited by Paul Marris and Sue Thornham, 246–251. New York: New York University Press, 2000.

Ellis, John. *Seeing Things: Television in the Age of Uncertainty.* London: IB Tauris, 2000.

Fiske, John. *Television Culture.* New York: Routledge, 1987.

Gauntlett, David, and Annette Hill. *TV Living: Television, Culture and Everyday Life.* New York: Routledge, 1999.

Gray, Jonathan. *Television Entertainment.* New York: Routledge, 2008.

Harmon, Gary. "On the Nature and Functions of Popular Culture." In *Popular Culture Theory and Methodology: A Basic Introduction,* edited by Harold E. Hinds, Jr., Marilyn F. Motz, and Angela M.S. Nelson, 62–74. Madison: University of Wisconsin Press, 2006.

Hartley, John. *Television Truths.* Malden, MA: Blackwell Publishing, 2008.

Hermes, Joke. *Reading Women's Magazines.* Cambridge: Polity Press, 1995.

Hoffman, Alison, and Chon Noriega. "Looking for Latino Regulars on Primetime Television: The Fall 2004 Season." 1–25. UCLA Chicano Studies Research Center, 2004.

Jameson, Frederic. "Reification and Utopia in Mass Culture." *Social Text* 1, 1 (1979): 130–148.

Kenny, Charles. "How TV Can Still Save the World." *Foreign Policy* (November 2009): 70–74.

Lears, T.J. Jackson. "Making Fun of Popular Culture." *American Historical Review* 97 (December 1992): 1417–1426.

Levine, Lawrence. "The Folklore of Industrial Society: Popular Culture and Its Audiences." *American Historical Review* 97 (Dec. 1992): 1369–1399.

Lipsitz, George. *Time Passages: Collective Memory and American Popular Culture.* Minneapolis: University of Minnesota Press, 1990.

Lughod, Lila Abu. *Dramas of Nationhood: The Politics of TV in Egypt.* Chicago: University of Chicago Press, 2001.

Macdonald, J. Fred. *One Nation under Television: The Rise and Decline of Network TV.* New York: Pantheon, 1990.

Modleski, Tania. "Rhythms of Reception: Daytime Television and Women's Work." In *Regarding Television: Critical Approaches,* edited by E. Ann Kaplan, 67–74. Santa Barbara, CA: Praeger, 1983.

———. "The Search for Tomorrow in Today's Soaps." In *Media Studies: A Reader,* edited by Paul Marris and Sue Thornham, 582–595. New York: New York University Press, 2000.

Morley, David. "At Home with Television." In *Television after TV: Essays on a Medium in Transition,* edited by Lynn Spigel and Jan Olsson, 303–323. Durham, NC: Duke University Press, 2004.

Nadal, Alan. *Television in Black-and-White American: Race and National Identity.* Lawrence: University Press of Kansas, 2005.

"9/11 Five Years Later: President Bush One-on-One." *Today Show* (NBC), 2006.

Rousseau, Jean Jacques. "The Social Contract (1763)." August 1997. http://www.fordham.edu/halsall/mod/rousseau-soccon.asp.

Stanley, Alessandra. "Where Cholera and the Good Life Rub Shoulders." July 11, 2012. *New York Times,* http://www.nytimes.com/2012/07/12/arts/television/in-haiti-tv-tries-to-educate-with-mixed-results.html?_r=2&nl=todaysheadlines&emc=edit_th_20120712.

Takacs, Stacy. *Terrorism TV: Popular Entertainment in Post-9/11 America.* Lawrence: University of Kansas Press, 2012.

CHAPTER 4

What Is the Object of Popular Culture Study?

If culture is the process of generating and circulating meanings and pleasures within a social system, how do we access those meanings and pleasures? Through what vehicles? What objects or works should we examine in a popular culture course, and how should we go about examining them? In general, the study of popular culture is about the study of systems of representation, but scholars often use the word "text" as a substitute for this clunky phrase. While most people think of a book or written work when they hear the word "text," the term can be used to describe all sorts of representational systems—photographs, movies, clothing choices, and musical performances, as well as books. Anthropologists have used it to talk about kinship systems, food-ways, even cockfights. Clifford Geertz goes so far as to define culture as an "ensemble of texts, themselves ensembles, which the anthropologist strains to read over the shoulders of those to whom they properly belong."[1] Clearly, these are metaphoric uses of the term "text" designed to articulate cultural activity to practices of representation and communication. They imply that culture is about signification, or the process of conveying meaning through signs.

This chapter will address the assumptions and methods that accompany such textualism. Textual analysis offers a vital approach to popular culture, which focuses on the structures of narration and discourse. It is closely identified with the methods of "close reading" in literary studies, but the emphasis on representation and communication directs attention to the actions of producers and audiences, as well. Scholars now acknowledge that texts—however meaningful in themselves—are also the products of particular social relations and contexts. As much time is spent studying the interactions between authors, texts, readers, and contexts, as is spent parsing the meaning of the lines on the page, the lyrics of the song, the composition of the film, or the formal conventions of the performance. This chapter will explain how "textualism" developed as a method. It will describe how textual methods were adopted and altered by cultural scholars and social scientists, and how the approach has been criticized and complicated in recent scholarship. According to some, the density and complexity of contemporary digital cultures undermines the coherence of any single text and strains textual methods to their limits, but, as we will see through a study of the Harry Potter franchise, textual analysis still has an important role to play in the study of popular culture.

HOW DOES REPRESENTATION WORK?

Cultural studies scholars assume the study of popular culture is really about the study of texts, or systems of representation. A **representation** is a sign, image, or picture that stands for, or depicts, something else. The key insight, from a cultural studies standpoint, is that there is always a gap between the entity depicted and the depiction. No representation, no matter how faithful, provides an objective reflection or simple re-presentation of reality. The best it can do is gesture toward that reality and call it to mind. Even a reflection in a mirror inverts and distorts the thing before it. When we talk about representation, then, we are talking about a process of mediation, whereby the real is rendered in symbolic form. According to cultural theorist Stuart Hall, there are two steps to this process. First, we assign signs and symbols—words, pictures, or sounds—to the things we've encountered in the world and hold in our memories. In our heads, we try to make sense of these things by naming, classifying, and organizing them in relation to each other. The second part of the process involves communicating our ideas with others, which, again, requires the use signs and symbols. At both ends, the sign systems we use to name, classify, and speak of the world are shared systems that pre-date our existence. We do not invent them; they invent us. As we learn language, we learn to name and classify things according to the rules our society has already laid out. These rules, or social **codes**, shape our ways of looking at and thinking about the world.

So, cultural studies scholars use the term "representation" to refer to the processes by which meanings are produced and exchanged through shared sign systems. These sign systems are what we refer to as texts, but a text could be a book, film, TV program, song, dance, or ritual. Even objects may be considered texts if they take on meaning. A rock, for example, is just a piece of stone until it is thrown through a window, at which point it sends a message and becomes a text susceptible to interpretation. Cultural studies scholars assume that sign systems are socially and historically constructed and that, therefore, meanings are socially and historically constructed, too. So, even a rock thrown through a window has more than one potential meaning. In the film *It's a Wonderful Life* (1946), for example, George Bailey (Jimmy Stewart) and his future wife (Donna Reed) each make a wish and throw a rock at a rundown mansion because local lore has it that breaking a window in the house will make one's wishes come true. In *Forrest Gump* (1994), by contrast, Jenny Curran (Robin Wright) throws rocks at her father's house to vent her rage and hostility toward the man who abused her, and, in *Remember the Titans* (2000), racist thugs throw a rock through Coach Boone's (Denzel Washington) window to encourage him to quit his job as coach of the town's racially mixed football team. In each case, the rock clearly has a meaning, but the meaning depends upon the context surrounding the gesture of throwing it. We cannot determine the meaning of the rock by looking at it in isolation. We must examine the signs and signals that surround it, as well.

This approach to representation comes from a field of study known as **semiotics**. Semiotics (from the Greek *semeion* meaning "sign") involves the study of signs and processes of signification, or meaning-production. It was pioneered by Swiss linguist Ferdinand de Saussure, whose structural analysis of language eventually became a model for cultural scholarship in a wide variety of disciplines. Saussure argued that **signs** were complex units comprised of a **signifier** (word, image, or sound) and a **signified** (the meaning or concept in your head), whose relationship was relatively arbitrary. There is no natural connection between the sequence R-E-D and the color red, for example. We know this because different societies use different words to describe the same color (e.g., *roja* in Spanish, *rouge* in French, *rosso* in Italian). The association between R-E-D and the color is conventional, or socially constructed, and so may be constructed differently in different societies. We cannot make sense of representations without knowing the social codes that link certain signifiers to certain signifieds within a given context. In a real way, then, meaning does not reside in the signifier or the signified but in the codes that connect them.

Semioticians use the stoplight to illustrate this point. A stoplight is a symbolic system (a text) with an internal structure that you must know in order to interpret the meanings of the various colors. The color red, within this system, has no meaning in and of itself. It gains meaning only when we think about it in relation to the other signifiers within that system. First, we notice that red is different from green, which is different from yellow; thus, there are three signifiers we must assign concepts to, and, since it would be redundant to use all three to say the same thing, we can guess that each stands for a different concept. Then, we might notice that the lights are arranged in a particular sequence and triggered in a particular order. Through convention (by watching others or reading a manual), we learn to associate each color with a particular meaning or behavior (red with stop, yellow with slow, and green with go). Yet even those meanings may shift if the context changes. For example, Americans sometimes struggle to understand British stoplights because, in Britain, the yellow and red lights illuminate simultaneously. Whereas the British find this extra code polite (a semiotic plea to "think about slowing down now, please"), Americans find it confusing ("should I slow down or go? which is it?"). As these examples illustrate, the meaning of a stoplight is neither obvious nor universal. It shifts with the context.

As Hall argues, the semiotic "approach to language unfixes meaning, breaking any natural and inevitable tie between signifier and signified. This opens representation to the constant 'play' or slippage of meaning." If meanings are not fixed, but socially and historically constructed, then "'taking the meaning' must involve an active process of interpretation," which can never be guaranteed. "The meaning we take, as viewers, readers or audiences, is never exactly the meaning which has been given by the speaker or writer or by other viewers." Moreover, language has a history of use, and "we can never cleanse [it] completely, screening out all other, hidden meanings which might modify or distort what we want to say."[2] Representational systems, then, are not closed systems that possess a single meaning to be deciphered; they are open systems comprised of many potential meanings, which individuals must work to activate. How might we go about interpreting these meaning-systems, then? Using what methods or approaches?

METHOD ONE: LOOK TO THE AUTHOR

One way to approach the interpretation of texts is to look to the author as the source of meaning. According to this approach, representations are the embodiment of the intentions of an author, creator, or speaker, and, if we can just figure out what that person intended to say, we can decipher the meaning of the text. We will call this the **intentional approach** because the author's intentions are all that seem to matter when it comes to interpreting texts. Reading involves "translating" or "absorbing" what the author has to say and acting as if it is both obvious and true. This approach is enticing because it seems easy enough to accomplish: we can just ask the author, or read what he or she has said about the work.

Is it really so easy to identify the author's intentions, though? If we think about translating this method into practice, some obvious limitations begin to emerge. For one thing, as French philosopher Michel Foucault has shown, the concept of the author is a relatively recent invention. It was not until the late eighteenth century that authors started signing their works because it was only then that "strict rules concerning author's rights, author-publisher relations, rights of reproduction, and related matters were enacted."[3] Before then, works often served a ritual or communal function and, thus, were not the property of an individual. Folk ballads and epic poems, for instance, were designed to convey the news of the day or provide moral instruction. They were carried from village to village by bards who performed the stories live, thereby creating new texts with each performance. Such works were not signed because they did not reflect the intentions of an individual or express a creative vision; they expressed communal values and relations. The audience was as much the author of those texts as the bard.

This example raises other questions: What happens to texts that have no author or whose authorship is disputed? Do they also have no meaning? Alongside these questions, we might add the following: Can we ever really know an author's intentions? Do the authors themselves always know what they are doing? Most importantly, if the author's intentions determine the meaning, why do different people interpret the same text in different ways? Shouldn't we all be arriving at the same meaning? As these questions demonstrate, the intentional approach posits a rather static conception of communication as a kind of hypodermic transfer whereby the author injects meaning into the reader via the text. Hall, among others, has criticized this model for oversimplifying the processes of production, distribution, and reception that define communication. For one thing, the model fails to consider how the author and reader are always already shaped by the linguistic and cultural codes of their society. For another, it ignores the many ways communications might go awry or get redirected. As we have seen, the arbitrariness of language ensures that texts carry many potential meanings, whose salience may wax and wane as circumstances change. Authors and readers rarely apply exactly the same codes when interacting with and through texts. Thus, the author's intentions are (a) not really his alone (they are an embodiment of social experience internalized through language) and (b) not always legible to readers who might bring their own combination of codes to their encounter with a text. To Hall, and most cultural theorists today, the text does not contain a univocal, authorial meaning. It is a site of many potential meanings, which have to be activated, or realized, by the reader.

The intentional approach is particularly problematic as an approach to mass-produced cultural forms because it cannot account for the corporate nature of said production. Commercial texts are often produced through the collaborative efforts of dozens of people and affected by decisions that have little to do with creative intentions. For instance, decisions about the size of the budget may influence the content and style of a film or TV program as much as any individual's "vision." Additionally, hundreds of people may participate in the creation of a film or television program, so who should we say is the author? The scriptwriter, the producer, the director, the cinematographer, the actors, the editor? Each of these people contributes to the form of the final product, but can any of them be said to control the process so absolutely as to be the author of it? Whose intentions matter under these conditions?

Though the Romantic conception of the author has been in crisis for some time, the notion of authorship continues to shape the way we approach and negotiate the meanings of texts. Foucault describes the author, not as a real person, but as a discursive figure whose function is to limit the potential meanings of a text. We invoke the **author-function** whenever we want to control and direct the way people read a text or set of texts. For example, the author's name may be used like a brand to differentiate products in a crowded marketplace. When network executives promote a new TV series with the phrase, "from the creators of . . ." or identify the producer as the anchor of meaning ("from acclaimed producer J.J. Abrams"), they are using the author as a selling point. Likewise, the names "Danielle Steel" and "James Patterson," while they originally designated people who authored books, have become little more than logos today. The real James Patterson no longer writes all of the books that appear under his signature; instead, the writing is farmed out to ghost writers who work from a template, or story formula.[4] Under these circumstances, the author serves a function not unlike that of the **star** or **genre**. He or she is a brand identifier whose purpose is to minimize the risks associated with commercial cultural production. "James Patterson" now references a type of story, not a person with intentions that matter to our reading process.

Instead of asking "what does the author mean," then, we should ask *"how is the idea of the author being mobilized?"* How does authorship function as a discourse or mechanism that shapes knowledge and interpretation? If authorship is being touted, how and why is this being done? What is the function of the author in this scenario? And, in the case of multiply authored texts, why is one creative genius being advanced over others? What is the effect of selecting one author over another potential candidate? Why praise the director of a film rather than the writer or producer, for example? At the very least, we should learn to be skeptical of arguments that locate meaning in the hands of an author when it comes to industrially produced cultural commodities.

METHOD TWO: LOOK TO NARRATIVE AND GENRE

A second way to approach the interpretation of cultural works is to look at the structure of the **narrative** and compare it to others of its type, or genre. A narrative is basically a story. More specifically, it is a written, spoken, or performed account that shapes the raw events of life into a meaningful tale of cause and effect. Narratives unfold through time (they have a beginning, middle, and end) and involve conflict and change. To study narrative structure, we should ask how the elements of a particular story are arranged in a particular way to achieve a particular effect. *How does the narrative work to prefer certain meanings and direct our attention to those preferences (and away from other options)?* In popular culture, the construction of a particular narrative is often highly formulaic and determined by the codes that govern the genre, or story-type. Thus, it is difficult to study narrative without also attending to questions of generic similarity and difference. What are the conventions that govern the classification of a film as a Western, for example, and how might understanding those conventions help us better understand a particular film in that category? Ultimately, we should study issues of narrative and genre because someone else is making choices that shape our experience of the world. We should ask about the politics of these choices: How is information being selected and framed for our benefit? What is the likely impact of these choices?

Narrative Theory

So, how do we go about studying narrative? What should we look for and why? Narrative theorists usually begin by distinguishing between the **story**—what happened in its entirety—and the plot, or the way elements of the story are selected and organized. Most stories contain much more detail than the plot can hold, so some events must be omitted or downplayed in favor of others. In film, for example, the events of a story may take weeks, months, or years to unfold, but the plot is usually 100–120 minutes in duration. Choices have to be made about what to include, what to leave out, and how to proceed in telling the tale. Where should the plot begin? Where should it end? How long should it take to get between these points? Should the plot proceed chronologically (from beginning to middle to end), or should time be reordered to emphasize certain plot points or themes? Each of these choices impacts our interpretation of events by directing our attention to certain details and away from others.

Films often shorten or expand time for dramatic impact, for example. Incidental human behaviors, like eating or going to the bathroom, may be cut out of the story to make space for the more salient plot points. The goal is to focus audience attention on the actions that matter most to deciphering the *meaning* of the story (at least this is true of Hollywood films). A film may also stretch time to create suspense or repeat elements to draw attention to important issues. At the conclusion of *Back to the Future* (1985), for instance, Marty McFly has four minutes to get the DeLorean time machine to a particular spot if he wants to return to the future. In screen time, however, the period is stretched beyond four minutes to increase the tension. In *Groundhog Day* (1993), the same day is repeated over and over again until the protagonist learns the lessons he needs to learn in order to become a better person. Time may also be scrambled using flashbacks, flash-forwards, slow motion, fast motion, and other tricks of the trade. For instance, the film *Memento* (2000) moves backward in time so that we arrive at the beginning of the story only at the end of the film, after the central character, who suffers from short-term memory loss, has reconstructed his own role in the murder of his lover. A good starting point for narrative analysis, then, might be to ask: Why does the plot start here? Why are the events of the story arranged in this order? What if the story started at a different point? What if it were told in a different way? How might such changes alter our interpretation of story?[5]

According to literary theorist Tzvetan Todorov, most narratives move from a state of equilibrium, through disruption and delay, to a new state of equilibrium.[6] The equilibrium is the normal state of affairs for that story world, and it may differ depending on the setting or type of story. For example, science fiction narratives may be set in space or involve aliens, neither of which is "normal" in the real world. Within the confines of the science fiction narrative, however, we are to assume that both space travel and aliens are plausible. Again, this consistent narrative pattern—from equilibrium to disruption to equilibrium—provides a means to recognize and interpret the difference that different choices make. We should ask: What is considered "normal life" at the beginning of the narrative? What threatens this state of normality? Who or what disrupts the state of normalcy, and what does the disruptor stand for (or against)? Finally, where do we end up? Is the end just like the beginning or has something changed? If something changes, what is it? Are we to celebrate that change or lament it? By asking these sorts of questions, we can get a better sense of the ideological thrust of the narrative (i.e., its dominant messages or preferred meanings).[7]

In addition to questions about temporal order and duration, narrative theorists often ask about the roles available in a given story and who occupies those roles. In "The Morphology of the Folk Tale," Russian literary scholar Vladimir Propp identified seven roles characters could play: hero, heroine, false hero, villain, dispatcher, donor, or helper. The hero is usually the main character, or **protagonist.** He (or she) is sent on an errand or assigned a project, whose completion constitutes the narrative. The villain is usually the hero's opponent and is referred to as the **antagonist.** His (or her) job is to disrupt or delay the hero's progress and to cause general mayhem. Other characters may play the role of helper or obstacle, but the thrust of the narrative is toward the attainment of the hero's goal (rescuing a girl, recovering a treasure, solving a problem, learning something) and the re-establishment of equilibrium. These narrative roles are defined by a set of actions, not by factors like gender, race, class, or humanity. So, for example, a male character can be the "heroine" of a story if he is the object of a search (this being the definition of the heroine in narrative theory). A female character can be the "hero" if she is the subject doing the searching (if her actions drive the narrative). Nature can play the villain if its actions (storms, drought, etc.) impede the hero's attempts to secure his (or her) goal. Thus, which characters get assigned to which roles in the narrative may hint at certain **themes,** or underlying messages.

An easy way to uncover some the central themes in a narrative is to perform something called a **commutation test.** As literary critic Alan McKee explains, "this is a thought experiment where you replace one element of a text with a similar but different" instance of it.[8] So, for example, we might substitute different characters into and out of the role of hero to learn what social codes or ideologies are being preferred in the text. Consider the Western film. The classic Western narrative begins with a shot of the hero, usually a white male, riding into town on his trusty horse. The town is an oasis of civilization in a savage land; it is typically populated by white families, who worship a Christian god, believe in education, and respect the concept of law and order. Into this equilibrium, ride the villains, often played by Native Americans, Mexicans, or "ignorant" (lower class, uneducated, etc.) white men. They lie, cheat, steal, and kill indiscriminately, thereby threatening the social order. The hero must take up the gun to defend the town, but he does so reluctantly and sparingly; he only kills when provoked or as a last resort. The typical Western narrative thus celebrates social order and implies violence is sometimes necessary to secure it. Moreover, it associates righteous violence almost exclusively with white masculinity, thereby reaffirming the social codes that already attach positive connotations to whiteness and maleness. What would happen to the message of "righteous violence" if we re-cast the roles of hero, heroine, and villain? What if a female character occupied the role of hero as in *Giarrettiera/Garter Colt* (1968) or *The Quick and the Dead* (1987)? Given the tendency in Euro-American societies to associate women with weakness, cowardice, and irrationality, would the turn to violence seem as reasonable if a woman were wielding the gun? What if an Indian character became the victim or hero, rather than the villain? What if the white people represented savagery and death, as in *Broken Arrow* (1950), *The Last Wagon* (1956), and *Dances with Wolves* (1990)? How would our perception of the righteousness of the gunslinger's violence be altered by these narrative changes? The commutation test allows us to see how narrative and social codes interact and how that interaction favors certain interpretations while discouraging others.

Narrative theory offers a starting point for analysis that draws our attention to the rules for the selection and arrangement of story elements within a system. Different narrative systems may work according to different rules, however, so you should always start by asking: what is typical of this *type* of narrative system? For example, non-fictional sources, like the news or documentary films, may employ narrative strategies to organize their information, but the codes of these systems will differ from those of fictional treatments. Compare the way newspapers depict crime stories as simple morality tales—innocent victim harmed by savage villain and redeemed by courageous policeman/hero—with the way novels like Jeff Lindsay's *Darkly Dreaming Dexter* (2004; the basis of the TV series *Dexter*) use personal history and social context to explain the villain's actions. Because news bulletins and novels have different tolerances for elaboration (news stories must be brief and to the point; novels may be long and winding), different narrative choices must be made. These different choices may lead us to think differently about the victims, villains, heroes, and crimes. We might be able to forgive a character like Dexter because we know his history, and we know he only murders serial killers and other "bad guys." Are we likely to be as forgiving of characters identified as "criminals" on the news?

Genre Theory

Genres are systems of classification that enable us to group texts together for comparison purposes. Genre classifications are usually built upon shared stylistic or narrative conventions (rules or codes). Conventions may include matters of content—shared character types, settings, costumes, and actions—or they may involve shared narrative choices—certain ways of organizing the story elements and character relations. For example, police procedurals usually take place in urban locales, involve the methodical investigation of crime, and feature dark lighting schemes, guns, violence, and the restitution of law and order at the end. Works of science fiction usually contain futuristic technologies (weapons, space ships, robots, and computers), are set in the future or in an alternate universe (i.e., time and space are dislocated), and investigate the moral implications of scientific development. Romantic comedies focus on heterosexual romance, involve a lot of dialogue, and are resolved through a much delayed marriage or coupling. And we have already seen how Westerns work.

From a production standpoint, genres comprise ready-to-use packages of plot, character, and design. Generic formulas mean producers do not have to invent a completely new story each time out. They can draw upon a stock set of plots and reuse the same technicians, artists, props, and settings over and over again. It is a highly economical mode of storytelling. From an audience standpoint, genres give people a way to sift through the entertainment clutter and identify things they are likely to enjoy based on past experience. They are also reassuringly familiar and, therefore, comforting. We know what to expect from a generic text and can take pleasure in the fulfillment of our expectations (or the avoidance of surprises). Finally, the highly conventional structure of most genre texts directs our attention to matters of execution and variation. Generic formulas provide a solid ground against which we can measure and delight in innovation. What makes the Scream films fun, for example, is their witty deconstruction of the rules of the "slasher film" even as the rules continue to play out. The formula remains the same—normality is disrupted by a monster, and all of the main characters die except the plucky "final girl"—but the tale is told with a nudge and a wink, which is innovative. Much of the pleasure associated with generic texts lies in this tension between convention and invention. We know what the conclusion is likely to be, but we want to know how we get there.

The formulaic nature of genre texts makes them easy for audiences to access and understand, which has often led critics to condemn them as inferior forms of "mass culture." Are genre texts really as simplistic as the critics say, though? Are the people who consume them really just stupid and lazy, or is there something else going on here? Many critics believe genre texts are popular because they address issues that are "historically, socially, and culturally significant."[9] They deal with real-world social tensions and offer imaginary resolutions to those problems. For example, Westerns are structured by a tension between the individual and society. In real life, this tension is unresolvable; our rights as individuals will always conflict with our responsibilities to others. But, in the fantasy world of the Western, the hero manages to fight for the community while remaining self-sufficient. He reconciles these irreconcilable social tensions and provides viewers with the means to think through their own social situations. Genres may be formulaic, then, but they are not necessarily simple or clichéd. Clever producers play with the conventions of the genre, stretching them in new directions and offering new ways to think about the social codes and contradictions embodied in the formula. Indeed, one could argue that formulas force producers to be *more* creative in order to distinguish their works in the marketplace. At the very least, genres provide a stable benchmark against which to measure difference and change.

In sum, a focus on narrative and genre teaches us to appreciate how story forms work to shape our processes of interpretation. An awareness of form makes us better "readers" of popular culture in that it requires us to think more consciously about how information is being selected and framed in a particular way. It draws our attention to the politics of representation. As a form of "close reading," however, these approaches often locate meaning in the text itself and ignore both the author and the reader as contributors to meaning production. Moreover, as we have seen, the meanings a narrative can convey are inherently unstable because language is unstable. We can say of a narrative the same thing Hall has said of language: every narrative is historically and socially situated and has a history of use, which we cannot erase completely. Texts are conventional arrangements of signs that are haunted by alternative possible arrangements.

All texts, as semiotician Roland Barthes would eventually come to realize, are really intertextual in nature, meaning they borrow from a cultural stock of stories about the world and knit these stories into a new whole.[10] Since all texts quote from and make reference to other cultural scripts, they are, by definition, open and **polysemous.** That is, they carry many (*poly*) possible meanings (*seme*), and most of these meanings come from "outside" the work itself (from the culture, from social codes, from the reader's prior experience, etc.). In order to understand the text, then, we need to look beyond the structure of the work itself.

METHOD THREE: LOOK TO THE READER

The recognition that all texts are intertextual and polysemous led to the development of reader-response criticism, or **reception theory**. Reception theory, which emerged in the 1970s, held that readers are not just passive consumers. They are active producers of meanings. If we want to understand how culture works, then, we need to better understand how readers process information and construct interpretations. This theory embodied a fundamentally different conception of the communicational process than the linear author-text-reader (sender-message-receiver) model. Scholars began to discuss communication as a multidimensional process involving encoding, decoding, and feedback loops. Authors were not fully in control of the message, and their works were not stable containers of meaning. Readers played a central role in decoding messages, and, depending on their desires and experiences, they might decode texts in unpredictable ways.

Stuart Hall described three possible styles of reading: dominant, negotiated, and oppositional. **Dominant readings** occur when the author and reader (sender and receiver) use similar codes to interact with the text. The author might encode the text with assumptions about the legitimacy of patriarchal authority—for example, an image of a benevolent father figure—and the reader, who also invests in the notion of patriarchal authority, would decode the text in a similar fashion. Author and reader would largely agree on the meaning of the text. What makes the reading "dominant" is that it is the preferred message of the text and also of the culture from which the text is created. The representation of benevolent fatherhood affirms and reproduces social norms. A **negotiated reading** involves a slight disjunction between the encoding and decoding processes, such that readers take some of the intended meanings but ignore others. A teenager might identify with the notion of benevolence in the benevolent father image, for instance, but chafe at the assumption that father always knows best. His reading largely agrees with the encoded meanings of the text, but he selectively tunes out or misdirects those aspects of the text that do not seem relevant to his situation. **Oppositional readings** occur when there is little to no overlap between the encoding and decoding processes. The author's experiences and encoded intentions are just too remote for the reader to acknowledge or accept. For instance, a feminist whose experience of life under patriarchy has taught her to be suspicious of benevolent father figures might read the image of the kind father as an alibi for male power. She might laugh at the text or deconstruct its underlying assumptions, thereby assembling a completely different text out of the materials her culture has made available to her.

This view of the communication process treats the text as an interface where the author's horizon of understanding meets the reader's and a dialogue ensues.

Reader-response criticism within literary studies took a similar tack. It drew attention to the processes of interpretation and insisted the text was produced through the act of reading. Inspired by new work on hermeneutics (the study of interpretation) in Germany, reader-response critics argued that the sense we make of a work is as much influenced by our prior knowledge and experience as it is by what is "inside" the work. For example, we may have some expectations about how a new mystery novel works because we know how the mystery genre works. This prior knowledge might condition us to pay more attention to incidental details, for we know they often prove to be decisive clues. Alternatively, we might have read other works by the same author, so our knowledge of prior themes and concerns in his or her body of works might affect how we approach the new story. We also bring social experience to our encounter with a text, and this can sometimes condition what we see or don't see. For instance, US readers of the *Harry Potter* series might not understand what a "public school" is, thereby missing important clues about social status inherent in the setting of the novels (in Britain, a public school is an exclusive private academy). Likewise, Italian viewers of the US sitcom *The Nanny* (1993–1999) did not understand the ethnic and class-based humor of the show until it was translated into Italian terms. When Fran Drescher's nanny character became a southern Italian, rather than a Jew, the jokes suddenly made sense.[11] The process of reading, thus, involves an exchange of information between the text, which is encoded with a wealth of social knowledge and experience, and the reader, who brings his or her own cultural baggage to the encounter.

The virtue of reception theory is that it conceives of the reader (or viewer in media studies) as an active participant in the production of meaning. The danger, however, is that it may license some to argue that interpretations are relative and entirely subjective. If interpretation begins with the reader's prior experience, and each reader has different experiences, then won't it be impossible to reach consensus about the meaning of a text? And, what is the difference between a "good" and "bad" reading under these conditions? Reception theorists tend to answer these questions in one of two ways: either they focus on the operations of the text or they focus on the training of the reader.

Hans Robert Jauss argues that the work cues our interpretation. A text "predisposes its audience to a very specific kind of reception" through "announcements, overt and covert signals, familiar characteristics, or implicit allusions" that activate certain of the reader's repertoires of knowledge and leave others dormant.[12] Thus, the text sets limits on what we can read into it. If we read *Hamlet* as a romance, for instance, we are willfully ignoring the cues the text is giving us. Hamlet pledges himself to vengeance and is uninterested in his would-be fiancée, Ophelia; Ophelia kills herself midway through the play; and the play does not end with a marriage (as is conventional) but with mass death. These are all signs of a tragedy, not a romance. If we choose to think of it as a romance, then this is a "bad" reading because it is utterly unsupported by the evidence in the text. Other theorists, like Stanley Fish, argue that our interpretations tend to be relatively similar because we are conditioned by **interpretive communities** to read in a certain way. When we read *Hamlet,* for example, we probably do so in a literature class, and what we learn from our interactions with the teacher and others in the class will shape our personal interpretations of the play. A consensus will form, not because the text limits interpretation, but because we listen to and are influenced by the interpretations of our teachers and friends.

As you might expect, each of these theories possesses some limitations. The attempt to locate consensus in the patterns of the text impinges on the reader's power to read against the grain or interpret in non-orthodox ways. Theorists like Jauss may overstate the case for textual coherence, ignoring the competing messages that all texts carry. They may identify the "dominant" reading as the "correct" reading, thereby limiting the reader's freedom to make alternative sense of the work. Fish's theories go to the other extreme, however, stripping the text of any power to influence the reader's processes of interpretation. According to Fish, there are no texts, only readers; yet, surely the language and organization of a work helps condition the sense readers make of it? Fish also ignores the wider contexts of production, circulation, and promotion within which texts are situated. Isn't it important to consider how these broader contexts impact our access to and interpretation of the texts?

Cultural studies theorists Janet Woolacott and Tony Bennett offer a slightly more sophisticated version of both arguments in their work on the popularity of the James Bond novels and films. They argue that there is no such thing as the "text-in-itself." All texts are really inter-textual mélanges, "humming with reading possibilities which derive from outside [their] covers."[13] Likewise, readers are social subjects whose identities are shaped by their experiences with other cultural systems. Thus, neither the text nor the reader has an independent existence that can serve as the ground of Truth or meaning. "Rather, text and reader are . . . co-produced within a **reading formation**."[14] A reading formation is much more extensive than an interpretive community, which is localized and rooted in peer-to-peer interaction. A reading formation, by contrast, consists of the broader social and cultural relations that prevail in a particular context, and shape what gets put into the text and what readers take out of it.[15] So, in addition to examining the structure and content of the work, we need to examine the production, distribution, and marketing decisions that helped ensure (or doom) its circulation. We need to think about how the work interacts with and is shaped by various intertexts (cultural scripts) and **paratexts** (texts about the text), including similar works (by the same author, in the same series, or in the same genre), promotional materials (cover pages, trailers, ads, interviews with producers or stars, etc.), public discourses (reviews, cultural references, media panics or debates, etc.) and private conversations (shared interpretations, gossip, "**fan** talk," and fan productions, etc.). In a nutshell, examining a reading formation involves asking how our personal interpretations are shaped by a variety of social and industrial factors.

Bennett and Woolacott's approach shifts the focus of cultural research from textual analysis (how to read a text) to the analysis of textualization (how to identify a text and understand people's interactions with it). In place of questions about the authorial intentions and aesthetic merits of a work, they substitute questions about how texts come to be meaningful in practice. They begin by asking about the textual environment that organizes the reception of a work: Where do readers congregate and why? What objects do people invest in and treat as "texts," and what forces (industrial, social, cultural) lead them to so? These questions help determine where study should begin and end. Once the text is identified, they ask about the processes of interpretation: How is the work read by actual readers? Which meanings are preferred by readers and why? How is that process conditioned by other discourses? In a way, the concept of reading formations returns us to Clifford Geertz's conception of culture as an ensemble of texts, comprised of other texts, to be read over the shoulders of actual readers. As Geertz cautions, this is a daunting task whose results can only ever be partial and contingent. The factors that explain the popularity of Sherlock Holmes in the nineteenth century will not be sufficient to account for his popularity today. Still, such an approach will prove far more manageable and much more engaging than trying to divine "Arthur Conan Doyle's message."

CASE STUDY: THE HARRY POTTER PHENOMENON

The Harry Potter phenomenon shows the value of these methods, for it is both a sprawling, intertextual franchise and a touchstone for debates about issues of literacy, authorial control, and textual primacy. The Potter franchise is defined by what Matt Hills calls "hyperdiegesis," or an extra-large storyworld (the term **diegesis** refers to the world inside a fictional creation).[16] The scope and complexity of the Potterverse (Potter universe) ensures that it could never be made to fit inside a single work. Instead, stories about the world proliferate across multiple episodes (sequels), in different media (books, films, soundtracks, videogames), and through amateur fan productions (including informal talk about the stories). To date, the Potterverse encompasses eight books (including *Tales of Beadle the Bard*), eight films, one theme park, a dozen videogames, thousands of promotional intertexts, and perhaps millions of fan texts. Though author Joanne "J.K." Rowling penned the last novel in 2008, and the last Warner Bros. film premiered in 2011, enthusiasm for the franchise has hardly diminished. Like James Bond, Harry Potter and his friends are well on their way to becoming popular heroes—heroes whose presence suffuses the culture to the point where one need not read the book or see the films to know who the characters are or what they stand for.

The pervasiveness of the Potter phenomenon presents some problems for traditional methods of textual analysis. What, for example, is the text of *Harry Potter and the Philosopher's Stone*? Is it the content of the book? If so, which book—the original British version, the US version (in which the "philosopher's" stone becomes the "sorcerer's" stone), the Russian version (starring Garri Potter), or the Hindi version (featuring Hari Puttar)? And where does the film fit in? What about J.K. Rowling's many discussions of the book—are these part of the text? Are fan discussions? What about fan fiction, Wizard Rock, and real-life Quidditch tournaments? Are these parts of the text, and, if not, why not? How do we isolate a text in the midst of this intertextual abundance? Harry Potter offers a test case, then, for our argument that textual analysis should give way to the analysis of textualization. Instead of asking what Harry Potter means, as if that could be determined once and for all, we must ask how people make sense of Potter and how their processes of interpretation are influenced by various discursive, ideological, and institutional forces. What reading formations shape the interpretation and deployment of the Potterverse?

An inquiry of this sort might start with the construction of the individual works. What do the books say and how do they say it? What themes are evident in the series, and how do the works themselves ask to be interpreted? What is the preferred (dominant) reading, and what alternatives seem possible? The first thing we should notice is that the Potter novels together tell a single story—that of the conflict between the forces of good, embodied by Harry Potter and his allies, and the forces of evil, embodied by Voldemort and his henchmen. Harry Potter's biography is a small slice of this larger story, which is itself sliced up and doled out over the course of seven novels. The story is this historical conflict between good and evil, whose beginnings predate Harry's birth (hence the first novel begins, not with Harry, but with life on Privet Drive as it was before he came into the picture). Each novel then tells a different piece of the story, featuring a unique plot. As the protagonist, Harry connects these plots across the series and provides a focus for audience identification. Though the novels address supernatural phenomena, they are written in a realistic manner that invites readers to accept the people, places, and events of the story-world as plausible.

What does it mean to say that the books are realistic? What are the codes of **realism**, and how do we see them in the Potterverse? First, in a realist text, events unfold in a linear, or chronological, fashion and adhere to the logic of cause-and-effect. The HP novels start with Harry and friends at age 11 and end with them at 17. There are few unexplained breaks in chronology, and, with the exception of a few narratively motivated flashbacks, we do not jump around in time. The plot advances through a sequence of cause-effect scenarios, as, for example, in book one, when Harry and Ron win a game of wizard's chess and unlock the door that leads to the philosopher's stone. The second convention of realism has to do with the consistency of the diegesis, or story-world. Realistic tales feature worlds that are spatially and temporally coherent unto themselves. A good story-world need not follow the laws of physics in the real world, as long as it follows its own rules consistently and faithfully. It is not possible in the real world for photos to move or for cars to fly, but it is possible in the world of the Harry Potter novels because this is a magical realm with its own internal logics. Rowling not only provides vivid descriptions of these magical spaces; she offers plausible explanations for the crazy events that take place there (for example, photos move when treated with a special chemical solution). These incidental details exist to lend color to the world and make it "feel" real.

Most importantly, realistic narratives focus on ordinary people and use character psychology and motivation to explain events. In the Potter novels, the abstract concepts of good and evil get assigned names and faces, and the cosmic battle between these forces gets played out through the actions of the hero (Harry Potter), the villain (Voldemort) and their various helpers. Harry and Voldemort are very similar and share many characteristics. They are both orphans, and both are resourceful, daring, and eager to prove themselves. Voldemort's backstory is as well-developed as Harry's, and we see clearly how their respective choices led them onto different paths. Still, we are privy to Harry's thoughts and feelings far more than we are to Voldemort's, which makes us want to identify with Harry and against Voldemort. Like Harry, we are to pity Voldemort (which shows our own good character), but we are not meant to identify with him.

By personalizing an abstract moral conflict in this way, the Potter novels at once simplify complex social tensions (good / evil, love / hate, tolerance / intolerance) and privilege one option above the other. The realist narrative thus works as a force for closure, reducing the potential meanings and pleasures available in the texts and preferring a narrow range of readings. We are invited to identify with Harry and his allies because we have greater access to their thoughts and feelings, and their actions do more to drive the narrative forward. The villains are either inaccessible to us or depicted in an unflattering light, and they work to block the progress of the narrative, which induces a feeling of frustration in the reader. Harry is so identified with the good that virtually anything he does comes to be associated with goodness. When Harry accidentally sets a snake on his adoptive brother, for example, we are supposed to view this as a just comeuppance, rather than a mean-spirited prank. When he isolates his friends and runs off alone, we are supposed to see this as a protective gesture, rather than an act of petulance. By positing Harry as the main point of identification, the narrative subtly structures our interpretation of the moral quandaries at the heart of the novels.

Another powerful force that controls our interpretation is the author-function. Fans know the story of the series' origins as well as they know the novels themselves. According to fan lore, impoverished, single-mother Joanne Rowling dreamed up the idea for the Potterverse while sitting on a London-bound commuter train in 1990. It took her four years to find a literary agent interested in the project and several more to finish the manuscript and secure a UK publisher. During that time, she was living on the dole (state welfare). However, Rowling's persistence eventually paid off, and she became an overnight success. Such lore both humanizes Rowling and validates the rags-to-riches ethos of meritocratic capitalism that the Potter books also celebrate (in the form of the Weasley twins, Fred and George). The origin-story is a way of touting Rowling's uniqueness as an author and has been used by fans and critics alike to explain the content of the books. For example, Rowling's focus on class inequality and intolerance in the Potter novels is attributed to her own experience of poverty and social marginalization. The origin story thus becomes a way of legitimating a certain reading of the novels.

More importantly, Rowling herself has interjected her personal insights into debates about the meaning of the novels. She has given numerous interviews in which she discusses everything from Dumbledore's sexuality (she insists he's gay) to the prominent themes of the novels. "My books are largely about death," she has said to one interviewer while, to another, she has described them as "a prolonged argument for tolerance, a prolonged plea for an end to bigotry." On still other occasions, she has said her intention was to encourage people to "question authority."[17] Yet, her statements appear to have had the opposite effect on her fans. Faithful fans collect, memorize, and redistribute her every word, multiplying the reach of these paratexts and ensuring they become part of the official Harry Potter canon. A **canon** is a sanctioned body of approved works, which is designed to regulate reading behaviors. Potter fans have readily embraced the notion of the canon and have used the "author's intentions" to judge what should or should not be included in it.

Websites like *The Leaky Cauldron* and *HPLexicon*—two of the oldest and most active fan sites—pride themselves on protecting "Rowling's vision." *The Leaky Cauldron,* for example, provides all manner of resources to help fans better understand the textual universe, from timelines, character biographies, and dictionaries to interpretive essays that situate Rowling's work in relation to literary history and philosophy. *HPLexicon* includes much of the same information but in more elaborately detailed forms. So, for instance, there is an Atlas of Wizarding Places, a Handbook of Quidditch, Encyclopedias of Spells and Potions, and a Who's Who of the Wizarding World. Both sites also provide "In Her Own Words" sections devoted to Rowling's interviews and publicized thoughts, and one site called *Accio-Quote!* touts itself as "The Largest Archive of J.K. Rowling in the News on the Web." Its home page is labeled "What JKR says about Books 1–7."

On the one hand, this cult of authorship and canon helps clarify the details of the Potterverse and fosters a richer engagement with the texts. On the other hand, "canonists" tend not to question Rowling's role as the source of meaning, and they make few allowances for alternative interpretations. Thus, they have engaged in flame wars on fan fiction sites over what is or is not "ooc" (out of character). They have maligned fan authors who focus on unconventional relationship stories (those featuring Harry and Hermione or Sirius Black and Remus Lupin, for instance) because Rowling has come out against such stories (though in 2014, she reversed herself on the first). They have even staged debates with fan authors at Potter conventions in order to validate and further publicize their own narrow interpretations of the novels.[18] The author's intentions have thus become a loaded weapon in the struggle for meaning within the Potter fanverse.

Canonists are not just invested in preserving "the facts" of the Potterverse; they are interested in policing behavior within it. They have turned Rowling and her novels into idols to be worshipped, which has stifled alternative interpretations and alienated other fans. These less-reverent fans have not taken such abuse lying down, however. They have created their own fan enclaves where they can speculate to their hearts' content about unconventional relationships, alternate realities, and "what would happen if . . ." scenarios not strictly sanctioned by Rowling or her texts. They have even coined a term to describe the more open parameters of their Potterverse—"the fanon." As these debates illustrate, the author is really a discursive construct, which can be built, shaped, and reshaped to suit a variety of needs (for example, "J.K." Rowling was born of an editor's need to mask Joanne's gender to appeal to young male readers). Under these conditions, we would be better served by asking how discourses about the author and authorship work. How do they attract (or repel) readers and shape their interpretations?

What other forces shape our entry into and interpretation of the Harry Potter "text"? Marketing paratexts—ads, cover art, critical reviews, movie trailers, posters, etc.—play a powerful role in shaping readings in today's commercialized cultural environment. As Jonathan Gray argues, such paratexts are more than simple add-ons: "They create texts, they manage them, and they fill them with many of the meanings that we associate with them."[19] Trailers for the Harry Potter movies, for example, give us clues about how to read the films and may reshape our impressions of the novels. The trailer for *Harry Potter and the Deathly Hollows*, Part 2 (2011), with its eerie grey-toned color scheme and imagery of death (cemeteries, gravestones, fire), looks like an ad for a horror film and implies that Voldemort, whose voice is privileged in the trailer, will triumph. By comparison, the cover art for the US release of the novel features a bright orange and yellow color scheme and only references Voldemort on the back. A battered Harry occupies the center of the image, with arm upraised, leaving the impression that Harry will be the last man standing. The film trailer and cover art thus define very different horizons of expectation that literally alter the shape of the text. The one we encounter first will likely over-determine our sense of the showdown and what it means. Gray calls these "entryway paratexts" because they frame our approach to the text and fix its initial parameters.

Paratexts may also unsettle or shift our impression of a text and its meanings *in medias res*. For example, so-called making-of DVD extras give us insights into the production of a film, which may alter our interpretation of the text in the middle of things. Theoretically, each novel or film in the Potter series may act as a "textual shifter" in this way, "selectively organizing and reorganizing the frameworks of ideological and cultural reference" that shaped our original interpretation of a work.[20] As both text and paratext, each installment in the Potter series orbits around the other texts and opens them up to new interpretations. While *Philosopher's Stone* may conclude, for example, with the defeat of Voldemort/evil and the celebration of Harry/good, each successive novel features the return of evil. Indeed, evil grows stronger and more powerful as the series goes on, making any narrative closure appear tentative, at best. We quickly realize that each installment in the series is subordinate to the larger story, which goes on and on. Like a television soap opera, the Potter novels seem to privilege disruption over resolution. The characters never achieve a state of equilibrium; instead, "their world is one of perpetual disturbance and threat."[21]

Such constant disturbance throws our faith in the status quo into crisis and can lead us to reexamine things we take for granted about the world. This is perhaps why "normality" is a dirty word in the Potterverse. (The first book begins with a satirical dismissal of the Dursley family's reverence for "normality.") The themes of tolerance and service to others clearly speak to ideological tensions within contemporary British society, particularly tensions around New Labor's anti-racism campaigns of the early 2000s.[22] In other parts of the world, these themes may be interpreted and applied in different ways, but we can safely say that similar tensions (between the individual and society and between different groups within society) are prevalent everywhere. The Potter series' open interrogation of the status quo thus becomes one of its primary selling points. That different people can invest in these broad themes in different ways is clearly one of the reasons it has become so popular globally.

This brief excursion into the Potterverse should demonstrate how texts are cobbled together out of a variety of inter- and paratexts, some of which work toward closure and others of which work toward openness. If the narrative structure, author-function and introductory paratexts all work to prefer certain meanings over others, the serialization of the story and its relation to a variety of other paratexts work to foster openness and speculative play. Arguably the key to the Potter franchise's success is its ability to make different types of reading pleasures available to different readers. Some may revel in the moments of narrative closure and seek validation for their interpretations in the author's intentions while others may bask in the associative pleasures of the story—its depth, complexity, and open-endedness, its interrogation of the status quo. The tension between closure and openness invites different groups with different reading strategies to engage with the text in different ways and helps explain why the series appeals to both boys *and* girls, children *and* adults, people in England *and* people in other locales.

The complexity of the texts-in-themselves cannot fully explain the popularity of the Potter franchise, however. Rowling's publishers obviously had the resources to promote the series and ensure broad access to the franchised works. Being on the *New York Times* best seller list helped spread the word about the novels to a range of readers who might otherwise never have noticed a children's series. And Warner Bros. Studios bankrolled the films and ensured their success through saturation marketing, a wide release strategy, cross-promotions, and merchandising deals. These institutional forces ensured it would be hard to miss the Potter series. Still, market saturation is no guarantee of popularity, as Philip Pullman found out when Scholastic and Warner Bros. tried to turn his children's series (called His Dark Materials) into the next Potter franchise. Both the novel and the film of *The Golden Compass* (originally called *Northern Lights*) failed to find an audience outside of England, and plans to invest in future film and videogame adaptations were quickly scrapped. As sociologist David Grazian reminds us, a popular work does not become popular just because it has the full might of the entertainment industry behind it. Far more influential are the actions of individuals (i.e., do they embrace and share the work with others?).[23]

Harry Potter benefitted, in this respect, from a shift in the media landscape, which enabled groups of fans to find each other and advocate for the text. Specifically, the series run coincided with the growth of the internet as a tool for social communication. The first Potter novel was published during the dot.com boom years of the late 1990s, and Harry Potter fans were some of the first to take advantage of the new graphical-user interfaces and web-building tools to self-organize and grow. The first Harry Potter fan site, The Unofficial Harry Potter Fan Club, was launched in 1997, and the first fan fiction site, Harry Potter's Realm of Wizardry, came online soon thereafter (1999). Since then, Harry Potter fan fiction has surpassed even the venerable Star Trek series in volume and internet presence. Today, a search for "Harry Potter Fan Site" on Google results in over 20 million hits. A more specific search of "Harry Potter Fan Fiction" results in 8 million hits. Even allowing for glitches in the search algorithm, this is a prodigious amount of online activity undertaken in the name of the Potterverse. Social media sites like MySpace and Facebook have only enhanced the process of community formation by allowing fans to exchange music, information, and commentary at the touch of a button. Indeed, superfan Melissa Anelli credits the direct marketing capabilities of MySpace for the growth of "Wizard Rock" (the hundreds of bands who now write and perform music based on Potter characters and themes). Clearly, the web has helped turn isolated fans into a "community of imagination" with a shared passion for Harry Potter and a willingness to advocate on behalf of the series and its author.[24] Their every effort, in turn, constitutes a type of free publicity for the franchise, spreading the good word about its complexity and richness and recruiting new readers.

The internet has worked equally well to promote counter-publics, however. Fundamentalist Christians have used it to communicate and share their objections to the novels and to organize censorship campaigns against it. These groups believe the books valorize witchcraft and may encourage children to seek out information on sorcery and alternative religions. Most of these critics have not even read the series, but they have brought a variety of other texts to bear on their interpretation of it. For instance, most have seen the video *Harry Potter: Witchcraft Repackaged—Making Evil Look Innocent* (2002), which discusses the first novel's references to real-world sorcerers (like Nicholas Flamel) and suggests that kids will be driven online to look for information about these individuals. From there, the fear is, they will be lured into the world of alternative religion (specifically Wicca) and "devil-worship." Though conservative Christian organizations like Focus on the Family and The Family Research Council have come out in support of the novels, arguing that they feature the triumph of good over evil and can be used to promote a discussion of Christian values, such statements have not persuaded the true believers. Instead, the statements have been used to illustrate the corruptive influence of the "mainstream" and to justify a rejection of these more moderate Christian approaches (remember from Chapter 1 that the "mainstream" is always in the eye of the beholder).

For Christians who oppose the Potter series, the inter- and paratexts prove more decisive in determining meaning than the novels themselves. They do not need to read the novels, they say, because they already know everything they need know about them from the Bible (which denounces witchcraft) and *Witchcraft Repackaged.* While their version of the Harry Potter text may seem vastly different from mainstream accounts, it does highlight the constructed nature of truth and the political nature of interpretation. Like other readers, the Christian anti-fans treat the Potter novels and films as meaningful units (texts) laden with ideological messages about social normality and moral good. They just disagree on how to evaluate and apply those messages.

The variety of interpretations testifies to the plurality of cultural texts, but it need not lead to the conclusion that a shared interpretation is impossible, or that "everything is relative." In fact, some meanings are more plausible than others, and meanings tend to converge around a few socially relevant issues because they are created from within shared social settings. The Potter novels *are* encoded with questions about morality, and the various paratexts *do* invite viewers to read them in religious or allegorical terms. Many fan activities reinforce these preferred readings by highlighting the moral dilemmas, working them over in public forums, and even using the text's moral lessons to inspire real-world social activism. The Harry Potter Alliance, for example, is a fan network whose members work for various social causes, from pro-literacy and anti-censorship campaigns to campaigns for worker's rights and humanitarian aid to Darfur, Sudan. Thus, it is not surprising that readings of the Potterverse would tend to cluster around questions of morality like "What is good and what is evil?" and "What should we do about evil when we encounter it?" Christian anti-fans participate in and help shape this cluster of meanings, even though their perspectives on these matters differ from those of most other fans.

The Harry Potter phenomenon offers a salutary reminder that meanings do not inhere in texts and are not the property of authors, corporations, or even fans. They are complex constructions produced through the collective efforts of individuals located in various social contexts. Semioticians tell us that every text is really an intertextual mélange, or tissue of quotations, which readers must make sense of using the cultural scripts and codes available to them. Any meanings constructed are always partial and provisional; they are subject to change and reinterpretation if circumstances change. Thus, instead of looking at texts, we should look at the processes of textualization that bring them into being; instead of focusing on readings, we should look at reading formations. What a text means is an impossible yet essential query, which can only be answered by looking at texts in their social contexts of production, circulation, and reception.

CONCLUSION

The textual approach to culture outlined in this chapter has prevailed in cultural studies since the 1990s, but it is not without contestation and amendment. There have been two main objections to this approach, which the next few chapters will take up. The first objection has to do with a tendency in textual approaches to celebrate the work of readers in an uncritical fashion. Critical theorist Jim McGuigan, for example, has accused textual criticism and reception theory of promoting a type of "cultural populism," which views every act of reading as inherently resistant or politically progressive. He and others suggest that more attention should be paid to the economic structures and political regulations that shape the interaction between popular cultural producers, texts, and readers.[25] Chapter 5 will review the history of debates about power and agency within cultural studies, and Chapter 6 will discuss the mechanics of commercial cultural production.

The other primary objection to the semiotic approach has to do with its over-weening emphasis on meaning and sense-making. As scholars like Joke Hermes, Matt Hills, Steven Shaviro, and others note, not every practice of cultural engagement can be reduced to a metaphor of textuality and reading. Not only do we undertake some activities precisely to avoid the injunction to "make sense," but the separation of knowledge from physical pleasure/displeasure artificially separates the mind from the body and stifles the latter in favor of the former. Where is the "love," we might ask? Do not cultural objects and practices engage the body as well as the mind? Chapters 7 and 8 will consider how and why popular cultural forms resonate for individuals—the first by examining processes of identity construction and identifica-tion; the second by asking how popular forms appeal to our senses and sensibilities.

SUMMARY

- A text is a system of representation that constructs a perspective on reality. Because there is a gap between the representation and the real, there is always room for interpretation.

- There are various ways to pursue the interpretation of texts. We might look to the author, the text, the reader (processes of reception), or the reading formation (which combines all of these plus an awareness of social and cultural context).

- To study the author, we should focus less on what the author intends and more on the way a discourse of authorship shapes the reading process. How does the *idea* of the author influence the circulation, valorization, and interpretation of a work?

- To study the text, we should consider how the narrative is organized to achieve a particular effect. How does the structure of the work direct our attention to certain meanings and away from other possible meanings?

- To study the processes of reading or reception, we should look at the way readers decode texts. How actively do they impose their own meanings on a work, and what forces (history, experience, training) influence their choices?

- To study a reading formation involves asking all of the above ques-tions, plus questions about the contexts of circulation, promotion, and valorization. It means looking at how various intertexts, para-texts, and interpretive communities shape the reading processes for individuals and groups.

NOTES

1 Clifford Geertz, "Deep Play: Notes on the Balinese Cockfight," *Daedalus* 134, 4 (2005), 86.
2 Stuart Hall, "The Work of Representation," in *Representation: Cultural Representations and Signifying Practices,* ed. Stuart Hall (Thousand Oaks, CA: Sage Publications, 1997), 32.
3 Michel Foucault, "What Is an Author?," in *The Foucault Reader,* ed. Paul Rabinow (New York: Pantheon Books, 1984).
4 Jonathan Mahler, "James Patterson Inc.," *New York Times*, January 20, 2010, http://www.nytimes.com/2010/01/24/magazine/24patterson-t.html?pagewanted=all&_r=0 (accessed April 1, 2013).
5 Horace Newcomb, "Narrative and Genre," in *The Sage Handbook of Media Studies,* ed. John Downing (Thousand Oaks, CA: SAGE Publications, 2004), 416.
6 Tzvetan Todorov, "Structural Analysis of Narrative," *Novel* 3 (1969).
7 John Fiske, *Television Culture* (New York: Routledge, 1987), 180.
8 Alan McKee, *Textual Analysis: A Beginner's Introduction* (Thousand Oaks, CA: Sage, 2003), 107.
9 Newcomb, "Narrative and Genre," 424.
10 Roland Barthes, "The Death of the Author," in *Image/Music/Text*, ed. Stephen Heath (New York: Hill & Wang, 1977), 146.
11 Chiara Ferrari, "The Nanny in Italy: Language, Nationalism and Cultural Identity," *Global Media Journal* 3, 4 (Spring 2004).
12 Quoted in Karin Littau, *Theories of Reading: Books, Bodies, and Bibliomania* (Malden, MA: Polity Press, 2006), 110.
13 Tony Bennett and Janet Woollacott, *Bond and Beyond: The Political Career of a Popular Hero* (New York: Methuen, 1987), 90.
14 Ibid., 64–65.
15 Ibid., 263.
16 Matt Hills, *Fan Cultures* (New York: Routledge, 2002), 137–138.
17 Geordie Greig, "'There Would Be So Much to Tell Her . . . ,'" January 10, 2006, *Daily Telegraph,* http://www.telegraph.co.uk/news/uknews/1507438/There-would-be-so-much-to-tell-her....html (accessed March 27, 2013); "JK Rowling Outs Dumbledore as Gay," BBC News, 2007.
18 On these canon-preserving activities, see Chapter 10 in Melissa Anelli, *Harry, a History* (New York: Pocket Books, 2008).
19 Jonathan Gray, *Show Sold Separately: Promos, Spoilers, and Other Media Paratexts* (New York: New York University Press, 2010), 6.
20 Bennett and Woollacott, *Bond and Beyond*, 58.
21 For a description of the dynamics of soap serials, see Fiske, *Television Culture*, 179–184.
22 Andrew Blake, *The Irresistible Rise of Harry Potter* (New York: Verso, 2002), 24–25.
23 David Grazian, *Mix It Up: Popular Culture, Mass Media and Society* (New York: W.W. Norton & Co., 2010), 69.
24 Hills, *Fan Cultures*, 180.
25 Jim McGuigan, *Cultural Populism* (New York: Routledge, 1992).

REFERENCES

Anelli, Melissa. *Harry, a History.* New York: Pocket Books, 2008.
Barthes, Roland. "The Death of the Author." In *Image/Music/Text,* edited by Stephen Heath, 142–148. New York: Hill & Wang, 1977.
Bennett, Tony, and Janet Woollacott. *Bond and Beyond: The Political Career of a Popular Hero.* New York: Methuen, 1987.
Blake, Andrew. *The Irresistible Rise of Harry Potter.* New York: Verso, 2002.
Ferrari, Chiara. "The Nanny in Italy: Language, Nationalism and Cultural Identity." *Global Media Journal* 3, 4 (Spring 2004).

Fiske, John. *Television Culture.* New York: Routledge, 1987.

Foucault, Michel. "What Is an Author?" In *The Foucault Reader,* edited by Paul Rabinow, 101–120. New York: Pantheon Books, 1984.

Geertz, Clifford. "Deep Play: Notes on the Balinese Cockfight." *Daedalus* 134, 4 (2005): 56–86.

Gray, Jonathan. *Show Sold Separately: Promos, Spoilers, and Other Media Paratexts.* New York: New York University Press, 2010.

Grazian, David. *Mix It Up: Popular Culture, Mass Media and Society.* New York: W.W. Norton & Co., 2010.

Greig, Geordie. "'There Would Be So Much to Tell Her . . . .'" January 10, 2006. *Daily Telegraph,* http://www.telegraph.co.uk/news/uknews/1507438/There-would-be-so-much-to-tell-her. . . .html.

Hall, Stuart. "The Work of Representation." In *Representation: Cultural Representations and Signifying Practices,* edited by Stuart Hall, 13–74. Thousands Oaks, CA: Sage Publications, 1997.

Hills, Matt. *Fan Cultures.* New York: Routledge, 2002.

"JK Rowling Outs Dumbledore as Gay." *BBC News,* 2007.

Littau, Karin. *Theories of Reading: Books, Bodies, and Bibliomania.* Malden, MA: Polity Press, 2006.

Mahler, Jonathan. "James Patterson Inc." January 20, 2010. *New York Times,* http://www.nytimes.com/2010/01/24/magazine/24patterson-t.html?pagewanted=all&_r=0.

McGuigan, Jim. *Cultural Populism.* New York: Routledge, 1992.

McKee, Alan. *Textual Analysis: A Beginner's Introduction.* Thousand Oaks, CA: Sage, 2003.

Newcomb, Horace. "Narrative and Genre." In *The Sage Handbook of Media Studies,* ed. John Downing, 413–428. Thousand Oaks, CA: SAGE Publications, 2004.

Todorov, Tzvetan. "Structural Analysis of Narrative," *Novel* 3 (1969): 70–76.

CHAPTER 5

What Are the Politics of Popular Culture?

When former British Prime Minister Margaret Thatcher died in 2013, a group of British activists started a campaign on Facebook to make the song "Ding-Dong! The Witch Is Dead," from *The Wizard of Oz* (1939), the number one single on the UK pop charts. Within a week, the song reached #2 on the charts, forcing the vaunted British Broadcasting Corporation (BBC) to acknowledge the prank on the Radio 1 program *The Official Chart*. The prank disrupted the commemoration of Thatcher as a "great leader" and reminded authorities that Thatcher's policies were none too popular among average Brits. The controversy illustrates how popular culture may be used to contest the agenda-setting power of the socially dominant.

Popular culture is not just a weapon. It is also a field of engagement upon which opposing groups fight to make their particular views seem less particular and more like common sense. During Thatcher's reign, her handlers used tabloid journalism and the British heritage industries to craft an image of her as a patriotic defender of British traditions. Her opponents on the left used songs, films, books, puppet shows, and comics to critique her policies and code them as draconian. In a very direct way, then, culture served as an arena of political debate during Thatcher's term in office. Culture need not be partisan to have political effects either. When ex–Spice Girl Geri Halliwell celebrated Thatcher on Twitter as "our 1st lady of girl power, . . . a green grocer's daughter who taught me anything is possible," she sought to re-frame Thatcher as a woman and a role model, rather than a politician. Activists on the left viewed this as an attempt to divert attention from Thatcher's legacy and Twitter-bombed Halliwell's account. When she removed the "offending" post, she was publicly shamed by conservatives for failing to stand her ground. Halliwell quickly learned that all words—no matter how seemingly innocent—have power and, under the right circumstances, can become a site of struggle. One need not speak directly about politics to send political messages or inspire political debate.

This chapter will take up the question of the politics of popular culture and consider how issues of power have been theorized within cultural studies. Our conception of politics will be broad, encompassing partisan speech but also examining broader questions of representation and voice. We will ask: Whose interests are being served in and through various representational practices? What social agendas are being promoted, how, and to whose benefit (or detriment)? Who has the power to speak and be heard in society and who does not? What role do institutions play in determining whose views will predominate? And, how much power do individuals have to evade, resist, or reconstruct the normative view of society? In short, how do cultural systems shape our thoughts and habits, and can they be shaped, in turn, by our actions?

Because they involve more participatory forms of cultural engagement, Web 2.0 platforms, like YouTube, will constitute the primary examples for this chapter. We will use them to discuss how new media both shape our sense of reality and enable us to take more control over the production of culture, and we will try to determine what this new mode of control amounts to in practical terms. Does the emergence of **prosumers** (media users who are both consumers *and* producers of culture) signal the waning of corporate authority over cultural production? If so, is this to be celebrated or lamented? Do new media platforms empower the people or the corporations who have traditionally controlled the means to shape reality, or have the terms of the debate shifted completely as the walls between producers and consumers have come tumbling down?

HOW DO CULTURAL STUDIES SCHOLARS THINK ABOUT POWER?

Cultural studies scholars think about power as a complex interaction between various structural forces and the human agents who must navigate those structures. In this, they follow German philosopher Karl Marx, who argued that "men make their own history, but they do not make it as they please; they do not make it under circumstances chosen by themselves."[1] This means people have the power to change or influence society (they have **agency**), but their thoughts and actions are inevitably constrained by the economic and social structures around them. They can act but only in relation to existing social forces; they cannot wish those forces away. In theory, cultural studies scholars seek to examine the tensions *between* structural power and people power, but, in practice, they often favor one end of the binary over the other. Some emphasize the power of structural forces to constrain popular agency while others emphasize the capacity of people to evade or resist those forces and nudge social relations in new directions. Crudely put, they ask one of two questions: "how does popular culture help oppress us?" or "how does popular culture help liberate us?" We will use these questions to organize the discussion that follows.

CRITICAL THEORY AND THE QUESTION OF OPPRESSION

Critical theory developed out of the Marxist tradition of materialist critique. **Materialism,** in this case, does not refer to a covetous desire for things, but a philosophical orientation that sees the material relations of society as the basis of thought. Karl Marx argued that the economic **base** of society—its mode and relations of production—determined the political, legal, and cultural mores of the society, which he called the **superstructure**. The function of culture within this formulation was to reproduce the dominance of the already dominant economic groups by spreading their ideologies. Marx put it this way:

> The ideas of the ruling class are in every epoch the ruling ideas, i.e. the class which is the ruling material force of society, is at the same time its ruling intellectual force. The class which has the means of material production at its disposal, has control at the same time over the means of mental production, so that . . . generally speaking, the ideas of those who lack the means of mental production are subject to it.[2]

In this model, the ruling ideas are forced upon the majority of the populace, who have little choice but to accept them. That these ideas do not serve the interests of the working classes means that ideology represents a type of **false consciousness**. It conveys misleading information about the real conditions of existence, which people accept as true either out of ignorance or out of a belief that they might one day make it into the ruling class themselves.

Marxism informed the work of later theorists like Theodor Adorno and Max Horkheimer, who were members of a loose affiliation of German scholars known as the Frankfurt School. Adorno and Horkheimer were both Jewish intellectuals forced to flee to the US after the Nazis came to power in Germany. Much of their suspicion of the new tools of mass mediation came from their experience of witnessing the stirring propaganda of the Nazi regime. They saw firsthand how mass media could be used to rouse individuals to act against the social good, and they perceived little difference between the state-controlled propaganda of the Nazis and the privatized propaganda of commercial culture in the US. Adorno and Horkheimer believed that culture should stand apart from economic and political influences and serve as a source of enlightenment and critique. They worried that the capitalist takeover of cultural production would stifle the growth of true art and replace enlightenment with "mass deception."

Adorno and Horkheimer criticized capitalist cultural production on two primary grounds: (1) it resulted in the standardization of cultural goods and a decline in their quality; (2) these standardized and stunted goods, in turn, produced standardized and stunted individuals. "Movies and radio need no longer pretend to be art," they fumed. "The truth that they are just business is made into an ideology in order to justify the rubbish they deliberately produce."[3] Adorno and Horkheimer did not buy this "we're giving the public what it wants" rationale. Instead, they argued that the choices allowed to the public were deliberately constrained. People are free to choose, but only from a limited slate of repetitive and formulaic offerings cloned from prior successes. They viewed such standardization as a natural outcome of the industrial need to minimize financial risk, but they lamented the effects of such strategies on the quality of the art and the humans who consumed it. "Culture now impresses the same stamp on everything," they argued. "Films, radio, and magazines make up a system which is uniform as a whole and in every part. . . . Under monopoly capitalism all mass culture is identical."[4] This does not mean that music is the same as film or radio or TV. Rather, it means that all mass-produced cultural goods are equally formulaic. They all construct an illusion of novelty by offering only slight variations on the same thing.

Adorno coined the term **pseudo-individualization** to describe the effects of such standardization on individuals. He argued that the mass address of consumer culture—the way it targets everyone with the same message—inevitably under-mines individuality by offering it in the same form to everyone. Starbucks, for example, provides a range of beverage options and sells merchandise that will allow you to tailor your coffee-drinking experience to "your style." "Choose from among our classic coffee mugs or seasonal designs," its website reads. "Find a new favorite Starbucks mug to enjoy coffee at home or when taking it to-go." Not only does this appeal assume you drink coffee (like everyone else), but it offers you the same chance to express your individuality as everyone else. We can all be individual in the same way—by buying tailored Starbucks merchandise. Expressed as a matter of consumer choice, Adorno argued, individuality is always and only partial; it repre-sents a "pseudo," or false, individuality that helps neutralize true difference, thereby undermining the basis of political solidarity and dissent.

The standardization of the product does not just lead to the standardization of individuals, however. It also harms their intellectual development. As Adorno and Horkheimer put it, the formulaic amusements of the cultural industries "[stunt] . . . the mass-media consumer's powers of imagination and spontaneity." "The sound film," for example, "leaves no room for imagination or reflection on the part of the audience."[5] Instead, audiences merely react to what they see and hear, like dogs trained to salivate at the sound of a bell. They quickly learn what to expect from formulaic films and come to expect no more. Their capacity for discernment withers as a result. Adorno's assessment of popular music offers the clearest expression of this criticism. Standardized music, he argued, "forcibly retards" the listening capac-ity and leaves audiences "arrested at the infantile stage": "Not only do the listening subjects lose, along with the freedom of choice and responsibility, the capacity for conscious perception of music, . . . but they stubbornly reject the possibility of such perception. . . . Regressive listeners behave like children. Again and again, they demand the one dish they have once been served."[6]

Such pronouncements embody the best and the worst of Adorno and Hork-heimer's thought. On the one hand, they capture an important aspect of the com-mercial cultural industries, which is that they thrive on formula and repetition and care only about making money. On the other hand, they fail to distinguish "the power of the culture industries . . . [from] the power of their influence."[7] They assume individuals consume cultural commodities passively and tire of them quickly. Adorno and Horkheimer focus so much on the processes of commercial production and exchange that they forget to ask how people use or relate to the commodities they purchase.

Adorno and Horkheimer's criticisms may seem overly pessimistic and one-sided—focusing on industries, rather than people—but they continue to matter because they draw attention to the role of culture in the production and reproduction of power relations. Their insights have influenced two main strands of critical analysis within the field of popular culture studies: **political economy**, which examines the organization of the systems of cultural production, and **ideology critique**, which explores the role of cultural products as vehicles of ideological norms. Let's look at each of these in turn.

Political Economy

Political economy is often confused with economics, but it actually developed as a critique of the instrumental aims of that discipline. As David Hesmondhalgh explains, orthodox economics "is not concerned with determining human needs and rights, nor with intervening in questions of social justice. Instead, it focuses on how human wants might be most efficiently satisfied." Political economy, by contrast, is centrally concerned with ethical and moral questions of right. It does not just describe the workings of the cultural industries; it describes how these operations affect access to the public sphere or the resources of representation. The main goal is to understand how capitalist relations condition political, social, and cultural life. Political economists of culture "see the fact that culture is produced and consumed under capitalism as a fundamental issue in explaining inequalities of power, prestige and profit."[8] By and large, they follow Adorno and Horkheimer in criticizing commercial cultural industries for serving the interests of the wealthy and powerful over those of the people.

We will use the insights of political economy to inform our discussion of cultural production in the next chapter, but a brief example might help clarify the outlines of the approach. Much of the discussion of Web 2.0 social media platforms has centered on their capacity to enhance popular participation in political and cultural life. YouTube, for instance, provides a free, user-friendly means of distributing videos. Anyone with access to a cellphone and the internet can theoretically create and share a video with the whole world. Thus, there is something of a democratic, or at least demotic (populist), ethos to YouTube, which promises to pluralize political and cultural discourse. When *TIME Magazine* declared "You" person of the year in 2006, the editors celebrated this capacity for popular empowerment, describing it as "revolutionary." According to them, social networking sites like YouTube, MySpace, and Facebook are "about the many wresting power from the few," and they congratulated "us" for "seizing the reins of the global media, for founding and framing the new digital democracy, for working for nothing and beating the pros at their own game."[9] Rather than focusing on the mechanics of production and consumption—how these corporately owned sites actually work—*TIME*'s editors focused on the power of individual expression, as if that power had no limits.

A political economist of culture would try to add nuance to this portrait by examining several interlocking questions: who owns these media sites, how are they run (what do the labor, wage, and profit relations look like?), how do political regulations influence these sites, and how do economic and social inequalities affect access to these sites? They might point out, for example, that YouTube is now owned by Google, one of the largest multinational media corporations in the world. Google's role as the largest search engine on the internet reinforces its attempts to become the go-to destination for streaming video content by directing user searches toward YouTube and away from other platforms. Google has also been trying to monetize the free content its users provide by embedding advertisements in the interface and in the videos themselves. Like a traditional television network, Google wants to attract eyeballs, which it can sell to advertisers. Very few amateur producers get a share of these profits, however, and those who do, labor under very tenuous conditions. Users with large followings may be paid a pittance per view to regularly update their vlogs (videologs). These wages are dependent on a steady viewership and can be suspended without notice if the viewing numbers drop. Some political economists describe these flexible labor relations as exploitative and liken YouTube and other social media sites to "digital sweatshops" whose profits depend on the unpaid labor of "net slaves."[10]

A political economist might also note that the YouTube interface is designed to re-enclose this potentially open digital space by folding it back within the logics of capitalist promotion and exchange. Google has revamped the YouTube interface to minimize its potential for randomness, for example. The homepage now carefully structures viewer attention and directs it toward the many commercial channels that litter its site. YouTube no longer lists the "most discussed" and "most responded" videos on the homepage—a tactic that favored amateur productions. Instead, it recommends videos in a narrow range of media genres: music, sports, (video)gaming, movies, TV shows, and news. Anything that does not fit in these categories is grouped in the "spotlight" category, which is also last on the list. Thus, the structure of the interface promotes viewer engagement with commercial cultural forms—those channels devoted to promoting already established stars and products—rather than amateur ones. Google's current business plan calls for the expansion of professionalized offerings via a slate of "original channels" featuring big name producers and stars. They have devoted an estimated one hundred million dollars to create ninety-six such channels featuring works by creators like Justin Lin, of the Fast & Furious movie franchise, and Anthony Zuiker, co-creator of the CSI franchise.[11] What will happen to amateur productions as the commercial cultural model grows? They are likely to be further sidelined and hidden from view. Political economy encourages us to think about these developments and their likely effects on democratic discourse. Do we want a YouTube that is just another space for shopping and promotion? What will be lost as a result of the incorporation of digital space?

A political economist would also consider how political regulations help restrict who can access the site and for what purposes. As Henry Jenkins, Sam Ford, and Joshua Green note, "YouTube's strategies for copyright management are generally focused on forging relationships with large copyright holders."[12] As part of this strategy, and as required by the Digital Millennium Copyright Act, they have adopted a copyright monitoring system called ContentID, which detects and eradicates copyright infringement on the site automatically. The system uses "digital fingerprinting" to search for special content codes embedded in the music or video files of copyright holders. When it finds these codes, it removes the offending material proactively, without regard to fair use. When YouTube had trouble negotiating a new licensing deal with Warner Music Group (WMG) in 2008, it used this system to pull down all videos that included WMG songs, even if the songs were clipped and used in a non-infringing way. Thousands of amateur producers suddenly found their videos censored or their accounts blocked. YouTube is less interested in protecting its amateur users' rights to sample copyrighted material for educational or transformative purposes. Such a narrow interpretation of copyright law once again favors corporate producers of culture over amateur ones and threatens to turn YouTube into just another outlet of professionalized culture and commerce.

Finally, a political economist would point out how social inequalities affect basic questions of access to social networking opportunities. The so-called digital divide—the gap between users who have easy access to internet connections and those who do not—remains a substantial impediment to full participation in the online "social revolution." The availability of mobile phones with smart technology has helped close this gap, but only so much. As of 2012, 66 percent of the world's population still did not have access to the internet. In Africa, only 15 percent of the population had regular access, and broadband speeds in the developing world remain so slow as to be unusable as a conduit for video streaming.[13] The majority of internet content is transmitted in just two languages—Chinese and English—and those with handicaps still face significant barriers to access.[14] If users cannot get online in a reliable fashion, or communicate once they get there, they cannot participate in the digital revolution so hyped by *TIME*. A politico-economic approach to culture shows how basic structures of ownership, remuneration, regulation, and access circumscribe the uses people can make of new technologies. It is one way to show how people make history but not necessarily under conditions of their own choosing.

Ideology Critique

In addition to political economy, the theories of the Frankfurt School fostered the critical tradition of ideological analysis that was particularly influential during the 1960s and 1970s. Ideology, you will recall, refers to a socially conditioned way of looking at the world. Members of a social group share certain common sense assumptions (ideologies) that they take for granted as right and true. American students often refer to all authors as "he," for example, even when the author's name is Nancy or Susan. They have been conditioned to assume that authority figures are male, and they jump to conclusions as a result. This is ideology at work. The students' beliefs unconsciously shape the way they look at the world.

Early attempts to critique ideology adhered a little overly closely to the Marxist definition of ideology as "false consciousness." Adorno and Horkheimer, for example, treated ideology as monolithic (*the* ideology of capitalism) and akin to a veil pulled over the eyes of unsuspecting individuals. Their writings were devoted to "lifting the veil" and exposing the way capitalist control of cultural production worked to standardize commodities and consumers alike. They hoped such exposure might spur a movement for social change. In the 1960s, French philosopher Louis Althusser merged Marxism with the new methods of structural analysis to produce a more sophisticated approach. Instead of examining specific instances of ideological expression, Althusser sought to define the mechanics of ideology as a system of social incorporation. To him, the important question was not "how does capitalism work," but "how does it continue to work despite its inherent contradictions and flaws?" He attributed the reproduction of capitalist relations to the work of ideology and various ideological state apparatuses (ISAs). The term *ISA* refers to those quasi-private institutions, like the family, the school, the church, and the media, charged with introducing individuals to the rules of their society. Ideology, in this sense, is not a "big lie" told to mask the "truth" of social relations; it is, rather, an agent of social subjectification and positioning. It turns individuals into social subjects by fitting them into the existing power relations.[15] We are so thoroughly imbued with ideology, according to Althusser, that there is no demystifying it, no way of getting outside or around it. Ideology is us; it suffuses our identities and shapes our social relations through and through.

Althusser's theories informed much early work in cultural studies. One of the most famous examples is French literary critic Roland Barthes's volume *Mythologies* (1957). While myths are often associated with ancient tales of gods and heroes, Barthes defined myths as the dominant ideologies of society, and he sought to explain how mythic assumptions were communicated in and through all sorts of popular forms from toys to food to professional wrestling. For example, he analyzed French toys as texts that conveyed a set of meanings to children and helped naturalize aspects of French social life. For him, the most obvious, or denotative, meaning of the toy—a toy is an object to be played with—was less important than the secondary, or connotative, meanings that became associated with the toys as a result of their form and texture. French toys, he noticed, were usually miniature copies of real-world objects (lifelike dolls, soldiers and military equipment, doctor's kits, etc.), designed to prepare children for the eventualities of adult life. By socializing children into their future adult roles, the toys helped make contingent social arrangements—the fact that women care for infants and men fight wars, for example—seem natural and inevitable. This, he argued, is the work of ideology—to naturalize and fix social relations that are really subject to contestation and change.

Barthes's work helped popularize Althusser's ideas and spread their influence well beyond France. Most prominently, in Britain, a group of scholars associated with the film journal *Screen* began applying semiotic and structural approaches to the organization of the cinematic **apparatus**—the cluster of technologies and social regulations that governed film production and exhibition. Christian Metz identified three basic "looks" in the cinema—the camera's look at the profilmic event, the looks exchanged between characters on screen, and the spectator's look at the screen—and postulated that the orchestration of these looks resulted in a certain ideological positioning of the subject. Decisions about camera placement and editing produced a particular perspective on the scene, which the spectator could not help but take up. In this way, the film proscribed the ways it would be watched and interpreted.

The most famous example of this work is probably feminist scholar Laura Mulvey's essay "Visual Pleasure and Narrative Cinema."[16] Mulvey argued that Hollywood film-making unconsciously privileged a male perspective by giving men a more active role in the narrative and framing women in ways that subordinated them to a male gaze. Because most Hollywood protagonists were men, male characters were responsible for driving the narrative forward and providing the audience with a point of identification. Women, when given agency at all, were either villains in need of punishment or sexual spectacles to be looked at. John Berger summed up these relations with the memorable aphorism: "men act; women appear."[17] Repeated over and over in Hollywood films, such patterns helped reinforce existing assumptions about the capacities (or incapacities) of men and women in society. That is, they reaffirmed the social dominance of men by making the male perspective the one that mattered. Everything about the film was designed to make the spectator see through male eyes. Even female viewers were invited to identify with male characters and adopt male perspectives by virtue of the film's orchestration of the gaze.

Ideology critique remains a powerful approach, particularly within textual analyses of popular culture. It has been modified and updated significantly since the 1970s, however. Few scholars today would assume that the gendering of roles on screen automatically translates into an identification with a "male" or "female" perspective, for instance. Actual viewers do not necessarily take up the positions they are offered, and they may identify across gender lines without necessarily identifying with the other sex. Carol Clover has shown, for example, that male viewers who identify with the "final girl" in slasher films like *Halloween* (1978) or *Texas Chainsaw Massacre* (1974) are not necessarily identifying with the perspectives of women or feminism. After all, most women fare poorly in slasher films, and identifying with the "final girl" is not like identifying with a "regular girl" since she embodies many characteristics associated with masculinity (her name is often masculine, and she enjoys math, science, and sports, is serious, and actively fights the villain). If the slasher film has a progressive political impact, according to Clover, it lies in the blurring of the rigid binaries that have traditionally ordered Western concepts of gender. It does not lie in the promotion of a female perspective because there is no such promotion.

FIGURE 5.01 *The rules explained above have become known as the Bechdel Test; the test exposes the gender politics of Hollywood films. From* Dykes to Watch Out For *(1985). Courtesy of Alison Bechdel.*

New media complicate these traditional ideological approaches still further by restructuring the ways we interact with media texts. No longer are viewers presumed to be passive spectators or mere consumers of media experiences. Instead, viewers are now positioned as users and invited to become more active participants in the entertainment experience through various processes of **interactivity**. Interactivity refers to the increased ability of users to select, control, and shape their media experiences, either through commenting and sharing (as in Web 2.0 technologies) or through immersive play (as in videogames). With interactive media, we are not just invited to identify with a pre-given character or subject position. We are invited to *become* the actor/character and thus to mark out our own subject position.[18] In new media forms, the process of ideological positioning becomes more personal and intense, but it is not necessarily more flexible. There are still technological protocols and rules that govern our interactions with new media, and these rules are not without ideological impact.

For example, sites like YouTube invite us to do more than just watch videos. We are asked to subscribe to channels and follow them constantly. Information about new videos is pushed to us on our phones and through our e-mails, and we are invited, as well, to comment and pass on links to videos. Active engagement with media texts is no longer an option; it is a mandate. This could be seen as a type of ideological interpellation—we are being hailed as "users" and "pushers" of new media, which is simultaneously positioned as a "drug" to which we have become "addicted." Those of us privileged enough to have access to these new media increasingly feel like we have to be "always on" and find ourselves adjusting our lives to suit the technologies that surround us. We internalize the mandate to "perform" or "curate" the self in online spaces, crafting personas that might appeal to others, rather than ourselves. While we may be addressed differently through new media forms, then, we are still being socialized to accept certain assumptions about the world. In that we do not leave the realm of the social when we enter virtual spaces, we are not free from social ideologies.

Scholars today also reject the notion that there is a single "dominant ideology" that drives social relations. Instead, they assume each society hosts many ideologies, which are constantly shifting in relation to each other as social groups jockey for power and resources. Cultural texts and practices are one place where we see the interplay of these worldviews. Post-structural theorists like Jacques Derrida and Michel Foucault were among the first to think of representational systems as fields of political contestation in this way. Derrida argued, for example, that no message is ever simple, straightforward, or politically neutral because (following Saussure) the relationship between signifiers and signifieds is inherently unstable. Any meaning assigned to a word or image can only ever be fixed temporarily through an act of interpretation. Interpretation is, thus, a contentious process, which we should learn to pay more attention to. If meanings are not fundamentally fixed, it matters who is doing the fixing, how, and for what ends. We need to consider representation and interpretation as forms of power.

Foucault and Discourse Analysis

Michel Foucault's work on discourse has been most influential in directing attention to these questions of power in recent years. Discourse refers to the social application of language, or how it is used to organize and delimit knowledge about the world. For Foucault, it includes language and representations, but also various practices and techniques for applying knowledge in the world. So, for example, he examines the architecture of the mental hospital or prison system in eighteenth-century Europe to help explain how distinctions between sanity and insanity, criminality and "proper" citizenship were enforced. In both cases, the architecture bolstered a process of pathologization whereby "sick" individuals were identified and locked away, in part, to affirm the "normality" of the rest of society. The internal structure of these facilities then communicated certain assumptions about proper behavior that helped discipline the subjects held there.

Foucault's concept of discourse connects the construction of knowledge (ideas about criminality) to the exercise of power (the disciplining of the criminal). According to him, a discourse need not be true to be effective. So, for example, copyright law makes no distinction between amateur and professional productions, but YouTube's *interpretation* of the law privileges the latter over the former. The site administrators go to great lengths to protect the rights of corporate stakeholders and make no allowance for the "fair use" of these materials by amateurs. This narrow interpretation of the law may not be accurate, but it is effective. It successfully narrows the range of representations available on the site and disciplines amateur producers to internalize certain norms of conduct. In that YouTube has the power to impose its definition of copyright on the rest of us, that definition becomes true for all intents and purposes. Foucault's work directs our attention to these questions of practice and power. How do discourses get activated in society? How do they structure social relations and to whose benefit?

CULTURAL STUDIES AND THE QUESTION OF AGENCY

The recognition that power is conditional—that it requires work to produce and sustain—has led some scholars to focus on the ways power and ideology may be resisted in and through popular culture. These theories depart from traditional critical theory in two key ways: (1) they view power as relational and fluid (never complete or total); and (2) they view resistance as tactical and contingent (involving small shifts, rather than revolutions). For example, contemporary theorists resist the notion that the economic base of society determines the political, legal, and cultural superstructure in some simple or direct way. They argue that the base is neither coherent enough to determine the superstructure, nor immune to determination itself. Indeed, knowing about the economic relations of production tells us little about the way people think about or live these relations. The proper work of cultural studies is to explain the latter, not the former.

British cultural studies scholar Raymond Williams proposed that we view the economic base of society as a living system comprised of human beings. Because the interests of different human beings often conflict, the base is unstable and supports a variety of political, ideological, and social perspectives. He uses the term **dominant culture** to describe the perspective that is most widely held at any given time, but he acknowledges that the dominant culture is never total. **Residual** and **emergent** perspectives—those that draw on past experience or anticipate a future state of being—coexist within the dominant culture and may assume importance if the dominant perspective no longer seems to explain the world adequately. Williams also rejected the notion that the economic base influenced, but was not influenced *by*, the superstructure. He viewed the flow of influence as multidirectional and argued that, by shaping men's minds, the superstructure (politics, the law, culture, and the arts) could reshape economic relations. "Social being determines consciousness," Williams argued, but not in any simple or direct way.[19]

To explain how power really works, Williams moved away from theories of structure and ideology and toward the more nuanced thinking of Italian neo-Marxist Antonio Gramsci. For Gramsci, individuals are not just oppressed by ideology or power relations; they choose to consent to those relations, which means they can always choose differently. Gramsci tried to explain how modern societies enforce power relations, not through repression, but through persuasion and cooptation. He used the term **hegemony** to describe this style of rule, which works as much through compromise as through subordination. According to Gramsci, those who want to gain or hold social power in today's societies must convince other groups that such a situation serves their own interests. They must win the consent of the governed by making their particular worldview seem natural and universal. Popular culture, as we have seen, is an important vehicle through which to effect this transformation of ideology into common sense. For this reason, Gramsci viewed popular culture as an important terrain of social struggle, a space where competing views of the world would, of necessity, meet and clash.

Consent, according to Gramsci, is hard to win and even harder to sustain. Those in power must meet at least some of the needs of at least some of the disempowered or risk rebellion. Meanwhile, the disempowered must agree to at least some of the rules set by the powerful in order to get their needs met. Because hegemony involves compromise on all sides, no one is ever fully satisfied with the resulting equilibrium, and everyone continues to fight for additional power and resources. This conception of power—as a never-ending struggle between competing social groups—proves very useful for understanding the relationship between the cultural industries and cultural consumers because it understands that both sides have some control over the production of popular culture. The cultural industries dictate what gets produced and distributed, and this gives them an enormous amount of power to set the social agenda and shape the prevailing common sense. Economic control does not automatically translate into cultural influence, however. People still have the power to choose which products succeed or fail, and they have the power to interpret and use the products in unexpected ways. They may even use them to speak back to those in power or to contest the prevailing common sense (as in the case of "Ding-Dong! The Witch Is Dead").

Hegemony theory has informed a range of approaches to popular culture, most of which are interested in the ways audiences transform commodities into culture through processes of **appropriation** and (re)articulation. For example, Dick Hebdige used hegemony theory to explain how British **subcultures** like the punks, Mods, and Teddy Boys used cultural commodities to forge alternative identities and communities of support. Punks, in particular, specialized in taking ordinary objects, like safety pins and trash bags, and using them in new and shocking ways (as jewelry or clothing). Punk music likewise embodied a do-it-yourself ethos that undermined traditional standards of musical quality. Punks valued the rawness of amateur production for its own sake—as a democratization of musical expression—and preferred noise to melody because it captured shared feelings of rage and frustration. Together these symbolic practices enabled punks to distinguish themselves as a group with a shared identity and counter-hegemonic, or oppositional, worldview. A critical theorist, like Adorno, might dismiss the significance of such subcultural rebellion by describing it in terms of **inoculation.** That is, the subculture represents a small, easily tolerated dose of rebellion, which ultimately helps forestall a full-scale attack on the health of the capitalist system. Hebdige (and Gramsci) would argue, instead, that even a small dose of rebellion alters the system in meaningful ways.

True, the punk look and sound were eventually coopted by the capitalist system—commodified and sold to non-punks as a generic expression of angst—but this cooptation could also be interpreted as a sign of the subculture's success. The punk critique of capitalist conformity became so influential that it had to be accommodated by the system. The political impact of such accommodation may be hard to measure, but it *is* real. For one thing, the incorporation of punk has kept the movement alive as a residual cultural formation. Commodified punk aesthetics may eventually drive individuals to search out the "real thing." Likewise, the use of punk rebellion as a marketing gimmick is contradictory in its appeals. In the process of using capitalist angst to sell commodities, corporations also reproduce anti-capitalist sentiments that may pose a threat to the smooth operation of the system in the future. Certainly, the punks' tactics of ironic *détournement* have inspired a range of contemporary culture jamming and hacking activities with an explicitly political edge. (We might think of the activities of the Anonymous collective as a legacy of punk, for example.) Finally, at the local level, punk continues to change hearts and minds and to draw people together around a shared set of beliefs and practices. It forges community. For all of these reasons, we could say the commodification of punk has been as troubling to capitalism, as it has been to punks themselves. The hegemonic compromise has left no one satisfied and everyone ready to continue the struggle.

John Fiske offers the most thorough-going and important deployment of hegemony theory in the study of popular culture, and, as David Marshall argues, his work is well-suited to the analysis of emerging media systems. As I explained in Chapter 1, Fiske defines culture in terms of popular agency. He explicitly rejects the notion that "people are . . . helpless subjects of an irresistible ideological system,"[20] but he also does not imagine they are completely free to make their own choices. What people can do, who they can be, how much freedom they have to express themselves, these are all influenced by the economic and social systems that surround them. He is particularly interested in how individuals maneuver in and around these systems, working with what they are given but transforming it into something far more meaningful. Thus, he is less interested in the commodity forms produced by cultural industries than in what people do with these forms.

While he champions popular agency, however, Fiske never forgets that the micro-level power to make meanings pales in comparison to the macro-level power of economic and social forces to shape existence. If popular culture is the "art of making do" with what the cultural industries provide, contained in that idea "is an acceptance of the ideological [and social] boundaries of one's activities and a sense of . . . resignation and lament. . . . The lament underscores the power imbalances present in contemporary culture."[21] Fiske is always careful to distinguish between the economic activities that result in the production and exchange of cultural resources for profit and the popular activities that result in the production and exchange of meanings for enjoyment. He is also highly attuned to the way power operates in and through processes of social categorization. Thus, he examines how discourses about race, gender, age, and sexuality circulate in society and shape processes of interpretation and affiliation (we will discuss this further in Chapter 7).

Finally, Fiske insists that the political value of any popular practice is determined by its location within a field of social tensions. Culture is about struggle, and different groups may be aligned differently on different issues, so "on some occasions the politics of popular cultural practices are contradictory, as when racial or class progressiveness is accompanied by gender conservatism." For Fiske, no cultural form is inherently or eternally "progressive" or "conservative." The political value of the form can only be determined in context, based on a careful study of its social mobilization. "The role of the critic-analyst," he says, "is not to reveal the true or hidden meanings of the text, or even to trace the readings people make of it; rather, it is *to trace the play of power in the social formation,* a power game within which all texts are implicated and within which popular culture is always on the side of the subordinate."[22]

The claim that "popular culture is always on the side of the subordinate" has led some of Fiske's critics to accuse him of depicting all popular activity as a form of political resistance. Much of this criticism derives from Fiske's own tendency to establish clear distinctions between producers and consumers, the powerful and the subordinate. At its most absurd, Fiske's discussions of power are so abstract as to appear depopulated, as if there are no people responsible for the articulations of power (only resistance) and anyone who resists power in any form is to be celebrated. If his theorizations are sometimes over-simplified, however, his analyses of cultural forms are usually more attuned to the interconnectedness of production and consumption, power and resistance. He views power relationally, as an on-going struggle to define social reality, and he takes seriously the capacity of individuals to change the contours of the system, slowly but surely. While he knows that radical social reform requires a change in material conditions, he insists that popular cultural activity can "fertilize the growth of those conditions" by expanding people's horizons and providing them with greater control over their everyday lives.[23]

Fiske's work was ultimately a polemic designed to get cultural critics to pay more attention to the way culture works in practice, not just in theory. Ideological purity only prevails under laboratory conditions, he maintained. In real life, people play with their mental food. They appropriate and use cultural resources to resist, evade, or negotiate with the dominant formation, and they pluralize discourse in productive ways through their creative activities. Aren't these activities at least as interesting and important as the activities of the cultural industries? Shouldn't we grant popular creativity and agency just as much legitimacy as the structural forces that shape the field of cultural engagement? Cultural studies theorists now assume the answer to both questions is "yes," so Fiske's championing of the power of the subordinate now seems old-fashioned. Yet, many of his ideas—about texts, agents, and semiotic struggle—seem more relevant than ever in the age of the internet and social media. How would Fiske assess a phenomenon like YouTube, then? How would his approach differ from other, more structural approaches to culture?

REASSESSING THE POWER OF YOUTUBE

As we have seen, most early discussions of YouTube have come from either the business realm, where the site is celebrated for its inventive way of monetizing attention, or from political economists, who have characterized the site's reliance on user-generated content as a type of exploitation. Both perspectives take a purely economistic approach to the evaluation of YouTube that focuses more on structural forces than on texts and agents. Cultural theorists like Fiske would try to add complexity to these discourses by challenging the assumptions about labor, value, and reward they take for granted. As Jean Burgess and Joshua Green argue, "YouTube needs to be understood as both a business . . . and as a cultural resource co-created by its users."[24] Its status as a platform provider, rather than a content provider, means that it must satisfy a range of users, from premium content producers, amateur creators, and advertisers to a variety of casual and not-so-casual users. In the process, it must mediate between "various competing industry-oriented discourses and ideologies and various audience or user-oriented ones."[25]

Certainly, Google and its premium content providers and advertisers view the site as a space where audience attention can be aggregated and sold for profit. They are interested in making money, rather than meanings, pleasures, or artistic statements. However, the amateur users of the site see things quite differently. Many see it as a communal space of sharing and describe their activities as "gifts" to be valued and reciprocated according to a different set of logics. YouTube's "value" to amateurs is cultural and social, not economic. They tend to view the sharing of content as a means of forging, strengthening, or managing identities and relationships, not so much a vehicle for delivering eyeballs to advertisers. In reality, though, YouTube is both at once. Cultural theorist Paul Booth has coined the term "digi-gratis economy" to capture the "mashed-up" character of YouTube as a financial, cultural, and social economy. While YouTube fosters monetary exchanges, Booth argues, these exchanges are also predicated on the symbolic, sentimental, or social value of the "goods" exchanged.[26] Advertising and entertainment companies need viewers to make their wares meaningful, or they will be lost in the flood of video content on YouTube. In industry parlance "if it doesn't spread it's dead," and what helps it spread is user investment. For these reasons, the cultural and social dynamics of YouTube are at least as important to understand as the financial ones. Any approach that fails to account for these dynamics will also fail to explain YouTube.

So, how does YouTube work as a **cultural economy**? How does it foster the circulation of meanings and pleasures? The site was originally built to allow users to share videos with one another. With the exception of a ban on shocking and pornographic content, and a mandate that videos comply with copyright and a ten-minute time limit (now lifted), there were few restrictions on the number or types of videos that could be uploaded. The low barriers to entry were designed to encourage viewer participation in the creation of site content. YouTube thus began from the assumption that people are cultural agents, capable of wielding the tools of symbolic creation in and for themselves. Google's purchase of the site, as political economists note, has changed this dynamic somewhat. The homepage has been redesigned to promote premium content at the expense of amateur production, and the presence of corporations, advertisers, and political authorities on the site is now so pronounced as to be unavoidable. Still, these are structural features of the site that creative users can easily maneuver through or around if they choose. For example, "YouTube's architecture and design invite individual participation, rather than collaborative activity," but YouTube users easily circumvent these limitations by remixing and responding to each other's videos, using "shout-outs" to acknowledge each other, and responding directly to viewer comments in the videos.[27] These tactics turn the site into a more communal and collaborative space where users can speak to and work off one another's insights.

In general, the YouTube interface is easy to use and designed to solicit participation, sharing, and commentary. Fiske might describe it as producerly in that it invites viewers to become active co-producers of meaning and value. YouTube promotes a "continuum of cultural participation" ranging from mere viewing to commenting, favoriting, responding, producing, and sharing. None of these activities should be viewed as passive or inconsequential, for they all "leave traces, and therefore they all have effects on the common culture of YouTube as it evolves."[28] Viewing and favoriting, for example, contribute to the filtering of the site content and help direct user-attention. Commenting transforms a one-way communicational flow into a two-way, dialogical exchange of views, pluralizing the potential meanings of the work while sharing recontextualizes video content in ways that might shift the interpretation of the work. All of these activities add layers of meaning to the video-texts and constitute acts of co-production, and all of them should be considered part of the meaningful content of YouTube.

YouTube's semiotic excess ensures that no single entity can determine what matters on the site or impose a particular interpretation of content on others. In fact, the surest way to get into trouble on YouTube is to try to constrain user participation. When the US Office of National Drug Control Policy (ONDCP) set up a YouTube channel in 2006 to distribute its anti-drug spots to teens, for example, it grossly underestimated the YouTube community's tolerance for didactic broadcasting. The ONDCP's big mistake was to shut off the commenting functions on the channel in an attempt to control the message. Outraged YouTube users grabbed the videos and re-posted them with the commenting functions turned back on. Once allowed to speak, commentators challenged the ONDCP's conflation of recreational drug use with addiction, offered economic arguments for the legalization of marijuana, and labeled the ONDCP's attempt to stifle the free exchange of ideas as "fascism." Other users posted parodies of the videos in an attempt to undermine the abstinence-only message of the original. The spot "Pete's Couch," for example, showed "Pete" sitting on a couch all day and missing out on life because he preferred to smoke marijuana. One parody filled the background outside the window with injuries, arguments, and general mayhem, thereby making life look far more dangerous than drugs. Pete's decision to "drop out" seemed rational in light of the recontextualization. Most of the parodies were equally light-hearted, eschewing radical politics in favor of cheeky humor, yet, by disrupting the ONDCP's intended message and reminding viewers of the on-going debate surrounding these issues, the parodies did do political work. The example demonstrates how YouTube's producerly affordances can be used to turn closed texts back into opportunities for dialogue and discussion.

Most video makers accept YouTube's participatory ethos and actually try to get their content flagged, discussed, and spread. They want their videos to "go viral," or become self-replicating cultural phenomena. Yet, they do not all succeed at this task, which raises the questions: What features of the video "text" make it conducive to cultural diffusion? What are the cultural logics that help videos spread? The recent video hit "Gangnam Style," by Korean rapper Psy, might provide some insight. "Gangnam Style" is a fairly conventional music video, featuring a portly rapper, rapping in Korean about the rampant materialism of South Korean elites. Yet, it became an international sensation and the most popular video in YouTube history at over 1.9 billion hits (as of January 2014). Why?

First, as a music video, the text is familiar and accessible to most people. Like other music videos, "Gangnam" features a carefully choreographed performance by the artist, which is edited in a rapid-cut fashion to match the rhythm of the music. The music itself is catchy and contagious; it sticks in your head whether you know Korean or not. The video also parodies certain features of the rap subgenre, including the flaunting of material wealth, male machismo, and female sexuality. Viewers familiar with rap (or commercial culture, in general) can access this parody even if they are unfamiliar with the Korean language or the Gangnam District of Seoul. Finally, the video is parodic, performance-based, and playful in every way. The dance alone might have made the song a hit, for it invites imitation, and each new iteration of the performance ensures the song will be re-posted. As a whole, "Gangnam Style" succeeds because it offers viewers multiple points of entry into the text and leaves abundant loose ends or gaps for them to work with. It is not just eye- or ear-catching; it is grabbable, remixable, and spreadable. It invites users to play along, but in their own ways and for their own reasons.

Unlike the ONDCP, Psy understands the basic communal and social norms of YouTube and has done little or nothing to stop the spread of his video. As a result, "Gangnam Style" has become a catalyst for a wide range of creative endeavors from clever commentary ("Now we know why North Korea wants to bomb the South") to parodic reenactments. Most such reenactments involve lip-synching and dancing along to the original video (run a Google video search for "Gangnam Style Dance Video" to see thousands of hilarious reenactments), but some involve more creative acts of appropriation. "Annoying Orange: Orange Nya-Nya style," for instance, is a classic "YouTube poop" video, which borrows the Gangnam tune, rescripts the lyrics, and cuts them together with nonsensical images to create a meaningless expression of humor. The first stanza reads: "I am an orange. People say that I'm annoying. Say what you want 'cause I'm certainly not boring. I hang out in the stables with a bunch of unicorns, and I ride 'em into outer space honking uni-horns." The pleasure of such videos comes, not from the content of the lyrics, but from the bravura recombination of elements—the wash of imagery and sound and the way it stimulates the senses. It is a celebration of pure creativity.

Other parodies, like CollegeHumor's "Mitt Romney Style," are more explicitly political in intention. "Romney Style" depicted 2012 Republican presidential candidate Mitt Romney and his running mate Paul Ryan as out of touch with the economic struggles of "real Americans." It featured a chorus of: "Affluence, Extravagance! That's Mitt (hey). Yeah, that's so Mitt (hey). Profits, Investments! That's Mitt (hey), Yeah, that's so Mitt (hey). You should elect me cause I got so much mo-nayayayayayayayay . . . Mitt Romney style." Meanwhile, Ryan was portrayed as a preening hustler who wants to cut the social safety net and leave "losers" like grandma with nothing. In this case, the act of repurposing Psy facilitated political talk about the relative merits of the Republican and Democratic platforms. It is a literal example of how popular culture may serve as a site of social struggle.

FIGURE 5.02 *A classic YouTube "poop" video, "Orange Nya-Nya Style" remixes Korean rapper Psy's hit "Gangnam Style" (2012) as a celebration of absurdism.*

FIGURE 5.03 *"Mitt Romney Style" remixes Psy's "Gangnam Style" to condemn the 2012 Republican Presidential candidates Mitt Romney and Paul Ryan. From CollegeHumor.com.*

Finally, as these examples illustrate, a proper understanding of YouTube requires some analysis of its **social economy**, or role in establishing connections between people. Most people stumbled upon "Gangnam Style," not because of Psy's marketing campaign or because they were Googling "K Pop," but because they heard about the video from a friend or acquaintance. The parodies, too, have been circulated through informal, word-of-mouth networks of "chattering individuals."[29] As we have discussed, YouTube's design makes it easy for users to communicate with each other on the site or through the ancillary circulation of video links and codes. This leads Burgess and Green to propose that, on YouTube, "content creation is probably far less significant than the uses of that content within various social networks."[30] Most users do not, in fact, upload content, but they do share it with colleagues, friends, and family. In such cases, the content hardly matters. What matters is the act of touching base or connecting others. John Hartley calls this **phatic communication**, and notes that its purpose is largely hegemonic—to affirm and reproduce existing social bonds.[31]

Can YouTube also be used to foster new social connections? Can it be used to mobilize people? What are the possibilities and limitations of YouTube for revitalizing democratic culture? There is much debate about such questions. Certainly, YouTube's accessibility as a broadcast platform has brought new voices into the political public sphere. Cranky libertarian politician Ron Paul has a huge following on YouTube, for example, and his name-recognition has increased among all Americans as a result. Denied access to mainstream media coverage, Paul has successfully used the site to get his message out there. Henry Jenkins has described, as well, how political activists on the right and left have used videos to disseminate their messages. For example, in 2006, the Harry Potter Alliance, a group of progressive Potter fans, teamed with the Service Employees International Union to help expose Walmart's unfair labor policies. Together, they produced a series of videos of Harry and company clashing with "Lord Waldemart," "whose sinister practices included exploiting his house elves, driving out local competitors, and refusing to provide health care to his underlings."[32] The videos provoked meaningful conversations around Walmart's labor practices and helped drive viewers to SEIU's Walmart Watch website, where they could get even more information. Such activities can work both ways, however. Conservative activists in the US have used hidden camera, agitprop tactics to entrap liberal politicians and community activists in compromising situations, then uploaded the videos to YouTube as a provocation. The goal in such cases is to rally the troops, not to provide information or stimulate rational debate. Is such agonistic, or conflict-based, communication ultimately good or bad for democracy (a question pursued more actively in Chapter 10)?

Another problem is the difficulty in determining the source or motivation of YouTube posters. Corporations have become adept at **astroturfing**, or using fake grassroots videos to promote their products and causes. In a famous example, a group sponsored by General Motors and Exxon Mobile produced an amateur-style spoof of Al Gore's global warming documentary *An Inconvenient Truth* (2006) with

FIGURE 5.04 *"Harry Potter and the Dark Lord Waldemart" (2006), a campaign by The Harry Potter Alliance and the Service Employees International Union to raise awareness of WalMart's unfair labor practices. With permission of The Harry Potter Alliance.*

the aim of undermining the documentary's message. Both companies had a vested interest in derailing the push for new environmental legislation, but many users assumed this was a "genuine" grassroots critique. How can we trust YouTube as a site for political information when we cannot reliably determine who is speaking and why?

Finally, there are significant limitations and biases built into the architecture of the site, which results in the privileging of certain voices over others. The voluntary basis of participation, for instance, weeds out those who lack the technology, skill, or time to contribute. The structural bias toward shocking and controversial material also sidelines more complex issues and may alienate some users. For example, comments on videos are often deliberately offensive, using inappropriate references to gender, sexuality, race, and class status, to provoke a reaction. Such **trolling** upsets women, especially, and drives many of them to stop participating, thereby reducing the diversity of speech and opinion on the site.[33] The "popularity index" that drives YouTube traffic also favors majoritarian groups and issues while marginalizing minority ones. As a result, the content of YouTube's most popular videos evinces "far less racial diversity than [even] broadcast television," which, as we have seen, is dominated by representations of whiteness.[34] Finally, the sheer volume of entertainment material on the site may swamp serious messages in a flood of noise. As Aaron Hess concludes, "any serious discussion found on YouTube is likely lost in the ether, ineffective in its ability to assist in deliberation."[35]

These are serious limitations. Still, Hess and other critics may be using an overly narrow definition of politics to support their pessimistic conclusions about the political potential of YouTube. For one thing, videos need not be directly about politics to be political. Politics is really about the rightful disposition of people, power, and resources, and YouTube is quite adept at aggregating publics, connecting individuals, and setting social priorities. It is "a noisy, messy place that brings people into strange new forms of contact with other people (and not merely with brands, with mainstream media and with those in power)."[36] For another thing, cultural content need not be serious or stilted to be political. As Jonathan Gray observes, "dividing the world into serious politics and non-political fun is foolish" because politics is not divorced from everyday life. Many YouTube videos, like the Potter parodies or "Mitt Romney Style," use a playful approach to get at serious issues, and popular culture, in general, gives people resources to think through their everyday lives. By making politics feel accessible and relevant, YouTube videos can help alienated citizens re-engage with political subject matter. Finally, by providing a space for the expression of popular creativity, skepticism, and resistance, YouTube provides individuals with hope. The relationships forged and strengthened through YouTube may enlighten, inspire, and sustain individuals during hard times. They may even move individuals to make positive changes in their own lives (there is an active weight-loss culture on YouTube, for example), and these micro-level changes should be viewed as political, too.

CONCLUSION

In the end, if YouTube has a politics, it is a politics of multiplicity. It works against the desire of the socially dominant to stifle debate and present their worldview as the common sense. Its "noisiness" makes difference and dissent legible, thereby reminding people that power is never total. It is always subject to contestation and revision. Corporations, politicians, and advertisers may prefer to increase YouTube's signal to noise ratio to maximize their influence, but ordinary users are no longer content to be silenced in this way. They want to produce, speak, and be heard. They want to debate, discuss, and connect. They want to play with cultural resources and make them personally and socially meaningful.

Corporations are slowly adjusting to this new state of affairs, but cultural theory has yet to fully catch up to these changes. What we need, as Jenkins and his colleagues argue, is "a more refined vocabulary for thinking about the reality of power relations between companies and their audiences."[37] The next chapter will contribute to this project by examining changes in the material relations of cultural production. It will look, particularly, at the growing tension between corporations and fans over the question of "who owns culture?" and will attempt (a la Fiske) to trace the play of power in this emerging social formation.

SUMMARY

- This chapter examines the relationship between politics and popular culture. By politics we mean both actual partisan discourse and questions of representation and voice: who can speak and be heard in society and who cannot?

- Cultural studies scholars think of power as a complex interaction between various structural forces and the human agents who must navigate those structures.

- There are various ways to approach the study of power.

  - Some look at the institutions responsible for producing popular culture (political economy).

  - Some look at the normative messages conveyed by popular culture (ideology critique and discourse analysis).

  - Some look at how popular culture becomes a terrain of struggle where the powerful and powerless negotiate the values that will prevail in society (hegemony theory).

- Cultural studies scholars treat popular culture as a key site of struggle. They are interested in how human agents impose and/or challenge the norms of society using popular forms as weapons or delivery vehicles.

- Power is never complete or total, but also never absent. Power relations are subject to renegotiation but only within limits. How social groups negotiate those limits is the key analytical question.

NOTES

1 Karl Marx, "The Eighteenth Brumaire of Louis Bonaparte," in *The Marx-Engels Reader*, ed. Robert C. Tucker (New York: W.W. Norton & Co., 1978), 595.
2 Marx, "The German Ideology: Part I," 172.
3 Theodor W. Adorno and Max Horkheimer, *Dialectic of Enlightenment* (New York: Continuum, 1997), 121.
4 Ibid., 120.
5 Ibid., 126.
6 Theodor W. Adorno, "On the Fetish Character in Music and the Regression of Listening," in *Adorno: The Culture Industry*, ed. J.M. Bernstein (New York: Routledge, 1991), 46.
7 John Storey, *Cultural Theory and Popular Culture* (New York: Pearson/Prentice Hall, 2001), 189.
8 David Hesmondhalgh, *The Cultural Industries*, 2nd ed. (Los Angeles: Sage Publications, 2009), 33.
9 Lev Grossman, "Time's Person of the Year: You," December 13, 2006, http://www.time.com/time/magazine/article/0,9171,1569514,00.html (accessed May 31, 2011).
10 Titziana Terranova, "Free Labor: Producing Culture for the Digital Economy," *Social Text* 18, 2 (2000).
11 Ryan Nakashima, "YouTube Bets $100 Million on Original Content," *USA Today* (2012), http://usatoday30.usatoday.com/tech/news/story/2012–02–20/youtube-original-content/53170394/1.
12 Henry Jenkins, Sam Ford, and Joshua Green, *Spreadable Media: Creating Value and Meaning in a Networked Culture* (New York: New York University Press, 2013), 51.
13 "Internet Usage Statistics: The Internet Big Picture," June 30, 2012, http://www.internetworldstats.com/stats.htm (accessed March 18, 2013).

14 "Internet World Users by Language," June 30, 2012, http://www.internetworldstats.com/stats7.htm (accessed March 18, 2013); Kathryn Zickuhr and Aaron Smith, "Digital Differences," April 13, 2012, http://pewinternet.org/Reports/2012/Digital-differences/Overview.aspx (accessed March 18, 2013).

15 Louis Althusser, *Lenin and Philosophy and Other Essays*, trans. Ben Brewster (New York: Monthly Review Press, 1971), 170.

16 Laura Mulvey, "Visual Pleasure and Narrative Cinema," in *Feminisms: An Anthology of Literary Theory and Criticism*, eds. Robyn R. Warhol and Diane Price Herndl (New Brunswick, NJ: Rutgers University Press, 1993).

17 John Berger, *Ways of Seeing* (London: Penguin Books, 1972).

18 P. David Marshall, *New Media Cultures* (New York: Oxford University Press, 2004), 22.

19 Raymond Williams, "Base and Superstructure in Marxist Cultural Theory," *New Left Review* 82 (Nov–Dec 1973), 3.

20 John Fiske, *Understanding Popular Culture* (New York: Routledge, 2011), 37.

21 Marshall, *New Media Cultures*, 9.

22 Fiske, *Understanding Popular Culture*, 36.

23 Ibid., 126.

24 Jean Burgess and Joshua Green, *YouTube: Online Video and Participatory Culture* (Malden, MA: Polity, 2009), 35.

25 Ibid., 37.

26 Paul Booth, *Digital Fandom* (New York: Peter Lang Publishing, 2010), 24–30.

27 Burgess and Green, *YouTube*, 65.

28 Ibid., 57.

29 David Grazian, *Mix It Up: Popular Culture, Mass Media and Society* (New York: W.W. Norton & Co., 2010), Chapter 4.

30 Burgess and Green, *YouTube*, 58.

31 Quoted in Burgess and Green, *YouTube*, 135.

32 Quoted in Burgess and Green, *YouTube*, 115.

33 Amanda Hess, "Why Women Aren't Welcome on the Internet," January 06, 2014, http://www.psmag.com/navigation/health-and-behavior/women-arent-welcome-internet-72170/ (accessed February 14, 2014).

34 Quoted in Burgess and Green, *YouTube*, 124.

35 Aaron Hess, "Resistance up in Smoke: Analyzing the Limitations of Deliberation on Youtube," *Critical Studies in Mass Communication* 26, 5 (2009), 429–430.

36 Luke Goode, Alexis Mccullough, and Gelise O'Hare, "Unruly Publics and the Fourth Estate on Youtube," *Participations: Journal of Audience & Reception Studies* 8, 2 (November 2011), 612.

37 Jenkins, Ford, and Green, *Spreadable Media*, 165.

REFERENCES

Adorno, Theodor W. "On the Fetish Character in Music and the Regression of Listening." In *Adorno: The Culture Industry,* edited by J.M. Bernstein, 29–60. New York: Routledge, 1991.

Adorno, Theodor W., and Max Horkheimer. *Dialectic of Enlightenment.* New York: Continuum, 1997.

Althusser, Louis. *Lenin and Philosophy and Other Essays.* Translated by Ben Brewster. New York: Monthly Review Press, 1971.

Berger, John. *Ways of Seeing.* London: Penguin Books, 1972.

Booth, Paul. *Digital Fandom.* New York: Peter Lang Publishing, 2010.

Burgess, Jean, and Joshua Green. *YouTube: Online Video and Participatory Culture.* Malden, MA: Polity, 2009.

Fiske, John. *Understanding Popular Culture.* New York: Routledge, 2011.

Goode, Luke, Alexis McCullough, and Gelise O'Hare. "Unruly Publics and the Fourth Estate on YouTube." *Participations: Journal of Audience & Reception Studies* 8, 2 (November 2011): 594–615.

Grazian, David. *Mix It Up: Popular Culture, Mass Media and Society.* New York: W.W. Norton & Co., 2010.

Grossman, Lev. "Time's Person of the Year: You." December 13, 2006. http://www.time.com/time/magazine/article/0,9171,1569514,00.html.

Hesmondhalgh, David. *The Cultural Industries.* 2nd ed. Los Angeles: Sage Publications, 2009.

Hess, Aaron. "Resistance up in Smoke: Analyzing the Limitations of Deliberation on You-Tube." *Critical Studies in Mass Communication* 26, 5 (2009): 411–434.

Hess, Amanda. "Why Women Aren't Welcome on the Internet." January 6, 2014. http://www.psmag.com/navigation/health-and-behavior/women-arent-welcome-internet-72170/.

"Internet Usage Statistics: The Internet Big Picture." June 30, 2012. http://www.internetworldstats.com/stats.htm.

"Internet World Users by Language." June 30, 2012. http://www.internetworldstats.com/stats7.htm.

Jenkins, Henry, Sam Ford, and Joshua Green. *Spreadable Media: Creating Value and Meaning in a Networked Culture.* New York: New York University Press, 2013.

Marshall, P. David. *New Media Cultures.* New York: Oxford University Press, 2004.

Marx, Karl. "The Eighteenth Brumaire of Louis Bonaparte." In *The Marx-Engels Reader,* edited by Robert C. Tucker, 594–617. New York: W.W. Norton & Co., 1978.

———. "The German Ideology: Part I." In *The Marx-Engels Reader,* edited by Robert C. Tucker, 146–202. New York: W.W. Norton & Co., 1978.

Mulvey, Laura. "Visual Pleasure and Narrative Cinema." In *Feminisms: An Anthology of Literary Theory and Criticism,* edited by Robyn R. Warhol and Diane Price Herndl, 432–442. New Brunswick, NJ: Rutgers University Press, 1993.

Nakashima, Ryan. "YouTube Bets $100 Million on Original Content." *USA Today* (2012), http://usatoday30.usatoday.com/tech/news/story/2012–02–20/youtube-original-content/53170394/1.

Storey, John. *Cultural Theory and Popular Culture.* New York: Pearson/Prentice Hall, 2001.

Terranova, Titziana. "Free Labor: Producing Culture for the Digital Economy," *Social Text* 18, 2 (2000): 33–58.

Williams, Raymond. "Base and Superstructure in Marxist Cultural Theory," *New Left Review* 82 (Nov-Dec 1973): 3–16.

Zickuhr, Kathryn, and Aaron Smith. "Digital Differences." April 13, 2012. http://pewinternet.org/Reports/2012/Digital-differences/Overview.aspx.

CHAPTER 6

How Is Popular Culture Made and Valued?

As we learned in Chapter 1, the term "culture" refers to the active process of generating and circulating meanings and pleasures within a social system. The resources from which people create meanings and pleasures may be more or less commercial in origin, but most become entangled in some way with capitalist systems of cultural production. This chapter is devoted to understanding how such cultural industries work. How are they organized, and how does this organization influence the shape of cultural commodities they produce? How do creative decisions get made in these environments, and what happens to the texture of our shared cultural life as a result? How might the **gatekeeping** role of the cultural industries—their power to determine which texts enter the media stream—affect the diversity and vigor of our common culture? The first part of the chapter will take up these questions.

The second part will examine the relationships between "producers" and "consumers" of culture within this system. I place these terms in quotation marks because the distinction between them has always been somewhat artificial. As we have seen, people are not passive consumers of cultural resources; they are active producers who make inert cultural resources come alive with meaning and value. Likewise, cultural industries are not just producers of culture; they are avid consumers of it, who make new things by repurposing old resources. Thus, both "producers" and "consumers," corporations and the people, engage in similar processes of **redaction** and **remixing**, meaning they create new forms of culture by interpreting, editing, and recombining existing cultural forms.

The similarities between the activities of producers and consumers have been exposed by the emergence of Web 2.0 platforms, like YouTube, Instagram, and Twitter, which allow ordinary people to display and disseminate their creative activities alongside those of commercial producers and professionals. These developments not only threaten the traditional gatekeeping functions of the cultural industries; they also bring competing discourses of ownership and value into conflict. Historically, as Lawrence Lessig explains, "the law protected the incentives of [professional] creators by granting them exclusive rights to their creative work, so that they could sell those exclusive rights in a commercial marketplace."[1] Increasingly, these copyright laws are being used to extend regimes of ownership into noncommercial spheres of cultural production, which means ordinary individuals are now being prosecuted for doing what they have always done with cultural resources—make them meaningful through appropriation and recirculation. The second part of this chapter will examine how emerging technologies are bringing producers and consumers closer together and reshaping the field of power relations as a result.

The music industry, past, present, and future, will comprise the dominant case study for this chapter because it best crystallizes the relevant tensions between commercial and noncommercial production, professional and amateur culture, the political economy of ownership and the moral economy of sharing. It is both a representative example of how most commercial culture industries function, and a stellar example of how technological changes have threatened these industries. As we will see, the accommodation of fan activity may challenge some of the gatekeeping authority of the cultural industries, but it hardly represents a diminution of their social status or power to influence. Their cultural authority must simply be consolidated in new ways and against an organized push-back from "the people formerly known as the audience."[2]

THE POLITICAL ECONOMY OF THE CULTURAL INDUSTRIES

> We have no obligation to make history. We have no obligation to make art. We have no obligation to make a statement. To make money is our only objective.
>
> —Michael Eisner, CEO, Walt Disney Co.[3]

How do cultural industries work? Political economy (discussed in the previous chapter) can be a very useful approach to answering this question because it takes former Disney CEO Michael Eisner at his word and focuses on the structures, logics, and practices that shape the *business* of making cultural resources. Political economists argue that commercial producers of culture, no matter what specific industry they are in, all work under a similar set of economic constraints and have developed similar ways of dealing with those constraints. Unlike other types of products, cultural commodities are semi-public goods, which means their availability may be restricted, but not because the goods are scarce. Cultural goods, like recordings, are not used up in a single act of consumption; they continue to circulate even after they are used, and new copies may be made fairly easily.[4] Because it is expensive to produce new content, but less costly to reproduce existing content, cultural industries tend to focus on hit-making. In economic terms: one big hit that sells to millions costs less over time than one hundred small works that only sell to thousands.

Hits are notoriously hard to produce, however. In the TV industry, for example, network executives may hear 5,000 "pitches" (ideas for series) a year and commission just five series from that pool. Of those five, only one is likely to last beyond the first season, thereby constituting a "hit." That is a 0.0002 percent success rate.[5] According to Dan Glickman, CEO of the Motion Picture Association of America, hits in the film industry are equally rare. In 2007, the "average cost to make and market a studio film was over $100 million," and "six out of ten movies never recoup their original investments in their domestic runs."[6] Finally, the Recording Industry Association of America (RIAA) estimates that the average cost to develop a new pop act is now $1 million, yet only one record in ten breaks even, and the majority of industry profits come from just a handful of hits.[7] According to Chris Rojek, "only 250 album releases sell more than 10,000 copies a year and fewer than thirty achieve platinum status (one million [in] sales)."[8] These statistics should give you a feel for how risky cultural production can be, so it is no surprise that commercial cultural industries have developed numerous strategies for minimizing their exposure to risk. What are some of these strategies?

Risk Minimization Strategy One: Go Big or Go Home

One way to minimize risk is to become bigger and more diversified as a company. Big companies can monopolize markets, driving smaller operators out of business and reducing the competition for their products. Their size also allows them to dictate the conduct of an industry by determining things like pricing structure. Moreover, by diversifying, these large companies can generate revenue in multiple ways and spread the risks and rewards of innovation across the corporation. Today's cultural industries are marked by a high degree of **concentration**, which means ownership and control of the different industries is dominated by just a handful of corporations. The five largest media corporations are Time Warner, Disney, Viacom (now split into Viacom and CBS Corporation, but under the same management), News Corporation, and Bertelsmann, and, together, they control the lion's share of the global market for cultural goods. These corporations are all multinational, multimedia **conglomerates**, which means they combine multiple industries and businesses under one corporate roof. For example, Time Warner owns book and magazine publishing interests (including Time Inc., *Sports Illustrated, People Magazine,* and DC comics), film and television production studios and distributors (under the Warner Bros. Entertainment umbrella), broadcast and cable television networks (including the CW, HBO, CNN, and TBS) and transmission outlets like Time Warner Cable (and formerly America Online).

Most of these subsidiary businesses are strategically interrelated, which means they are designed to support each other and thereby maximize the profit-making capabilities of the parent corporation. Integration of this sort may be vertical, horizontal, or both. **Vertical integration** happens when a corporation controls all aspects of production, distribution, and transmission within a particular media industry. For example, Time Warner now owns DC comics, which gave it easy access to the story material (Batman comics) needed to produce the latest Batman picture, *The Dark Knight Rises* (2012). Warner Bros. Pictures produced and distributed the movie, which was also screened in Warner-owned theatres and distributed via Warner-owned cable franchises to Warner-owned cable networks (namely HBO and TBS). These patterns of ownership gave Time Warner enormous control over the film's production and profits and virtually guaranteed it would find an audience (since Time Warner could book the film in its own theaters and on its own networks).

In addition to owning businesses along each step in the production chain, a conglomerate might try to buy up competing businesses within the same tier of the production chain. So, for example, a movie studio might buy up a small independent production house to get an infusion of new talent and reduce competition. They might also try to acquire holdings across multiple, related media industries, in the hope of creating **synergy** around a successful cultural property. Both tactics may be described as **horizontal integration** because they are about gobbling up nearby or closely related businesses. Horizontal integration allows a conglomerate like Time Warner to eliminate the competition and keep the potential profits from a "hit" in house. For example, Time Warner can take *The Dark Knight Rises* and spin it off into multiple ancillary products, like a soundtrack, a DVD, a cartoon series, a comic book, or a novelization, without ever involving an outside player. The profits from the film and its ancillary commodities all go to Time Warner and its stockholders.

Finally, these conglomerates are increasingly multinational in scope, which means they have a presence in markets all over the world and try to produce and distribute products on a global scale. The impetus to go abroad in search of markets is not necessarily new—the US film industry has dominated global film markets since at least World War I—but it has become easier and more profitable in recent years to target multiple international markets simultaneously. New technologies of communication and transportation have enabled a tighter integration of formerly distinct national economies, political systems, and cultural tribes (for lack of a better word). These integrative processes, known collectively as globalization, have altered the terrain in which cultural industries operate in significant ways. For one thing, they have made it very hard for national governments to shut out "foreign" content. Governments cannot keep satellite television signals from entering their countries, for example, and they struggle to filter the content that comes in over the internet or through social media sites. On the other hand, the same technologies that make it easier to cross national borders also make it easier and cheaper to produce cultural commodities, thereby lowering the barriers to entry in the cultural industries. A bevy of local and regional firms have thus emerged to compete with the Big Five in this new environment, and they have done well in capturing local and regional markets, especially in non–English speaking regions. The Korean media industries now dominate Asian regional markets in film, television, and recorded music, for example, beating the US-based multinational conglomerates at their own game.

Still, the multinational multimedia conglomerates have been around longer and have more resources than these newcomers, which ensures they will continue to be important players in most local markets and the top players in the global mass market. These companies view global markets as a source of growth and have taken steps to ensure their strategies of vertical and horizontal integration extend across national borders. For instance, Bertelsmann, the fifth largest media corporation in the world, is based in Germany but also operates in the US and dozens of other countries. Time Warner has particularly strong holdings in Europe and Latin America while Disney operates theme parks on three continents, owns a cruise line to travel between them, and has spun its ESPN and Disney cable channels off into over forty local iterations (each), including twenty-one Disney channels for Europe and sixteen ESPN channels for Asia. All of these players engage in **joint ventures** with overseas producers and distributors, which enables them to take advantage of local tax breaks and share some of the costs of production. In 2004, for instance, Bertelsmann joined with Sony to create Sony BMG Music Entertainment, which is now one of the four largest music producers in the world. According to Robert Mack and Brian Ott, the merger allowed the two companies to shed two thousand jobs and save $350 million a year.[9] It also gave them a 30 percent share of the US market in recorded music and a 25 percent share of the global market.[10] One company sold over a quarter of the music consumed in the world for 2011, and the four largest companies together accounted for 72 percent of global sales! That means the thousands of independent producers together only accounted for 28 percent of global sales.

As such statistics demonstrate, the strategies of concentration, integration, and globalization enable a few corporations to lock out competitors and limit the number of media offerings, thereby maximizing the potential audience for their own goods. Political economists may be right to worry about the effects of such concentration on the diversity of culture and opinion in the public sphere. Large and powerful gatekeepers certainly can restrict the free exchange of information within our common culture, and, as we will see, their desire to maximize profits does seem to result in a reluctance to innovate.

Risk Minimization Strategy Two: Shift the Risk to Others

Another strategy cultural industries use to minimize their exposure to risk involves shifting the risk down the value chain, onto subcontractors or the artists themselves. Most commercial cultural industries operate on a deficit-financing model whereby content creators must contract with the major corporations to get their works distributed broadly. These contracts may be drawn up on a case-by-case basis or as a long-term development deal, in which creators are bound to make a certain number of records, films, or television programs over a period of time. The contracts rarely cover the full costs of production, however, which means independent producers go into debt to finance their operations (hence "deficit" financing). Contracts also tend to be structured to the advantage of the corporations so that costs for the development of the project—from prints to promotions—will be born by the creative firms or individuals, not the corporations. How does this work in practice?

The recorded music industry offers a case in point. In 2012, just four major music labels—Universal Music Group (Vivendi), Warner Music Group (Time Warner),

Sony-BMG Music Entertainment (Bertelsmann), and EMI—controlled the market for the production and distribution of recorded music (in late 2012 Warner and Bertelsmann each purchased parts of EMI, dropping the number of firms controlling the recording industry to three). These labels also own or control most of the independent music labels, which they use to identify and cultivate new talent. Independent firms must contract with the majors to gain access to mass-market distribution; if they do not, they may struggle to bring their products to the consumer. Independents lead a precarious existence in relation to the larger corporation, however. As contract labor, they get revenue from the major label to run their day-to-day operations, but they are not a permanent part of the corporate structure, which means, if the corporation decides to downsize, these independents are expendable.

Rap producers, in particular, have suffered from this flexible relationship. Historically, major labels have been reluctant to create in-house rap divisions because their personnel (most of whom are white) do not understand the genre and worry about its economic potential. Rap's reliance on sampling, for example, makes it hard to copyright the work and actually drains potential profits since anything sampled must be licensed (i.e., paid for). Industry insiders also feel the genre has limited potential for international sales; it is both "too local" (i.e., too black) and "too vocal" (i.e., too dialogue-driven) to travel well. Instead of creating their own rap divisions, the major labels have contracted with independent producers, who are presumed to be "closer to the street" and so better able to judge talent and assess potential. The contract arrangements usually benefit the major labels far more than the independents, however. Independents must bear the costs of talent development, for example, which, according to the RIAA, are now around $1 million per act.[11] If an act becomes successful, the majors also have the exclusive right to sign the artists away from the independent label, which means few long-term residuals will accrue to the independent producers. Virtually all that the independents get from these deals is operating expenses.

Artists usually fare even worse under these conditions, especially those who sign with the major labels. "The crux of traditional contracts," as Rojek notes, "is the assignment of copyright."[12] Artists who want the exposure a major label can provide must sign away the copyright to their works in exchange for a 10–15 percent share (on average) of the record sales and backend licensing deals. They are usually given an advance to record an album or several singles, but they must also pay that money back, and then some, before they can begin to earn royalties. Other costs include the studio rental, crew salaries, video production expenses, tour support, and the costs for promoting the songs. Sometimes artists even have to put money into a reserve fund to cover the cost of "unsold units" returned by record stores.[13] So, for example, a band that sells five hundred thousand units (the benchmark for a "gold" record) might make as little as $149,000 at a 10 percent royalty rate.[14] That money must be split among the band members, which can leave the artists with very little for their trouble.

Such exploitative practices are routine in the industry, and contracts are notoriously hard for artists to renegotiate once they have been signed. Even mega-stars like Prince, George Michael, The Clash, and David Bowie have had to sue to get their contracts altered. The most egregious example in recent years might be the hip-hop group TLC, which had to file for bankruptcy because an unfair contract left them $3.5 million in debt. Despite receiving the first ever Diamond certification from the RIAA for sales over ten million for their album *CrazySexyCool* (1994), the band's members only took home around $35,000 each after paying the managers, producers, tour expenses, and taxes.[15] Moreover, while labels are free to drop artists as and when they please, artists can be stuck with a bad contract for life. All of the leverage in this contractual relationship belongs to the corporations. The average musician has very little control over his or her work and receives very little profit from his or her labor.

Of course, new technologies have made it cheaper and easier to produce and distribute recorded music, which has led to a boom in independent production and direct-to-market distribution over the internet. Artists like Radiohead, Jane Siberry, and Amanda Palmer have experimented with offering albums for digital download at a price point to be determined by the consumer, and Radiohead purportedly made between $6 million and $10 million on their direct-to-consumer, flexible pricing scheme for the album *In Rainbows* (2007).[16] Social networking sites like MySpace, Facebook, and SoundCloud allow bands to interact with consumers directly while online radio services like Rhapsody, Last.fm, and Spotify provide a new source of revenue for artists to tap.

All of this might lead one to question why artists still need the major labels. The answer is two-fold: (1) these online streaming sources do not, in and of themselves, replace the revenues generated by record sales; and (2) major labels are better positioned to leverage an artist's work across this cluttered marketplace. The entertainment marketing firm First Class Alliance estimates that for an artist to make a minimum wage salary of $1,100 per month, she would have to sell 1,161 retail CDs per month; on Spotify, she would have to sell 4,053,110 downloads per month. Thus, digital distribution alone will not provide a living wage. Artists need to maximize their exposure and diversify their revenue streams. Major labels have the resources to do this. They can more efficiently distribute and promote records, and they are better positioned to negotiate lucrative licensing deals for the placement of songs in commercials, videogames, and television programs.

Such performance rights—the right to use a song in multiple media platforms—are the new focus of the industry, and major labels now judge artists less for their musical abilities than for their potential to become a popular cultural phenomenon. Recording contracts, as Keith Negus reports, "have been modified to enable companies to claw back money from an artist's earnings through films, books, or games to cover any lost investment from musical recordings."[17] Thus, when the R&B/pop singer Rihanna licenses a song for use in a television show like *Ugly Betty* (2006–2010), contributes to the soundtrack for a film like *The Hangover* (2009), appears on a reality program like *The X Factor* (2011–), or stars in a movie like *Battleship* (2012), her label gets a 50 percent cut of the royalties, along with its regular cut of her record sales. As record sales have fallen (30 percent from 2004–2009), the major labels have adapted by ceding the riskier terrain of musical production to independent artists. They are happy to wait for an artist to succeed then buy into the distribution and performance rights and wait for the backend deals to pay off.

Risk Minimization Strategy Three: Play It Safe

Another set of strategies for minimizing risk involves tightly controlling the number and quality of the texts produced. Cultural industries tend to overproduce products for the market and to tailor the products to certain formulas in the hopes that audiences want more of the same. As we've seen, the TV industry routinely develops five series for every one hit it achieves. That means 80 percent of what they develop ends up being junked within a matter of months. The recording industry, likewise, acquires a repertoire of thousands of artists in dozens of genres in order to satisfy conflicting consumer tastes. Rojek estimates that less than 10 percent of these artists ever recoup their royalties, and many are dropped from their contracts after one attempt.[18] Why so much waste? Because overproduction increases the chances of scoring a hit. As the saying goes, if you throw enough mud at a wall, some of it is going to stick. One hit can mitigate the damage caused by dozens of flops. It can keep a company, and sometimes an industry, afloat during down times, and there are always downtimes. Increasingly, cultural industries are using social media to try to streamline the processes of hit-production, but the sense that "all hits are flukes" still prevails in many industries, which means overproduction will continue for the foreseeable future.

Because they cannot predict what will succeed, most commercial cultural industries concentrate on minimizing the number of failures through formatting and repetition. The goal is to make it easy for audiences to identify and consume new texts by connecting them to past experiences. Genres, stars, and **pre-sold commodities** are all ways of facilitating these experiential connections. Genres are formulas that allow audiences to categorize texts according to certain representational codes and narrative patterns. Everyone knows, for example, that a pop song will be three to five minutes in length, alternate between a verse and a chorus (usually with an emphasis on the chorus), and be driven by its rhythm line. The chorus will contain a "hook," which is designed to be catchy and will be repeated often enough to stick in the head. Part of the pleasure of listening to pop music involves knowing these codes and being surprised when the formula is worked out in new ways. For example, Queen's song "Bohemian Rhapsody" (1975) delights, in part, because it starts out as a standard rock ballad but incorporates operatic and choral pieces in the mid-section, where the chorus should be. From the audience's perspective, genres provide a stable ground against which to measure innovation. From a marketing standpoint, genre labels help consumers distinguish between products in a crowded marketplace. Labels like "rock" or "rap" help customers identify music they might like through comparison to their past preferences.

Stars are another way to facilitate an immediate connection between consumers and commodities. Actors and performers are the most familiar types of stars, but authors, directors, or producers may also be used to brand and promote a cultural product, as, for example, when we are told that a new television program comes "from the creators of *Lost*." It is important to recognize that stars are not actual human beings; they are carefully manufactured texts, or personas, that offer distinctive points of identification for audiences. Rihanna, to return to an earlier example, embodies a mix of sexuality and vulnerability that many of her songs and album titles describe explicitly. She is the "Good Girl Gone Bad," a "Fool in Love" with a penchant for "S&M" but an insistence that her life choices are "Nobody's Business" but her own. Her abusive relationship with boyfriend and singer Chris Brown reinforces this image of confused, but defiant womanhood, even as it builds his image of tough masculinity. She remains cocky ("Cockiness") and "Unapologetic" about her lifestyle even as controversy swirls around her. Stars are another way to brand commodities in a crowded marketplace, but they are also more than that. A successful star persona becomes a template for the production of future stars. Thus, Rihanna's image is modeled on precursors like Lil' Kim, Trina, and Beyoncé, and her success has spawned a bevy of new imitators like Ke$ha and Azealia Banks. The idea is that if we identify with the image once, we will be likely to do so again.

Finally, commercial industries like to literally reproduce prior cultural successes in the hopes that the new iterations will also succeed. A pre-sold commodity is a text, story, or concept that is already well-known to audiences. The idea is that, by remaking, copying, or extending an existing body of cultural works, producers will have a built-in audience for new products. Fans of those earlier texts can be counted on to buy into the new one. *The Avengers* (2012) movie exhibits several of these tactics for tapping fans and building audiences. The film is a **re-make** of the Marvel comic book series of that name, which was itself a **spin-off** from a series of other Marvel comics (*The Hulk, Iron Man, Thor, Nick Fury, Black Widow, Captain America*). In some ways the film is also a **sequel** to the second *Iron Man* film, for the characters of Black Widow and Nick Fury show up in *Iron Man 2* (2010) to assess Tony Stark's viability for inclusion on the Avengers team. Finally, *The Avengers* is something of a **copy-cat text** in that it follows a string of very successful blockbuster film series based on other comic books (notably *X-Men, The Incredible Hulk, Spider Man,* and *Iron Man*). Re-making beloved stories, spinning-off new versions of them with familiar characters, creating sequels that extend the stories, and copying the formulas of prior success are all ways to ensure audiences will recognize—and love—your new products. In politico-economic terms, standardization and repetition are an inevitable result of the corporation's need to maximize audiences.

Repetition cannot guarantee success, however. To do that, corporation's need to add a little mustard to the mix.

Risk Minimization Strategy Four: Maximize Exposure

Commercial cultural production revolves as much around marketing and promotion as its does around the production of cultural commodities. The RIAA's breakdown of a typical contract for new artists includes a $200,000 advance, for example, and *$300,000* for marketing and promotion. If we add in the costs of making videos to promote the artist (a separate category in the table, but clearly a marketing expense), the total expenditure on marketing and promotion jumps to 50 percent of the contract (or $500,000).[19] Where does this money go? Much of it goes toward drafting various gatekeepers and social influencers—those with the capacity to "spread the word" about an artist. For example, the music industry has a long history of bribing disk jockeys with money, gifts, and sex to play their artists on the air. Such "payola" schemes were formally outlawed in the US in the 1960s, but major distributors simply used "independent record promoters" to get around the restrictions until that practice, too, was declared illegal in 2006. Promoters may also go directly to "social influencers" like club DJs, music reviewers, lifestyle bloggers, and even prominent Twitter users to promote an artist, event, or song. Often this involves the exchange of cash, free merchandise, or a "meet-and-greet" for a positive review.

Since word-of-mouth advertising is generally more effective than corporate advertising, record promoters also use "street teams" of youthful fans to promote bands and concerts in a seemingly unmotivated fashion. In the past, this has involved spreading band stickers and posters around town, wearing band merchandise in the "right" locales, and passing out free CDs ("ripped" to look authentically user-generated). Today, however, it involves social networking. Promoters enlist fans to participate in online chat forums, post videos on MySpace or YouTube, tag and comment on the artist's material on these sites, and even produce band-oriented podcasts or blogs themselves. In Italy, for example, Universal Music Italia hosts a web portal for its street teams called UTeam.[20] Managers construct "missions" for fans to enact in exchange for receiving CDs, concert tickets, or a meet-and-greet with the artist. One mission to support Lady Gaga asked her fans to incorporate Gaga's portrait into their Facebook pages; another promoted a "download day" in which fans buy copies of a designated single on iTunes in hopes of pushing it into the iTunes top ten. Promoters may also try to inspire "flash mob" activity by distributing video tutorials of an artist's choreographed dance routines and inviting fans to go out and perform the routines in public. They may offer prizes for the best flash mob videos posted on YouTube. All of this activity is designed to seem spontaneous, and fans are hardly compensated for their efforts, but the marketers who facilitate the activity are highly paid apparatchiks of the major labels. As we will see, these attempts to transform fan love into labor are the new trend, but they are also unpredictable and can sometimes backfire.

Multimedia conglomerates have much easier means to get the word out about their products—namely, forms of **cross-promotion** and synergy. Cross-promotion refers to the use of one product or service to promote another. Sometimes cross-promotion happens through licensing deals with outside companies, as, for example, when McDonalds signs an exclusive contract to offer Star Wars toys at its restaurants, or Harley Davidson Motorcycles licenses the use of the Iron Man character to promote their machines and be promoted, in turn, in a Marvel comic (as happened with *Iron Man 3*). More often than not, though, such deals are kept strictly in-house. So, for example, Disney, which owns both Marvel comics and the ESPN network, used scenes from *Iron Man 3* to introduce its flagship sports program *Sportscenter* throughout the month of May 2013—the month of the film's release. Synergy involves an even more strategic integration of content such that the potential for spin-off merchandise is taken into account in advance when selecting artists or projects. New recording artists are often "broken" on reality television series sponsored by multimedia conglomerates, for example. The prize for winning *Pop Idol, American Idol, The X Factor,* and other series is a recording contract with a subsidiary of the conglomerate and the "opportunity" to tour incessantly to promote the show, its affiliated recording label, and its sponsors, who also co-produce the show in most cases. The conglomerate makes money by selling advertising space in and alongside the program, *and* it gets to test market new talent for future economic cultivation. Contestants are pre-selected for participation based not just on their talent, but on their image, their social poise, and their marketability (which group of fans are they likely attract). They are then groomed through a grueling process of performance and critique that strips the would-be stars of their original personality and replaces it with a carefully manufactured image. As Su Holmes notes, by the time voters choose a winner, they are merely selecting from the same slate of pre-packaged genre representatives the industry always gives its fans. The finalists are all equally ready to be launched to stardom as the industry defines it, and many of the "losers" also receive recording contracts and invitations to tour in support of the show.[21] The conglomerates can generate multiple revenue streams from one source. This is the essence of synergy.

All in all, these strategies of risk minimization help to routinize and standardize the processes of cultural production. The goal is to transform a messy and unpredictable procedure into something manageable and factory-like. Political economists make much of this factory metaphor, conjuring images of alienated labor from the early days of mass production. "This is the way these music companies work," according to Robert McChesney. "They're not interested in the ideas behind the music, they're not interested in the spirit that moves the music, the passion. They're just interested in making money, and they have no regard for the music otherwise."[22] Political economists also worry about the effects of concentration and conglomeration on the quality and diversity of our cultural resources. If three or four large corporations control 72 percent of the market for recorded music in the world, will this not, of necessity, reduce the diversity of the offerings available?

What will happen to local acts or cultural practices that do not fit the mold of the commercial cultural industries? Will they just disappear? And, if all of these companies use the same production strategies to reduce their exposure to risk, won't this mean we get the same type of song (or book or film or TV show, etc.) churned out over and over again? The Australian musical comedy band Axis of Awesome provides a compelling illustration of this fear in the piece "Four Chord Song" (2009). The work demonstrates precisely how standardized commercial musical production has become by morphing from one major hit song to another—from Journey's "Don't Stop Believing" to Alphaville's "Forever Young," Jason Mraz's "I'm Yours," U2's "With or Without You," and even Bob Marley's "No Woman No Cry"—without ever changing the tune.[23]

WHAT ARE THE LIMITS OF THE POLITICAL ECONOMY APPROACH?

The political economy approach, with its emphasis on macro-level structures of ownership and control, draws attention to the economic calculations that drive the cultural industries. It shows quite clearly how corporate decision-making is constrained by bottom-line thinking, and how such thinking can reduce cultural diversity, constrain consumer choice, and favor social consensus. Still, like all approaches, political economy has some limitations. For one thing, macro-level accounts of the cultural industries "often forget the less orderly organizational life within the companies . . . [and] the human beings who inhabit the corporate structure."[24] Different sectors of a corporation may vie with each other for customers, and they may pursue competing agendas all in the name of the corporate interest. Even within the home office, there may be some contention between, say, the legal department of the corporation, whose job is to protect copyright by locking down user-activity, and the marketing department, which views user-activity as a vital means of generating interest in a media property. These corporations have shared strategic aims, but the aims are not always realized efficiently in practice. Political economy is not really concerned with how the processes of capitalist cultural production are actually lived, which sometimes leads them to over-generalize their claims. For example, political economists tend to apply the Anglo-European model of production to all commercial cultural industries, making it difficult to understand how these industries function differently in different societies. As Jocelyne Guilbault shows, the Caribbean calypso industry's preference for performance over recording changes the economic calculations leaders in these industries make. So, traditional politico-economic analyses would provide little insight into the calypso industry's operations.[25]

Political economists are also not concerned with non-commercial modes of cultural production. As we have seen, culture proper consists of a broad range of behaviors—from play-acting and performing to remixing and gossiping—that are not necessarily commodified or commodifiable. If I play a guitar in my spare time to amuse myself and my friends, no one is profiting from that behavior but me and my friends. Moreover, the music, even if it was originally produced for commercial consumption, becomes something new when I perform it in this context. Not only might the interaction with an audience alter the shape and quality of the song, but the function of the music changes—the song goes from being a product for sale to being a ritual expression that draws me and my pals closer together. I share this music; I do not own or profit from it, nor, really, do the corporations. Political economy is ill-equipped to address these alternative modes of cultural production because it thinks of value in narrowly economic terms. To understand the social dynamics of cultural exchange, we should look to more historical, sociological, and ethnographic modes of inquiry.

THE MORAL ECONOMY OF FANDOM: A DIFFERENT VIEW OF OWNERSHIP AND INDUSTRY

The term "industry," as Raymond Williams notes, refers to more than just "a set of institutions for the production of trade." It refers also to "the human quality of sustained application and effort."[26] Narrowly economic conceptions of industry, ownership, labor, and value make it difficult to think about the role of audiences in the creation of culture. Fans, and the scholars who study them, have long contested this narrowly economic framework, arguing instead that cultural consumption is a type of production that adds value to commodities and helps them succeed. Fans frequently feel a sense of "ownership" over their favored cultural objects, and they expect the institutional producers to acknowledge their "debt" to the fans for their "labors" of love. "We made you; you owe us" is the general philosophy of the fan. What fans want, however, is rarely monetary reward. They want loyalty and devotion, acknowledgement and praise. They want producers to care as much about their favorite cultural texts, objects, and stars as they themselves do. In this respect, fans draw upon a different set of social and cultural principles—a different moral economy—than commercial cultural producers do.

For one thing, the commercial producers tend to think of consumers only as consumers—atomized buying units who make purchasing decisions based on rational calculations. They often weigh decisions about what acts to sign, films to produce, and books to promote based on assumptions about the "purchasing power" of target markets that fail to speak to the investment and energy of fans as co-promoters of the brand. For example, the music industry has historically under-supported both the heavy metal and rap genres due largely to calculations about the potential purchasing power of the target audiences of working-class youth. They failed to recognize the cross-over potential and global appeal of both forms and left it up to fans to do the labor of spreading the good word. That both forms eventually became global hits had little to do with the efforts of the commercial recording industries. It had to do with the "industry" of the bands and their fans.

Early metal bands toured almost incessantly, generating interest in the music and establishing the basic outlines of what would eventually become a full-fledged subculture. This subculture developed its own uniform (long hair, tight jeans, concert T-shirts, tattoos) and gestural language (the devil horns, "fuck-you" attitude, head-banging, and moshing), which it spread through performances, fan zines and underground "metal shops" around the world. Metal fans in the US military have been an important source of global diffusion in recent years, spreading metal to locales like Japan, North Africa, and Iraq.[27] Meanwhile, the internet has enabled indigenous examples of metal from places like Brazil (Sepultura, Ozone) and Norway (various "death-metal" bands) to reach audiences in Britain and America and reenergize the form. In the absence of industry support, metal fans have been the agents charged with "appraising" and "selling" the form to new audiences. They undertake this "labor" out of love for the bands, the music, and the community that surrounds it. Economic theories of cultural production might describe these fans as "alienated" or "exploited" because they receive no financial benefit in exchange for their labor, but fans see things quite differently. They give their labor freely in exchange for a variety of alternative rewards—subcultural prestige, social connection, and personal empowerment. As this example demonstrates, audiences are not merely consumers, and their activities cannot be reduced to a series of economic transactions. They are active agents who produce meaning and value, identity, and community, from otherwise inert cultural commodities.

Another difference between the commodity logic of the commercial producers and the social logics of audiences and fans is that corporations look at cultural commodities as goods to be hoarded. For them, value derives from the exclusivity of ownership. They want to control the circulation of the commodity as tightly as possible in order to leverage profits at every step of the value chain. Such exclusivity, however, is at odds with the values of reciprocity and sharing that define most modes of user engagement, and there is a fine line between controlling the circulation of a cultural property and choking off user access and interest. New technologies make this line even finer by inviting users to participate in the circulation and marketing of cultural goods on platforms like Facebook, YouTube, and Last.fm. As Henry Jenkins and his co-authors argue in *Spreadable Media,* corporations who cling to notions of exclusivity and centralized ownership in this new network system risk alienating their audiences and undermining their profits. Tight control over distribution may undermine the desire of users to share media content, and sharing has become vital to success in the contemporary distributed media environment.

They use the Susan Boyle phenomenon to illustrate the concept. In 2009, Boyle auditioned to perform on the reality television series *Britain's Got Talent.* Her amazing voice, coupled with her unconventional appearance (she was older and decidedly frumpy), made her performance interesting to fans, who quickly posted the audition tape to YouTube where it was viewed over 77 million times (that's two times as many views as the 2009 season finale of the popular US series *American Idol* attracted). Boyle's tape was then copied and posted by users in Brazil, Japan, China, and others locales, making her a global phenomenon. What made Boyle's video "spreadable" had little to do with the cultural industries that "discovered" and initially displayed her (they had no plans to distribute the program beyond Britain). It had to do with audience interest and energy.

Her performance provided multiple points of entry for audience engagement. For Christians, she became an inspiration and "the focus of online prayer circles. Science blogs discussed how someone with her [small] body [size] could produce such sound. Karaoke singers debated her technique . . . reality television blogs debated whether her success would have been possible on U.S. television . . . [and] fashion blogs critiqued and dissected the makeover she was given for subsequent television appearances."[28] New technologies and skills, meanwhile, made it possible for users to clip Boyle's performance, upload it to the web, and share it easily via html link or embed code. Many users in the US and other markets "found" Boyle, not through *Britain's Got Talent,* but via email bulletins, Facebook sites, and blog posts set up to serve other communities of interest. If FreemantleMedia, the corporation who owns the rights to *Britain's Got Talent,* had decided to clamp down on such user-activity, it would have undermined the growth potential of its latest star. Instead, the company let such circulation happen and ended up profiting in the end.

The recording industry's early response to online file-sharing offers a counter-example, which illustrates the relative incompatibility of commercial and fan economies. Early file-sharing sites like Napster or Grokster provided a space where users could upload and swap content of interest to them. The operators did not upload content themselves or profit from any of the exchanges on the site; all they did was build a space where users could connect and share resources. Still, in 2000, Napster was sued by the RIAA for copyright infringement and forced into bankruptcy. (They were eventually bought out by Roxio and redesigned as a pay-per-download distribution service, which is now owned by electronic retailer Best Buy.) The RIAA case rested on the claim that Napster's existence encouraged fans to illegally copy and trade music, thereby undermining the sales of recorded music. Industry lawyers compared file-sharing to the theft of a CD from a store shelf and claimed such services were primarily responsible for the 30 percent drop-off in CD sales between 1999 and 2003 (more likely, the decline resulted from file-sharing plus a range of other factors, like a decrease in CD releases, inflated prices, and competition from other media).[29] In their claims of "piracy," the RIAA made no distinction between young teens sharing music with friends and the sophisticated copy-and-distribute operations responsible for flooding international markets with unauthorized, low-cost versions of official CDs. Lessig has likened the industry's tactics to those of a mob boss who sends lackeys to break the kneecaps of anyone who threatens his dominion. This punitive strategy may have cooled user enthusiasm for illegal downloading in the short term, but in the long run it tarnished the industry's public image and drove younger consumers, who were already loathe to buy CDs, even further away from recorded sales. The lawsuits also had a negligible effect on file-sharing sites, most of which simply stopped hosting files on a centralized server and went underground or overseas to avoid industry scrutiny.

The failure of the industry's efforts to stop file-sharing can be related directly to their refusal to understand the social and cultural aspects of the practice from the perspective of participants and audiences. For one thing, most musicians do not make music solely for financial gain and see little harm in file-sharing. We have already discussed several cases of musicians offering albums for online distribution for a price-point to be determined by the fans. Trent Reznor of Nine Inch Nails went one better and posted his 2008 album *The Slip* on his website for free, telling fans "this one's on me." As Jenkins explains, the album may not have cost fans money, but it did entail a social obligation—to continue supporting the band in the future. Likewise, fans swap music files, not necessarily out of a selfish desire to get something for nothing, but because it may be socially damaging not to. As Ian Condry explains, "Unlike under-wear or swimsuits, music falls into that category of things you are normally obligated to share with your dorm mates, family, and friends. . . . In fact, if asked directly by a friend to share music, sharing is the only reasonable thing to do."[30]

Music is not just a commodity; it is a means to establish, explore, and cement social relationships. That is why so many people from so many different demographic groups (according to the last Pew Research Center poll on the subject, up to 30 percent of Americans, and Condry cites 66 percent of Japanese) participate in some form of illicit downloading or file-sharing. Moreover, fans insist their sharing activities serve a promotional function that helps the industry. File-sharing is a type of personal endorsement that drives consumers to purchase more, not less, music. According to economic research, they may have a point. An early study by economists at Harvard and North Carolina universities concluded that "free" music downloads had an effect on record sales that was "indistinguishable from zero."[31] They found that the ability to sample content actually drove consumers to purchase CDs, and this activity offset any losses from the original "crime."

If the recording industry had actually studied the *culture* of file-sharing, they might have thought twice about taking such a hardline approach. At the very least, they might have anticipated the consumer backlash that resulted. Condry's research suggests, for example, that many file-sharers view themselves as modern-day Robin Hoods, correcting the economic imbalances that enrich the industry at the expense of artists and fans. Knowing that CDs cost only about a dollar to reproduce, Condry's students questioned why CDs cost consumers fifteen times that amount. They characterized the bundling of songs into albums as a deceptive marketing practice that forces consumers to purchase ten bad songs for every good one. Finally, knowing that musical contracts are unfairly structured, they asked why a bunch of "middle-men" should make so much more than the artists who create the music. For the industry to suddenly assume the moral high-ground and accuse their customers of being "thieves" and "pirates" struck many fans as hypocritical.

Based on these cultural lessons, what might a more effective response to file-sharing look like? Condry's research again provides some insight. After repeatedly failing to make his students feel guilty about file-sharing, he decided to ask them, instead, what music they would always pay for. They responded with a variation on a single theme: we would pay for music that we connect to or are passionate about.

Record companies err, as one Japanese executive put it, when they try to reduce music to a token of commercial exchange. By focusing on "hit songs, rather than developing fan relationships with artists and groups," the industry trains consumers to think of music as "a commodity, not a piece of the soul of an artist or group." This executive calls on the industry to stop punishing those who share music and start fostering the "relationships" between audiences and artists that might make illicit file-sharing feel morally untenable.[32] After all, most people would not cheat or steal from their loved ones. The trick for corporations, then, is to help spread the love by fostering more intimate and intensive relations between audiences and artists.

AFFECTIVE ECONOMICS, OR THE CONVERGENCE OF PRODUCER AND CONSUMER RELATIONS

The major music corporations have finally learned this lesson. They are beginning to embrace online delivery platforms and establish social networks to build brand loyalty and direct illicit consumer behavior into legal channels. They call this strategy "customer relationship management," or CRM, but Jenkins more aptly describes it as a form of **affective economics**. For our purposes, **affect** refers to the physical sensations and feelings that connect people to cultural goods (see Chapter 8). The goal of affective economics is to tap consumer passion and use it to raise the profile of commercial brands. As Coca Cola president Steven J. Heyer explains, savvy corporations now try to "break into people's hearts and minds. . . . We're moving to ideas that elicit emotion and create connections."[33] Thus, the website that Coke built to accompany its sponsorship of the TV program *American Idol* uses social media tools—identity profiles, personalized playlists, crowd-based ratings systems, games, quizzes, and contests—to promote (and control) the types of "connections" fans can make with the brand, the show, and each other. Taco Bell recently took this approach to its logical conclusion by "marrying" eight of its most ardent fans. The promotion mixed consumer familiarity with the Beyoncé Knowles song "Put a Ring On It" with the fans' pre-existing "love" for the Taco Bell brand in an attempt to generate a viral internet meme that might draw in more female consumers.

As Jenkins notes, however, this new touchy-feely commercial strategy can be a double-edged sword for both audiences and corporations. For fans, it represents an acknowledgement of the moral economy of gift-giving and blurs the boundaries between producers and audiences in productive ways. Corporations now actively solicit and reward fan involvement in the promotion of the brand. Fan labor gains both economic and institutional value within media corporations, as fans become important "test markets" and "multipliers" of promotional messages. Yet, affective economics is ultimately about selling things. Corporations want to understand human emotions so that they can better control and direct consumers' behaviors in the marketplace. Too often corporations speak the language of love and friendship (often literally on Facebook and other sites where "friending" is the operative

FIGURE 6.01   *Taco Bell "weds" its fans to promote the brand (2013).*

modality) without accepting the moral obligations that come along with genuine human relationships. The corporations foster what sociologists call **weak ties**, or social relationships that are shallow, transitory, and demand little in the way of reciprocity. Such ties are great for bridging the differences that keep social groups apart, but they are not great for fostering intimacy and trust among those parties. Fans often feel betrayed or used by corporations who fail to attend to the obligations that come with emotional attachment.

An example from China might help illustrate the fraught nature of Customer Relationship Management. China has its own version of the popular amateur singing competition format called *Super Girl* (or *Super Boy*).[34] As in other countries, the program was developed and supported by the Chinese recording industry, which was desperate to find new sources of revenue after a slump in CD sales, and new ways to test market future stars. Like other such formats, the show actively engages its audience in the process of star production and promotion in the hope of inspiring increased consumption. In 2005, a young, tomboyish singer named Li Yuchun won the contest thanks to her avid fan following. Since then, her fans, called "Corns" in English (a rough translation of *yumi* or "Yuchun fan"), have continued to promote her career using their collective buying power to drive up CD sales and sophisticated public relations strategies to generate grassroots enthusiasm for the star. For example, Corns organize "chart beating" and "trial listening" actions designed to drive Li's singles up the Chinese pop charts (which are indexed to measures of online voting and consumer sampling). They hand-deliver marketing packets, containing a fan-created magazine and Li Yuchun desk calendar, to major media outlets to promote each new album release. They visit local record stores to give away free Li Yuchun merchandise and badger the store owners into stocking more Li Yuchun CDs. Finally, in a country where the internet piracy rate is 99 percent,

Corns make sure to purchase every Li Yuchun CD available (and often multiple copies) in order to prove there is value to the industry in supporting the star. Their slogan is "prove your love for her with sales numbers," and they have worked to combat piracy in China by spreading this message. In 2006, three of them organized a twenty-city bicycle tour to raise awareness of the industry's anti-piracy efforts. The banner they carried on the trip read: "Piracy stops at true love. Please support legal audio-video products and support good music."

Unfortunately for them, the local talent agencies and record companies have not responded with similar devotion. They seem to view fans as a free pool of labor from which to draw for promotional services. They will not sign new acts without an existing fan base, but they also will not respond to fan demands for more financial support or creative independence for the artist. More often than not, they exploit fan love by selling cheaply produced records by their star attractions at a higher price point. They know fans will buy the album regardless of its quality or cost. Likewise, promoters inflate the price for concert tickets for star acts while under-supporting the tour financially, leading to equipment malfunctions, poor sound quality, and sometimes cancellations. Fans view these actions as deliberate attempts to exploit their wealth and devotion at the expense of the star's long-term career. More specifically, Corns accuse Taihe Rye, Li Yuchun's promoters, of pricing mainstream consumers out of the market for Li Yuchun's CDs and concert tickets. This harms her mass-market appeal and may keep her from achieving greater stardom. Corns are ambivalent about their devotional activities, then, because they know their financial support of the singer enables the company's neglect. They are not duped by the system; they persist because they feel a genuine connection to the star, whom they characterize as a "little sister" or "daughter."

Affective economics makes corporations vulnerable, too, however. The neglect or exploitation of fans can sometimes generate a full-scale consumer revolt. Corn fans dream of establishing their own music conglomerate devoted to developing Li Yuchun's star power, but also to upending the reigning Chinese business model, which they view as exploitative. The size and relative marginality of cultural fandoms in China ensures this will remain a dream for the foreseeable future, but other fan communities have successfully leveraged consumer affect to shame corporations or win concessions from those who fail to properly appreciate the scope or depth of fan love. When Sony hired new media consultancy Zipatoni to create a fake grassroots (aka astroturf) YouTube video to promote its Play Station consoles in 2006, gamers quickly discovered the videos were hosted on Zipatoni's servers. Game sites like Kotaku and Joystiq denounced the ploy as "sad" and quickly spread the word that "Sony marketers are horrible liars" (the title of Joystiq's review). They took great glee in ridiculing the videomaker's amateur attempt to appear amateur, eventually forcing Sony to issue the following apology:

> Busted. Nailed. Snagged. As many of you have figured out (maybe our speech was a little too funky fresh???), Peter isn't a real hip-hop maven and this site

was actually developed by Sony. Guess we were trying to be just a little too clever. From this point forward, we will just stick to making cool products, and use this site to give you nothing but the facts on the PSP.[35]

When Warner Bros. Pictures began shutting down Harry Potter fan sites after acquiring the rights to the film in 2001, Potter fans also got organized and launched a massive anti-censorship campaign designed to shame Warner Bros. into backing down. Teenage fans led the assault. Heather Lawver, proprietor of an online newspaper called *The Daily Prophet,* formed an organization called "Defense Against the Dark Arts" to paint Warner Bros. as a "dark force" and defend fellow fans from Warner's legal actions. She took her case to the media, and partnered with fans in other countries who did the same. Together, they forced Warner Bros. to change its policies and practices, relinquishing some control over their content in exchange for continued loyalty of the Potter fandom.

These are just two examples of how the new affective economics can be a double-edged sword for corporations. Fan love doesn't just enrich corporations. It also makes them vulnerable. If corporations betray the trust of fans, all of that fan energy and influence can be turned against the brand, and, once a brand is tarnished, it is often easier to start fresh than to rebuild consumer trust. Fans are not oblivious to the ways commercial producers try to constrain and direct their energies, and they are often the first to admit that their love of popular forms can be like addiction—an expensive habit that makes them vulnerable to manipulation. Yet, it is important to consider the alternative compensations fans receive for their activities and to resist the urge to reduce popular culture to the commercial logics of the cultural industries.

CONCLUSION

As Jenkins and his colleagues note, "social and cultural practices operate in an economic context, but economic practices also operate in a social and cultural context."[36] To better understand how meanings and pleasures are created and circulated in everyday life, students of popular culture should learn to trace the interrelations between these different systems. This means asking how cultural commodities are made and circulated by corporations but also how they are remade and recirculated by people. It means attending to the ways cultural commodities acquire "value" in the market but also how they acquire "worth" in the aftermarket of everyday life. Unlike value, which is determined by impersonal forces like institutions and markets, worth is a subjective and social measure of value based on use or sentiment. It refers to those qualities of an item that "you can't put a price on."

The "Priceless" series of MasterCard commercials offers a simplistic illustration of the difference (albeit one that seeks to translate worth back into value by selling you a credit card). In one version of the ad, we learn what it costs for a father and son to attend a baseball game. The game is pricey—costing over $100— but the experience of father-son bonding it enables is "priceless" in that it cannot be duplicated and will live a long afterlife in memory. Family heirlooms have a similar sentimental value, or worth, which may be at odds with their market value, as television programs like *Antiques Roadshow* repeatedly demonstrate. Viewers often bring in family heirlooms to be appraised on such shows only to discover they are value-less by market standards. Few are deflated by these conclusions, however, for few would part with their heirlooms even if they were economically valuable. The objects are "priceless" because they embody human relationships and memories.

The point here is that commercial value is only one way of measuring the meaningfulness of an object. As scholars of popular culture, we must understand the basic economic dynamics of the cultural industries, but we should never forget that human industry is what turns commodities into culture, value into worth. Especially in a media context that blurs the lines between producers and consumers and promotes a generalized ethos of remixability, we must examine how economic, social, and moral logics intersect. Our job, as John Fiske argues, is to trace the play of power as these different value systems and moral economies come into contact.

SUMMARY

- This chapter explains the workings of the commercial cultural industries and their attempts to adjust to recent changes in the media environment.

- Commercial industries are less concerned with making art than with making profit. They have developed a variety of strategies for minimizing the financial risks associated with cultural production while maximizing profits.

- These strategies involve producing "hits" through the use of stars, pre-sold commodities, and proven formulas.

- New strategies involve generating multiple revenue streams through the synergistic selling of spin-off merchandise, like toys, videogames, and soundtracks.

- Companies also try to gain economic advantages by shifting the costs of production onto artists and expanding their operations.

- Political economy can tell us about the conditions of production in these industries, but it tells us little about how people live with/within these conditions. To understand the lived experience of cultural production, we need historical, sociological, and ethnographic methods.

- The real question is: how do the economic, social, and moral logics of corporations and the people intersect? Around what issues, tensions, or points of agreement?

NOTES

1 Lawrence Lessig, *Free Culture: How Big Media Uses Technology and the Law to Lockdown Culture and Control Creativity* (New York: Penguin Press, 2004), 8.

2 Jay Rosen, "The People Formerly Known as the Audience," in *The Social Media Reader,* ed. Mandiberg, Michael (New York: New York University Press, 2012), 13.

3 Michel Eisner, quoted in "Mickey Mouse Monopoly: Disney, Childhood & Corporate Power," Media Education Foundation, 2001, DVD.

4 Philip M. Napoli, "Media Economics and the Study of Media Industries," in *Media Industries: History, Theory and Method,* eds. Holt, Jennifer and Alisa Perren (Malden, MA: Wiley-Blackwell, 2009), 165.

5 Jason Mittell, *Television and American Culture* (New York: Oxford University Press, 2009), 51.

6 Stephen J. Dubner, "Your Movie Industry Questions Answered," *Freakonomics,* September 9, 2008, http://www.freakonomics.com/2008/09/09/your-movie-industry-questions-answered/ (accessed May 1, 2013).

7 "Let's Play: The American Music Business" (Washington, DC: Recording Industry Association of America, 2012).

8 Chris Rojek, *Pop Music, Pop Culture* (Malden, MA: Polity Press, 2011), 136.

9 Robert Mack and Brian Ott, *Critical Media Studies: An Introduction* (Malden, MA: Wiley-Blackwell, 2010), 39.

10 "The Music Industry," 2013, http://en.wikipedia.org/wiki/Music_industry (accessed May 2, 2013). These figures are based on the official Nielsen Soundscan reports for 2011.

11 "Let's Play: The American Music Business."

12 Rojek, *Pop Music, Pop Culture,* 157.

13 Anita M. Samuels and Diana B. Henriques, "Does Going 'Broke' Mean Artist Really Doesn't Have Any Money?," February 5, 1996, http://web.archive.org/web/200410100 81842/http://mbhs.bergtraum.k12.ny.us/cybereng/nyt/rapper01.htm (accessed May 1, 2013).

14 For comparison, an artist who presses and distributes directly via the internet may make $4 million on the same volume of sales—problem is, such artists rarely achieve such volume. Henry Cedeno, "How Much Revenue Do Artist[S] Really Earn through Traditional/Non-Traditional Retail Outlets," *First Class Alliance Entertainment Marketing,* November 8, 2011, http://firstclassalliance.com/how-much-revenue-do-artist-really-earn-through-traditionalnon-traditional-retail-outlets.html (accessed May 1, 2013).

15 Samuels and Henriques, "Does Going 'Broke' Mean Artist Really Doesn't Have Any Money?"

16 Eliot Van Buskirk, "Estimates: Radiohead Made up to $10 Million on Initial Album Sales," October 19, 2007, http://www.wired.com/listening_post/2007/10/estimates-radio/ (accessed May 2, 2013). Amanda Palmer speaks about her experience with this pricing scheme in her TED Talk "The Art of Asking," http://www.ted.com/talks/amanda_palmer_the_art_of_asking (accessed May 22, 2014).

17 Keith Negus, *Music Genres and Corporate Cultures* (New York: Routledge, 1999), 33.

18 Rojek, *Pop Music, Pop Culture,* 136.

19 "Let's Play: The American Music Business."

20 The information that follows is based on Agnese Veller, "The Recording Industry and Grassroots Marketing: From Street Teams to Flash Mobs," *Participations: Journal of Audience & Reception Studies* 9, 1 (2012), 95–118.

21 Su Holmes, "'Reality Goes Pop!': Reality TV, Popular Music and Narratives of Stardom in Pop Idol," *Television & New Media* 5, 2 (2004), 155–158.

22 "Money for Nothing: Behind the Business of Pop Music," Media Education Foundation, 2001, DVD.

23 See the YouTube video and enjoy: http://www.youtube.com/watch?v=5pidokakU4I (accessed May 1, 2013). Thanks to Tony Harkins for the reference.

24 Negus, *Music Genres and Corporate Cultures,* 16.
25 Jocelyne Guilbault, "The Politics of Calypso in a World of Music Industries," in *Popular Music Studies,* eds. Negus, Keith and David Hesmondhalgh (New York: Oxford University Press, 2002).
26 Raymond Williams, *Keywords: A Vocabulary of Culture and Society* (New York: Oxford University Press, 1985), 165.
27 While much has been made of the military's use of heavy metal to induce stress in prisoners in Iraq and Afghanistan, the appeal of the music to youth cultures in those locales has received far less attention. See the documentaries *Global Metal* (2008) and *Heavy Metal in Baghdad* (2007) for details about global fandom.
28 Henry Jenkins, Sam Ford, and Joshua Green, *Spreadable Media: Creating Value and Meaning in a Networked Culture* (New York: New York University Press, 2013), 13–14.
29 See Lessig, *Free Culture,* 70–71.
30 Ian Condry, "Cultures of Music Piracy: An Ethnographic Comparison of the US and Japan," *International Journal of Cultural Studies* 7, 3 (2004), 348.
31 Felix Oberholzer and Koleman Strumpf, "The Effect of File-Sharing on Record Sales: An Empirical Analysis," March 2004, http://www.unc.edu/~cigar/papers/FileSharing_March2004.pdf (accessed June 10, 2013).
32 Katsuya Taruishi, quoted in Condry, "Cultures of Music Piracy," 352.
33 Quoted in Henry Jenkins, *Convergence Culture: Where Old and New Media Collide* (New York: New York University Press, 2006), 69.
34 The information that follows is based on Ling Yang, "All for Love: The Corn Fandom, Prosumers, and the Chinese Way of Creating a Superstar," *International Journal of Cultural Studies* 12, 5 (2009), 527–543.
35 "New Sony Viral Marketing Ploy Angers Consumers," December 14, 2006, *Guardian,* http://www.theguardian.com/technology/gamesblog/2006/dec/11/newsonyviral (accessed May 22, 2014).
36 Jenkins, Ford, and Green, *Spreadable Media,* 71.

REFERENCES

Cedeno, Henry, "How Much Revenue Do Artist[S] Really Earn through Traditional/Non-Traditional Retail Outlets." *First Class Alliance Entertainment Marketing,* November 8, 2011. http://firstclassalliance.com/how-much-revenue-do-artist-really-earn-through-traditionalnon-traditional-retail-outlets.html.
Condry, Ian. "Cultures of Music Piracy: An Ethnographic Comparison of the US and Japan." *International Journal of Cultural Studies* 7, 3 (2004): 343–363.
Dubner, Stephen J., "Your Movie Industry Questions Answered." *Freakonomics,* September 9, 2008. http://www.freakonomics.com/2008/09/09/your-movie-industry-questions-answered/.
Guilbault, Jocelyne. "The Politics of Calypso in a World of Music Industries." In *Popular Music Studies,* edited by Keith Negus and David Hesmondhalgh, 191–204. New York: Oxford University Press, 2002.
Holmes, Su. "'Reality Goes Pop!': Reality TV, Popular Music and Narratives of Stardom in Pop Idol," *Television & New Media* 5, 2 (2004): 147–172.
Jenkins, Henry. *Convergence Culture: Where Old and New Media Collide.* New York: New York University Press, 2006.
———, Sam Ford, and Joshua Green. *Spreadable Media: Creating Value and Meaning in a Networked Culture.* New York: New York University Press, 2013.
Lessig, Lawrence. *Free Culture: How Big Media Uses Technology and the Law to Lockdown Culture and Control Creativity.* New York: Penguin Press, 2004.
"Let's Play: The American Music Business." Washington, DC: Recording Industry Association of America, 2012.
Mack, Robert, and Brian Ott. *Critical Media Studies: An Introduction.* Malden, MA: Wiley-Blackwell, 2010.

Mittell, Jason. *Television and American Culture.* New York: Oxford University Press, 2009.

"Money for Nothing: Behind the Business of Pop Music." Media Education Foundation, 2001. DVD.

"The Music Industry." 2013. http://en.wikipedia.org/wiki/Music_industry.

Napoli, Philip M. "Media Economics and the Study of Media Industries." In *Media Industries: History, Theory and Method,* edited by Jennifer Holt and Alisa Perren, 161–170. Malden, MA: Wiley-Blackwell, 2009.

Negus, Keith. *Music Genres and Corporate Cultures.* New York: Routledge, 1999.

"New Sony Viral Marketing Ploy Angers Consumers." December 14, 2006. *Guardian,* http://www.theguardian.com/technology/gamesblog/2006/dec/11/newsonyviral.

Oberholzer, Felix, and Koleman Strumpf. "The Effect of File-Sharing on Record Sales: An Empirical Analysis." March 2004. http://www.unc.edu/~cigar/papers/FileSharing_March2004.pdf.

"Mickey Mouse Monopoly: Disney, Childhood & Corporate Power." Media Education Foundation, 2001. DVD.

Palmer, Amanda. "The Art of Asking." http://www.ted.com/talks/amanda_palmer_the_art_of_asking.

Rojek, Chris. *Pop Music, Pop Culture.* Malden, MA: Polity Press, 2011.

Rosen, Jay. "The People Formerly Known as the Audience." In *The Social Media Reader,* edited by Michael Mandiberg, 13–16. New York: New York University Press, 2012.

Samuels, Anita M., and Diana B. Henriques. "Does Going 'Broke' Mean Artist Really Doesn't Have Any Money?" February 5, 1996. http://web.archive.org/web/20041010081842/http://mbhs.bergtraum.k12.ny.us/cybereng/nyt/rapper01.htm.

Van Buskirk, Eliot. "Estimates: Radiohead Made up to $10 Million on Initial Album Sales." October 19, 2007. http://www.wired.com/listening_post/2007/10/estimates-radio/.

Veller, Agnese. "The Recording Industry and Grassroots Marketing: From Street Teams to Flash Mobs." *Participations: Journal of Audience & Reception Studies* 9, 1, (2012): 95–118.

Williams, Raymond. *Keywords: A Vocabulary of Culture and Society.* New York: Oxford University Press, 1985.

Yang, Ling. "All for Love: The Corn Fandom, Prosumers, and the Chinese Way of Creating a Superstar." *International Journal of Cultural Studies* 12, 5 (2009): 527–543.

CHAPTER 7

How Do We Relate to Popular Culture?

This chapter will more closely examine a set of questions first raised in our discussions of power. To wit: what is the relationship between our mental and material lives? As we learned in Chapter 1, cultural systems help identify us as members of a group and provide us with a shared vocabulary through which we can communicate with one another. They shape our sense of who we are and explain where (and with whom) we belong. In the process they also explain where and with whom we do *not* belong. They produce differences in perspective and experience that make it difficult for us to speak to or understand one another across cultural divides. Our job in this chapter is to trace the role popular culture plays in these processes of identification and differentiation. How do people use cultural resources to express themselves and forge connections with others? How do they use culture to distinguish themselves from others? What political or social ramifications do such processes have?

In keeping with our understanding of reality as a social construction, we will approach identity as an unstable social process, rather than a fixed property of the individual. Cultural studies theorists like to say *identity is something we do, not something we are.* As a social process, the mechanics of identity formation are neither fully within our control nor fully beyond our influence. We make our identities but not under conditions of our own choosing. It is easy to forget this lesson in societies like the US and Britain where the capacity to reinvent the self is so incessantly celebrated. Yet, not everyone has equal access to the tools of self-invention or the skills of impression management they require. Some subjects or groups are more bound to their identity categories than others, just as some identity choices are more celebrated than others. How identity is shaped in relation to social processes and material conditions will be the focus of this chapter.

We can learn a lot about these processes by looking at how identities are constructed in virtual contexts like video games and online worlds, for, in such contexts, a player must consciously construct an onscreen identity, or persona, using nothing more than written language and graphics. This may feel liberating, as if you can play with identity as you will, but, in fact, there are rules that limit the amount of freedom you have to (re)make the self. On Facebook or Google+, for example, you may register only one account per email address and must provide a real world identity to do so. This means your online actions are traceable to you, which might lead you to control your online persona for fear that it might impact your real-world life (prospective employers regularly check Facebook profiles to see what sort of worker they are hiring, for example. Do you really want those pictures of you guzzling beer at a frat party representing "who you are"?). In video games the constraints become much more obvious, for you are faced with a menu of identity choices (gender, race, class, occupation) that you cannot bypass. These choices shape your experience of the game by determining what powers you have and dictating how others will treat you. The real world has just as many constraints—expectations about how people of different ages, genders, sexualities, and races ought to behave in certain situations— but they are so commonsensical as to disappear from consciousness. Virtual worlds become potent "objects to think with," then, because they make the ordinary rules of identity construction obvious to us. They encourage us to ask how real-life rules of social engagement shape who we (think we) are and how we (think we ought to) interact with others.

WHAT DO WE MEAN BY IDENTITY?

When we speak of identity, we tend to do so in contradictory ways. On the one hand, we describe identity as the internally consistent core of a person's being—his or her essential personality. In this usage, identity is what makes us unique and different. We are presumed to possess a "true self" that is stable, distinctive, and quantifiable. We express this sense of identity when we talk about "being ourselves," "finding ourselves," or "revealing ourselves." On the other hand, we use the word identity to express our similarity to or affinity with others. We talk about having a national identity, an ethnic identity, or a gender identity, for instance, and presume our relationships with others shape who we are as individuals. Here, as cultural theorist David Buckingham puts it, "identity is about identification with others."[1] Yet, this is also where complexity enters the picture, for how can we be both internally consistent *and* defined by our relations to others? Don't our interactions with others, of necessity, inform our personal identities? And, if so, isn't personal identity fluid and dynamic, rather than static? More radically, aren't we sometimes identified with others against our wishes? How much choice do we have in the formation of our identities? Can we go on thinking of identity as a simple expression of "who we are inside"?

To clarify matters, cultural studies scholars often distinguish between the acts of self-definition we can control and the acts of social definition we cannot. They use the terms identity or individuality to refer to the processes of self-definition, and the term subjectivity to describe the ways we are positioned, defined, and sometimes pigeon-holed by social institutions or actors. This usage derives from Louis Althusser's conception of ideology. As explained in Chapter 5, Althusser treats ideology less as a myth to be debunked than as a force that shapes social relations through-and-through. For him, it involves a process of **interpellation**, or hailing, which works to define and locate us within the existing social order. He uses a simple metaphor of greeting to illustrate the process: I call to a friend on the street, and she turns and shakes my hand, thereby accepting my definition of her and of our relationship. In the act of hailing, my friend is both constituted as a subject and subjected to my (limited) sense of who she is. The example highlights the gap between the individual's sense of self and the world's sense of who she is and what she is capable of. It shows how every act of recognition also involves a certain amount of misrecognition. My friend is, no doubt, much more interesting and complicated than I know, yet my definition of her in that social situation prevails. In acknowledging me, she has agreed to play along with my limited conception of her, to play the part I've marked out for her.

This example may seem innocuous. Who cares if I think less of my friend than she thinks of herself? Does that really harm her? Can't she just shrug it off and go on with her life? Perhaps, but not every act of interpellation is so easily ignored. Identity documents, surveillance monitors, and body scanners all "hail" us in a similar fashion, but the way they fix our identities can have very real consequences for our freedom of movement. Such practices often define us on the basis of the most superficial differences—how we dress, what we weigh, how we walk, what skin color we possess, which religious symbols we wear, and so on. They then use these differences to determine who is a threat to security and who is not. How would it feel to go through the body scanners at an airport if you were transgendered or intersexed? The scanners only offer two options: male and female. Where would you fit if your gender display did not match your genitalia? Scanners also presume a "healthy" body. What if you have a pacemaker or a prosthetic limb? How are the security officials likely to react to people who do not fit neatly into the categories offered? Finally, what if you fit into the category of "suspicious character" based on the fact that you wear a turban, a veil, or a backward baseball hat? The affirmation of identity, in these cases, could lead to your being defined as a "suspect" by the screeners. Here, misrecognition has very real and potentially damaging consequences.

As these examples attest, every act of identification is also an act of subjection to the rules of the social context, so it also always involves questions of power. The fact that I, as a healthy, slender, middle-aged, white woman, can slip through security relatively easily is a sign of the privilege that accrues to those who (seem to) fit the normative categories. Those categories give me a kind of superpower—the power to become invisible and pass unnoticed. I benefit from the operative construction of the social order in Western societies, but, if I move to a place that values different categories, I might encounter problems. The social order is as much a construction as identity, and not every society creates the same subject positions or endows them with the same meanings. Indeed, the social order itself is fragmented and demands that we perform different roles in different social settings. Each setting—the home, the school, a restaurant, a bank, etc.—carries its own rules of decorum, which we are expected to known and adhere to. For example, a student may be expected to know and use text-speak when conversing with her friends electronically, but, if she composes an essay for class in the same language, she will likely fail the assignment.

Text-speak is simply inappropriate in a classroom setting. By knowing the rules and acting accordingly—that is, by responding as expected to the ideological summons—the student can save herself a lot of trouble and anxiety.

Yet, it is important to remember that interpellation is not fate. As feminist scholar Kathryn Woodward explains, social factors may influence the particular subject positions available to us, but "they do not explain what investment individuals have in particular positions and the attachments they make to those positions."[2] We can refuse to occupy the positions marked out for us, or we may perform the positions ironically or strategically to get what we want or need. If a mediocre student wants to get into a good college, for example, he might temporarily pretend to be a better student than he is. By playing to the expectations of the school's administrators, he might be able to bluff his way in, but, once there, he is free to relapse into mediocrity or to become the student that the administrators think he can be. There is always an element of agency involved, which is why Woodward prefers to think of identity as *the identifications we make with the subject positions available to us.*

Feminist philosopher Judith Butler best captures the tension between stability and instability, coherence and multiplicity, that defines the experience of identity. Butler views identity as a performance behind which there is no unified, coherent, or fixed self. Rather, the social agent is produced as such through the performance; *the performance creates the subject, not the other way around.* She uses gender as her primary example and argues that it "is in no way a stable identity or locus of agency from which various acts proceed; rather, it is an identity tenuously constituted in time—an identity instituted through a *stylized repetition of acts.*"[3] For Butler, we do not identify as a member of a gender first, then go out and act according to a cultural script. Rather, we act first, and based on the consistency of our performance, we are ascribed a gender identity. We do not *have* a gender; we *do* gender; we enact it day-to-day.

The fact that we *do* gender does not mean we are free to do it as we please, however. As Butler puts it, "gender identity is a performative accomplishment compelled by social sanction and taboo."[4] Western societies define gender according to a strict binary: you are either male or female in terms of your sexual characteristics, and masculine or feminine in terms of gender identity. Men and women are presumed to be different, and different behaviors are ascribed to the two categories. The binary also carries assumptions about sexuality, which privilege a heterosexual norm. Real men and women must work within the terms of the gender binary and the heterosexual matrix or suffer the consequences—ostracism, ridicule, or even physical abuse and death. Thus, subjects are constituted through a performance that is always shaped by social discourses and policed by other social agents. Such policing may be conscious, as in the case of physical abuse of those who act differently, or unconscious, as when we try to guess a newborn's sex based on its dress (pink or blue), hair length (long or short), or size (small or large). Even innocuous or reflexive behaviors, like calling a woman with short hair "sir," may shape the subject's sense of who she is or how she ought to perform.

In short, our ideas about gender and sexuality have a history and a material presence in real life. We cannot simply evade the structures and discourses that surround us, but we may subtly shift them through acts that fail to conform to expectations. Butler uses transvestism as an example. Transvestites, by virtue of their refusal to adhere to one category or another, call our attention to the constructedness of these categories. They remind us that the discourses that shape our society—including the idea of a gender binary and a heterosexual norm—have been created and can be recreated. Because discourses are well-entrenched, however, change does not happen suddenly. Still, small acts of confusion or defiance, repeated over the course of time, may accumulate and result in a shifting of the historical sediment.

Butler strikes a nice balance between recognizing the power of social discourses to shape identity and understanding the limits to such power. For her, subjects are not *just* inscribed or positioned by discourse; they *enact* the discourses in their everyday encounters with others. Individuals may not be free to act as they please, but they are also not condemned to act as society dictates. The individual serves as the critical point of articulation where discourses get expressed and applied to real-life social settings. As such, individuals have agency to redirect, challenge, or stretch the discourse in new directions. That they rarely do so—that most people invest most of the time in the established menu of subject positions—does not nullify the possibility of a different articulation.

WHY DOES IDENTITY MATTER TO THE STUDY OF POPULAR CULTURE?

Identity matters to cultural studies scholars because it is a central facet of social existence. Faced with "the blooming, buzzing confusion of reality," humans try to make sense of the world by categorizing individuals into groups and ordering groups in relation to each other.[5] Whether we like it or not, we become identified with certain people on the basis of similar features or experiences (similar racial features, for instance, or similar socio-economic statuses). Where we are "placed" within the social order is not up to us as individuals, but it does shape our sense of who we are, where we belong, and how we should live. Systems of representation play a key part in creating, disseminating, and naturalizing the categories available in a given society. That is part of the reason cultural studies scholars are interested in the subject of identity. They want to know how social relations are being imaginatively constructed and how these constructs relate to everyday experience.

Individuals also use cultural resources to craft their identities and connect with others who share similar experiences, ideals, or tastes. Cultural studies scholars are interested in how these articulations happen: how do people use cultural resources to express themselves and identify with or against others? The music we listen to, the films we enjoy, the rituals we practice—these choices ground our sense of who we are and what we stand for. Thus, the concept of identity matters because it draws attention to the processes of affiliation and disaffiliation that create formations of the people. It can tell us something about how groups come together and pull apart around various sense-making practices.

Most importantly, identity matters because it reminds us that all processes of cultural creation and interpretation embody particular perspectives and are, therefore, political. Though the term "identity" derives from the Latin *idem,* meaning same, identity is never just about similarity. Every similarity implies a difference. Who we think we are is always determined, at least in part, by the ideals, actions, and modes of being we reject (a process called othering). Indeed, as John Fiske argues, "the sense of oppositionality, the sense of difference, is [often] more determinant [of identity] than that of similarity."[6] Think, for example, of how much more intensely we live our national identities when the nation is at war. Faced with an "enemy," most people rally around the flag. National identity becomes momentarily unproblematic. When the war is over, however, tensions *within* the nation usually reassert themselves and assume greater importance. Still, tensions predominate. As a central mechanism of social ordering, identity is never neutral. Which members of society get folded into the mainstream (into "us") and which get marginalized (as "them") is a political issue. Social differences always involve power differences. Cultural studies scholars are interested in how discourses of identity and otherness work to locate people and allocate resources to (or away from) them. By drawing attention to these processes, they hope to make social inequality more visible so that it may become subject to revision.

HOW DO WE GO ABOUT STUDYING IDENTITY IN POPULAR CULTURE?

When we consider issues of identity in relation to popular culture, what exactly are we looking for? Implicit in many discussions of identity and popular culture is an assumption that representations invite **identification** with the characters and values depicted. Whenever we encounter narrative, in particular, we are asked to adopt the perspective of a character and to see the world through his or her eyes. Representation, in this sense, constitutes a type of interpellation, or hailing, that marks out the available subject positions and encourages us to occupy them. One way to study identity in popular culture, then, is to study the way cultural forms (texts) shape our sense of the world and the roles available within it. How exactly do we go about measuring the influence of texts on our identifications, though?

One approach (and a rather old-fashioned one) involves evaluating characters according to the criteria of accuracy or authenticity. How closely does the depiction correspond to the real-life experiences of individuals or groups? Is the story-world peopled with three-dimensional "individuals" or two-dimensional character "types" (i.e., representatives of a group)? If the latter, are the types aspirational or derogatory; are they role models or stereotypes? There have been many important studies of stereotypes and role models in popular culture. Books like Donald Bogle's *Toms, Coons, Mulattos, Mammies, and Bucks* (1973) or Vito Russo's *The Celluloid Closet* (1987), for example, work to identify the patterns of (mis)representation that have structured Hollywood portraits of blacks and gays respectively. Anita Sarkeesian's Kickstarter project "Tropes v. Women in Video Games" similarly focuses on the reductive depictions of women and femininity in video games.[7] By drawing attention to the conventions of representation, these authors hope to prompt the cultural industries to develop more well-rounded, thoughtful, and inclusive representations of the world.

One problem with such studies, however, is the difficulty in determining which representations are "positive" and which are "negative." Is the meaning of an image inherent to it, or is it constructed during the processes of interpretation? Can an image be "positive" or "negative" once and for all, or is the value of the image necessarily dependent on the context of its use? For example, the American television sitcom *The Cosby Show* (1984–1992) offered an abundance of positive images of black people and black life in America in the 1980s. To construct its positive images, the program deliberately ignored many of the social problems (poverty, racism, drugs, etc.) that were plaguing black communities at the time. Sociologists who studied the reception of the program found that many viewers interpreted the Huxtable family as proof that the struggle for civil rights had succeeded in securing equality of opportunity for all people. These "positive" representations thus had a "negative" effect on the struggle for social justice by suggesting that race was no longer a problem in America. If black people were struggling to find jobs, get a good education, feed their families, and accumulate wealth, the argument went, they were simply not trying hard enough. The government had no duty to intervene to correct social imbalances because there were no imbalances, only morally corrupt and lazy people. The example illustrates how even "positive" representations may have "negative" effects.

The stereotypes and role models approach also tends to take a rather narrow view of identification as a process. Its practitioners assume that individuals who share certain physical, psychological, or social traits must also share an identity. They further assume that your real-life traits will determine whom you decide to identify with in fantasy. So, for example, in worrying about the effects of hypersexualized imagery on the women and young girls who play videogames, such scholars often take it for granted that women will identify with and compare themselves to the female characters. The result will be to harm their self-esteem because very few "real" women can achieve the wasp-waisted, big-breasted look of the videogame avatars. But who is to say that women and girls actually *do* identify with the female characters? Most games offer a range of avatars for players to inhabit, and many allow you to switch roles during the game or run several different personae at once. To assume that female players will naturally adopt a feminine persona is to take for granted what ought to be investigated—namely, how identification happens.

Media Effects Research and the Question of Stereotyping

Research into stereotypes and role models often takes the form of quantitative studies called "media effects studies." Effects researchers look for patterns of presentation in media texts (like how much violence there is or what sort of stereotypes are used) and try to determine how those patterns will impact the behaviors or self-esteem of media users, especially children.

For example, effects research into videogames suggests the medium badly distorts issues of race, gender, and violence in society. The 2001 Children Now survey looked at 70 popular video games and found that 64 percent of the game characters were male, 19 percent were non-human, and only 17 percent were women. The quality of male and female roles was also stereotyped according to prevailing gender norms, with men being more often associated with competition and physical aggression and women being associated with verbal aggression or various forms of cooperation or sharing. Finally, 20 percent of female avatars exemplified "unhealthy or unrealistic body sizes." The survey also included measures of race, which showed very few non-white characters (less than half of all characters) and a hugely disproportionate number of black female victims (86 percent of black female characters were victimized). Omit the sports game category, and the stock of black and other non-white characters dwindled to nothing. Racial categorizations were also strongly linked to prevailing social stereotypes. White characters were more frequently portrayed as "heroic"; black males were usually more violent than their white counterparts, and black females were almost always prostitutes or sexual tokens. Such statistics demonstrate a clear pattern within the game industry of privileging white male characters and perspectives at the expense of other groups.

Such data seem very convincing, but there are problems with the methods used to gather, analyze, and apply the data. For one thing, such research tends to focus on the negative impacts of media on society and to ignore the positive effects. The result is a biased sample that proves only how devoted effects researchers are to the *premise* that media are bad. What if we counted all the instances of gamers helping, rather than hurting, each other? How might that change our perspective on the medium's effects?

Effects researchers also tend to treat media users, especially young people, as if they are incapable of distinguishing between representation and reality. Much of this research assumes users will simply absorb the imagery and carry what they've learned from the text over into real life. However, ethnographic research shows that children are sophisticated interpreters of media, capable of making all sorts of fine-grained distinctions between levels of reality and even constructing their own counter-representations. Because effects researchers fail to talk to their test subjects, they overlook the influence of social experience on media interpretation.

Finally, media effects researchers rarely consider gradations of meaning and context when they compile their statistics. So, for example, the claim that "violence was a predominant feature in almost all of the video games analyzed (89%)" was based on counting incidents of violence without regard to the scale or scope of the violence or the context in which it was expressed. One "violent" encounter in a game meant it would automatically be counted as a "violent game." Yet, isn't there a difference between an incident of pinching and an act of murder? And what of games that use violence to provoke ethical reflection? What if a player's choice of violence makes the game more difficult, for example? Doesn't this teach the value of non-violence? Should such a game really be treated like other "violent" videogames?

As Henry Jenkins says, representations are not simple stimuli that provoke automatic responses. Game players (and other media users) are not the equivalent of Pavlov's dogs, salivating on cue whenever a bell is rung. Rather than focusing on the "automatic effects" of stereotypes or violent representations, we would be better served by asking how "meanings emerge through an active process of interpretation."[1]

1 Henry Jenkins, *Fans, Bloggers and Gamers: Exploring Participatory Culture* (New York: New York University Press, 2006), 210.

If hunting stereotypes and role models is an inadequate approach, then, what other strategies are available to trace the play of identity and difference in popular culture? Alan McKee offers three additional strategies of textual analysis that may prove useful. First, we can learn to attend to processes of **exnomination.** Roland Barthes coined this term, which means "outside of naming," to account for the way the dominant group's perspective or experience may be taken for granted in representation. Harry Benshoff and Sean Griffin offer Hollywood films and comic book heroes as examples. A film like *You've Got Mail* (1998) is often described as a romantic comedy, but the same film starring two black leads—something like *Love Jones* (1997) or *Two Can Play That Game* (2001)—would be called a *black* romantic comedy. Likewise, "Spawn" is often described as a *black* superhero, but no one ever calls "Batman" or "Superman" *white* superheroes. The pervasiveness of these patterns indicates how thoroughly whiteness is presumed to be the norm in US society. In that this unconscious bias toward whiteness affects decisions about which films or comic books get produced, it helps perpetuate white power and privilege in Hollywood (and arguably in the broader society).

Lisa Nakamura offers a similar example with regard to early online social networking sites like LambdaMOO. Because graphics were unavailable at the time these sites were created, users had to build an online profile using text alone. This process of digital "selfing" involved answering a series of questions about gender, age, occupation, and the like, either truthfully or fancifully. Noticeably absent was a question about racial identification. Far from signaling the obsolescence of racial classification among the site's members, the absence of race masked the site's expectation of whiteness. As Nakamura explains, "in the absence of racial description, all players [were] assumed to be white."[8] Users of color who chose to identify their race—it being a central facet of their sense of self—often encountered harassment on the site, and, when they complained, the community consensus held that they had brought such harassment on themselves. As one member put it: "If you want to get in somebody's face with your race, then perhaps you deserve a bit of flak." Yet, this response presumes racial identity is something that both *can* and *should* be disavowed. It is easy for white Americans (and most LambdaMOO users were both white and American) to say "just ignore race" because their racial identity is the presumptive norm; it is much harder for blacks, Asians, Latinos, and other groups to disavow racial classifications in this way. Racial classifications are not just labels; they carry the weight of shared historical experiences, both good and bad, which many individuals are either reluctant or unable to shuck off. The presumption that one would *want* to deny the importance of race is itself a sign of racial privilege. In sum, what is exonominated, or unnamed, in a text can tell us something about whose identity and perspective are being privileged, whose experience comprises the norm against which others will be measured, who has power, and who does not.

The second strategy McKee recommends is called the commutation test. As we discussed in Chapter 4, the commutation test "is a thought experiment where you replace one element of a text with a similar but different" instance of it.[9] To better understand what Nakamura is talking about with regard to race in cyberspace, for example, we might try reversing the situation. How would it feel to "ignore race" if you were a white member of a bulletin board community called "Black Planet"? What if much of the discourse on that site centered on the stereotyping of white women or the derogatory treatment of white males (as happened with Asian men and women on LambdaMOO)? Would you choose to identify as "white" in such a space? Or would you want to remain silent about your racial classification for fear of being harassed? How would it feel to have to suppress your race under these conditions? Would you resent it?

To cite another example, the classic video arcade game *Donkey Kong* was built, like many other platform games of its era, around a damsel-in-distress scenario. The central character, Mario, the Plumber, had to rescue his lady Pauline from a keg-throwing ape named Donkey Kong. Over time, Mario and his brothers became a video game franchise, spawning dozens of different variations on the theme of Pauline's rescue. The damsel-in-distress, meanwhile, persists as one of the dominant "tropes" of video game adventures.[10] In 2012, a three-year old unwittingly performed a commutation test by asking her father, game developer Mike Mika, "How can I play as the girl? I want to save Mario!" Having the requisite skills to fix this problem, Mika modified the game and created a version where Pauline got to be the hero of the story and, by proxy, so did his young daughter. "She really did seem to enjoy the game more," he reported. "For whatever reason, she was more motivated to play as Pauline than as Mario." This little thought experiment eventually went viral touching off a firestorm of debate about the gender coding and implicit sexism in videogames. By trying to see the world through his daughter's eyes, Mika learned just how entrenched social assumptions about masculinity and femininity can be. "If something as innocuous as having Mario be saved by Pauline brings out the crazy," he concluded, "maybe we aren't as mature in our view of gender roles as we should be."[11] Properly applied, the commutation test can draw attention to the classifications that organize our societies and lead us to question the legitimacy of one mode of organization over another.

The final strategy for tracing the play of identity in cultural texts involves learning to ask what is *not* represented in a text. As McKee notes, "often texts will systematically exclude certain kinds of representations and not draw attention to this [process]."[12] We need to learn to look for these **structuring absences,** then. In Chapter 3, we discussed this in relation to the concept of symbolic annihilation and noted how US television systematically excluded blacks and gays from TV roles at different periods of time. A structuring absence involves more than just who is represented, though. It involves asking about the terms of a group's representation. If, for example, gays are now regularly included in TV programming (at least in Western societies), what are the limitations of these representations? What are such characters *not* allowed to say or do that straight, white characters are? The obvious omission involves sexual intimacy. Rarely, do we see gay characters kiss, hug, or even hold hands with their partners the way straight characters do, and we virtually never see gay characters in bed.

Alexander Galloway offers a more complicated example with regard to race and video game design. He notes that many adventure games use the term "race" to designate a pre-designed package of skills. In the massively multiplayer online role-playing game (MMORPG) *World of Warcraft,* for example, the society of Azeroth is divided into two opposing camps—The Alliance and The Horde. These camps are further divided into dozens of "races," and the races are further divided into "classes." Each race has a particular set of skills that are exclusive to it. If you choose to be a Night-Elf, for example, you have special magical powers, but you are not likely to prevail in a physical fight. If you become an Orc, you can fight but not heal or perform magic. The "races" of Azeroth may bear no *direct* relationship to real-life racial categories and assumptions, but real-life tends to creep in nonetheless. Most obviously, real-life assumptions about the dominance of whiteness as a social norm seem to have influenced the assignment of racial attributes within the game. The races of the Alliance include humans and a range of human-like figures (mostly white) whose skills tend more toward wizardry, the healing arts, and stealth combat. By contrast, the races that comprise the Horde tend to be more animalistic, ethnically "exotic," and better skilled in violent combat. For instance, the Horde-aligned

Trolls dance in a raunchy Jamaican dance-hall style and have Jamaican accents. The Taurens are coded as Native American by virtue of the trappings (totem poles, feathers, teepees, etc.) that surround them. And all Horde members are defined by physical strength and aggression, rather than cunning. As Jessica Langer puts it, "*World of Warcraft* carries out a constant project of radically 'othering' the Horde."[13]

Thus, Azeroth's world of racial distinctions is far from neutral or fantastic. The Alliance races are marked as both "whiter" and "more humane" than the Horde

FIGURE 7.01 World of Warcraft *characters. Above: A Tauren with teepees and totem poles. Below: Female Troll with "African" masks, drums and scenery.*

races, which suffer from a structuring absence of humanity. This absence is quite literal: all Humans are white, and all non-whites are not Human. Racial difference turns out to be indexed to species difference. The attributes of each "race" are also disturbingly fixed in the game. While you can stylize your avatar a bit, including lightening or darkening its skin tone, you cannot change the other attributes assigned to your race. A "brown" Human is still modeled on Eurocentric cultural norms of dress, speech, and behavior, and, even when "lightened," a Troll remains "black" in that he (or she) retains a Jamaican accent and cultural properties and continues to serve as a "synthetic site of racial tourism and minstrelsy" for the largely white designers and game players.[14] What do these in-game racial logics imply about race as a social construct?

Together, the structuring absence of non-white Humans combined with the absence of racial flexibility create the impression that racial categories are biologically determined. They imply that one's race defines one's being in some unavoidable way. *Is* race simply a matter of biology, though? Not according to current conceptions of race in the biological and social sciences. Biologists point out, for example, that there is more genetic variation between two fruit flies than there is between humans of different races. Meanwhile, sociologists and anthropologists insist that, while racial categories may be based on biological differences, which differences *matter*—skin color, eye color, hair quality, facial features, genetic codes—is entirely a function of social determination. Different countries possess vastly different systems of racial classification, some much more elaborate and fine-grained than others. History, too, refutes the claim that race is biologically determined. Not only does the historical record contain thousands of cases of racial "passing" (non-whites pretending to be white); it also suggests that the notion of "whiteness" has changed dramatically since the nineteenth century, especially in the US. The Irish, once the "blacks of Europe," are now full-fledged "whites," along with the once-"swarthy" Jews, Italians, and Eastern Europeans, but South Asians, who once belonged to the category "white" by virtue of their Aryan origins, were redefined as non-white, non-citizens in a famous US Supreme Court ruling in 1923 (*US v. Baghat Singh Thind*). Now, people of South Asian descent are labeled "Indian," and these "Indians" are different yet again from Native American Indians. Far from being a simple biological determination, then, race is a complex and contested social formation.

World of Warcraft's lack of racial flexibility is troubling because it ignores the contingent nature of real-world racial identity. Worse, it implies a fixed articulation between particular physical attributes, racial identity, and moral good, for the (white) Humans are also figured as more humane than the other races. As Langer notes, the association of the Alliance with the "good" and the horde with "evil" is not direct or absolute in the game, but many players interpret the game in this way because they have been trained by their (white, Western) cultures to "associate foreignness and insidiousness." This association "derives from Western colonial legacies," and these legacies structure most of the Tolkeinesque fantasy narratives on which role-playing videogames are built.[15] Put differently, European dominance is the unnamed norm against which all other races are measured in such games; it is the exnominated category.

That the text structures things in this way, does not mean all players will take up the positions outlined, however. We need to consider how they actually make sense of the game and its processes of social ordering. Do they merely buy into the racial re-enactment, or do they use the game as an "object to think [about race] with"? To answer these questions, we need to move beyond textual analysis to an analysis of textualization. How do people make sense of the representations they are offered? Do they or do they not identify with the positions offered, and what do we mean by "identification"?

WHAT IS IDENTIFICATION AND HOW DOES IT WORK?

It might be helpful, first, to describe what processes we are *not* concerned with when discussing identification. We are *not* concerned, for example, with the sort of distanced contemplation associated with aesthetic appreciation or political critique that seeks to distance us from the text. These modes of engagement demand that we bracket our emotional investments in order to concentrate on the work of interpretation (we must think, rather than react). We are also *not* concerned with passive modes of cultural engagement that involve little or no imagination or projection of the self. Sometimes, individuals merely consume texts without thinking much about them, or they become caught up in the physical "rush" and pay little attention to characters or their perspectives. While these are legitimate (and frequent) modes of cultural engagement, they are not our concern here because they neither require nor promote identification.

If identification is not about distanciation or passivity, then, what *is* it about? Identification involves some sort of imaginative extension of the self into the world of the text or ritual. Usually, though not always, this involves adopting the perspective of a particular character and seeing the world through that character's eyes. So, identification involves immersion and interactivity; it is both intimate and engaged. We both invest in the text or practice and personalize it in a way that makes it relevant to us. While many critical theorists are skeptical of the politics of identification—viewing it as a form of escape or denial that promotes political passivity—cultural studies scholars prefer to think of identification as a complicated mode of engagement whose political value can only be determined in context. Sure, sometimes identification involves taking up the subject positions offered to us, but sometimes the act of imagining oneself into the world of a text may inspire contemplation of and resistance to social norms. Context is everything.

Because people's identifications are rarely straight-forward or simple, we need to be cautious about assessing their investments. There are three big dangers to avoid when researching people's practices of identification. First, one should not assume social location determines people's preferences or thought processes. While

FIGURE 7.02 *"On Playing Well with Others," by Maki Nora of the online comic Sc.I.eN.Ce.* (http://sci-ence.org/on-playing-well-with-others/).

many video games are targeted toward young male consumers, for example, this does not mean women and young girls do not enjoy them or play them well. It also does not mean that young males *do* enjoy them (or play them well). Both the game industry and its critics operate on the assumption that young males are (a) alike, (b) "innately" attracted to images of violence and sex, and (c) unwilling or unable to be critical about them. In fact, many male gamers are just as critical as female gamers of the industry's reductive definitions of masculinity (as brute force) and femininity (as raw sex). Men and women alike have begun to chastise the industry for its "lazy" writing and over-reliance on social stereotypes. Clearly, while a person's similarity to a character may increase the likelihood of identification, similarity may be based on a variety of factors other than one's demographic profile. Some male gamers identify with a sense of social justice and appreciate games that embody principles of equality and fair treatment. Rather than assuming we know how people will think based on the social categories they (seem to) belong to, we should talk to them, read what they have to say, or observe their behaviors.

The second danger to avoid when researching people's practices of identification is assuming that identification is always earnest or complete. In fact, we often embrace cultural works in a negotiated fashion or with a touch of irony. For example, many female gamers identify with the character of Lara Croft from the *Tomb Raider* series, but not necessarily with her sexualized representation. They admire her because she is clever, capable, and competent, and selectively tune out the other aspects of her presentation. Meanwhile, many male gamers claim to enjoy the game because it does *not* ask them to fully identify with the female protagonist. Rather than seeing the game completely through Croft's eyes (as in subjective shooter games), players play behind or alongside Croft. The game's third-person perspective gives players the space to choose how they will identify with the character: Will they imagine *being* Lara Croft or *being with* Lara Croft? Will their identification be "sympathetic" or "associative," in the words of literary critic Hans Robert Jauss?[16] Ethnographic research suggests that, for many young, heterosexual, male gamers, the associative option is much more rewarding. Not only does it allow them to maintain some distance from "the female perspective," it offers them a perfect view

FIGURE 7.03 *The third-person perspective of the* Tomb Raider *videogame. You can imagine being Lara Croft or being a sidekick (with a view).*

of Croft's breasts and behind as she jiggles her way through her adventures. It would be a mistake to collapse these two very different modes of identification (sympathetic and associative) and assume they worked toward similar ends.

Likewise, it would be a mistake to assume an ironic identification with a cultural text, icon, or practice was the same as a sincere one. Many female gamers dress as versions of Croft at fan conventions, but not all of them do so earnestly. Some exaggerate the already exaggerated proportions of the character—inflating their breasts to gargantuan size or removing all but the barest strips of clothing—as a means of critiquing the systemic sexualization of female avatars in adventure games. By performing this hypersexualization, they seek to unsettle gamers who take such characterizations in stride when they appear in game form. This is a very different way of "playing with" Croft and what she represents. It requires an investment in the character, but it is certainly not an homage to her. Thus, we also need to pay attention to the *mode* of identification. We should not assume everyone is equally earnest or equally enthralled by the object of their identification. Instead, we should look at the social context to determine the type and quality of the attachment being articulated.

Finally, we should not assume people's personal preferences are truly personal. As French sociologist Pierre Bourdieu argues, "taste is an acquired disposition to 'differentiate' and 'appreciate.'"[17] It is never simply a reflection of someone's inner identity or "true feelings." Expressions of taste, or preference, always emerge from within a social context, and each social context is governed by its own rules and logics of value. These rules cannot help but influence the choices individuals make. In other words, we make our choices as much for the benefit of others, as for ourselves. On social networking sites like Facebook or MySpace, for example, users are hyperaware of the signals they send through their selection of "likes" and "friends." They know that identity is not produced only through conscious decision-making (the signals we "give"); it is also shaped by the unconscious signals we "give off." Teen users of these sites are particularly sensitive to the way their taste preferences look to others. They worry that choosing the wrong "friends" or "liking" the wrong bands or movies will lead them to be marginalized or ridiculed by their peers. (See the "You Have 0 Friends" episode of *South Park* for a humorous take on these anxieties).[18]

In addition to these informal social dynamics, Facebook and MySpace also have subtle differences in their interface design that can shape the projection of identity online. MySpace allows users to personalize their home pages to a much greater extent than Facebook, which is often described as a "minimalist" interface. According to researcher danah boyd, these design differences have reinforced the social migration of younger, lower-class, and "ethnic" users to MySpace and older, middle-class, and white or Asian users to Facebook. The example of the "ghettoization" of MySpace shows that "what is socially acceptable and desirable differs across social groups." Marginalized youth tend to understand their difference from the mainstream and embrace it as a mark of distinction; they appreciate the ability MySpace gives them to "express themselves." Members of or aspirants to a majoritarian lifestyle, on the other hand, appreciate the uniformity of the Facebook site because it constrains individuality and signifies their inclusion in the mainstream. While marginalized youth celebrate MySpace for its "bling" and "glitter," mainstream youth describe it as "gaudy," "tacky" or "cluttered." Mainstream youth describe Facebook as "clean" and "orderly," and marginalized youth describe it as "lame," "boring" and "elitist." Such disputes over taste show how variable aesthetic standards can be. Beauty is in the eye of the beholder, as they say, and individuals are usually drawn to styles that signal their relationship to a social group. If "one's values and norms are strongly linked with one's [group identifications]," then the way individuals choose to represent themselves online can never be a purely individual matter.[19] Rather, online embodiment is an expression or inflection of prevailing group norms. Thus, we also need to ask how social context influences the choices people are making with regard to the presentation of their identities.

As these discussions illustrate, identification is not a simple, direct, or easily deciphered process. It involves judgments about personal interest, social expectations, and the "proper" balance between these. It is not just about "expressing oneself" or claiming an affinity for persons, objects, or practices "outside" ourselves, as if the boundaries between "inside" and "outside" were clear, and our identities were stable. Rather, it is about *constructing* a self via such choices. In Butler's terms, identification is part of the process of performing identity, and, as such, it is always a thing we do for an audience; the social context shapes (and delimits) our choices. This means we need to shift our questions slightly. Instead of focusing on how aspects of identity (gender, race, class, etc.) are presented "positively" or "negatively" in cultural texts or practices, we should be asking how individuals use cultural resources to *do* gender, to *do* race, to *do* class, and so on. How do participants construct their identities and affiliations as a result of their interactions with cultural texts, objects, and practices? What are the possibilities and limitations of these identity formations? And, how does *doing* identity relate to questions of power, privilege, and social mobility? Only by looking at processes of identification in practice can we discern something of how people live their relation to the social positions marked out for them.

CASE STUDY: DOING RACE AND GENDER IN *WORLD OF WARCRAFT*

In this section we will return to a question raised earlier in the chapter: how do *World of Warcraft (WoW)* players make sense of the game's inflexible construction of race? We will add to that an inquiry into the game's construction of gender and the players' responses to it. Before we take on these questions, though, it might be useful to stop and contemplate the appeal of video games, more generally. Why do people play video games? What rewards or pleasures does this cultural form (potentially) offer?

The first thing to note is that games are explicitly interactive. They do not just invite players to take up subject positions; they demand it. Players *must* identify with a character and insert themselves into the "text" in order to start the game. Moreover, the player's avatar is never just a representation of the self; it is a proxy self. The character responds to your control; it acts in your name and with your assistance. The machine may even give you haptic feedback when your character is hurt or triumphs (that is, the controller may buzz or vibrate). Therefore, the relationship between video game avatars and players is much more intense than the relationship between, say, a reader and the central character in a novel. Part of the pleasure of playing games derives from this intensive mode of identification.

According to Robert Mack and Brian Ott, games as a medium evoke three principle types of pleasure. The first is the pleasure of *control*. By control, they do not mean a simple assertion of will over the text; rather, control involves a dynamic tension between manipulating the game and being manipulated by it. "One must feel that one has sufficient control to obtain an objective, but never so much control that the activity stops being challenging." Complete mastery makes the game boring, so games that delay gratification produce the most enjoyment. The second pleasure is the pleasure of *immersion,* which they characterize as a mode of escape: "digital games are especially effective at fostering elaborately simulated places in which we can forget our troubles and lose ourselves." Finally, there is the pleasure of *performance.* Video games provide on opportunity for people to play with identity. This aspect of games may be exaggerated, as we will see below, but it is true that some people view games as "safe spaces" in which to "try on" new identities and explore the limits of who they (think they) are.[20]

For example, I have a friend who plays *WoW* every day after work because she wants to blow off steam. She takes particular glee in "killing things." Though, in real life, she feels like a "frumpy old woman," in *WoW* she gets to fantasize about being a warrior and having the capacity to bend others to her will. You may be thinking "so what? It's just a fantasy," but research suggests that real life and virtual life are not discontinuous. Real life frequently spills over into the virtual realm and affects the gameplay, and virtual play may leak into real life, changing the ways people act for themselves and in relation to others. Women often report, for example, that game play increases their confidence and self-esteem, which may allow them to assert greater control over their life circumstances.[21] Likewise, men who gender-swap online report gaining greater insight into "what women go through"; they may become more sensitive to the needs of their female partners as a result.[22] At the very least, by treating identity as a dynamic mode of becoming (rather than a static mode of being), video games make it possible for players to "work on themselves" and have fun, too.

How many players actually embrace this opportunity, though? Early research on games tended to celebrate such identity play uncritically, viewing it as an inherently resistant and mind-altering practice.[23] But, of course, resistance is always contextual. We cannot ignore the myriad ways online worlds are structured by offline sensibilities and social classifications, and we must inquire into the motivations and contexts of identity play if we are to determine its political valence. We have already seen how race works in *WoW,* not just to distribute various skill sets, but to perpetuate long-standing associations between dark skin, inhumanity, and evil. The questions now are: How does the lack of racial "playability" (or pliability) affect the game and its players? How have players responded to the game's interpellation of them, and what does that activity suggest about identity construction, more broadly?

The results of such an inquiry are, in some ways, unsurprising. Research on the first two editions of the game showed that players chose to identify with the humanoid races of the Alliance by an almost two to one margin.[24] The binary structure of the game, coupled with the transcoding of race as species difference (human v. non-human), had the effect of driving players toward the Alliance and away from the Horde. What should we make of the fact that so many people heeded the games' racial logics, that they took up and invested in the subject positions marked out by the text? Does the politics of identification in *WoW* signal a desire for racial or ethnic purity on the part of the players? Or, is it a case of white guys unconsciously reenacting the European history of colonization (as Langer argues)?

Probably the latter, as most players do not even notice the racial logics of the game until forced to pay attention to them. Non-white players almost immediately recognize the racial and ethnic stereotypes as stereotypes and have trouble "playing" with or within those identities. Yet, as Langer notes, "*World of Warcraft* is not a fixed text: it is a game," which means it can be played in multiple ways simultaneously. Players contribute, through their actions, to the narrative of the game, and they are active in interpreting, and sometimes circumventing, the constraints of the game. While most players buy into the racial logics most of the time, some players work to expose or challenge them, and the game's open-architecture permits such challenge. For example, many players are uninterested in the conflict elements of the game and treat Azeroth as a glorified social network instead. The game designers encourage such play by asking players to choose an "occupation" (cook, blacksmith, miner, etc.) and to create a set of clothes to wear in non-combat situations. This more social modality has encouraged some players to break from the colonialist logics of the game and set up villages where members of the Alliance and the Horde live together in harmony. Other players identify with the Horde stereotypes and use them as a platform to launch in-game critiques of Human (i.e., European) racism and colonialism. As Langer notes, the inherently hybrid identity of the player/avatar has the potential not only to be used for **identity tourism** (the temporary trying on of "otherness"), but also for subversion of the expected norms.[25]

In addition to in-game critiques, gamers also hold lively debates about the political implications of the game's representational choices in online discussion forums. Such forums constitute a "meta-game," or game about the game, where players can work through their virtual experiences with identity play in a thoughtful manner. In 2006, for example, the blog Terra Nova hosted a discussion of "cultural borrowing" that focused on precisely these issues of racial representation: "I guess what I'm curious about," wrote Greg Lastowka, "is how people feel about cultural borrowing in *WoW,* and more broadly, about the appropriate limits (if any) of this kind of thing. Is there a point where crypto-cultural references become offensive? Can they be offensive if they are not perceived by the players?" The discussion that followed ran the gamut from disclaimers of player responsibility to a counter-discourse that depicted Humans as the incarnation of "evil" in the game. For instance, one respondent noted that the game's Humans enslaved the Orcs, depriving them of access to learning and magic and effectively making them into "savages." It is just as likely, he argued, that *WoW*'s designers are "using their fictional world's unfolding history to mimic the dissolution of traditional colonial narratives." Other respondents turned the discussion from issues of stereotyping and "cultural borrowing" to the game's exnomination of whiteness: "Even though you can pick a number of skin tones in *WoW* for your human character," one player noted, "the culture of humanity is clearly European. There is no existence of non-European humanity in Warcraft lore whatsoever."[26] Such discussions remind us that gamers are not just dupes, sponges, or transmitters of ideology. Many are self-reflective beings, who *make* sense of the cultural resources around them.

The construction of gender in *WoW* is equally complex. In *WoW* one must also choose a gender for one's avatar, and there are only two choices: male or female. The sexual differences are coded in conventional ways, largely as physical differences in muscle mass and waist size. While some of the races feature hypersexualized females (Humans and Elves especially), there are other options. Trolls are short, round, and not conventionally "beautiful," for example. One may also choose a costume that covers the breast cleavage and refuse to engage in "dancing" if one's avatar is associated with a sexual dance (as with Trolls). Warcraft lore also features several powerful female figures, and non-player characters are as likely to be active guardians as passive cooks or "props." Most importantly, the game does not discriminate on the basis of gender with regard to a player's skill-level or class-reference. Female avatars can be as powerful as male avatars, and there is no glass ceiling built into the world of Azeroth. Any avatar can ascend to the top of the social hierarchy as long as the players puts in the requisite time, money, and effort. Azeroth is the ultimate meritocracy in that respect (though its cash economy complicates matters a bit). At the level of design, then, gender differences seem much less significant to *WoW* than racial determinations.

When it comes to actual game *play*, however, gender remains a potent constraint on identity. The choice of gender may not determine one's skill set or proficiency, but it does change how other players treat a character. Most players who play as females report being offered more assistance than their male counterparts, for example. Many male players gender-swap in *WoW* for precisely this reason—to gain access to the advice and assistance of other players. Female players generally avoid gender-swapping for the same reason. As Nick Yee puts it, "men gain a functional advantage when they gender-bend [in role-playing games] whereas women lose that advantage." Heterosexual men may also choose to gender-bend for the titillation that comes from watching a sexy female body onscreen (call it the Lara Croft syndrome). Meanwhile, the sheer size and bulk of the male avatars in *WoW*—most of whom are scary huge dudes—may be a turn-off to female players (especially those who associate femininity with a certain "softness"). Thus, men and women are differently incentivized to play with gender in *WoW,* and research suggests that *WoW* is not unique in this regard. Men are three to five times more likely than women to gender-swap in MMORPGs and may account for half of the female avatars being played at any one time.[27]

Does this mean men who gender-swap are getting an education in what it feels like to be a woman (and consequently that women are being deprived of the reverse opportunity)? To some extent, perhaps, but we should be cautious about celebrating this trend uncritically. As Nakamura argues, identity tourism of this sort is often a sign of social privilege that ends up reinforcing and perpetuating stereotypes, rather than breaking them down. Men who play as women to gain a functional advantage are rewarded for playing up the helplessness or cluelessness of their female avatars, for example. Whether or not they glean life lessons from the experience, their *performance* of femininity reinforces existing assumptions about the inadequacies of female gamers vis-à-vis their male counterparts. Meanwhile, those who play "sexy" female avatars so they have something nice to look at while gaming are not really identifying with the social experience of being female; they are identifying with a male fantasy, and the perpetuation of such fantasies is not usually of great benefit to actual women. Witness the Chinese *WoW* player who recently bragged on the game site about his sexual escapades with various real-world female guild members. Undertaken, as he claimed, "in the name of the Alliance," the sexploits have unleashed a whirlwind of misogynistic discourse on Chinese game forums, which positions female gamers as incompetent sluts. Few have risen to the defense of the female players, though many have congratulated the man on his conquests and vowed to follow his example.[28]

In comparison to male players, female players are more restrained and constrained in their gender play on *WoW.* Few women choose to play as male despite finding the constant solicitation female avatars are subject to "intrusive" and "annoying." There are two possible explanations for this choice. First, more women than men come to the game through their romantic partners. According to Yee, only 16 percent of men regularly play MMORPGS with their partners compared to 60 percent of women. Women introduced to the game in this way report being advised to adopt more nurturing, less-aggressive avatars, like Paladins. The choice of avatar then constrains the character's style of play, leading to the assumption that women *prefer* to play more supportive, less-violent roles. Even after female players have "proven themselves" and gained enough skill to join a "guild," for example, many report being tasked with "crowd control," "mop-up," or "support" operations—the assumption being that women are "naturally better" at such things than men. Real-world gender assumptions thus frame women's access to the game and affect their ability to "play" with gender identity. Many women choose to "go along to get along" since their partners are nearby and the consequences of "rocking the boat" may be more immediate and more momentous (or so Lina Eklund's ethnographic study of Swedish gamers suggests).

The second thing to note about how and why women choose female avatars has to do with motivation. What do they want to get out of the experience of the game? As we have seen, many men choose an avatar for instrumental reasons—to maximize their success or pleasure within the game. In contrast, women tend to choose avatars they can identify with, and embodiment is a central element of this identification. As Eklund explains, female gamers feel as though they "[need] a female avatar to be able to identify with her, to be capable of creating a long-term relationship with her." Her subjects all reported "that they would not be able to feel kinship or identify with a male avatar; instead they chose a body familiar to themselves."[29] In addition to choosing an avatar who looks like them or someone they want to be (or date in the case of some lesbian players), many female players report selecting their avatars on the basis of aesthetic criteria. They claim to want to play "beautiful" or "sexy" avatars. How should we interpret this motivation? Are women just playing to the expectations of their male partners and friends, or is something else going on?

Research suggests that women may be conditioned to engage with texts in different ways than men. David Bleich has argued, for example, that women and men read differently and for different ends. When asked to recount a story, the men he studied tended to explain the plot structure while the women focused on character motivation and atmosphere. "Women enter the world of the novel, [and] take it as something 'there' for that purpose," he concluded. Men "see the novel as the result of someone's action and construe it's meaning or logic in those terms."[30] Jenkins and Justine Cassel documented a similar set of differences regarding boys and girls gaming preferences, with boys being more goal-oriented and girls focusing more on socialization and exploration.[31] Ethnographic research on MMORPGs supports these findings and extends them to adult populations. Eklund found that her female subjects were more interested in collecting pretty dresses for their avatars, flirting with other players, and chatting, than in fighting or questing.

The emphasis on embodiment and appearance may be heavier for female players, then, because they are playing a different game with different stakes. The tendency of female players to stylize their female avatars is reminiscent of the processes of profile construction on social networking sites. Thus, avatar construction may be less about playing with identity, than solidifying it—giving off the "right" signals about who one is and where one stands in the social hierarchy. It is less about self-invention, or play, than impression management, or survival. However unconsciously, Eklund's female gamers may be training themselves to survive in the patriarchal societies that exist outside of the game.

CONCLUSION

As *WoW* demonstrates, virtual spaces are saturated with real-world logics and social ideologies. By and large, we port our offline identities and social relationships into our online interactions, and this necessarily constrains our identity play. Constraint is not the same as determination, however. That games mark out certain subject positions for their players to occupy does not mean the players do occupy them. As we have seen, players may invest to different degrees in the characters as they are rendered. Some merely enact the roles marked out by the games; others negotiate them and still others use the game to reflect on real-world identities and social relations. The lesson is this: how we perform identity in these spaces—how we *do* gender or race or class, etc.—is neither entirely up to us nor entirely impervious to our actions. We are agents of articulation, expressing identity in and through these cultural resources and using them to draw connections to and conclusions about the world around us.

The next chapter will extend this discussion of identity by looking at the role of affect and emotion in the production of identities and social relations. As we will see, to analyze affect is to ask how popular forms *move* us, how they evoke emotion and put it to work. We will be particularly interested in the way affect functions as an engine of articulation. How do feelings (broadly defined) work to produce connections and disconnections? How do they align us with certain groups or agendas and against others? And, under what conditions might our affective alignments be redistributed?

SUMMARY

- Identity is not a property or "essence" we possess, but a tenuous performance we give for an audience of others whose expectations shape our actions.

- Identity always involves a tension between self-definition and social definition. Social norms, ideologies, and discourses try to pigeonhole us into a limited set of roles, but we have some say in determining which roles we will take up and how.

- Popular culture is both a mechanism through which social roles are constructed and an instrument people may use to elaborate or challenge those roles.

- The aim of cultural analysis should not be to hunt for "positive" or "negative" representations, but to ask how individuals use popular forms and practices to construct their identities and social affiliations?

- We should also ask: how does the way we *do* identity relate to questions of power, privilege, and social mobility?

- To help answer the latter question, we can ask: Whose perspective is taken for granted (i.e., exnominated) in a popular text? And whose is missing (i.e., whose is a structuring absence)? We can also flip the terms of the representation to determine the range of roles available (or not) to different social groups (commutation test).

NOTES

1 David Buckingham, "Introducing Identity," in *Youth, Identity and Digital Media,* ed. David Buckingham (Cambridge, MA: MIT Press, 2008), 1.
2 Kathryn Woodward, "Concepts of Identity and Difference," in *Identity and Difference,* ed. Woodward, Kathryn (Thousand Oaks, CA: Sage Publications, Inc., 2002), 42.
3 Judith Butler, "Performative Acts and Gender Constitution: An Essay in Phenomenology and Feminist Theory," *Theatre Journal* 40, 4 (1988), 519, emphasis mine.
4 Ibid.
5 Walter Lippmann, quoted in Richard Dyer, "The Role of Stereotypes," in *Media Studies: A Reader,* eds. Paul Marris and Sue Thornham (New York: New York University Press, 2000), 245.
6 John Fiske, *Understanding Popular Culture* (New York: Routledge, 2011), 24.
7 See http://www.kickstarter.com/projects/566429325/tropes-vs-women-in-video-games (accessed July 30, 2013).
8 Lisa Nakamura, *Cybertypes: Race, Ethnicity, and Identity on the Internet* (New York: Routledge, 2002), 38.
9 Alan Mckee, *Textual Analysis: A Beginner's Introduction* (Thousand Oaks, CA: Sage, 2003), 107.
10 See a dissection of this trope at: http://www.feministfrequency.com/2013/03/damsel-in-distress-part-1/.
11 Mike Mika, "Why I Hacked *Donkey Kong* for My Daughter," *Wired,* March 11, 2013, http://www.wired.com/gamelife/2013/03/donkey-kong-pauline-hack/ (accessed July 31, 2013).
12 Mckee, *Textual Analysis,* 110.
13 Jessica Langer, "The Familiar and the Foreign: Playing (Post)Colonialism in *World of Warcraft,*" in *Digital Culture, Play and Identity: A World of Warcraft Reader,* eds. Hilde Corneliussen and Jill Walker Rettberg (Cambridge, MA: MIT Press, 2008), 87.
14 Tanner Higgin, "Blackless Fantasy: The Disappearance of Race in Massively Multiplayer Online Role Playing Games," *Games and Culture* 4, 1 (January 2009), 16.
15 Langer, "The Familiar and the Foreign," 88.
16 Hans Robert Jauss, "Levels of Identification of Hero and Audience," *New Literary History* 5, 2 (Winter 1974).
17 Pierre Bourdieu, *Distinction: A Social Critique of the Judgment of Taste,* trans. Richard Nice (Cambridge, MA: Harvard University Press, 1984), 466.
18 Available at: http://www.southparkstudios.com/full-episodes/s14e04-you-have-0-friends (accessed May 22, 2014).
19 danah boyd, "White Flight in Networked Publics: How Race and Class Shaped American Teen Engagement with MySpace and Facebook," in *Race after the Internet,* eds. Lisa Nakamura and Peter Chow-White (New York: Routledge, 2012), 212.
20 Robert Mack and Brian Ott, *Critical Media Studies: An Introduction* (Malden, MA: Wiley-Blackwell, 2010), 256.
21 Scott Steinberg, "The Benefits of Video Games," December 26, 2011, http://abcnews.go.com/blogs/technology/2011/12/the-benefits-of-video-games/ (accessed February 5, 2014).
22 Nick Yee, "Gender-Bending," 2004, http://www.nickyee.com/daedalus/gateway_genderbend.html (accessed July 31, 2013).
23 See, for example, Sherry Turkle, *Life on the Screen: Identity in the Age of the Internet* (New York: Simon & Schuster, 1997).
24 Nick Yee, "WoW: Basic Demographics," 2004, http://www.nickyee.com/daedalus/archives/001365.php (accessed July 31, 2013).
25 Langer, "The Familiar and the Foreign," 105.
26 On the Terra Nova discussion, see Higgin, "Blackless Fantasy," 9.
27 Yee, "Gender-Bending."

28 C. Custer, "Chinese WoW Player Sleeps with Guild Members 'for the Alliance,'" *TechInAsia,* February 2, 2013, http://www.techinasia.com/chinese-wow-player-sleeps-guild-members-alliance/ (accessed July 31, 2013).
29 Lina Eklund, "Doing Gender in Cyberspace: The Performance of Gender by Female World of Warcraft Players," *Convergence: The International Journal of Research into New Media Technologies* 17, 3 (2011), 328.
30 Quoted in Henry Jenkins, "Star Trek Rerun, Reread, Rewritten: Fan Writing as Textual Poaching," in *Television: The Critical View,* ed. Horace Newcomb (New York: Oxford University Press, 1994), 476.
31 Justine Cassel and Henry Jenkins, *From Barbie to Mortal Kombat: Gender and Computer Games* (Cambridge, MA: MIT Press, 2000).

REFERENCES

Bourdieu, Pierre. *Distinction: A Social Critique of the Judgment of Taste.* Translated by Richard Nice. Cambridge, MA: Harvard University Press, 1984.
boyd, danah. "White Flight in Networked Publics: How Race and Class Shaped American Teen Engagement with MySpace and Facebook." In *Race after the Internet,* edited by Lisa Nakamura and Peter Chow-White, 203–222. New York: Routledge, 2012.
Buckingham, David. "Introducing Identity." In *Youth, Identity and Digital Media,* edited by David Buckingham, 1–24. Cambridge, MA: MIT Press, 2008.
Butler, Judith. "Performative Acts and Gender Constitution: An Essay in Phenomenology and Feminist Theory." *Theatre Journal* 40, 4 (1988): 510–531.
Cassel, Justine, and Henry Jenkins. *From Barbie to Mortal Kombat: Gender and Computer Games.* Cambridge, MA: MIT Press, 2000.
Custer, C., "Chinese WoW Player Sleeps with Guild Members 'for the Alliance.'" *TechInAsia,* February 2, 2013. http://www.techinasia.com/chinese-wow-player-sleeps-guild-members-alliance/.
Dyer, Richard. "The Role of Stereotypes." In *Media Studies: A Reader,* edited by Paul Marris and Sue Thornham, 246–251. New York: New York University Press, 2000.
Eklund, Lina. "Doing Gender in Cyberspace: The Performance of Gender by Female World of Warcraft Players." *Convergence: The International Journal of Research into New Media Technologies* 17, 3 (2011): 323–342.
Fiske, John. *Understanding Popular Culture.* New York: Routledge, 2011.
Higgin, Tanner. "Blackless Fantasy: The Disappearance of Race in Massively Multiplayer Online Role Playing Games." *Games and Culture* 4, 1 (January 2009): 3–26.
Jauss, Hans Robert. "Levels of Identification of Hero and Audience." *New Literary History* 5, 2 (Winter 1974): 283–317.
Jenkins, Henry. "Star Trek Rerun, Reread, Rewritten: Fan Writing as Textual Poaching." In *Television: The Critical View,* edited by Horace Newcomb, 470–495. New York: Oxford University Press, 1994.
Langer, Jessica. "The Familiar and the Foreign: Playing (Post)Colonialism in *World of Warcraft.*" In *Digital Culture, Play and Identity: A World of Warcraft Reader,* edited by Hilde Corneliussen and Jill Walker Rettberg, 87–108. Cambridge, MA: MIT Press, 2008.
Mack, Robert, and Brian Ott. *Critical Media Studies: An Introduction.* Malden, MA: Wiley-Blackwell, 2010.
McKee, Alan. *Textual Analysis: A Beginner's Introduction.* Thousand Oaks, CA: Sage, 2003.
Mika, Mike. "Why I Hacked Donkey Kong for My Daughter." March 11, 2013. *Wired,* http://www.wired.com/gamelife/2013/03/donkey-kong-pauline-hack/.
Nakamura, Lisa. *Cybertypes: Race, Ethnicity, and Identity on the Internet.* New York: Routledge, 2002.
Steinberg, Scott. "The Benefits of Video Games." December 26, 2011. http://abcnews.go.com/blogs/technology/2011/12/the-benefits-of-video-games/.

Turkle, Sherry. *Life on the Screen: Identity in the Age of the Internet.* New York: Simon & Schuster, 1997.

Woodward, Kathryn. "Concepts of Identity and Difference." In *Identity and Difference,* edited by Kathryn Woodward, 7–62. Thousand Oaks, CA: Sage Publications, Inc., 2002.

Yee, Nick. "Gender-Bending." 2004. http://www.nickyee.com/daedalus/gateway_genderbend.html.

———. "WoW: Basic Demographics." 2004. http://www.nickyee.com/daedalus/archives/001365.php.

CHAPTER 8

How Does Popular Culture Move Us?

So far, much of our discussion of popular culture has centered on processes of signification and meaning. How do popular forms "speak to us," "what do they say," and "what do *we* speak through our use of them?" But popular culture is about more than just meaning and utility. It is about pleasure and sensation, feelings and attachments. We invest in popular forms personally and passionately, and we do so, in part, because they are suffused with both sentiment and sensuousness. We will use the term "affect" to describe these various "feelings" and their effects on our behaviors. As media theorist Brian Ott explains, affect consists of the sensual modes of response through which we engage the world. It includes "direct sensory experiences (of color, light, sound, movement, rhythm, and texture), along with the feelings, moods, **emotions**, and/or passions they elicit."[1]

The aim of this chapter will be to examine how popular culture works on and through forms of affect, or physical and emotional sensation. To analyze affect is to ask how popular forms *move* us. How do they work on the heart and the body, not just the mind? And, from a cultural studies perspective, what are the political and social effects of such appeals? How do they relate to questions of identity, social location, and power? We will begin with a detour through theories of affect before tackling the relationship between affect and the popular arts. How do popular texts or practices appeal to our senses artistically? How and why do individuals respond to these practices (often in different ways)? Specifically, we will examine the way movies *move* us, and the types of e-*motional* investments that fans make in their favored objects.

WHAT DO WE MEAN BY AFFECT?

As I've suggested, affect refers to our sensory experiences and the feelings, moods, emotions, or passions they elicit. British cultural studies scholar Raymond Williams was perhaps the first to identify affect as an important component of cultural processes. He argued that culture consisted not just of the interests, meanings, values, and activities of a society, but the way these were lived, or experienced. He used the phrase **structure of feeling** to describe this lived reality. The concept is often glossed quickly in cultural studies work, but it is worth taking a second to unpack it.

In speaking of a *structure* of feeling, Williams is implying that feelings are social, as much as they are personal, that they are a patterned response to certain organizations of social resources and relations. Different ways of organizing society will result in different configurations of experience and emotion. These patterns are not necessarily conscious, however. The structure is "one of feeling much more than of thought—a pattern of impulses, restraints, [and] tones" that constitutes (in the words of fellow Brit Richard Hoggart) "what it feels to be alive at a certain time and place."[2]

After the 2001 terrorist attacks on the US, for example, people had good reason to feel afraid. Fear became the officially sanctioned emotion of the US, and fear was used to reprioritize social policies, pumping up the military, police, and intelligence agencies at the expense of domestic affairs. If one stopped to think about the vulnerability of the US rationally, these fears would seem unwarranted. The US is the largest military power in the world with resources unmatched by the next ten nations combined.[3] Its intelligence capabilities are legendary and extensive, and its monetary resources are virtually unlimited. Attacks on the US have been, and continue to be, extremely rare because they are effectively suicidal. Though Americans may have known rationally that another attack was unlikely, they *felt* vulnerable. This experience of fear was neither idiosyncratic nor irrational. It was a collective experience stimulated through public policy, official discourse, and popular culture, all of which worked to modulate the public mood. People were encouraged—by official discourse, by color-coded terror alerts, by the visions of war on their television sets—to feel fearful. This was a *structure* of feeling fostered by a particular articulation of social resources and priorities. The study of affect involves studying these articulations, as well as the effects they produce.

To study affect does not mean prioritizing emotion over intellect, however. In much public discourse, mind and body are still conceived as separate and opposed aspects of being. The mind is said to be rational, logical, and trustworthy whereas the body is irrational, illogical, and suspect. This opposition derives perhaps from Rene Descartes's definition of the modern subject as a "cogito"—a thinking being. Descartes is the guy who proposed that thinking defines existence: "I think therefore I am." Since the modern age, scholars (at least in the West) have acted as if that truth were incontestable, and this has frequently fueled a reflexive condemnation of popular culture for being too "sensational." Allan Bloom neatly captures the danger of this binary-thinking in *The Closing of the American Mind*:

> Picture a thirteen-year-old boy sitting in the living room of his family home doing his math assignment while wearing his Walkman headphones or watching MTV [Note that this was written when Walkmans were the portable music player of choice, and MTV still showed music videos]. He enjoys the liberties hard won over centuries by the alliance of philosophic genius and political heroism, consecrated by the blood of martyrs; he is provided with comfort and leisure by the most productive economy ever known to mankind; science has penetrated the secrets of nature in order to provide him with the marvelous,

lifelike electronic sound and image reproduction he is enjoying. And in what does all of this progress culminate? A pubescent child whose body throbs with orgasmic rhythms; whose feelings are made articulate in hymns to the joys of onanism or the killing of parents; whose ambition is to win fame and wealth in imitating the drag-queen who makes the music. In short, life is made into a nonstop, commercially prepackaged masturbational fantasy.[4]

Bloom clearly imagines the mind and body at odds here and feels justified in prioritizing the former over the latter. The mind, he says, has brought us political liberty, wealth, and technologies to sustain our health and well-being. The body, on the other hand, brings us nothing but distraction and death, masturbation, and murder.

Like other critics of popular culture, Bloom seems to want to wish the body away, but such fantasies are neither realistic nor helpful. The body is not just a vessel for the mind; affect, emotions, and sensations direct our attention and help determine the sense we make of the world. There is no rational cognition without physical and emotional stimulation. As cultural critic Jonathan Gray puts it, "We only chose to think about things or to act upon them because of emotions and affect," because we *care*.[5] This does not mean, however, that we should just invert the binary and study the body or affect at the expense of intellect. Rather, as Williams argues, we must look at the "affective elements of consciousness" together with the intellectual ones: "not feeling against thought, but *thought as felt* and *feeling as thought*."[6] How do we feel, or live, the reigning ideas of our society, and how do our feelings direct the ways we think and act? How do feelings help reshape our societies' ideals and relations?

Of course, this is not the only way to think about or study affect and emotion. Psychologists, cognitive scientists, and neuroscientists often conceive of these as properties of the individual mind or body, rather than socially conditioned responses to the world. They are interested in diagnosing, measuring, and regulating "feelings" for therapeutic purposes. Philosophers like Gilles Deleuze reach in the other direction. Instead of reducing affect to emotion and locating it in the mind, they define it as a set of lived intensities that traverse the social field and influence the disposition of our bodies in imperceptible ways. For Deleuze, affect is not a thing we can measure or pin down in a laboratory; indeed, to do so is to translate affect back into emotion and to locate it in an individual body. As American philosopher Brian Massumi explains, affect is about an experience of intensity "disconnected from [both] meaningful sequencing . . . [and] vital function." It is not susceptible to narration or causation. All attempts to qualify it—to give it a clear meaning—translate it into another essence (mere emotion).[7] Indeed, for Massumi, affect and cognition operate on different frequencies and relate inversely, so that any amplification of intensity comes at the expense of meaning and vice versa. By emphasizing the *experience* of intensity and movement, rather than the interpretation of it, these philosophers hope to change the ways we think about subjectivity and power relations. They hope to shift the focus from questions of stasis (how our identities are "fixed" and "located" by ideological and discursive processes) to questions of movement and change (how our identities and social locations remain fluid and subject to transformation).

These are all legitimate approaches to affect, of course. From a cultural studies perspective, however, they are limited because they fail to consider the inter-subjective aspects of affective experience. That is, they treat affect as either a reflexive property of the individual body (the scientific approaches), or a free-floating miasma that overwhelms the body and resists conceptualization (the philosophical approaches). Cultural studies scholars insist that affect and emotion are interrelated and have a social dimension. They are socially conditioned experiences that also effect (or change) social relations. Our "feelings" are not ours alone but derive from our interactions and our cultural milieus. We learn how to feel from the people and the culture that surrounds us, and we use our feelings as resources through which to generate new meanings and connections. Cultural studies scholars are interested in these processes of stimulation, connection, and change. Instead of treating affect and emotion as individual possessions (things we have), they treat them as social agents (things that *do*). They ask how sensibilities circulate and accumulate significance as a result of that circulation. How do emotions derive from and help construct our social formations? How do they invest our relations with meaning and power?

For example, racist hate groups in the US often position the white body as an object of love, and black or brown bodies as objects of fear, loathing, and disgust. The more they do this, the more attention they get, and the more the associations become contagious. Even people who think of themselves as non- or anti-racist might begin to wonder why blacks (or Indians or Arabs or Hispanics, etc.) are so feared and loathed. They might begin to think subconsciously "is there something about black people that merits this treatment. Is there a reason for it?" At that point the associations take on a life of their own, one that builds on and extends the history of race relations in the US. People may start to make their own connections—to historical incidents, to news reports, to images on TV, etc.—all of which start to look like confirmation that "something is wrong with black folk." Eventually, the emotional response of "disgust" or "fear" becomes naturalized and enters the cultural common sense. It becomes the reflexive understanding of who and what black folk are. In other words, the reflex reaction of fear or loathing directed at black people (or other non-white groups) in the US is not born in the bodies of white people; it is produced through social experience.

This "contagiousness" is why cultural studies scholar Lawrence Grossberg declares affect "the engine of articulation."[8] Affect is what creates social connections, but it is also what can undo those connections. If we love someone who is black, we see quite clearly how prevalent and hurtful the common sense assumption that "black folks are scary" can be. Thus, the key questions from a cultural perspective are not descriptive but functional. Rather than asking about the type or quality of affective experience in the abstract, cultural studies scholars focus on the work affect does in a given time and place. How do feelings (broadly defined) work to produce connections and disconnections? How do they align us with certain groups or agendas and against others? And, under what conditions might our affective alignments be redistributed?[9]

WHY IS AFFECT IMPORTANT TO THE STUDY OF POPULAR CULTURE?

Affect is important to the study popular culture because it is a primary feature of mass cultural forms. Theorists and historians of the popular arts have long identified "sensationalism" as a feature that distinguishes the "popular" from the "high" arts. For instance, literary scholar Harold Schechter describes popular fiction as visceral and gut-grabbing: "Popular fiction . . . [is] mass-produced art whose primary goal . . . is to reach out to (and into) the widest possible audience by telling a story that triggers a very basic and powerful emotional response: wonder or terror, laughter or tears, suspense or erotic arousal."[10] Late nineteenth-century dime novels, in particular, were a school for scandal and sensationalistic one-upmanship. Each new edition was bloodier and more thrilling than the last, as publishers tried to make the formulaic fare appear distinctive in a competitive marketplace. According to one historian, "twenty deaths per novel was not unusual and the formula demanded at least one dangerous crisis per chapter."[11]

In *The Unembarrassed Muse,* a magisterial survey of American popular forms from the moment of colonization through the 1960s, Russel Nye argues that all forms of popular art, from printed fiction and stage melodramas to movies and television, share two ingredients: relevance and sensationalism. The popular arts comment on events, ideas, and values of the day but use sex, violence, and overwrought emotionalism to help the medicine go down.[12] Sensationalism makes popular entertainment accessible to the masses. Emotions and physical sensations require little formal training to understand, and they provide a much-needed type of release after a hard day's work. In contrast, the high arts are said to be "edifying, elitist, refined, [and] difficult."[13] They seek to distance the mind from the body in order to provoke a heightened state of mental concentration. Popular forms reject this neat bifurcation of the self and, instead, stimulate the mind by targeting the body. Their stories are simple, repetitive, and formulaic but also vivid, emotional, and hard-hitting. They require little concentration and even less commitment of time, energy, and intellectual resources. Their pleasures are often physical—the jolt of the action film, the goosebumps of the horror story, the tears of the melodrama. In short, they make an impact by privileging "force over finesse."[14]

Critics of popular culture worry that such sensationalism panders to emotion and over-stimulates the body at the expense of the mind (a la Allan Bloom). Such criticisms ignore the importance of relevance as a criterion of popular enjoyment, however. Relevance refers to the way popular forms draw from and relate to everyday life, the way they express real social tensions and offer resources for surviving those tensions. For example, John Fiske once observed a group of homeless men at a local Minneapolis shelter cheering with glee every time the criminals in *Die Hard* accomplished some spectacularly violent mayhem. He argued that their support for the violence (and the villains) was related to their immediate experience of shelter life, where their every move was policed, and to their broader experience of life as a cut-throat competition, which they were "losing." *Diehard* stages a conflict between the powerful and the powerless that resonated with these men because of their experiences. It gave them an opportunity to revel imaginatively in the rejection of order and authority. They rooted for the criminals, not because they admired the men or wanted to see people get hurt, but because the criminals seemed to oppose the capitalist system. The identification was with the experience of "rebellion," not necessarily with the activities of the villains.[15] Other people watching this film—people with different histories or experiences—might take different lessons, feeling for the "underdog cop" as he battles to restore social order, for example. The point is that viewers recognize the conflicts in *Die Hard* as relevant to their lives and respond accordingly. They invest in the story because it *feels real,* and the more real it feels, the more it becomes relevant. Physical and intellectual stimulation are not opposed here; they feed into each other.

Soap operas offer perhaps the clearest example of how sensations and sense-making interact in productive ways in the popular arts. One of the most emotionally excessive of all popular forms, soap operas have long been known to impact viewer behavior in the real world. Their emotional content can literally move people to do things. Narratively and visually, soap operas focus on the intimate lives of families. The slow pacing and open-endedness of these series mimics the temporal structures of everyday life and makes the implausible events that befall the characters feel real despite their absurdity. Fans of soap operas live with the characters for so long they come to think of them as family members. Soap operas have often used the empathetic connection between viewers and characters to promote social change in the world outside the screen. In a famous example, the US series *Guiding Light* depicted one of its character's struggling with uterine cancer, and health officials across the country reported a huge increase in the number of women seeking cancer screenings.[16] Jonathan Gray notes that depictions of gay teens and coming-out narratives on programs like *All My Children* have also impacted social attitudes toward gays and lesbians.[17]

Recent studies in Brazil suggest that telenovelas (a form of soap opera) have "helped shape women's views on divorce and childbearing," with divorce rates increasing and fertility rates declining as access to television has been democratized.[18] The Peruvian telenovela *Simplemente María* ("Simply Maria," 1969), which told the story of country girl's rise from poverty through education, was credited with increasing the demand for literacy classes exponentially. More recently, Kenya's *Makutano Junction* has featured heart-breaking storylines about the dangers of spending money on drink rather than malaria medicines. All over the world public health officials and educators are using soap operas to reach people with social messages about AIDs prevention, family planning, domestic violence, and how to handle one's personal finances. Key to this campaign is the recognition that the power of stories lies in the connections they foster between characters and viewers. The messages are not didactic but emotional: "A safe-sex message, for example, is more powerful if H.I.V. isn't an abstract idea but something that happens to a beloved character."[19] So, sensationalism can serve very real purposes and have effects beyond mere emotional and physical stimulation. The stories popular forms convey are often over-wrought and may simplify complex issues to the point of incoherence, but they grab people's attention and create opportunities for empathy and understanding—with racial and ethnic "others," with A.I.D.s victims, with the poor and illiterate.

Popular forms are also known to stimulate physical sensations, and much has been made of the liberation of the body enabled by sensational cultural forms. Music, amusement rides, horror films, pornography, the more ecstatic forms of religious practice, all of these are noted, and beloved, for their capacity to transport us beyond our ordinary states of being. Such popular forms produce pleasure by stimulating, or encouraging the stimulation of, the body, rather than the mind. The thrill, the frisson, the tingle, even the pain, can provide a temporary release from everyday reality. Whether that temporary release enables us to tolerate our routines or allows us to transcend them is a matter of usage and context, but either way, such pleasure is an important aspect of the engagement with popular culture, and not to be ignored. Thus, Richard Dyer celebrates the physical bravado and energy of Hollywood musicals and argues that the affective elements of the performance often work against the messages of the films. Many musicals are about corralling female energy and initiative within the bonds of marriage. They are about containment. In the musical numbers, however, women fly about the stage, grandly occupying space and even occasionally defying gravity. The dance numbers are all about breaking bonds and taking wing. They work at odds to the narrative, creating a utopian feeling of freedom that belies any message of restraint and self-effacement.

Dyer lauds disco for similar reasons. He notes that, in the 1970s, discotheques gave people an opportunity to lose themselves in pure rhythm, forget about the drudgery of the workday, and experience a type of liberation denied to them elsewhere in society. As a focus of gay party rituals, moreover, disco songs and dance routines encouraged a fluidity of movement that complemented the group's political conception of sexuality as a fluid continuum. Affect did not just promote an evasion of ideology in this instance; it fostered new forms of identity and collectivity. In both cases, Dyer shows how popular forms of entertainment can serve a utopian function by tapping into affect. This is a unique and tenuous form of utopia, however. Unlike utopian novels, which might sketch out a plan for how to organize a new society, music, dancing, and spectacle offer no sense of orientation; they provide no coherent or obvious rules for living. What they do is convey "what utopia would feel like."[20] They express what it would *feel like* to live outside of the systems that ordinarily constrain us, what it would *feel like* to live in a society that more fully accommodated our needs. They allow us to "be critical of the way things are by feeling how they might be."[21]

Such physical and emotional release is not inherently political or progressive, however, and we would be wrong to imagine that the capacity to mobilize bodies is only or inevitably emancipatory. As Michel Foucault reminds us, the body is also the site where social discipline is inscribed and enforced. Fiske puts it this way: "the body is where the power-bearing definitions of social and sexual normality are, literally, embodied, and is consequently the site of discipline and punishment for deviation from those norms."[22] The mobilization of affect, energy, and mood that occurs in popular forms may work to reinforce, as well as challenge, these processes of normalization.

For example, Lawrence Grossberg and Todd Gitlin both show how mood music may be used to modulate popular emotions and attune individuals to the rhythms of the workday or the shopping experience. As Gitlin details, the Muzak corporation has made a business out of mood modulation, experimenting with various arrangements of songs in order to maximize the efficiency of the workplace. The optimal balance, they discovered, is to start slowly and gradually build pace and volume as the day goes on so that the music may lift workers spirits as their bodies start to fatigue. Muzak now provides individualized soundtracks for retail outlets, doctor's offices, airports, and most public spaces, being careful to offer variety "so that it never seems that Big Brother or the Wizard of Noise is in charge."[23] Clearly, though, this is a carefully calibrated form of control, designed to discipline our minds and

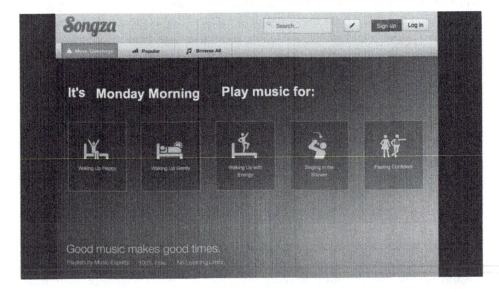

FIGURE 8.01   *Music apps like Songza, whose interface is depicted here, make it easy for us to program our own moods.*

bodies for the day's routines. And, we don't need Muzak to do this work anymore. We happily program our own soundtracks on our iPods to help us get through our workouts, our workdays, even our downtime with the family. Streaming music platforms like Songza or Spotify make such self-regulation even easier by offering pre-selected playlists arranged by "mood." All we have to do is push a button, and we can program ourselves to feel better (or worse).

Such activities do have a political effect: they allow us to carve out a zone of privacy in a crowded existence and to evade some forms of social discipline. But the politics of evasion and release are never pure; they are always tied to the systems of power we seek to flee. They carve out a space *within* those systems for some "me-time," but they never carry us completely beyond the social formation. At best, the pleasures of bodily release and evasion associated with affect and mood management are "progressive pleasures" concerned with redistributing power within the existing social structures; they are not "radical" forms of resistance concerned with tearing those structures down.[24] The social field within which evasion operates determines its political utility. To paraphrase Fiske, "tuning out" is not in itself liberatory, but under certain social circumstances (when those in authority seek to discipline our labors or direct our emotions, for example) it might be.[25]

HOW SHOULD WE STUDY AFFECT IN POPULAR CULTURE?

To study affect is to ask what sensibilities, or structures of feeling, govern relations in a particular context and to think about how those sensibilities are embodied in particular works. There are two basic ways cultural studies scholars have approached such inquiries. One has been to look at the formal properties of texts to determine how they evoke physical and emotional responses. How do texts use technique to appeal to the senses? Which moods or feelings does a particular work make available, how, and to what end? The other has been to examine audiences and their activities in relation to popular forms. How do audiences feel about cultural objects, and how do these feelings produce connections to other people and agendas? The first approach asks how passions, emotions, moods, and sensations are embodied in the text, and the second asks how such affective sensibilities work on people and shape their relations.

The first approach is commonly associated with aesthetic and rhetorical forms of analysis. The study of **rhetoric** involves examining of the way language (including figural languages like song, film, or art) persuades, or moves, individuals. Aesthetic approaches to rhetoric focus less on the content of messages than on their material form and artistic properties. For example, an aesthetic study of music would look less at the lyrics of songs and more at the ways rhythm, melody, harmony, and the grain of voice are used to create a particular sensation in the audience. Likewise, in the study of film, an aesthetic approach would focus on the formal properties of the audio-visions projected on screen. It would look at both the way a scene is staged, filmed, edited, and augmented (by visual and audio effects) *and* the materiality of the medium itself. (Was the image shot digitally or on film? If film, what type? At what speed? How was the film exposed? How much grain or texture does the resulting image have?). As cultural studies scholar Arthur Asa Berger notes, these aesthetic decisions "[convey] a great deal of information and [give] us a sense of the importance of what we are seeing relative to other images and events."[26] They both focus our attention and provoke our emotional engagement with the characters and actions.

From an affective standpoint, aesthetic decisions may also give the film an overall tone or mood, which we may not consciously experience, but which works on us nonetheless. Deidre Pribram argues, for example, that the film *Crash* (2004) is structured by a pervasive mood of anger and frustration.[27] It uses the metaphor of the car crash to configure contemporary urban America as a land of increasing socioeconomic and racial segregation, which offers no basis for prosocial forms

FIGURE 8.02   *The top two images from the movie* Crash *(2004) depict Officer Ryan (Matt Dillon) sexually assaulting Christine Thayer (Thandie Newton). In the remaining frames, all four characters react to the incident. Note the dark lighting and tight framing.*

of engagement. Instead of interacting, contemporary Americans career into each other with explosive results. This narrative theme is enhanced by the use of a dark lighting and color scheme and intensely claustrophobic framing. The framing is so tight, at times, that the characters appear isolated from each other even as they are interacting. For example, during an early scene, when police officers John Ryan (Matt Dillon) and Tom Hansen (Ryan Philippe) stop a black couple, Cameron and Christine Thayer (Terrence Howard and Thandie Newton), for a traffic violation, the encounter devolves into an incident of sexual abuse, as Officer Ryan punishes Christine Thayer for challenging his authority. This assault is captured in tight shots of all four participants, as they separately recognize what is happening. Even Officer Ryan and Christine Thayer are captured in isolation despite the most intimate nature of their contact at that moment.

The visual separation of the characters in the early parts of the film heightens the emotional impact of their encounters when they are thrown together later. In one of the final scenes, for example, Officer Ryan arrives on the scene of a car crash and tries to rescue the female occupant of the vehicle. She happens to be Christine Thayer, making the would-be rescue feel like a traumatic reenactment of the original assault. To heighten the anguish and transfer her discomfort to the audience, the scene is blocked and framed in the most intimate fashion, as a grotesque simulation of a sexual encounter. This intimate sequence in the car also lasts for nearly four minutes of screen time, which is double the length of most scenes in contemporary Hollywood cinema (David Bordwell estimates that the average

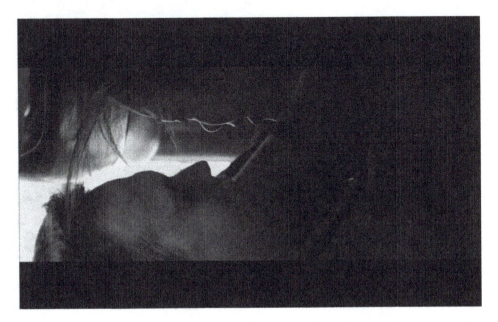

FIGURE 8.03 *Officer Ryan must cut Christine Thayer free from her seat belt. The scene is blocked like a grotesque simulation of sex; it is designed to shock viewers.*

scene now lasts between one and half and two minutes).[28] By prolonging the rescue in this way—even having bystanders pull Ryan from the car at one point to delay the resolution—director Paul Haggis makes viewers sweat it out along with the characters.

The musical score provides an eerie contrast to the visuals, thereby heightening the traumatic sensibility of the scene. The shot of Ryan pulling Thayer from the car is scored to Mark Isham's haunting (and aptly named) jazz song "Flames." The lyrics of the song are in multiple non-English languages (Farsi and Welsh), but, roughly translated, they speak of love and nostalgia. Though few people in the audience would be able to understand the lyrics, the uncredited female vocalist manages to convey the sense of longing and desire through her vocal inflections and tone. The grain of her voice evokes confusion and heartache. While Ryan does eventually rescue Thayer, no one, including the audience, really knows how to feel about it. The imagery and soundtrack leave us feeling bewildered and bereft. This matches the decidedly downbeat ending of the film, which features a few examples of incipient human empathy, but only a few. In the end, we are literally left where we began. The narrative has circled back to the death that opened the film, and the final sequence of images depicts yet another LA car crash.

At the opposite end of the emotional spectrum, we might think of a film like *Love, Actually* (2003), which tells ten interlocking stories of love and loss but manages to stay relentlessly upbeat throughout. Reviewers called it "doggedly cheery" and "sweet," a cinematic "confection" calculated to delight.[29] The film makes us

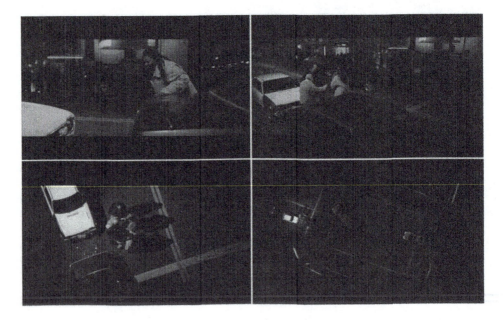

FIGURE 8.04 *The final sequence in the film* Crash *(2004) depicts yet another car crash, yet more violence and anger, and the God's eye view evokes "frustration."*

feel happy despite the disappointing resolution of several of the narrative strands, and it does this because it is visually and aurally "bright." The cast is handsome and homey; their performances convey warmth, even in the midst of despair, and the lighting, costuming, and color scheme are so vibrant they might have been ripped from a high-toned fashion magazine. The soundtrack features recognizably fuzzy pop hits from Britain and the US (both classics like the Pointer Sisters' "Jump (For My Love)" and new hits by the likes of Kelly Clarkson and Dido), which are employed strategically to warm our hearts. Even as Andrew Lincoln's character Mark expresses his unrequited love for his best friend's wife, for example, the sticky sweet Christmas carol "Silent Night" plays over the scene. Finally, the director, Richard Curtis, gently accelerates the pace of the editing as the film draws to a close, generating a sense of unstoppable momentum akin to a sugar rush. The epilogue features all ten couples at the bright, white Heathrow Airport greeting newly arrived friends and family home for the holidays. As the Beach Boys song "God Only Knows" plays on the soundtrack, the screen fragments into dozens of boxes, each containing a similar scene of "love actualized" by ordinary people. The love literally overflows

FIGURE 8.05 *The final sequence from the film* Love, Actually *(2003). Love is all around, as the film closes. Viewers are left feeling happy and warm.*

the screen. So, just as *Crash* leaves its audience little room to feel good about anything that happens in the film, *Love, Actually* leaves no room to feel bad. We cannot help but smile at the warmth and humanity of the film.

In addition to examining the portrayal of emotion in individual films, we might acknowledge that certain genres of film (and entertainment) *move* us more than others. The so-called body genres of pornography, melodrama, and horror, for example, are all designed to provoke an excessive physical and emotional response from us.[30] Genres like the musical and the action film, likewise, use excessively spectacular set-pieces (either musicals or action sequences) to disrupt, and often counter-act, the flow of the narrative. Many critics still lament the popularity of these genres, especially the popularity of blockbuster action cinema. Film critic Thomas Schatz, for example, dismisses the New Hollywood blockbuster formula as "increasingly plot-driven, increasingly visceral, kinetic, and fast-paced, increasingly reliant on special effects, increasingly 'fantastic' (and thus apolitical), and increasingly targeted at younger audiences."[31] He assumes that an over-abundance of visual spectacle must necessarily crowd out substance and laments the decline in the "quality" of Hollywood's output under this formula. Feminist film scholar Yvonne Tasker argues, however, that critics like Schatz are guilty of "textual contempt" for failing to assess these movies on their own terms. Moreover, their critical biases toward narrative and character progression blind them to other facets of the movie-going experience, namely its sensuousness and celebration of motion (we do call them *movies* for a reason). Instead of lumping all action films together in a category labeled "dumb movies for dumb people," she says, we ought to consider how such films work.[32] How and why do they appeal to audiences? How are their appeals constructed in different ways, for different purposes, and with differential effects?

What do action films *feel like*, and what types of pleasures do they evoke? Sociologist Todd Gitlin (who is no fan of the genre, mind you) has described the experience as something akin to the rush of intoxication—fleeting but powerful. He argues that the excessive and dynamic quality of the action set-pieces, coupled with the harried pace of the editing, produces a feeling of temporary transcendence, which he calls the "kinetic sublime" (for its awe-inspiring power). When we watch an action film, he explains, we get carried away by the sights and sounds and experience a potent fantasy of liberation, "a cutting loose from the terrestrial gravity of everyday life into a stratosphere of pure motion, suspense, and release."[33] He believes these sensations are too "disposable" to be good for us; they will undermine our capacity to sustain "genuine" human feelings and relationships and distract us from the work of political organizing. Other scholars are not so concerned, however. Film critic David Bordwell, for example, has celebrated the hyper-kineticism of the Hong Kong action cinema as a masterful contribution to classical film form. Like Tasker, he is interested in the *experience* of film, not just its ideological messaging, and his comparison of Hong Kong action cinema to Hollywood's new post-classical, post-continuity style of action masterfully demonstrates how different aesthetic choices produce different affective experiences.

As Bordwell argues, both Hong Kong and Hollywood filmmakers use the quick cutting, rapid editing, and mobile camerawork that defines today's international film style, but Western filmmakers, like Michael Bay or Tony Scott, use these tools to produce disorientation and an illusion of energy. They are less concerned to have the audience follow the action than in generating a raw physical sensation. So, for example, in the action sequences of the Transformers (2007, 2009, 2011, 2014) films, Bay uses swish pans to flash from subject to subject, pulls focus without explanation, and rarely matches the cuts for continuity. These choices throw the spatial integrity of the scene out of whack, inducing a feeling of vertigo in many viewers. Bordwell describes the style as "impressionistic" or "lumpy" because it renders combat and pursuit sequences as "a blurred confusion." Instead of a continuous sense of motive and motion, "we [get] a flurry of cuts calibrated not in relation to each other or to the action, but instead suggesting a vast busyness. Here camerawork and editing [don't] serve the specificity of the action but [overwhelm], [and] even [bury] it."[34] Such pictorial "energy," he claims, is an undisciplined sort of "energy" that seems to breed confusion for its own sake.

Hong Kong filmmakers, on the other hand, balance speed with stasis in a "pause/burst/pause pattern" that amplifies the expressive potential of the images. Each shot is carefully orchestrated to enable us to grasp, quickly, but decisively, the heart of the matter. The extended shoot-out at the end of John Woo's *Hard-Boiled* (1992), for example, takes place as the gunmen run through a series of hospital corridors, shooting everything in sight and throwing up a blinding confusion of bodies, dust, glass, and flames. Yet, we never lose sight of the action because it is carefully choreographed, filmed, and edited. Instead of two to three second cuts, Woo alternates between quick cuts and long takes, sometimes of a minute or more. As they travel down the corridors, Woo's police officers advance-pause-shoot, advance-pause-shoot, providing time for viewers to re-orient themselves. Woo also uses slow-motion sequences to emphasize important details (like the identity of a police officer killed by friendly fire) and distinguishes between the good and bad guys by assigning different guns and gun noises to them. The result: we are never confused, no matter how fast-paced the action gets.[35]

Instead of immersing viewers in an extended, often nauseating, experience of pure speed, Woo gives his action scenes a rhythm and a purpose. The rhythm expresses the emotions of the characters and produces a lyrical effect that tells viewers how to *feel* about the violence on screen. Rather than celebrating mindless destruction, the balletic arrangements of gunplay, gore, and grisly death convey a sense of wistful regret for what the world might have been like were it not so violent. Woo and other masters of the Hong Kong actioner do not just produce mindless spectacles, then. They use their action sequences to reinforce the narrative emphasis on nihilism. The result is what we might call (a la Dyer) "a feeling of dystopia." This feeling links transcendence, not to escape or rebellion, but to death. It is a bleak sensation, but one that clearly resonates for many filmgoers.

Fans of the action genre believe it is misunderstood because it defies conventional notions of "what film art is or could be."[36] Action films remind us that much of the beauty and meaning of film "comes from the expressive use of non-representational signs" like "color, music, movement," and the careful orchestration of these.[37] An affective approach to cinema draws attention to such non-representational dynamics and asks us to take them seriously not for what they mean (or fail to mean), but for what they *do*. How do aesthetic choices create a "structure of feeling," tone, or mood? How do they move us emotionally and what do they connect us to? This brings us to the second phase of our affective analysis: the examination of the audience and its affective investments.

HOW DOES AFFECT BUILD CONNECTIONS?

As the previous discussion demonstrates, different cultural works and practices attract different levels of devotion from audiences. The action genre has its fans, like Bordwell and José Arroyo, who believe it represents the height of filmic art due to its exploitation of the full palette of cinematic techniques. It also has its anti-fans, such as Schatz and Gitlin, who detest the genre because it seems to promote feeling over thinking. Such differences develop because, as Ott explains, different "experiencing bodies" bring different "bodies of experience" to the same films.[38] Bordwell's obsession with action cinema enables him to see fine-grained distinctions between the works of Michael Bay and John Woo while Gitlin's antipathy toward the genre leaves him blind and deaf to such distinctions. The debates between these scholars show just how much our mental evaluations of cultural works depend on our physical and emotional responses. If a film (or other work) is to resonate for us, we need to be responsive to the cues it gives us, and what pre-disposes us to be responsive is a history of prior emotional and affective experience. That is, how we have been socialized to think about sensation and emotion affects our sense of who we are and what we ought to value. Affects and emotions contribute to the formation of identities and power relations.

Fan and anti-fan practices clearly demonstrate the interplay of affect, identity, and power, for fandom is marked by a passionate attachment to a particular text (or type of text), icon, or practice. Such passion sometimes borders on obsession, which is why fans are often pathologized in mainstream discourse as "loony tunes." In truth, fans are just people who are so moved by an object, event, individual, or experience that they want to share their feelings with others. These feelings may be feelings of love or hate, but the point is that the individual is moved—both emotionally and physically—to create larger communities of affinity around the object. These communities of affinity, or **fandoms**, provide mutual aid and support to their members, give them an outlet for their passions and their creativity, and help them expand their horizons by putting them in touch with like-minded but experientially different individuals.

Affect plays a powerful role in the primary fan experience. If we look at teen idols and their fans, for example, we can see how the disposition of the star's body called to the fans, who responded in kind. Bodily performance worked, almost in a ritualistic fashion, to cement the emotional attachments between idol and fan. In the 1950s, Elvis shook his hips, and the girls swooned in their seats. Some cut their hair in a ducktail to emulate the star while male fans studiously imitated his movements and postures, becoming the first Elvis impersonators (the film *Forrest Gump* lampoons this habit by having a teenage Elvis copy the moves of the disabled youngster Forrest. The joke: Elvis dances liked a "cripple"). In the 1960s, the Beatles rattled their mop-tops, and female fans in the UK mobbed them, tearing the men's clothes from their bodies. By the time they hit the US in 1964, thousands of fans greeted them at the airport, and hundreds more surrounded their hotel. At their concerts, thousands of teenage girls wept, screamed, and peed their pants at the mere sight of the "Fab Four," and the noise was so deafening that it purportedly drowned out the sound of the music. What drew the fans to their favorite celebrities was the physicality of the performance style; what cemented their relationships was a shared affective disposition toward "unruliness," or rebellion. And, lest we think only modern music fans are guilty of such physical disorder, Daniel Cavicchi tells us that nineteenth-century opera fans also "expressed overwhelming visceral ecstasy" in response to musical performances. They often described "the music 'filling their souls' to the point of losing composure" and conceived of the experience as "excitingly dangerous and cathartic."[39]

Today, Canadian pop singer Justin Bieber is the primary object of preteen hysteria throughout the world. As with Elvis or the Beatles, Bieber's fans are noted for their emotive expressions of devotion and their physical paroxysms of delight in his presence. The official fan club is called "Bieber Fever," and fans freely acknowledge that they may be delirious with love for the singer. A mocking entry on Urbandictionary.com describes the symptoms of Bieber Fever as: "Obsessive thoughts of Justin Bieber, stroke, heart attack, and seizure possibilities if meeting him, crying hysterically, screaming at a shrieking tone, fainting, and falling in love. Falling in love is most likely permanent and irreversible." Recently a biologist and a mathematician from the University of Ottawa determined (tongue in cheek) that Bieber Fever operates like a real disease and may be "even more contagious than the measles." Indeed, it may be "the most infectious disease of our time" based on its current rate of dissemination and the possible multiplying effects of the media.[40]

Such jokes are obviously ways of dismissing the unruly bodies of both the performer and his fans. As with other forms of negative discourse, these jokes belittle as a means of containment, for the preteen, female fan's boisterous body defies the rules of social decorum associated with youth and femininity. Ordinarily, girls are to be seen and not heard; they are to act primly and remain chaste. The girl-fan's loss of bodily control is a long, loud raspberry directed at these requirements. Their paroxysms of delight challenge the common sense rules designed to put girls in their place. As Barbara Ehrenreich, Elizabeth Hess, and Gloria Jacobs argue regarding Beatlemania, for young teen girls "to abandon control—to scream, faint, dash about in mobs—[is], in form if not in conscious intent to protest sexual repressiveness, [and] the rigid double-standard."[41] Likewise, Bieber fans may not intend, in any direct way, to challenge authority, but their bodily insubordination does defy the various attempts to define and subordinate them as a class. Moreover, it may serve utopian purposes, allowing the girls to experience what defiance feels like.

As these examples demonstrate, fans feel intensely for their objects of adulation; this feeling is manifest in the postures, actions, and adornments of the fan body, but it is also expressed and transmitted in the **vernacular creativity** of fan cultures. Fans differ from mere enthusiasts in that they translate their love (or hate) into various forms of publicly shared texts or performances. They create fan fiction, tribute websites, artwork, songs, videos, and discussions devoted to their favorite subjects and share their work online, in fan clubs and at conventions. These texts are laced with emotional language that affirms the fan's identification with their idol. The fan "vid," for example, is all about "love." Vidding involves mixing a favorite, emotionally charge song with clips from a favorite film or TV show to create a new montage that communicates one's love of these texts. Not coincidentally, the subject matter of many vids is also love, specifically relationships between favorite film and TV characters. Sometimes these relationships are legitimized by the text, as in the case of Twilight fan vids that compile scenes of the central characters, Bella (Kristin Stewart) and Edward (Robert Pattinson), mooning at each other. But sometimes they are illicit compilations that evoke a fantasy relationship or seek to raise a subtext to the position of primacy, as in Harry Potter fan vids that mix scenes of affection between Harry and Hermione together with a love song to imply a romantic relationship between them (a relationship J.K. Rowling and her "fanonites" sought to suppress until very recently).[42] The fan vid is thus a labor of love that is also about the love of texts and the love of love.

Anti-fans—those who express dislike for a particular fan object—use similarly emotional language and gesture to disqualify the fan's admiration of the object. There are dozens of Bieber anti-fan clubs on Facebook, and a Google search of "Bieber anti-fan" results in over twenty *million* hits. Most of these express their distaste for Bieber using jokes about his age, gender, and sexuality, thereby using the affective appeals of laughter or the smirk to recontain the excesses of the star and his fans. These jokes affirm existing age, gender, and sexual norms as a means of pulling the fan back into line and countering the singer's outsized influence on contemporary culture. For example, Bieber is often dismissed for being a "fag," or, more outrageously, a "lesbian." What can this be other than a way of policing masculinity and sexual propriety? "Hating on" Bieber offers a way of defining masculinity in opposition to femininity and thus of repositioning girls (and those who entertain their whims) on the bottom of the social hierarchy.

These examples show how affect works as an engine of articulation, defining identities, forging social connections, and generally helping people determine what or whom to care about (often as a response to what their peers care about). Affect is the primary means through which fans express their personal interests and forge bonds with others. In the words of a prominent Lord of the Rings fan, fans follow their "strong attraction" to the franchise and "their feelings [point] them toward new friends, new pastimes, new talents, new jobs, new countries, a new life entirely."[43] Affect is also the means through which the excesses of fandom get policed, through laughter, rolled eyes, sneers, and sniffs of disdain. In both cases, affective behavior is the hinge that connects individuals to the social order. It is the vehicle through which they articulate their interests and are, in turn, articulated to other interests, both popular and hegemonic.

As we have seen (in Chapter 6), those who make and distribute popular culture are newly hip to the power of affect to cut through the media clutter and effect connections that can be turned to profit. Film producers, distributors, and promoters have been some of the first to understand and exploit this model of affective economics, courting fans in active ways to generate buzz for their films. In response, fans have become extremely fickle about their affinities, discriminating between those shallow attempts to pitch them something and the more dedicated attempts to engage them as co-creators. For example, fans of the *Star Wars* franchise have been up in arms ever since the Disney Corporation purchased Lucasfilms in 2012. Disney has a long track record of protecting its properties by suppressing fan activity, and many worry the same thing could happen to Star Wars that has happened with the Disney animated characters (namely, no one can use them for any purpose without Disney's consent). Already fans feel shut out of the creative process surrounding the next installment of the film franchise, which is being developed under a veil of secrecy (as of this writing). If Disney wants Star Wars fans to show up for the next film as expected, fan Marcus Doige suggests, they need "to show us they know how to cater to the *Star Wars* fans' requirements and throw some goodwill gestures at us."[44]

In this, they could take a lesson from Peter Jackson, director and producer of the Lord of the Rings trilogy (2001, 2002, 2003). Those films were based on a much-beloved series of novels created by the British author J.R.R. Tolkien. By buying the rights to the series, Jackson and his distributor, New Line Cinema (a division of Time-Warner), were also buying the loyalties of those fans, and thus considerations of fan affect figured prominently in the development of the films. While Jackson did not want to offend the fan base, he knew he could not include every character or incident in the novels and still create an engrossing narrative for a general audience. So, he came up with a compromise solution: for the general audience, the story would be streamlined to foreground the spectacular action sequences, but, for the fans, the atmospherics would be dense, lush, and absolutely faithful to the books. The New Zealand crews hired native artisans to design the armor, weapons, clothing, and sets using authentic materials and folk knowledge to add a sense of historical depth to the set design (no plastic props or synthetic fabrics were used, for example). Jackson also gave each ethnic group inhabiting the fictional Middle Earth a unique language and look, based on the fragments of language and description used by Tolkien himself in the novels and companion texts. Much of this density can only be captured by freezing the film frame or listening carefully for the linguistic differences, but for fans this density provided a much-needed reassurance that Jackson understood their passion for Middle Earth. For non-fans, Jackson and the script-writers beat a relentless pace through the narrative, often shunting aside the character-building, relationship-based elements of the fiction in favor of breath-taking action sequences. In the end, the films managed to satisfy just about every-one, fans and non-fans alike. Even the American Academy of Motion Picture Arts & Sciences—a body that rarely rewards genre films—acknowledged Jackson's feat with a clean sweep of the major categories for 2004.[45]

Merchandising tie-ins for the films extended the narrative universe outward and into the home, offering mood music (albums, CDs, songs), entertainment (not one but three official DVD sets and multiple trading card, board, and video games), information (several "making of" documentaries available on TV or DVD), and high-end collectibles designed to replicate the world of Middle Earth (chess sets, jewelry, replica swords, and statues of the characters designed by Jackson's in-house miniatures-studio Weta Workshop). The style guide created for the merchandisers included the same attention to detail and density as the film guide, right down to the different skin tones of the various races. In striking these deals, New Line was careful to avoid association with tacky merchandise, like bobble-heads, that might offend the sensibilities of Tolkien fans.

For promotions, Jackson and New Line contacted fan producers and turned them into sales people. At the time of the first film's release (2001), websites were relatively new, and social media technologies were still on the horizon (MySpace was "born" in 2003, Facebook in 2004, YouTube in 2005, and Twitter in 2006). Jackson and New Line Cinema were really the first major film industry players to try using fans and fan networks to promote their films (though they took their cue from independent producers Daniel Myrick and Eduardo Sanchez who used online fan buzz to promote their 1999 film *The Blair Witch Project*). To stoke fan ardor, Jackson and company gave regular reports and inside information to a small group of loyal fans who then acted as "multipliers," authenticating and disseminating the information to the larger fan base. New Line's George Paddison (Senior Vice President for Worldwide Interactive Marketing) downplayed the strategy, saying "we go where the fans are and give them stuff," but the courting of fans went far beyond mere giveaways.[46] Jackson and New Line's promotions staff invited key website producers to the set in New Zealand and let them blog about their adventures on their fan sites. Several fan bloggers were invited to the premiere event at Cannes in 2000, and Jackson, the cast, and some of the crew showed up to fan parties organized around the Academy Awards events in LA. At least one fan parlayed his Lord of the Rings insider status into a career in popular journalism (Harry Knowles of *Ain't It Cool News* secured sponsorship for his media blog through the "scoops" Jackson and Paddison provided) while others gladly spent thousands of dollars and untold man-hours toiling for the franchise out of their love and respect for the Tolkien brand.

As we have seen, such "free labor" is not properly described as exploitation because it is freely given and rewarded in other ways. Most fans are not looking for monetary compensation from media producers but for acknowledgment and a stake in the process. From each other, they are looking for connection, support, and prestige. So, while these relationships may seem exploitative from an economic perspective, *they are not necessarily lived that way by the fans.* For example, the authors of TheOneRing.net accrued over $70 thousand of debt to produce a lavish Oscar party for *The Return of the King,* the final film in the sequence. Jackson and New Line clearly received some publicity and a few feel-good pats on the back from the event, but they did not offer to help the fans with their debts. That may seem exploitative, but only if we wish to deprive fans of any **agency** or control over the process. In truth, neither Jackson nor New Line asked the fans to go to these lengths, and they did not benefit that much from the publicity (this was, after all, at the tail end of the trilogy's run). Why should they be held responsible for the work these fans did of their own accord?

More importantly, the fans felt the effort was worth every penny. Their investment in the franchise was not ultimately centered on their interest in Jackson, New Line, or the films. They were fans of the books before the films, and what they professed to "love" about the experience of celebrating the films was the chance to meet—not Jackson or the cast members—but each other. "Because of these four folks, who met for the first-time in 'real-life' on Oscar Sunday," said one of the organizers, "we have all discovered that we are not alone; that we are part of an immense worldwide community."[47] That community should not be dismissed as inconsequential or naïve. Like most fans, these ones understood their relationship to Jackson and company was tenuous and strategic. They were not duped into thinking they were economic partners in the creation of the franchise; rather, they used the "Frodo franchise" as a vehicle to articulate their own forms of partnership. For these fans, the experience, the emotion, the love of the "Frodo Franchise" was always about more than the corporate bottom line. It was about identity and connection, culture and community. Their individual love for the Tolkien stories was enhanced, not diminished, by the experience of sharing their affinities with others.

CONCLUSION

In the end, an awareness of affect and emotion—and the work they do—can help us better understand our own attachments to cultural objects, icons, and practices, and, let's face it, we are all fans of something. It reminds us that our behaviors are not always rational or conscious, nor do they need to be. In fact, much of the pleasure of popular culture derives from letting ourselves go a little, surrendering occasionally to the tides of sensation and emotion, letting the images wash over us, succumbing to the rhythm of the beat. This is not to say that affect is always or inevitably about liberation, however. As film critic Steven Shaviro says, "power works in the depths and on the surfaces of the body, and not just in the disembodied realm of 'representation' or of 'discourse.'" We need to talk about how a medium like film "arouses corporeal reactions of desire and fear, pleasure and disgust, fascination and shame" because "such affective experiences directly and urgently involve a politics."[48] Our feelings and emotions articulate relationships that matter; they have force. They move us to do things—to believe things and to fear things, as well as to embrace things. Learning to attend to affect means learning to understand how our feelings shape our identities and relations in both good *and* bad ways.

The next chapter will continue this conversation by focusing on the way cultural goods circulate globally and produce new forms of desire, fear, envy, and love. It will concentrate, in particular, on the tensions between identity and difference that emerge as cultural resources traverse the geographic and linguistic boundaries that once made nations (seem) so distinct. How well do cultural artifacts and customs travel? What happens to local cultures when "foreign" goods, people, money, and ideas invade? Will globalization result in the homogenization of cultures, or will it lead instead to an increasing hybridization, as locals selectively appropriate global goods for their own local purposes?

SUMMARY

- Affect consists of the sensual modes of response through which we engage the world, including direct sensory experiences and the feelings, moods, emotions, or passions they elicit.

- Like identity, feelings are not entirely subjective or individual. They are socially constructed, change over time, and differ from context to context.

- Affect may not be rational or intellectual, but it does aid thought by directing our attention and giving us an investment in the outcomes of knowledge production. It teaches us what to care for and about.

- One way to study affect is to ask how popular forms *move* us. How do they evoke emotions or sensibilities artistically? And, how and why do people respond to such appeals as they do?

- Another way to study affect is to consider the political and social ramifications of such appeals. What *work* do affect and emotion do? How do they influence our identities and determine our social locations?

NOTES

1 Brian Ott, "The Visceral Politics of *V for Vendetta*: On Political Affect in Cinema," *Cultural Studies in Media Communication* 27, 1 (March 2010), 5.
2 Raymond Williams, *Politics and Letters* (New York: Verso, 1981), 159. Richard Hoggart, qtd. in Lawrence Grossberg, "Affect's Future: Discovering the Virtual in the Actual," in *The Affect Theory Reader,* eds. Melissa Gregg and Gregory J. Siegworth (Durham, NC: Duke University Press, 2010), 310.

3 Andrew Bacevich, *The Limits of Power: The End of American Exceptionalism* (New York: Metropolitan Books, 2008), 219.

4 Quoted in Lawrence Grossberg, *We Gotta Get out of This Place: Popular Conservatism and Postmodern Culture* (New York: Routledge, 1992), 4.

5 Jonathan Gray, *Television Entertainment* (New York: Routledge, 2008), 143.

6 Raymond Williams, *Marxism in Literature* (New York: Oxford University Press, 1977), 132.

7 Brian Massumi, *Parables of the Virtual: Movement, Affect, Sensation* (Durham, NC: Duke University Press, 2002), 25.

8 Grossberg, "Affect's Future," 327.

9 Examples include: Grossberg, *We Gotta Get out of This Place*; Grossberg, *Dancing in Spite of Myself: Essays on Popular Culture* (Durham, NC: Duke University Press, 1997); George Marcus, *The Sentimental Citizen: Emotion in Democratic Politics* (University Park: Pennsylvania State University Press, 2002); Sara Ahmed, "Affective Economies," *Social Text* 22, 2 (Summer 2004), 117–139.

10 Harold Schechter, "The Bosom Serpent," in *Popular Culture Theory and Methodology: A Basic Introduction*, eds. Harold E. Hinds, Jr., Marilyn F. Motz, and Angela M.S. Nelson (Madison: University of Wisconsin Press, 2006), 313.

11 Russel Nye, *The Unembarrassed Muse: The Popular Arts in America* (New York: Dial Press, 1973), 205.

12 Ibid., 250.

13 Richard Dyer, *Only Entertainment* (New York: Routledge, 2002), 6.

14 David Bordwell, *Planet Hong Kong: Popular Cinema and the Art of Entertainment,* 2nd ed. (Madison, WI: Irvington Way Institute Press, 2011), 4.

15 John Fiske, *Power Plays, Power Works* (New York: Verso, 1993), chapter 1.

16 "Interview with Agnes Nixon" in Robert Kubey, *Creating Television: Conversations with the People Behind 50 Years of American TV* (Mahwah, NJ: LEA, 2004), 73.

17 Gray, *Television Entertainment*, 121.

18 "Brazilian Soap Operas Shown to Impact Social Behaviors," January 29, 2009, http://www.iadb.org/en/news/webstories/2009–01–29/brazilian-soap-operas-shown-to-impact-social-behaviors,5104.html (accessed June 17, 2012).

19 Sarika Bansal, "Soap Operas with a Social Message," January 26, 2012, http://opinionator.blogs.nytimes.com/2012/01/26/steamy-plots-with-a-social-message/ (accessed June 17, 2012).

20 Dyer, *Only Entertainment*, 20.

21 Ibid., 179.

22 John Fiske, *Understanding Popular Culture* (New York: Routledge, 2011), 73.

23 Todd Gitlin, *Media Unlimited: How the Torrent of Images and Sounds Overwhelms Our Lives* (New York: Henry Holt and Company, 2002), 62.

24 Fiske, *Understanding Popular Culture*, 46.

25 Fiske, *Power Plays, Power Works*, 256.

26 Quoted in Robert Mack and Brian Ott, *Critical Media Studies: An Introduction* (Malden, MA: Wiley-Blackwell, 2010), 116.

27 Deidre Pribram, *Emotions, Genre, and Justice in Film and Television* (New York: Routledge, 2011).

28 David Bordwell, *The Way Hollywood Tells It: Story and Style in Modern Movies* (Berkeley: University of California Press, 2006), 57.

29 Susan Wloszczyna, "Love's Actually Funny to Curtis," November 5, 2003, http://usatoday30.usatoday.com/life/movies/news/2003–11–04-curtis-profile_x.htm (accessed February 18, 2014).

30 Linda Williams, "Film Bodes: Gender, Genre and Excess," *Film Quarterly* 44, 4 (1991), 2–13.

31 Quoted in Bordwell, *Planet Hong Kong*, 5.

32 Yvonne Tasker, *Spectacular Bodies: Gender, Genre and the Action Cinema* (New York: Routledge, 1993), 60, 56.

33 Gitlin, *Media Unlimited*, 195.

34 David Bordwell, "A Glance at Blows," November 28, 2008, http://www.davidbordwell. net/blog/2008/12/28/a-glance-at-blows/ (accessed February 20, 2014).

35 For a comparison of the two styles, Bay versus Woo, see Matthias Stork's video "Chaos Cinema" at http://vimeo.com/28016047 (accessed May 22, 2014).

36 José Arroyo, ed. *Action/Spectacle Cinema* (London: British Film Institute, 2000), ix.

37 José Arroyo, "Mission: Sublime," in *Action/Spectacle Cinema*, ed. José Arroyo (London: British Film Institute, 2000), 24.

38 Ott, "The Visceral Politics of *V for Vendetta*," 49.

39 Daniel Cavicchi, "Loving Music: Listeners, Entertainments, and the Origins of Music Fandom in Nineteenth-Century America," in *Fandom: Identities and Communities in a Mediated World*, eds. Jonathan Gray, Cornel Sandvoss, and C. Lee Harrington (New York: New York University Press, 2007), 241.

40 Valerie Tweedle and Robert. J. Smith, "A Mathematical Model of Bieber Fever: The Most Infectious Disease of Our Time?," *Transworld Research Network* 37, 2 (2012), 8.

41 Barbara Ehrenreich, Elizabeth Hess, and Gloria Jacobs, "Beatlemania: Girls Just Want to Have Fun," in *The Adoring Audience: Fan Culture and Popular Media*, ed. Lisa A. Lewis (New York: Routledge, 1992), 85.

42 Sam Marsden, "Harry Potter Should Have Married Hermione, Admits JK Rowling," February 2, 2014, *Telegraph*, http://www.telegraph.co.uk/culture/harry-potter/10612719/ Harry-Potter-should-have-married-Hermione-admits-JK-Rowling.html (accessed February 25, 2014).

43 Kristin Thompson, *The Frodo Franchise: The Lord of the Rings and Modern Hollywood* (Berkeley: University of California Press, 2007), 190.

44 Marcus Doige, "Star Wars: 10 Treats We Want from Disney before 2015," March 8, 2013, http://whatculture.com/film/star-wars-10-treats-we-want-from-disney-before-2015.php#HAvj3pUFryxpeetD.99 (accessed February 25, 2014).

45 *Return of the King* won eleven Oscars in total including Best Picture, Best Director, and Best Adapted Screenplay. In total, the series garnered 30 Academy nominations and took home 17 awards, most for effects, design, and costuming.

46 Thompson, *The Frodo Franchise*, 141.

47 Quoted in Thompson, *The Frodo Franchise*, 190.

48 Steven Shaviro, *The Cinematic Body* (Minneapolis: University of Minnesota Press, 1993), viii.

REFERENCES

Ahmed, Sara. "Affective Economies." *Social Text* 22, 2 (Summer 2004): 117–139.

Arroyo, José, ed. *Action/Spectacle Cinema*. London: British Film Institute, 2000.

———. "Mission: Sublime." In *Action/Spectacle Cinema*, edited by José Arroyo, 21–25. London: British Film Institute, 2000.

Bacevich, Andrew. *The Limits of Power: The End of American Exceptionalism*. New York: Metropolitan Books, 2008.

Bansal, Sarika. "Soap Operas with a Social Message." January 26, 2012. http://opinionator. blogs.nytimes.com/2012/01/26/steamy-plots-with-a-social-message/.

Bordwell, David. "A Glance at Blows." November 28, 2008. http://www.davidbordwell. net/blog/2008/12/28/a-glance-at-blows/.

———. *Planet Hong Kong: Popular Cinema and the Art of Entertainment*. 2nd ed. Madison, WI: Irvington Way Institute Press, 2011.

———. *The Way Hollywood Tells It: Story and Style in Modern Movies*. Berkeley: University of California Press, 2006.

"Brazilian Soap Operas Shown to Impact Social Behaviors." January 29, 2009. http:// www.iadb.org/en/news/webstories/2009-01-29/brazilian-soap-operas-shown-to-impact-social-behaviors,5104.html.

Cavicchi, Daniel. "Loving Music: Listeners, Entertainments, and the Origins of Music Fandom in Nineteenth-Century America." In *Fandom: Identities and Communities in a Mediated World,* edited by Jonathan Gray, Cornel Sandvoss, and C. Lee Harrington, 235–249. New York: New York University Press, 2007.

Doige, Marcus. "Star Wars: 10 Treats We Want from Disney before 2015." March 8, 2013. http://whatculture.com/film/star-wars-10-treats-we-want-from-disney-before-2015. php—HAvj3pUFryxpeetD.99.

Dyer, Richard. *Only Entertainment.* New York: Routledge, 2002.

Ehrenreich, Barbara, Elizabeth Hess, and Gloria Jacobs. "Beatlemania: Girls Just Want to Have Fun." In *The Adoring Audience: Fan Culture and Popular Media,* edited by Lisa A. Lewis, 84–106. New York: Routledge, 1992.

Fiske, John. *Power Plays, Power Works.* New York: Verso, 1993.

———. *Understanding Popular Culture.* New York: Routledge, 2011.

Gitlin, Todd. *Media Unlimited: How the Torrent of Images and Sounds Overwhelms Our Lives.* New York: Henry Holt and Company, 2002.

Gray, Jonathan. *Television Entertainment.* New York: Routledge, 2008.

Grossberg, Lawrence. "Affect's Future: Discovering the Virtual in the Actual." In *The Affect Theory Reader,* edited by Melissa Gregg and Gregory J. Siegworth. Durham, NC: Duke University Press, 2010.

———. *Dancing in Spite of Myself: Essays on Popular Culture.* Durham, NC: Duke University Press, 1997.

———. *We Gotta Get out of This Place: Popular Conservatism and Postmodern Culture.* New York: Routledge, 1992.

Kubey, Robert. *Creating Television: Conversations with the People Behind 50 Years of American TV.* Mahwah, NJ: LEA, 2004.

Mack, Robert, and Brian Ott. *Critical Media Studies: An Introduction.* Malden, MA: Wiley-Blackwell, 2010.

Marcus, George. *The Sentimental Citizen: Emotion in Democratic Politics.* University Park: Pennsylvania State University Press, 2002.

Marsden, Sam. "Harry Potter Should Have Married Hermione, Admits J.K. Rowling." February 2, 2014. *Telegraph,* http://www.telegraph.co.uk/culture/harry-potter/10612719/Harry-Potter-should-have-married-Hermione-admits-JK-Rowling.html.

Massumi, Brian. *Parables of the Virtual: Movement, Affect, Sensation.* Durham, NC: Duke University Press, 2002.

Nye, Russel. *The Unembarrassed Muse: The Popular Arts in America.* New York: Dial Press, 1973.

Ott, Brian. "The Visceral Politics of *V for Vendetta:* On Political Affect in Cinema." *Cultural Studies in Media Communication* 27, 1 (March 2010): 39–54.

Pribram, Deidre. *Emotions, Genre, and Justice in Film and Television.* New York: Routledge, 2011.

Schechter, Harold. "The Bosom Serpent." In *Popular Culture Theory and Methodology: A Basic Introduction,* edited by Harold E. Hinds, Jr., Marilyn F. Motz, and Angela M.S. Nelson, 313–317. Madison: University of Wisconsin Press, 2006.

Shaviro, Steven. *The Cinematic Body.* Minneapolis: University of Minnesota Press, 1993.

Tasker, Yvonne. *Spectacular Bodies: Gender, Genre and the Action Cinema.* New York: Routledge, 1993.

Thompson, Kristin. *The Frodo Franchise: The Lord of the Rings and Modern Hollywood.* Berkeley: University of California Press, 2007.

Tweedle, Valerie, and Robert. J. Smith. "A Mathematical Model of Bieber Fever: The Most Infectious Disease of Our Time?" *Transworld Research Network* 37, 2 (2012): 1–21.

Williams, Linda. "Film Bodes: Gender, Genre and Excess." *Film Quarterly* 44, 4 (1991): 2–13.

Williams, Raymond. *Marxism in Literature.* New York: Oxford University Press, 1977.

———. *Politics and Letters.* New York: Verso, 1981.

Wloszczyna, Susan. "Love's Actually Funny to Curtis." November 5, 2003. http://usatoday30.usatoday.com/life/movies/news/2003–11–04-curtis-profile_x.htm.

CHAPTER 9

Is There a Global Popular Culture?

This chapter will examine in greater detail the tensions between unity and diversity, identity and difference raised in earlier chapters by looking at the global circulation of cultural goods. As we have seen, critics of popular culture have long worried that the industrialized production of culture will lead to a standardized and bland society where everyone looks the same, acts the same, and thinks the same. The intensified integration of social life on a global scale has only exacerbated these concerns by bringing traditional ways of life into contact with powerful outside influences. Many critics of globalization fear that once-distinct cultures will become homogenized, as global brands "invade" and remake societies from within. Other critics fear the opposite—that the threat of homogenization will lead to an uncritical defense of tradition as a mark of difference. In the memorable phrasing of political scientist Benjamin Barber, we will be left with either a bland McWorld or a chaotic Jihad.[1] But are these really our only options? Aren't there other ways to think about how cultural forms and practices circulate?

This chapter will provide an overview of debates about the global circulation of culture and its impact on identity construction. It will focus, in particular, on the recent processes of economic globalization and how they have enabled the transmission of cultural goods, services, and ideas across formerly rigid geographic and linguistic barriers. How do societies react when new cultural forms "invade" their space? What happens to older, more traditional identities and practices when people encounter new options? Because sport involves explicit rituals of identification and belonging—rituals that may differ depending on whether one is a player or a spectator but which invariably meld the individual into a group—various examples of sporting life will constitute the primary examples for this chapter. Global sports like basketball, cricket, and soccer, which are highly corporatized, commercialized, and mediatized, can provide some insight into the workings of the new global capitalism and its ethos of branding. Yet, as we will see, sports are not just about money and power. They are also about processes of identification and belonging that knit communities together and link them across time and space. If globalization often incites a panic about the "who we are question," sports provide a regular opportunity for people to confront and (try to) resolve that question.[2] By using sports as a cultural lens, we can examine the processes and effects of globalization in more minute detail.

WHAT IS GLOBALIZATION, AND HOW DOES IT RELATE TO CULTURE?

A standard definition of **globalization** might look something like this: "Globalization refers to the rapidly developing and ever-densening network of interconnections and interdependences that characterize modern social life."[3] New technologies of transportation and communication have not only enabled the cross-border flows of money, goods, people, ideas, and images; they have enabled such exchanges to proceed at a much faster pace and on a much more routine basis. While most studies of globalization focus on the economic and political effects of these intensified flows—how globalization has enabled the rise of transnational corporations, for example, or affected the capacity of nation-states to govern themselves, regulate the economy or protect the environment—we will be particularly concerned with the impact of globalization on cultural life and experience. How does the material fact of globalization change the way we think about the world and our place in it? How does it alter our sense of identity, our experience of place, and our commonsense assumptions about others in the world?

Generally speaking, the intensification and routinization of global flows reshapes our experience of local places and traditions by putting us in touch with the products, ideas, images, and life experiences of others. Even though we continue to live life locally, we *feel* as if our lives are economically, politically, socially, and culturally intertwined with the lives of distant others. It is important to remember that such interconnection is not experienced in the same way in all locations, however. Some peoples and places are more plugged in to the global circuits of capital than others. Some societies have more political sway than others, and some cultural resources travel more easily than others. In short, global connectivity is unevenly developed. The interconnections between the US and Europe are quite dense, and it is fairly easy for people from those countries to jet around the world, Skype with friends in distant places, and shop for exotic foods in their local supermarkets. Such privileged individuals likely experience globalization as a form of liberation from the everyday—a "spicing up" or enhancing of the local.

Yet, for other individuals and societies, living the global life is neither easy nor liberating. There are large swaths of the continents of Asia, Africa, and South America that are bypassed completely by the existing networks of global communication and transportation, for example. These are "fly over" spaces, only tangentially connected to the circuits of global capitalism. Most people in these regions experience globalization, not as a release from the confines of the local, but as an intensified form of social marginalization. They may feel as if globalization estranges them from their local roots and traditions, thereby robbing them of what little control they have over their lives. From their perspectives, it may seem like distant events and influences are "invading" the local and re-making it from within. Thus, they may perceive the social and cultural proximity of others as a threat, rather than a boon, and they may cling all the more tightly to traditions in the hope of preserving a sense of solidarity and security.

It is important to remember that globalization is not one process but many; it unfolds in fits and starts and moves in sometimes unexpected directions. As such, it may be experienced by different peoples in different ways. To some, "foreign" ideas are inherently antithetical to "local" cultures and identities. Iranian religious authorities, for instance, have long tried to block the influx of Western popular culture by banning everything from Madonna albums and Barbie dolls to satellite dishes. The belief is that Western cultural decadence will creep in alongside these amusements and undermine Iranian cultural traditions (most notably, the practice of Islam). Likewise, China recently began censoring reality television programs because their emphasis on individualism and materialism was perceived to be "too Western" (or insufficiently socialist). Others feel quite differently about the influx of new influences. They view "foreign" materials as vehicles for fresh thinking that can help break cultural stalemates, such as the one between tradition and modernity. Brian Larkin argues, for example, that Bollywood musicals became popular in Nigeria because they offered a new, but non-Western, way to think about modern relationships. They were different enough from traditional Nigerian films to be thought-provoking, but not so different as to be alienating (Indians and Nigerians both struggle with traditions of arranged marriage, for instance). By walking a fine line between modernity and tradition, Indian films were able to offer Nigerians resources for thinking about the effects of modernization in new ways. They provided a much-needed third way of being and belonging for Nigerians trapped between tradition and modernity, Nigerian ways and Western ones. As these examples suggest, globalization is not a uniform process that elicits a uniform response. The meaning and impact of globalization can only be determined through careful study of specific cultural interactions.

IS GLOBALIZATION A TYPE OF CULTURAL IMPERIALISM?

The uneven development of globalization and, specifically, the historical dominance of the global North and West over these networks of trade, transport, and communication, has led some to describe globalization as a form of **cultural imperialism**, which seeks to swamp local cultures in a sea of foreign goods and false idols. Proponents of the cultural imperialism thesis believe globalization involves homogenization, or the "synchronization [of experience] to the demands of a standardized consumer culture." The result of globalization, according to such arguments, is to "make everywhere seem more or less the same," that is, more or less like the US.[4] For many around the world, America has come to symbolize the processes of globalization. As *New York Times* columnist and globalization guru

Thomas Friedman puts it, "globalization often wears Mickey Mouse ears; it eats Big Macs, drinks Coca Cola or Pepsi and does its computing on an IBM PC, using Windows [software], with an Intel Pentium . . . processor and a network link from Cisco Systems." As a result, "people [outside the US] cannot distinguish anymore between American power, American exports, American cultural assaults, . . . and plain vanilla globalization."[5]

This fear of global cultural standardization relates to earlier fears about the influence of "mass culture" articulated by people like Dwight Macdonald (see Chapter 1) and the Frankfurt School critics, Theodor Adorno and Max Horkheimer (see Chapter 5). Recall that, for these men, commercially produced culture is formulaic and empty of genuine insight; its consumption dulls the senses and works to infantilize and pacify the population. Proponents of the cultural imperialism thesis worry about the damage such mass-produced culture can wreak overseas, on publics who are not trained from birth to recognize themselves in the reflections of Hollywood or Madison Avenue. They fear "authentic" cultures everywhere will be swamped in a tide of tawdry foreign schlock, or, worse, local publics will willingly toss aside local traditions in favor of foreign distractions. The result will be a type of "spiritual dry-rot" that hollows out the local culture and leaves no basis for community organizing.[6]

A variation on this argument, and one that has some utility in understanding the globalization of sport, is George Ritzer's **McDonaldization** thesis. Ritzer argues that contemporary life processes are being colonized by a particular kind of systems logic—the same logic the McDonalds Corporation uses to run its retail empire. The term "McDonaldization" does not just refer to the spread of McDonald's franchises around the world. It refers to the way "the principles of the fast-food restaurant are coming to dominate more and more sectors of American society as well as the rest of the world." These principles include an emphasis on efficiency, calculability, predictability, and control.[7] Every McDonalds restaurant in the world shares the same emphasis on the swift delivery of meals (efficiency); in mass quantities (calculability); of a uniform shape, size, and quality (predictability). Moreover, the interior of every McDonalds is carefully designed to control the flow of the food to the customer and to minimize human deviations from routine on either end (control). So, for example, the food production line is automated to ensure a uniform product and minimize the amount of human tinkering with the food. Seating space in the dining room is limited, and the furniture is decidedly uncomfortable (usually hard plastic) to discourage customers from lingering. Disposable plates, cups, and utensils also signal consumers that this is a meal to be gulped, rather than savored, and it all makes the maintenance of the dining area quicker and easier for the harried workers. Control, in this scenario, is ensured by the technological systems that precondition our every move. We do not need austere managers or fast food police to enforce the rules of decorum, for the tyranny of the system makes actual tyrants redundant. This is the essence of Ritzer's concerns—how we are increasingly controlled by the systems we ourselves have created.

More than the influence of American fast food habits on local cultures, Ritzer worries about the social and environmental impact of the irrationalities built into these rational systems. True, McDonalds' rationalization of the fast food process has made it quicker and easier to consume food of a predictable quality for little money (i.e., there is some good to the system), but it has also created economies of scale that are unsustainable in the long term. For example, McDonalds' need for large quantities of standardized food products (beef, potatoes, tomatoes, etc.) promotes large-scale, monocultural farming practices that are bad for the environment and drive down prices, making it hard for small farms to survive. Likewise, its preference for unskilled, temporary labor drives down wages and benefits and leaves workers vulnerable to economic, social, and psychic hardship. Many of these workers must turn to social service agencies to supplement their meager incomes, thereby straining the social safety net. In practical terms, the lower the cost of these workers to McDonalds, the higher their cost to society. Ritzer asks us to pay more attention to the long-term social consequences of implementing these structural changes.

In the end, what makes Ritzer's arguments about McDonaldization different from standard arguments about cultural imperialism is the emphasis on the structural changes wrought by American companies. According to Ritzer, this quintessentially American way of doing business, when exported, requires the complete overhaul of the material environment. In favoring a certain way of doing business, it makes other ways of doing business difficult to sustain.

CASE STUDY: THE McDONALDIZATION OF SPORTS

A similar argument could be made about the influence of globalization on local sporting traditions and cultures. According to historians of sport, the global diffusion of sport really took off during the late nineteenth century when the first international governing bodies were created and began to sanction international competitions and tours. Since then, "a global network of tournaments has grown in tandem with developments in air travel and television coverage."[8] As it became easier to stage and screen these international spectacles for global consumption, it also became desirable to monetize the whole exchange through broadcast rights and corporate sponsorship. Large multinational media corporations vie with each other for the right to carry global sporting events because they are "live" and watched by millions, sometimes billions, of adoring fans. Advertisers will pay a premium to rent airtime on such programs, believing they have a captive and receptive audience for their commercials. In addition to buying airtime on television, large corporations also bid against each other for the right to sponsor events like the Olympics and the FIFA (Fédération Internationale de Football Association) World Cup.

2010 FIFA World Cup in South Africa

The McDonaldization of global sports is most evident in global sports competitions like the Olympics or the FIFA World Cup. Such events are highly centralized, rationalized, commercialized and tied to televisual mediation. They provide efficient, calculable, predictable, and controlled entertainment. But how do such events affect local people?

The 2010 World Cup offers an interesting case study. The event was held in South Africa, the first (and perhaps last) African nation to host the tournament. Thirty-two teams from Europe, Asia, Africa, and the Americas participated in the event. Culturally, it was a very "global" event. The theme song, "Waka Waka," was performed by Colombian pop star Shakira (with the South African band Freshlyground) while the designated anthem, "Sign of Victory," featured American pop star R. Kelly (with the Soweto Spiritual Singers). A Brazilian fan trumpet called the "vuvuzela" briefly became a global fad as a result of the games, and the televised matches were watched by record crowds all over the world. FIFA estimates that 3.2 billion people watched at least some of the events; that is 46.4 percent of the global population! Almost 900 million watched at least a minute of the final between Spain and the Netherlands (won by Spain 1–0), and 619 million watched at least twenty minutes.[1] In Spain, 15.6 million people, or 86 percent of the viewing audience tuned into the final match, setting a record for the country. In the Netherlands, 8.5 million people, or 90 percent of the viewing audience, watched. Germany, France, Britain, Italy, and the US also broke viewing records during the tournament.[2]

Matches were held in ten stadiums, located in different cities throughout South Africa. Five of the stadiums had to be built for the event, and transportation infrastructure had to be upgraded to accommodate the crowds at a cost of 2.4 billion dollars (US). In all, the cost of the event was estimated to be 3.5 billion dollars. One hundred fifty thousand fewer foreign tourists showed up for the games than expected, and few local business people benefitted from the events since FIFA priced local food and souvenir vendors out of the market for stalls around the sporting venues. As with other major world sporting events, the host nation evicted local residents living in shantytowns near the venues and resettled them in scandalously bad public housing developments far away from the tourists. In the end, FIFA, which pocketed most of the money for television rights and sponsorship deals, made 2.5 billion dollars from the event compared to South Africa's 3.5 million dollars.[3]

Still, supporters claim the event produced intangible benefits for the country and the continent. In South Africa, it united the population around a central goal, lifted people's spirits, and created a positive buzz about the country, which organizers hope will lead to greater tourism. For the continent, the event showcased the emerging African societies and generated global good-will that should help with future economic development.

1 "Almost Half the World Tuned in at Home to Watch 2010 FIFA World Cup South Africa," July 11, 2011, http://www.fifa.com/worldcup/archive/southafrica2010/organisation/media/newsid=1473143/ (accessed March 1, 2014).
2 Todd Lamansky, "2010 FIFA World Cup Draws Record Ratings in USA, Europe, and Beyond," July 13, 2010, http://bleacherreport.com/articles/419916-2010-fifa-world-cup-draws-record-ratings-in-usa-europe-and-beyond/page/3 (accessed March 1, 2014).
3 David Goldblatt, "Footing South Africa's World Cup Bill " June 4, 2010, http://news.bbc.co.uk/2/hi/africa/8718696.stm (accessed March 1, 2014).

Thus, the globalization of sport has proceeded in tandem with the commercialization of competition, and it has reached a point where one commentator describes the overlapping interests as a "sports-media complex."[9] Within this complex, the meaning of sport has been transformed. It no longer means just "competitive physical activity" (a common dictionary definition of the term); sport now means "professionalized competition between commercially-sponsored teams, which is also susceptible to televisualization." If a sport can't be packaged, branded, and sold on TV, it hardly counts as a sport anymore. Similarly, if a leisure activity *can* be packaged, branded, and sold on TV, it may suddenly *become* a sport. Witness the emergence of poker, fishing, cheerleading, and Crossfit as "sports" regularly covered on the global cable sports channel ESPN.

How does the growth of this sports-media complex affect local sporting cultures? As you might expect, the results are highly uneven. For many individuals, teams, and sports, the increased attention has been a welcome boon, underwriting larger salaries and better working conditions for the athletes and increased profits for owners, advertisers, and broadcasters. Certainly, the global trade in sports stars enables some individuals from depressed economic regions to escape poverty and the insecurity that comes with it. The commercialization of sport also provides a second revenue stream for many athletes whose professional leagues would otherwise not pay a living wage. Female athletes, Olympic hopefuls, and athletes in non-traditional sports, like skateboarding or motocross, have all benefitted from the new emphasis on branding within the sports-media complex.

Still, the increasing standardization of what counts as sport has negative effects, as well. For one thing, it tends to favor the already well-established and wealthy leagues over emerging leagues in poorer locales. For example, in football (known as soccer in the US), the European leagues have benefited most from the new sports-media complex, and they have been able to poach star talent from leagues in North and South America, Asia and Africa. Leagues in those countries are being systematically underdeveloped, as stars leave for higher salaries and better sponsorships. Moreover, the emphasis on making money off of sports investments has altered the traditional workings of many sports leagues. When media mogul Rupert Murdoch invested five hundred million dollars to create an Australian Rugby Super-League in 1995, he also implemented new rules to help "rationalize and modernize the game along strictly commercial lines."[10] A casualty of this process was the working-class favorite South Sydney Rabbitohs (aka "The Souths"), a founding member of the original Australian Rugby League and beloved local club. The club's lack of profitability was cited as a rationale for eliminating it, and the plot would have succeeded but for a massive local outcry (more on the resistance later).

Entire sporting traditions are also being endangered by the move toward commercial rationalization and televisualization. In the US, baseball has been eclipsed as "America's pastime" by the more spectacular and faster-paced sport of football. Major League Baseball has attempted to accommodate this change by speeding up the game and adding a designated hitter (in 1973 to the American League) to ensure higher scoring. The desire to recapture lost audience share might also explain the rampant steroid use among players during the 1990s, and the baseball association's willingness to look the other way. Still, baseball continues to decline in popularity relative to the more telegenic sports of football and basketball. The decline of speed skating in Northern Europe offers another example. As anthropologist Thomas Hylland Eriksen notes, "speed skating was an undisputed national sport in Norway and the Netherlands" for over eighty years. "Swedes, Finns, Russians, Germans and others also competed in a serious way and their domestic media duly covered the international championships in a serious way."[11] Today, television channels only broadcast edited versions of the international meets and hardly cover local ones at all. As a result, speed skating has become "a quaint and old-fashioned activity in the eyes of many Norwegians" and is often side-lined in favor of more telegenic sports like free-style skiing and short-track skating (which is briefer, faster, and more of a contact sport). "Speed skating has too much complexity—the cultural entrance ticket is too expensive," Eriksen claims, to enable it to succeed in a competitive media environment.[12] And so, it has become another casualty of the sports-media complex.

These examples draw our attention to what may be most useful about the cultural imperialism thesis—its focus on the differential power relations at the heart of globalization. It may seem unfair to liken increased cultural influence to a type of imperial domination. Yet, by doing so, theorists of cultural imperialism have drawn much needed attention to the economic, political, and social systems that enable such influence. The term reminds us to attend to these structures and the ways they channel global flows in unequal ways. If cultural influence flows only in one direction or flows with such force as to, tsunami-like, wipe out local institutions and traditions, then domination may not be too strong a word to capture its effects.

WHAT ARE THE LIMITATIONS OF THE CULTURAL IMPERIALISM THESIS?

While the cultural imperialism thesis can help us attend to the structural forces that shape the global system, its practitioners often oversimplify the networks of cultural exchange and fail to ask about the impact of these forces on the ground. There are three major critiques of cultural imperialism with which you should be familiar: (1) it assumes that culture flows mainly from the West to the rest (and so ignores the way the West has been equally dis-located by global forces); (2) it ignores the flows of culture that circumvent the West entirely; and (3) it assumes local populations are passive, helpless, or unwilling to resist the onslaught of "foreign" goods. Let's look at each of these critiques in turn, using global sport as our primary lens.

First, by focusing exclusively on how developed nations influence others, proponents of the cultural imperialism thesis often ignore the way global flows have dis-located the West, as well. They assume the "West" remains a stable center of power even as globalization undermines the coherence of all spaces and abets the rise of new nodes of economic, political, and social authority. Consider, for instance, how the influx of foreign-born players into European national football clubs has affected the racial climate of Europe. The poaching of foreign stars, while designed to help the clubs succeed on the field, has also created a crisis of identity for many fans, who have responded by circling the wagons and attempting to repel the "foreign invaders." The result is that "in many European countries, soccer stadiums have become theaters of hatred; platforms from which neo-Nazis and racists can peddle their ideology."[13] Examples are not hard to find. In France, far right politician Jean Marie Le Pen and his National Front party have frequently denounced the national soccer team for having "too many black players." In Germany and Poland, neo-Nazis have used soccer matches to organize attacks on local ethnic minority communities, and in Italy fans frequently taunt their own players using racial slurs and monkey chants. This includes superstar Mario Bolatelli who, though of Ghanian descent, was born in Palermo and is an Italian citizen. During the Euro2012 finals in Poland, fans went so far as to hurl bananas at black players on the field. The Union of European Football Associations (UEFA) has started imposing fines on clubs who cannot control their fans, but it is fighting an uphill battle given the rise of far-right nationalist political parties across the region. These parties give expression to the fears of "ordinary" (white) Europeans that their countries are under attack by foreign influences. Unfortunately, the remedies they offer are both cruel and counter-productive. The genie of globalization is out of the bottle, and the boundaries that once distinguished here from there, us from them, and West from rest no longer hold. Proponents of the cultural imperialism thesis are so intent on measuring Western power that they fail to grasp the degree to which the West has become both de-Westernized and de-centered.

A second and related problem with the cultural imperialism thesis involves the failure to account for the local, regional, and global flows that by-pass the powerful Western networks of culture and commerce. As we have seen (in Chapter 6), regional cultural producers often hold more sway in non–English speaking regions than US or European producers, even the large multinational corporations. The popularity of the Korean wave in Asia, of Nigerian films in North Africa, of Mexican telenovelas in Latin American, of Turkish TV in the Middle East—all point to the growth of new centers of power within some sections of the global economy. Such regional transactions build connections between far-flung locales and disparate cultures just as surely as Hollywood films and the American recording industry do, but they happen without the interference of Western media corporations. Proponents of the cultural imperialism thesis rarely even see, let alone study, these cross-currents. It is a very Western-centric approach to global cultural transformations.

If soccer illustrates the way Western spaces are being dis-located from within, cricket might best illustrate the way Western powers are being dis-placed from without. Cricket, for those unfamiliar with the sport, is a complicated game played with a bat, a ball, and two eleven-man teams who alternate between batting and fielding. Any resemblance to American baseball is purely coincidental, however, as cricket matches can last for days and are played according to rules that may seem inscrutable to non-fans. As a game, it demands both physical grace and mental acumen from its players and endurance and discipline from its spectators. Cricket originated in Britain in the sixteenth century and became the national game by the nineteenth, though it was played primarily by the wealthy and used to teach the next generation the proper respect for order, discipline, and decorum. During the heyday of colonialism, British functionaries carried the game to the empire's far-flung colonies in Africa, Asia, and the West Indies, where it was used to instill a sense "Britishness" among the troops and reinforce a sense of British superiority over the local populations (who were new to the game, hence, bad at it).

However, this most British of games was quickly embraced by the indigenous populations and infused with local sensibilities and meanings. In India and Jamaica, for example, cricket became a focus of national identity and was used to express resistance to British rule. Now, former British colonies (namely, India, Pakistan, Bangladesh, Jamaica, Kenya, and South Africa) dominate the global game and regularly export their superstars into Britain. The International Cricket Council is currently run by authorities from South Asia and recently moved its headquarters from Britain to Dubai to be closer to the new seats of power in the game. Cricket—once a thoroughly "British" game—now circulates beyond the purview, sanction, or notice of British cultural authorities. It has become thoroughly de-Westernized and glocalized, or incorporated into various local sporting traditions to the point that it no longer seems "foreign." Rather than training colonial subjects in the art of "being British," it now articulates what it means to be Indian, Bangladeshi, South African, or Jamaican.

This brings us to the third and final criticism of the cultural imperialism thesis: it underestimates the capacity of local populations to select, use, alter, and even reject cultural influences. As Jonathan Inda and Renato Rosaldo argue, "Third World consumers faced with an imported text, media, or otherwise, will not simply or necessarily absorb [the] ideologies, values, and life-style positions [it carries]. Rather, they will bring their own cultural dispositions to bear on such a text, interpreting it according to their own cultural codes."[14] The glocalization of cricket is one example of this process, and, as we will see later, American baseball has become equally hybridized and localized, integrated into local sporting traditions in the

Caribbean, South America, Japan, South Korea, and many other locales. We might also look at the way in which American-style football has been *rejected* by most populations outside the US and Canada. Beginning in the 1990s, the American National Football League (NFL) attempted to increase the reach and impact of the game by financing various developmental leagues around the world. The first attempt, the World League of American Football, involved a handful of teams from smaller US cities, Canada, and Europe and folded after only four years (1991–1995). The second attempt, NFL Europe, lasted a bit longer (1995–2007) but never achieved the kind of popularity the NFL owners had hoped for. Except for Germany, which was able to sustain five teams and won most of the European football championships, the European franchises struggled with low attendance and had to fold for lack of revenue. Since then, the NFL has scrapped its overseas franchises and decided just to market the game through event programming, like the Super Bowl (the championship game of the NFL season) and the occasional regular-season game played overseas.

Lane Crothers attributes the failure of American-football abroad to the high cultural and economic barriers to entry.[15] Unlike soccer or basketball, which can be played with minimal investment, football requires large teams, lots of space, and expensive equipment. It also exacts a high toll on the body of the players, making it distasteful to many people. Finally, the rules of the game are arcane, its teams are unknown outside the US, and its stars are invisible behind their helmets and masks. Many Europeans mistake it for rugby and are confused when the rules play out differently. They do not recognize or celebrate American football stars and, according to one French fan, think the players are "steroid addicts and [wimps] for wearing helmets."[16] There is simply nothing familiar for foreign fans to grab onto, and so they largely haven't. There may also be some hostility to the game related to fears of Americanization. For example, the NFL never discussed a possible franchise in France perhaps because the French government has frequently blocked US attempts to extend the doctrine of free trade into the cultural arena, calling free trade a harbinger of American cultural imperialism. As this example illustrates, the economic power to project one's culture abroad does not automatically translate into cultural acceptance or influence.

Ultimately, proponents of cultural imperialism assume that the power to disseminate one's culture broadly will inevitably generate acceptance or influence. They treat culture as if it were a virus encoded with instructions for living, which, once injected into a host society, will replicate unchecked. Yet, societies have built up powerful cultural antibodies (traditions, rituals, and beliefs) through years of shared history and experience. When foreign matter enters the social system, these antibodies leap into action to block, neutralize, or absorb the threat. The case of NFL Europe offers a reminder that culture does not inhere in the products of the cultural industries; it is created by the people who encounter, interpret, and use those products.

The US cultural industries certainly do have a comparative advantage over others when it comes to flooding the global market with commodities; they do not have a monopoly over the processes of meaning-making, however. Certain preferred meanings may be encoded into cultural products, but there are always other possibilities available, and users may actively de- and re-construct these products to suit their local needs and desires. Thus, the result of globalization is not homogenization so much as cultural hybridization: new cultural mixtures, or mélanges, get produced as cultures travel and influence each other. Anthropologists call this process of cultural intermingling **transculturation**, or hybridization, and they argue that it is the norm, rather than the exception to the rule of cultural contact. One of the more interesting things to do when studying popular culture, then, is to study how cultural objects and practices meet, mingle, and get altered in the processes of contact.

HOW DOES TRANSCULTURATION WORK?

The cultural imperialism thesis is premised on an outmoded view of cultures as containers of tradition (we might call this the essentialist view of culture). In this model, when two cultures meet, one must give way before the other because neither can change in any substantive way. So, for example, American culture is singular and static. It is what it is for all time, and, when it travels, it merely imposes itself on others (swamping the local in a wash of "foreign" values) or exploits them for its own gain (stealing their assets and undermining their cultural infrastructure). Most anthropologists now reject this essentialist view of culture and favor an understanding of cultures as living systems that evolve and change. They would point out that "American culture" is really a *mélange* of cultural influences drawn from all over the world—from Europe, the Americas, Africa, and Asia. These influences have mingled over time and become so melded together that it is hard to discern an origin point for most American traditions. Moreover, as the main proponent of globalization, the US is very active in the world, and each point of contact results in new in-flows of immigrants, ideas, and customs, which remake the culture anew. Things that we now consider quintessentially American—jazz, rock 'n roll, French fries, pizza, mixed martial arts—all either came from elsewhere or were shaped by immigrant traditions from elsewhere. And, as practiced in America, these traditions are also not the same as they once were; they have been transformed as they have traveled. Something new has been created from the admixture and blending of cultural traditions and practices.

The term "transculturation" is designed to capture this process of intermingling and to focus on the new, hybrid cultural formations that result from a history of global contact. It asks how people selectively appropriate and recontextualize the semantic resources made available through global trade, and how their cultures and identities are altered in the process.[17] As an example of the process we might look at the global circulation of American baseball. Like soccer and cricket, baseball was formalized as a set of rules and activities in the nineteenth century and "travelled the colonial, military, and mercantile circuits of the world . . . creating a global sportscape of local followings, national pastimes and international rivalries."[18] Unlike soccer and cricket, however, it remains fairly localized in its development and resistant to integration at the global level. While there has been an International Baseball Federation (IBAF) since 1938, the organization largely oversees amateur competition. It rarely holds a Baseball World Cup (only thirty-five times in the last seventy-five years) and does not attract significant global attention when it does. Rather than a global sport, baseball represents a disjointed system of loosely interconnected national traditions, and most fans remain fairly localized in their tastes for the game.

For these reasons, anthropologist William Kelly likens the game of baseball to a language with many vernaculars. The US organization, Major League Baseball (MLB), may have originated the language of the game—codifying its rules and normalizing the practices of nationalization, commercialization, and professionalization, which others have copied—but most nations do not speak MLB baseball as a primary language. Players and fans learn their local baseball argot first and tend to prefer it strongly to other dialects. Cuban baseball fans do not care about the MLB or its teams and players, for example. They care about Cuban league dynamics, follow Cuban teams, idolize Cuban stars, memorize Cuban baseball statistics, and recite Cuban baseball history. That history often includes politically charged tales of victory over their arch-nemesis the US and colors the treatment of Cuban baseball stars who defect to play in the US (such players are described as "traitors," not just to the team, but to the nation). Baseball may have been brought to Cuba by Americans, but it has been utterly transformed in the process into a symbol of national heritage. Even communist leader Fidel Castro is a baseball fan, and he famously subsidized the sport as a national pastime after the Revolution.

CASE STUDY: JAPANESE BASEBALL

The process of transculturation is perhaps most evident in the development of Japanese baseball. Next to the US, Japan has the longest history of playing baseball and the largest spectatorship. The game was first introduced to the Japanese in 1872 by Horace Wilson, an American hired by the Japanese government to help modernize the Japanese school system. Wilson taught the game to his high school students because he thought they needed more exercise. It quickly caught on with the boys, and an amateur league formed as early as 1878. The growth of the sport was aided by a series of friendly matches between the local Ichiko team (the First High Schoolers) and the American-led, "whites only" Yokohama Athletic Club, which took place between 1896 and 1904. The Japanese squad took eleven out of thirteen games from the Americans (clubbing them twenty-nine to four in the first game). Those games were quickly imbued with nationalist sentiment and viewed as confirmation of the superiority of Japanese manners and methods. Between 1900 and 1930, intermittent "friendlies" between American and Japanese college and semi-professional teams helped to spread baseball fever and led to the formation of the first Japanese professional league in 1934. Now called the Nippon Professional Baseball (NPB) league, this organization systemized, rationalized, and commercialized the game, bringing it into line with its American cousin the MLB.[19]

Still, there are profound differences between baseball as played in the US and baseball as played in Japan. The rules are basically the same, but, in Japan, the ball is smaller, the strike zone is wider, and the fields are less ample (making some of them technically illegal in the US). Games are time limited and ties are allowed and even encouraged. Most importantly, the sport is practiced, played, and appreciated in a uniquely Japanese way. The Japanese consider *Yakyû*, or field ball, a martial art, rather than competitive sport. They believe the game teaches tenacity, discipline, and moral character and liken baseball players to the samurai warriors of medieval Japan. The sense of baseball as a martial art derives from the early Ichiko teams, who were known for their grueling practice schedules and intense discipline. Suishû Tobita, a legendary coach from Waseda University (now remembered as the "God of Baseball" in Japan), adopted this ascetic style and married it to a "team-first" ethic of absolute obedience to authority. According to historian Robert Whiting, Tobita viewed practice as the most important element of the game and demanded "the constant cultivation of tears, sweat and bleeding" from his players. "If the players do not try so hard as to vomit blood in practice," Tobita said, "they cannot hope

FIGURE 9.01 *Japan's Waseda University Team, 1916. Courtesy of the Library of Congress, Prints & Photograph Division.*

to win games. One must suffer to be good." Tobita's methods were so extreme they were called *shi no renhu,* or death training, but they were also so successful that the dedication to the ethos of practice remains fundamental to the Japanese game. To this day, games will be cancelled if players are unable to warm up and practice beforehand.[20]

In addition to the intensive training regimens, Japanese baseball is also played differently on the field than American baseball. The team comes first, and players, coaches, and fans alike value team spirit, or *wa,* above individual statistics or success. This impacts the game in a variety of ways. Americans see baseball as a straight-up, man-to-man competition along the lines of "Throw me your best pitch and let me see if I can hit." The Japanese play strategically, to avoid assertive competition and promote team goals.[21] Thus, homeruns and strikeouts, though spectacular and appreciated, are not the center of the Japanese game. According to one American journalist, "Strategy is what [the Japanese game is] about—bunting, hit and run, moving the man over. Giving yourself up for the good of the team."[22] The emphasis on strategy over spectacle, team over individual, is obviously very different from the American game and has led at least one former US player to say of the Japanese game: "This isn't baseball—it only looks like it."[23] Perhaps most galling, from an American perspective, is the Japanese tolerance for tie games. If neither team scores more runs in the allotted time frame, the teams earn a tie. In the minds of many Japanese fans, this is the preferred outcome because neither team loses face; in the minds of many Americans, however, it is sacrilege because no one came out on top. America loves a winner. The Japanese love the fight, and they will applaud the collective efforts of everyone involved regardless of the outcome if the fight was executed with admirable dedication.

This is not to say that Japanese fans lack discrimination or fail to play favorites. They are incredibly passionate about their teams, and the inter-squad rivalries can be incredibly intense. But it is to acknowledge that fandom may be enacted in different ways in different locales. This satirical take on the American song "Take Me Out to the Ball Game" captures some of these crucial differences:

> Oh, take me out to the besuboru game
> Take me out to the dome
> Buy me some dried squid and yakitori on a stick
> The orange-colored rabbit mascot is really a kick
> For it's bang the taiko drum for the home team
> But if they tie the other team, it'd be great
> One, Two, Three 'sanshin,' bow to the ump, and you're out
> At the old besuboru game.

Such a song might be sung during the seventh inning stretch in an American ballpark, but the Japanese do not practice that tradition. Instead, they beat pots and pans and taiko drums loudly throughout the game, and they break into local chants at seemingly random intervals. These chants are specifically designed for the local team and its fans and are far more colorful than the programmed music played between innings at a US park (one example is the Yomiuri Giants song "To the Sky with Fighting Soul, Ah Giants"). Such fervor has led one journalist to describe baseball in Japan as a religion, and the fans as devotees.[24] That sort of passion seems lacking in the US where baseball has been so thoroughly standardized that fan behaviors are cued by in-house organs, sound systems, and dynamic scoreboards. Even "Take Me Out To the Ball Game," which has been sung in US stadiums since 1908, is subtitled for fans who may not know the words. Such casualness with regard to baseball fandom would be utterly foreign in a Japanese stadium.

Cultural imperialism might explain how the NPB league has come to resemble MLB in its organization, administration, and financing, yet it cannot account for the way the US game has been translated by the Japanese into the local cultural idiom. Transculturation better captures this unpredictable process of translation and hybridization. US games were originally embraced by the state as a means of modernizing Japan. As such, baseball and other games have irrevocably transformed Japanese culture, but the transformation runs both ways. Major League baseball now looks to Japan for players and revenues. They have begun staging exhibition games between MLB teams in Japanese stadiums to cash in on the Japanese love of the sport, and most MLB teams have recruiters assigned to scout the Japanese leagues for new talent. Japanese players now regularly sign with American teams, and these players—men like Ichiro Suzuki and Yu Darvish—have injected a bit of Japanese style into the US game. Suzuki's work ethic, technical precision, speed, and high batting average (dependent mostly on singles) has earned admirers among US players and fans, and his "small-ball" style of play increasingly defines the post-steroids era of Major League Baseball. Darvish, meanwhile, commands an astounding array of pitches (eight, if you count his fast and slow curve as two), has incredible stamina on the mound, and, though he has one of the best fastballs in the game, prefers to use his off-speed pitches to strike batters out. In the US, pitchers are coddled and told to limit their pitching repertoire to "save their arms." Darvish has shown that there are other ways to preserve a pitcher's abilities (by building up stamina through practice and throwing a variety of pitches).

MLB has also been altered by the presence of foreign players from the Caribbean, Central and South America, Australia, and South Korea. Up to 30 percent of the players in MLB are now born outside the US, and their addition has inevitably altered the US game.[25] Currently, the debate centers around the flashy play of some Latino players, like young LA Dodgers right fielder Yasiel Puig or Milwaukee Brewers center fielder Carlos Gomez. US fans and sports writers criticize these players for celebrating home-runs, taunting the other team, and generally failing to "play the game the right way." As sports blogger Jorge Arangure, Jr., argues, however, "What exactly is the right way? . . . It may be that the [old-school] style of baseball that . . . was developed during a mostly all-white era, has been long-lasting, but that doesn't make it any better than another style of play. So far, no one has been able to convince me that admiring a home run or pumping a fist after striking someone out somehow damages the fabric of the game. It might be showy and, yes, in part egocentric, but it doesn't change anything about how baseball is actually played." He goes on to suggest that "baseball will have to adjust to the changing racial dynamic of the game."[26] As new players enter with different traditions and styles of play, the game will inevitably be altered, and some of these alterations will be for the good. As Arangure argues, we need to avoid the assumption that "foreign" automatically equals "bad."

CONCLUSION

Cultural anthropologists are not unaware of the power discrepancies that structure global flows. They know full well that the US has more power to influence others and to protect itself from unwanted influences. Yet, even the US cannot fully control the outcome of its attempts to spread its cultural values (witness the recent wars in Afghanistan and Iraq). When it comes to cultural goods, which are loosely tied bundles of semantic resources, a certain loss of control is virtually guaranteed. It may seem like the US dominates baseball globally—poaching players from overseas leagues, dominating the rule-governing organizations like the IBAF, and setting the ground rules for what counts as "baseball done right"—but, in fact, other baseball nations follow their own rules and traditions, and they sometimes actively contest US dominance in international forums. The World Baseball Classic, for example, is an American-engineered international competition rigged to profit MLB and help it conquer new markets for US-style baseball. The first Classic was held in 2006, only after Japanese objections to the US-centric format were addressed. The NPB rightly "felt that scheduling, logistics, rules and finances of the event" favored the MLB over other leagues and refused to participate until changes were made. Now an Asian nation hosts at least the first round of games in the Asian pool (otherwise, all venues are located either in the US or the US-province of Puerto Rico).[27] In 2013, the Japanese Players Union threatened to boycott unless the NPB were given a larger share of the sponsorship and licensing revenue. As Japan has won two of the first three events and their fans are the most avid, MLB had little choice but to capitulate.[28]

Similarly, Rupert Murdoch's scheme to create a new Australian rugby league backfired on him when he decided to expel the beloved South Sydney Rabbitoh's for underperforming economically. "The Souths" supporters fought back by organizing a massive demonstration that drew eighty thousand Australians, many of whom were not even rugby fans. As sociologists David Andrews and George Ritzer explain, the club's long-term association with the working-class community of Redfern turned "the South's travails . . . [into] something of a metaphor for working-class communities in Australia in general." According to the legendary Rabbitoh's coach George Piggins, "[People] were there because what had happened to us was a symbol of what was happening elsewhere in Australia . . . as giant corporations cut and closed, downsized and played havoc with the lives of ordinary people."[29] Sport, which is often portrayed as a form of distraction that breeds political passivity, here became a beacon around which to rally the troops. People turned out to support the Souths, but they also turned out to register their objections to the unrestrained form of economic globalization represented by Rupert Murdoch and his global media empire. In the end, Murdoch had to back down and reinstate the Souths in order to end the public relations nightmare.

What these examples illustrate is that globalization is neither natural nor inevitable in its progression or outcomes. People can and do intervene in the construction, interpretation, and use of global connections, and they will circumvent the authorities and the authorized channels if necessary. When confronted with forces beyond their control, most people will seek to maximize the positive effects those forces bring while mitigating the negative. Cultural forms are vital resources through which they try to do this. By following football/soccer, baseball, cricket, or the Olympics, people seek distraction, true, but they also learn to recognize, negotiate, and map the contours of the global systems that increasingly impinge on their daily lives (a la the "Souths" controversy in Australia). They also use sports rituals to forge (or renew) the identities and alliances that will sustain them through the social upheaval.

Oddly, ESPN seems to grasp this better than many economists. Its latest marketing campaign, "It's not crazy. It's sports," details the outlandish ways fans show their love for their favorite teams. The series is the culmination of extensive in-house research into fan practices, which, of course, ESPN has only undertaken as a means to better capitalize on fan love (see the section on affective economics in Chapter 6). Still, the commercials resonate because they capture something about the way fandom works. From the creation of colloquialisms like "Roll, Tide" to the branding of burial caskets and urns, the series shows how fans use rituals to cement their identities and social relations. One of my favorite spots, "Born To It," captures precisely the tensions between homogenization and hybridization at the heart of

FIGURE 9.02 *A frame from "Born Into It," one of the ESPN promotions in the series "It's Not Crazy. It's Sports" (2012).*

globalization. Using a split screen (that often merges into one), the commercial tracks two working-class British lads—one a fan of Manchester United (the Blues) and the other a fan of Manchester City (the Reds)—as they imagine their lives as a supporter of the other side. "If I'd a been born a Blue/Red," both lads say, "I'd a been . . . a miserable git." Their lives are essentially the same—they have families of the same size and temperament, work the same dead-end job, speak the same language with the same accent, and have virtually the same girlfriend (both named Becky)—but their love of the Blue or Red makes all the difference in their sense of who they are and what they can accomplish.

Proponents of the cultural imperialism thesis might look at this and see the similarities: both lads seem to be mindlessly consuming the bread and circuses offered by those in power to distract from the realities of their increasingly miserable lives. For the lads themselves, though, sports fandom provides a much-needed sense of purpose and social solidarity. It helps them understand who they are, where they came from, and how they fit into a changing society. The rituals may be essentially the same—and they may be underwritten by greedy corporations who simply want to profit from selling more tickets and jerseys—but these rituals still produce profound cultural differences for the individuals who engage in them. How people interact with the cultural resources globalization provides them, how they interpret and make sense of these resources—these are the questions that matter for the cultural study of globalization.

In the end, globalization is not likely to result in either homogenization (McWorld) or differentiation (Jihad), but both at once. In many ways, humanity will be drawn closer together culturally, and this will likely involve some degree of Americanization given the outsized influence of American governmental agencies, corporations, and products around the world. In other ways, our cultures will become more varied, more dynamic, and more plural, as we all encounter new ideas, new practices, new stories, and new people. Some of these changes will be for the good; others may be for the bad, but the only way we can assess the value of change is by studying it in context. Toward that end, I want to conclude this chapter with a series of questions students of popular culture might find useful when thinking about globalization as a cultural phenomenon.

QUESTIONS TO ASK OF POPULAR CULTURES IN CIRCULATION

- How do cultural mores or commodities travel? Along what routes and through what carriers (via people like migrants, institutions like the military, or media networks like film and TV distribution channels or the internet)?

- Who controls or directs these routes, and who is marginalized by them? What are the power equations involved in the processes of cultural dissemination?

- Why do some cultural resources travel better than others? What factors affect the accessibility and usability of these resources?

- How do people interact with, or use, the cultural resources globalization makes available to them?

That last question entails several additional questions, including:

- What meaning and value do people ascribe to these new influences or resources? How do they fit them into their everyday lives (or not)?

- Is the outcome of cultural contact best described as acceptance, rejection, or selective appropriation in any given instance? Do you find evidence of increased homogenization (a la McDonaldization), increased conflict (a la Barber's concept of Jihad), or increased hybridization (a la transculturation)?

- How should we assess the value of these possibilities? Is homogenization always "bad"? Is the preservation of local traditions always "good"? Is hybridization "good" or "bad" (and what would make it so)?

- Does it matter who controls the process of transculturation? What happens, for example, when corporations lead the charge for localization by indigenizing their global brands? How should we assess that?

- Finally, and most importantly, how do the people affected by or involved in these processes feel about them? *How do the people make sense of globalization?*

SUMMARY

- Globalization refers to the increased cross-border traffic in money, goods, people, ideas, and images enabled by new technologies of communication and transportation.

- A cultural approach to globalization asks how these new economic, political, and social ties are being experienced by people. How does globalization change the way people think about the world and their place in it?

- Globalization has been implemented unevenly and so is experienced by different peoples in different ways. Some experience it as liberating while others find it increases their marginalization and lack of control over their destinies.

- The cultural imperialism thesis enables us to see how certain structural forces can lead to cultural homogenization, but its proponents

> fail to account for backflows (the impact of foreign influences on the "powerful" nations); regional circuits of influence; and local practices of appropriation, transculturation, and resistance.
>
> • Globalization is neither natural nor inevitable in its progression or outcomes. People can and do intervene in the construction, interpretation, and use of global connections. How they do so is the interesting question.

NOTES

1 Benjamin Barber, *Jihad vs. Mcworld: How Globalism and Tribalism Are Reshaping the World* (New York: Random House, 1996).
2 Franklin J. Lechner, "Imagined Communities in the Global Game: Soccer and the Development of Dutch National Identity," in *Globalization and Sport*, eds. Richard Giulianotti and Roland Robertson (Malden, MA: Blackwell Publishing, 2007), 109.
3 John Tomlinson, *Globalization and Culture* (Chicago: University of Chicago Press, 1999), 2.
4 Ibid., 6.
5 Thomas L. Friedman, *The Lexus and the Olive Tree: Understanding Globalization* (New York: Anchor Books, 2000), 366.
6 Richard Hoggart, *The Uses of Literacy* (New Brunswick, NJ: Transaction Publishers, 2006 [1958]), 190.
7 George Ritzer, *McDonaldization of Society*, 5th ed. (Thousand Oaks, CA: Sage Publications, 2007), 1.
8 Barry Smart, "Not Playing Around: Global Capitalism, Modern Sport and Consumer Culture," in *Globalization and Sport*, eds. Richard Giulianotti and George Ritzer (Malden, MA: Blackwell Publishing 2007), 9.
9 Ibid., 18.
10 David L. Andrews and George Ritzer, "The Grobal in the Sporting Glocal," in *Globalization and Sport*, 38.
11 Thomas Hylland Eriksen, "Steps to an Ecology of Transnational Sports," in *Globalization and Sport*, 53.
12 Ibid., 54.
13 Richard Gizbert, "Racism at Italian Soccer Matches," July 1, 2012, *ABC News*, http://abcnews.go.com/WNT/story?id=130886 (accessed December 8, 2013).
14 Jonathan Xavier Inda and Renato Rosaldo, "Tracking Global Flows," in *The Anthropology of Globalization*, eds. Jonathan Xavier Inda and Renato Rosaldo (Malden, MA: Wiley-Blackwell, 2007), 16.
15 Lane Crothers, *Globalization & American Popular Culture*, 2nd ed. (Lanham, MD: Rowman & Littlefield Publishers, Inc., 2009), 146–147.
16 Clement Fockett, "NFL Crusade in Europe: A French View," April 9, 2008, http://bleacherreport.com/articles/16985-nfl-crusade-in-europe-a-french-point-of-view (accessed December 8, 2013).
17 Richard A. Rouse, "From Cultural Exchange to Transculturation: A Review and Reconceptualization of Cultural Appropriation," *Communication Theory* 16 (2006), 491.
18 William W. Kelly, "Is Baseball a Global Sport? America's 'National Pastime' as Global Field and International Sport," in *Globalization and Sport*, eds. Richard Giulianotti and George Ritzer (Malden, MA: Blackwell Publishing, 2007), 79.
19 Robert Whiting, *You Gotta Have Wa* (New York: Vintage Books, 1990), 27–51.
20 Ibid., 37–38. See also Kelly, "Is Baseball a Global Sport," 89–90.

21 Nick Canep, "Baseball Takes Funny Bounces in Japan," 1989, http://japanesebaseball.com/writers/display.gsp?id=41941 (accessed December 17, 2013).

22 Gary Warner, quoted in Kelly, "Is Baseball a Global Sport," 87.

23 Kelly, "Is Baseball a Global Sport," 88.

24 Canep, "Baseball Takes Funny Bounces in Japan."

25 "Percentage of Foreign Players Rises," April 5, 2012, *ESPN: MLB,* http://espn.go.com/mlb/story/_/id/7779279/percentage-foreign-major-league-baseball-players-rises (accessed December 17, 2013).

26 Jorge Arangure, "The Changing Face of Baseball," October 3, 2013, *Sports on Earth,* http://www.sportsonearth.com/article/62352290/ (accessed December 16, 2013).

27 Kelly, "Is Baseball a Global Sport," 82.

28 "Japan Baseball Players Back Off Boycott Threat," September 5, 2012, *New York Times,* http://www.nytimes.com/2012/09/05/sports/baseball/japan-baseball-players-back-off-boycott-threat.html?_r=0 (accessed December 20, 2013).

29 Andrews and Ritzer, "The Grobal in the Sporting Glocal," 38–39.

REFERENCES

Andrews, David L., and George Ritzer. "The Grobal in the Sporting Glocal." In *Globalization and Sport,* edited by Richard Giulianotti and George Ritzer, 28–45. Malden, MA: Blackwell Publishing, 2007.

Arangure, Jorge. "The Changing Face of Baseball." October 3, 2013. *Sports on Earth,* http://www.sportsonearth.com/article/62352290/.

Barber, Benjamin. *Jihad vs. Mcworld: How Globalism and Tribalism Are Reshaping the World.* New York: Random House, 1996.

Canep, Nick. "Baseball Takes Funny Bounces in Japan." 1989. http://japanesebaseball.com/writers/display.gsp?id=41941.

Crothers, Lane. *Globalization & American Popular Culture.* 2nd ed. Lanham, MD: Rowman & Littlefield Publishers, 2009.

Eriksen, Thomas Hylland. "Steps to an Ecology of Transnational Sports." In *Globalization and Sport,* edited by Richard Giulianotti and George Ritzer, 46–57. Malden, MA: Blackwell Publishing, 2007.

Fockett, Clement. "NFL Crusade in Europe: A French View." April 9, 2008. http://bleacherreport.com/articles/16985-nfl-crusade-in-europe-a-french-point-of-view.

Friedman, Thomas L. *The Lexus and the Olive Tree: Understanding Globalization.* New York: Anchor Books, 2000.

Gizbert, Richard. "Racism at Italian Soccer Matches." July 1, 2012. *ABC News Online,* http://abcnews.go.com/WNT/story?id=130886.

Hoggart, Richard. *The Uses of Literacy.* New Brunswick, NJ: Transaction Publishers, 2006 [1958].

Inda, Jonathan Xavier, and Renato Rosaldo. "Tracking Global Flows." In *The Anthropology of Globalization,* edited by Jonathan Xavier Inda and Renato Rosaldo, 3–46. Malden, MA: Wiley-Blackwell, 2007.

"Japan Baseball Players Back Off Boycott Threat." September 5, 2012. *New York Times,* http://www.nytimes.com/2012/09/05/sports/baseball/japan-baseball-players-back-off-boycott-threat.html?_r=0.

Kelly, William W. "Is Baseball a Global Sport? America's 'National Pastime' as Global Field and International Sport." In *Globalization and Sport,* edited by Richard Giulianotti and George Ritzer, 79–93. Malden, MA: Blackwell Publishing, 2007.

Lechner, Franklin J. "Imagined Communities in the Global Game: Soccer and the Development of Dutch National Identity." In *Globalization and Sport,* edited by Richard Giulianotti and Roland Robertson, 107–121. Malden, MA: Blackwell Publishing, 2007.

"Percentage of Foreign Players Rises." April 5, 2012. *ESPN: MLB.* http://espn.go.com/mlb/story/_/id/7779279/percentage-foreign-major-league-baseball-players-rises.

Ritzer, George. *McDonaldization of Society,* 5th ed. Thousand Oaks, CA: Sage Publications, 2007.

Rouse, Richard A. "From Cultural Exchange to Transculturation: A Review and Reconceptualization of Cultural Appropriation." *Communication Theory* 16 (2006): 474–503.

Smart, Barry. "Not Playing Around: Global Capitalism, Modern Sport and Consumer Culture." In *Globalization and Sport,* edited by Richard Giulianotti and George Ritzer, 6–27. Malden, MA: Blackwell Publishing 2007.

Tomlinson, John. *Globalization and Culture.* Chicago: University of Chicago Press, 1999.

Whiting, Robert. *You Gotta Have Wa.* New York: Vintage Books, 1990.

CHAPTER 10

Does Popular Culture Make Us Smarter or Dumber?

This chapter addresses concerns about the impact of popular culture on our critical sensibilities. As we will see, such debates have been with us for a long time, but they have taken on a new urgency in recent years due to the emergence of a wealth of new media technologies, like computers, the internet, and smartphones. According to new media enthusiasts, by making more information available to more people, these technologies have empowered individuals to become their own knowledge producers and curators. The result, according to *Time* magazine's editors, has been an" explosion of productivity and innovation" that promises to revolutionize the way we live. In naming "You" Person of the Year for 2006, the editors celebrated you for using Web 2.0 technologies to "[seize] the reins of the global media, . . . [found] and [frame] the new digital democracy, . . . [work] for nothing and [beat] the pros at their own game." In the very next breath, however, the editors outlined some of the potential problems with this "revolution": "Web 2.0 harnesses the stupidity of crowds as well as [their] wisdom. Some of the comments on YouTube make you weep for the future of human- ity just for the spelling alone, never mind the obscenity and the naked hatred."[1] Other critics cite the shallowness and group-think that arise as a result of a lazy use of Google to filter the plethora of information these technologies make available.

These sorts of debates date back at least to the time of Plato's *Republic* (B.C. 380). Using Socrates as an interlocutor, Plato famously banished poets from his ideal society because their works catered to the emotions, thereby undermining the capacity for rational thought and, by extension, just governance. Such a long history of debate might make it seem like the issues are unresolvable and, therefore, irrelevant. Critics should just agree to disagree and get on with their lives. I would argue instead that such debates recur because they are "good to think with." When we debate the role of popular culture in the good society, we are actively contributing to the formation of that society. Entailed in the debate are a whole raft of questions about what we want for ourselves and our communities: What should we value, and why should we value it? What are our most pressing problems, and what are the roots of those problems? What tools do we need to solve those problems, and how should we arrange things so as to maximize our potential as a society? Thus, the debates are not a dead-end, but a new start. They give us an opportunity to think about and adjust to social change.

Whether any particular instance of popular culture is bad for us or not, then, the debates we stage about popular culture are good for us, and we ought to spend some time engaging with the arguments. In what follows, we will do just that, using the title questions of key works on the subject to organize the material. One section will deal with Neil Postman's 1985 question: "Are we amusing ourselves to death?" Another will ask, ala more recent polemics by Nick Carr (*The Shallows*, 2011) and Mark Bauerlein (*The Dumbest Generation*, 2009): "Do digital media make us stupid?" Finally, following several discussions of social media and political mobilization, we will inquire: "Are digital media bad for democracy?" Before we get to those discussions, however, we must take a short detour through theory in order to understand the approach most of these authors take to the role of media in society. That approach is best described as **media ecology**, a term coined by Postman to capture the way media work *as* environments and also *shape* our environments.

MEDIA ECOLOGY: THE MEDIUM IS THE MESSAGE

Media ecology focuses on the ways different media influence our social lives. Media ecologists presume that each medium has different technological capabilities and limitations—often called affordances—and different rules of engagement, or protocols, which define their use. The goal of media ecology is to study the logics surrounding different media, rather than their messages. As Neil Postman puts it, "media ecology looks into the matter of how media of communication affect human perception, understanding, feeling and value." The word ecology is used deliberately to suggest "the study of environments: their structure, content, and impact on people in their daily lives."[2] If a medium is an environment—a complex integrated system for living—the question becomes: what are the components of that environment, and how do different environments shape our perceptions, values, and actions differently?

Two examples might suffice to demonstrate the method. The first is a simple illustration of the way different technologies exercise different parts of our sensorium, thereby affecting our behaviors, often without us even being aware it. In his book *The Shallows*, Nicholas Carr explains how philosopher Friedrich Nietzsche, ill and losing his sight at the age of 34, bought a typewriter and learned to compose by feel, so he could continue writing. Though he did not keep the machine for long, while he used it, it caused a subtle change in the shape and quality of his writing. His prose became "tighter, more telegraphic," and "there was a new forcefulness to it, as though the machine's power . . . was . . . being transferred into the words it pressed into the page." Instead of writing in long, detailed paragraphs, he began to write in aphorisms—short bursts of thought designed to convey truth with immediacy and impact, like the following: "What is done out of love always takes place beyond good and evil."[3] Nietzsche's typewriter illustrates how the technologies we use may also use us, subtly altering our behaviors to suit their logics.[4]

The second example illustrates how different media can alter the way we construct a vision of the world. According to Postman, the invention of the telegraph in the 1830s "destroyed the prevailing definition of information, and, in doing so, gave a new meaning to public discourse." Before the telegraph, the information conveyed through newspapers was local and functional, "tied to the problems and decisions readers had to address in order to manage their . . . affairs." After the telegraph, "relevance became irrelevant," as newsagents prioritized the novelty of information over its utility. Suddenly, what mattered most was how much information could be delivered, from how far away, and at what speed. Radio and television each exacerbated the emphasis on instantaneity and liveness, producing what Postman calls a "peek-a-boo world, where now this event, now that, pops into view for a moment, then vanishes again." How did this new definition of information affect people's ways of thinking? According to Postman, it changed the way we define and use our intelligence. In place of historical depth and context, electronic media provided breadth and speed. After the telegraph, intelligence came to be equated with "knowing *of* lots of things, not knowing *about* them."[5] Postman, for one, believes this transformation is bad for society because it leaves people ill-equipped to engage in the sort of informed debate that democracies require. We will come back to this argument in a minute, but, for now, the point is that electronic media have profoundly altered the way we look at and engage the world.

You'll note that neither of these examples refers to the content of the messages being transmitted via typewriter or telegraph. The emphasis is on the nature of the transmission process and how that affects the way we think and act. Media theorist Marshall McLuhan argued that the messages carried by media systems mattered far less than the systems themselves. "The medium," he argued, "*is* the message." According to McLuhan, different media possess different characteristics, or **media biases.** These biases produce different "sensory balances," which cause us to think and act in different ways. Cultures that rely on oral transmission, for example, tend to be tight-knit, group-oriented, and tradition-bound. Because they must retain information in their memories, they focus on building knowledge that is concrete, functional, and additive; ideas are passed from generation to generation and accrue weight only if they prove useful. Such societies are also highly participatory and agonistic, meaning they encourage active engagement and debate as a way of testing knowledge claims. Print societies, by contrast, emphasize abstraction, linear thinking, and rationality over sensory experience. They are able to preserve memories more effectively and so preserve more of them (i.e., they are less tradition-bound than oral cultures). The transition from oral media of communication to print ones also "shifted our sensory experience of the world from predominately one of sound, which is group-oriented, to one of sight, which is individually oriented."[6] The transition to a culture of reading enabled group ties to be stretched across time and space—newspapers and novels could help us imagine ourselves as part of a national community, for example—but those ties also became weaker. Such virtual ties lack the intimacy and intensity of the bonds forged through face-to-face encounters with others.

Electronic media have altered the sensory balance yet again, with what many perceive to be dire consequences. According to Robert Mack and Brian Ott, electronic media are nonlinear and decentered; that is, they do not have clear beginnings and endings and do not promote sequential thinking. They are also dynamic and open-ended; rather than fixed systems of meaning (like books), electronic media promote seriality and enable constant updating (as in film franchises or TV series). Instead of one-way communication from writer to reader, electronic media promote interactivity and collaboration between cultural producers and consumers; indeed, they make the distinction between producer and consumer somewhat obsolete. And, finally, electronic media rely on images and icons instead of text-based symbols to convey meaning; as a result, the message may be processed more quickly, easily, and in a more associational (rather than logical) fashion. Since many of the traits of electronic media recall traits of oral societies—the emphasis on group-orientation, participation, and associational thinking, for example—some theorists describe the electronic age as a second age of orality. Yet, significant differences exist between oral societies and electronic ones. For example, virtual communities foster "weaker" (i.e., more horizontal and temporary) ties than face-to-face communities of shared experience. They are not as tradition-bound as oral ones, and they nurture different forms of intelligence and discourse. What are the likely ramifications of these differences? What happens when we move from "strong" to "weak" ties? How will the embrace of the ever-new affect the way we live our lives and organize our resources? How does the function of memory change with the changed sensory balance? How is debate staged differently in these different environments? These are the sorts of questions that animate the on-going debates over the meaning and value of media changes.

ARE WE AMUSING OURSELVES TO DEATH?

What is the proper balance between the body and the mind, pleasure and discipline? Can the wrong mixture of these elements actually be bad for society? Is it possible to amuse ourselves to death, and, if so, which media are likely to lead us down that road and which are likely to lead us onto other paths? Critics of popular culture have long blamed new media for promoting entertainment and distraction over seriousness and rational thought. What is interesting, though, is that the type of media hardly matters to these debates; only its newness matters. Plato banished poetry from the ideal republic because it appealed to the emotions over the intellect and threatened to make the people irrational, hence ungovernable. His objection is that poetry, even when spoken orally, adheres to different protocols of use. As a mode of discourse, it foregrounds artistry as an end, rather than a means to an end. What a poem says matters less than how well the message can be wrapped and delivered. Plato feared that poetry would influence the construction of social discourse more broadly, moving it away from matters of substance and favoring matters of style.[7]

The development of writing and print elicited similar fears from social authorities. In a later dialogue called *Phaedrus,* Socrates (via Plato) objects to the notion that writing would improve human intelligence by enhancing human memory. Speaking through an interlocutor named Thamus, Socrates responds that "this invention will produce forgetfulness in the minds of those who learn to use it, because they will not practice their memory." He warns that writing is a tool "not of memory, but of reminding"; it fosters "the appearance of wisdom, not true wisdom."[8] When we write our thoughts down, according to Socrates, we relieve ourselves of the duty of constructing complex associations in our minds. As a result, our minds become weaker, and our capacity to weigh the social good is impaired.

Other arguments against writing, especially print, centered on its likely moral influence. Prior to the invention of the printing press in the fifteenth century, books were rare and expensive, and few people possessed the basic literacy skills necessary to read one. Only aristocrats and the clergy (priests and monks) had regular access to written material, and their social authority rested on this monopoly over information. The printing press enabled books and other material to be reproduced at a much faster rate and in many languages, making the printed word more easily available to more people and threatening the elite monopoly over knowledge. As Carr explains, Europe experienced a wave of teeth-gnashing at the prospect of commoners reading for themselves: "The Italian humanist Hieronimo Squarciafico worried that the easy availability of books would lead to intellectual laziness, making men 'less studious' and weakening their minds. Others argued that cheaply printed books and broadsheets would undermine religious authority, demean the work of scholars and scribes, and spread sedition and debauchery."[9] And, as the Protestant Reformation (1517–1648) proved, these critics were not entirely wrong: the print revolution did undermine the authority of the Roman Catholic Church and its preferred language (Latin).

The clamor over the printing press only grew louder in the eighteenth and nineteenth centuries, as printers began catering to the tastes of this enlarged public by printing travel accounts, political pamphlets, chap books, and eventually novels. As literary historian Cathy Davidson notes, "prose fiction [was] perceived as a subversive literary form in every Western society into which it was introduced," in part, because it required little formal education to access and, in part, because it "replaced the authority of the sermon or Bible with the enthusiasms of sentiment, horror, and adventure." While we now equate the arrival of print with the Age of Reason, back then social authorities, like the second president of the United States, John Adams, saw things very differently. Adams described the printing press as the harbinger of the "Age of Folly, Vice, Frenzy, Brutality, Daemons, Buonaparte, [and] Tom Paine." For him, it marked "the Age of the burning Brand from the bottomless Pit: or anything but the Age of Reason."[10]

Critics were particularly concerned about the effect of novel-reading on the impressionable minds of women and children. Novels, the critics claimed, were seductive. They could "soften hearts" and manipulate minds, and many a critic described novel reading as "a cause of female depravity" that unsuited women for their duties as wives and mothers. Others worried about youth culture more broadly: "The free access which many young people have to romances, novels, and plays has poisoned the mind and corrupted the morals of many a promising youth." Like many critics to follow, this one went on to liken popular fiction to intellectual junk food: "Parents take care to feed their children with wholesome diet; and yet how unconcerned about the provision for the mind, whether they are furnished with salutary food, or with trash, chaff, or poison."[11] Behind such arguments looms a fear of social change—the empowerment of workers, women and youth, for example—but also a presumption that entertainment and intelligence are inherently antithetical. One could either have fun or one could think, but one could not do both simultaneously.

Defenders of the novel understood the fallacy involved in the artificial separation of mind from body. Novels, they declared, extolled literacy, inspired a love of learning, and enabled deep thought about social and moral dilemmas, and they worked *more* effectively for tugging the heartstrings. Davidson examined hundreds of early American novels and found that most "inspired education by stressing the sentimental and social value of literacy." By offering literate characters as role models and ideals, they moved people to become better readers and taught them the value of introspection. Author Charles Brockden Brown similarly defended the novel as a type of moral instruction. By humanizing social dilemmas, he claimed, novels gave millions of readers who might otherwise have no access to moral philosophy a chance to ruminate on questions of life and death, right and wrong. Finally, at a time when access to the public sphere was highly restricted, novels gave many readers (especially women) access to meaningful information about the social and political events of the day, information that would otherwise have been withheld from them. Discussing a novel like *Uncle Tom's Cabin* (1852) was an approved way for women, children, and other subaltern groups to engage in social debates about the morality of slavery. *Uncle Tom's Cabin* showed that novels could do more than simply distract their readers; they could inform, enlighten, and uplift them. They provide what literary theorist Kenneth Burke called "equipment for living," symbolic resources that audiences can use to negotiate real-world dilemmas.[12]

Today novels and novel-reading fall mostly on the good side of the intellectual ledger, the presumption being that reading of any sort promotes literacy and encourages "deep thought." Here, for example, is American cultural critic Andrew Solomon extolling the virtues of "pleasure reading" in the *New York Times* in 2004:

> Reading is not an active expression like writing, but it is not a passive experience either. It requires effort, concentration, attention. In exchange, it offers the stimulus to and the fruit of thought and feeling. . . . The metaphoric quality of writing—the fact that so much can be expressed through the rearrangement of 26 shapes on a piece of paper—is as exciting as the idea of a complete genetic code made up of four bases: man's work on a par with nature's. Discerning the patterns of those arrangements is the essence of civilization.[13]

This paean to pleasure reading appeared in response to a 2004 National Endowment for the Arts survey, which found "reading for pleasure" was declining across all demographic groups in the US. Solomon and other critics, most notably Mark Bauerlein, attribute the drop in reading rates to an increase in screen time. They depict screen entertainments, not just as alternative forms of amusement, but as enemies who are actively waging a war on literate culture. "Television does not extend or amplify literate culture," Postman argued in his famous anti-television diatribe, *Amusing Ourselves to Death* (1985), "It attacks it." He presents TV as a cultural vortex that sucks in all manner of public discourse—from politics to religion—and transmutes it into entertainment. The bias of TV, according to Postman, is an image bias that decontextualizes, trivializes, and degrades every subject it comes in contact with. Unlike books, which promote contemplation and deep thinking, TV skims the surface of life, offering only those stories with the best visuals, the most drama, the warmest human-interest angle. It also offers them in rapid succession, without exposition or context, which, according to Postman, makes it difficult for audiences to forge meaningful connections between events. As a result of all this, "Americans may be the best entertained and . . . least well-informed people in the Western world."[14]

For Postman (and others), this proclivity for amusements has reached crisis proportions. Nothing less than the soul of the nation is at stake: "When a population becomes distracted by trivia, when cultural life is redefined as a perpetual round of entertainments, when serious public conversation becomes a form of baby-talk, when, in short, a people become an audience and their public business a vaudeville act, then a nation finds itself at risk; culture-death is a clear possibility."[15] Certainly, there is some truth to these claims. TV and other electronic media do promote distraction, and mass distraction does tend to lead to political quiescence. Moreover, TV's emphasis on good visuals and entertaining stories does make it difficult to speak about complex social issues that lack clear villains, victims, heroes, and resolutions.

Yet, as a logical argument about the impact of electronic media, Postman's analysis leaves a lot to be desired. For one thing, Postman is guilty of **technological determinism,** or the assumption that the tool determines its use. He attributes TV's penchant for entertainment to its technological preference for iconographic representation when he should probably be attributing it to the social and cultural protocols of commercialization that drive the TV *industry*. As many critics have pointed out, television can be made in a serious and sober fashion and has been so made in other nations. In the US, however, even the nightly news programs must make money, which has had a perverse effect on the type of news viewers have access to. Stories that lack good visuals, compelling characters, and clear resolutions get sidelined in favor of scandal-mongering, explosions, violence, and confrontational banter. The news becomes emptier not because it is graphically adorned (graphics can often be helpful), but because it must compete for viewer attention in a crowded media marketplace and so must be *over*-adorned. In this case, the protocols of commercial TV—not the affordances of the technology—explain its bias toward entertainment.

Another problem with Postman's argument is that he tends to position electronic media as the root of all our social ills. The binary structure of the argument carries an implicit value judgment: print is "good" and TV "bad." If we would just revert to a print-based culture, he implies, we would become an enlightened, rational, sober, "adult" society ready to solve all of our social problems. This flies in the face of both history and reason. There is nothing inherent to print-based media that guarantees an emphasis on seriousness. As we have seen, cultural authorities have been equally suspicious of writing and print culture at different times and for the same reasons (they diminish mental agility and become a distraction). In reality, most of these arguments had less to do with the form or content of print media than with on-going debates about whose cultural authority should count, who should be allowed to convert knowledge into power, and who should not.

This brings us to a third point: people have a variety of motives for embracing cultural forms, only some of which have to do with the joys of engaging the text. "Thumbing your nose at your betters" is often as good a reason as any for consuming "low" culture. Indeed, historian Neal Gabler makes a strong case that the embrace of mass culture in the US has been motivated as much by class warfare as by the desire for amusement. He reminds us that nineteenth-century workers were not the illiterate dullards reformers made them out to be. They read voraciously, listened to opera, loved Shakespeare (albeit in bowdlerized forms), and could sit for hours listening to political debates. "If they were fools," he concludes, "they were at least fairly knowledgeable ones." When they embraced "low" cultural forms, it was partially out of a desire to rebuff the elite social reformers who were constantly trying to curtail their appetites. Embracing low culture "would infuriate the aristocrats," and so it was embraced.[16] Similar arguments could be made about the subsequent skirmishes over film, comic books, television, rap music, and videogames in the United States, "American culture" abroad ("American" being equivalent to "trash"), and "overly entertaining" reality TV in China. (The Chinese government recently banned such programs for corrupting "socialist values" by promoting "money worship, hedonism, and extreme individualism"; in reality, the move is designed to reassert Communist Party control over the media industries).[17] Because Postman neglects to consider the social context of media consumption—how it fits into larger social debates—he risks over-stating the importance of popular media in intellectual life.

Finally, Postman and other mass culture critics mistakenly presume that amusement and seriousness are mortal enemies, that acting rationally requires foreswearing distraction. This is not only unrealistic, given the omnipresence of electronic technologies; it is counter-productive. As Kenneth Burke has shown, entertainments may enable serious thinking about moral, political, and social quandaries. Popular forms provide resources people can use to think through real-world dilemmas, thereby preparing them for the serious business of life. Moreover, popular forms sometimes use amusement as a Trojan Horse to sneak information through to viewers who may be alienated from conventional political and social channels of discourse. For example, satirical news programs like *The Daily Show* (Comedy Central, 1996–) and *The Colbert Report* (Comedy Central, 2005–2014) in the US, *The Late Edition* in the UK (BBC 4, 2005–2008), or *Al-Bernameg*/The Program (Capital Broadcast Center, 2011–2013) in Egypt often deliver very real information under the guise of "fake news." In fact, a 2004 study by the Annenberg Public Policy Center at the University of Pennsylvania showed that "viewers of late-night comedy programs, especially *The Daily Show with Jon Stewart* on Comedy Central, [were] more likely to know the issue positions and backgrounds of presidential candidates than people who [did] not watch late-night comedy." Political scientist Matthew Baum duplicated these results with questions about US foreign policy. In both cases, *Daily Show* viewers answered more questions correctly than both viewers of "serious" TV news programs *and* readers of newspapers.[18] Of course, this may mean *The Daily Show* attracts already knowledgeable viewers, but it may also be a sign that the show imparts information in a way that facilitates its absorption.

In addition to imparting information, most of these shows also promote **media literacy**, or the critical analysis of media texts, by regularly deconstructing the conventions of mainstream TV news programs. Unlike traditional news programs, "fake news" purveyors are unburdened by the need for objectivity and restraint, so they have "more freedom to comment on, and to counteract, the spin that . . . often accompanies news of the day."[19] For example, *The Colbert Report* caricatures pundit-driven news shows like *The O'Reilly Factor* (Fox News, 1996) in order to reveal the emptiness and self-absorption at the heart of such programs. Stephen Colbert shows how the punditry replace evidence-based reasoning with "truthiness," or the expression of gut-level beliefs that resist all appeals to facts, logic, or reason. His excessive performance shows just how corrosive such emotional appeals can be for deliberative democracy.

Likewise, John Stewart of *The Daily Show* repurposes clips from the nightly news programs and comments on them in such a way as to expose the mechanics of journalistic story-telling. During the Iraq War, for example, he mocked the use of red, white, and blue banners, theme songs and patriotic titles like "America At War" to package destruction as a feel-good spectacle of patriotic unity. He ridiculed Fox News for setting the opening salvo of the "Shock and Awe" campaign to a light jazz score and offering it to viewers as entertainment. And he had fake reporters provide fake news reports from "on location" in the studio. In one of these reports, "Senior War Correspondent" Stephen Colbert (who was then with *The Daily Show*) explained to Stewart that the media's role in wartime "should be the accurate and objective description of the hellacious ass-whomping we're handing the Iraqis." Such "reports" pushed the prevailing style of gung-ho journalism to its logical extreme in order to show how subjective and skewed the news had become in the US. *The Daily Show* not only provided important information about on-going combat operations, then, it provided daily lessons in how to view the "serious" news with a critical eye. While amusing, all of these programs are politically engaged and challenge viewers to become more self-aware and skeptical of their officials and journalists. In that sense, they may be said to work against, rather than for, the infantilization of the public.

In the end, the argument that we are "amusing ourselves to death" fails to convince because it is too absolute. There is no doubt that new media will bring change, but change is not inherently bad (just as tradition is not inherently good). The impact of any media change must be assessed in context. Moreover, new and old media are not necessarily opposed, and the emergence of new media will not necessarily drive old media from the cultural field. Oratory and oral performance persisted through the print revolution, and books and reading will persist through the electronic one. They may become residual cultural forms, rather than dominant ones, but our lives will continue to be shaped by their logics and lessons. There is no Gresham's Law of popular culture; it is not the case that "bad media" will inevitably drive "good media" from the cultural marketplace. It is still less true that "good" and "bad" are absolutes when it comes to cultural media. Different media have different strengths and weaknesses. Media ecology should be about assessing *both* qualities, not condemning the new out of deference to the old.

DO DIGITAL MEDIA MAKE US STUPID?

Closely aligned with these debates about amusement are arguments about the negative effects of media on our intellects. Socrates believed writing would harm people's memories, thereby undermining their ability to produce knowledge from facts. John Adams and other American critics feared print culture would promote "mobocracy," or rule by popularity. By drowning out official culture and promoting strident voices, like Tom Paine's, it would lead to "anything but the Age of Reason." Finally, television has long been blamed for stupefying those who consume it. In addition to Postman's concerns about entertainment crowding out serious thought, books like Marie Winn's *The Plug-In Drug* (1977) and Jerry Mander's *Four Arguments for the Elimination of Television* (1978) claim television produces "no cognition" among its viewers, who are likened to addicts and zombies. Indeed, Mander contends that television has a *negative* impact on cognitive functioning: "television shortens one's attention span, reduces interest in reading, promotes hyperactivity, impedes language development and reduces overall school performance."[20] That there is little empirical evidence to support such claims does not stop such critics from believing them fervently (which only proves that "truthiness" is unrelated to TV consumption).

These arguments about old media predict much of the discourse surrounding the development of the computer and the internet. People like Mark Bauerlein argue (a la Socrates) that the internet will deplete our stock of mental reference points, weakening our minds and making us less competent thinkers. More importantly, it will crowd out knowledge-building activities, like books, museums, and science shows, and leave us ill-prepared to evaluate the quality of the information that comes at us. If the trend continues, we will become a society of narcissistic idiots, knowing nothing but willing to believe anything we read on the internet.[21] Andrew Keen argues (a la John Adams) that the internet fosters a type of "digital Darwinism" where only "the loudest and most opinionated" survive. By undermining the cultural authority of experts and intellectuals, it will dilute public discourse and lead to rule by "the mob and the rumor mill."[22]

Most of these claims are easily dismissed as hysterical overreactions to the development of new media. They exhibit the same fear of change and hostility to competition as earlier indictments of new media. Other arguments about the impact of the new media on the shape of our thinking are . . . well . . . more thoughtful. Nicholas Carr, for example, is less concerned with the content or quality of the information conveyed over the internet than with the way its network structure may be altering our brains. He opens his article, "Is Google Making Us Stupid?" with an anecdote about his growing inability to concentrate:

> Over the past few years I've had an uncomfortable sense that someone, or something, has been tinkering with my brain, remapping the neural circuitry, reprogramming the memory. My mind isn't going—so far as I can tell—but it's changing. I'm not thinking the way I used to think. I can feel it most strongly when I'm reading. Immersing myself in a book or a lengthy article used to be easy. . . . Now my concentration often starts to drift after two or three pages. I get fidgety, lose the thread, begin looking for something else to do. I feel as if I'm always dragging my wayward brain back to the text. The deep reading that used to come naturally has become a struggle.

He suspects the internet may be to blame and sets out to determine if there is some truth to this suspicion. He turns to cognitive psychology and neuroscience for information about how the brain works, and how it might work differently under different stimuli. He adds to this a wealth of information about the historical and social contexts that have shaped our use of tools like print, electronic, and digital media. The result is a slightly more nuanced understanding of the way media influence our processes of cognition and shape our intellectual priorities.

While he personally believes that print culture promotes deeper thinking than electronic culture, he offers a rationale for this belief that goes beyond a simple nod to tradition. Namely, print is linear and hierarchical, and promotes analytical processing. When we read, we must make connections between what we know and what we think will come; we must speculate, test, and reflect on the accuracy of our guesses. In short, we must process information in a deliberate manner because it is doled out to us piecemeal. The time and concentration required to read something in print affords us the opportunity to move information from our short-term memory to our long-term memory, where it becomes available for later reference. The internet, by contrast, slices and dices our attention, distributing it among an array of hyperlinks, multimedia accompaniments, and interruptive companion apps like email and instant messaging. The plethora of distractions discourages contemplative thought by disrupting our concentration. We have neither the time nor the patience to focus and so we retain very little of what we read online. More importantly, we increasingly delegate the responsibility for building mental associations to our machines. We let Google, bloggers, online ratings systems, and recommendation algorithms determine the connections that matter to us because it is a convenient way to cut through the clutter.

Carr's question is simply this: "what if the cost of machines that think is people who don't?" If knowledge involves a process of selecting and synthesizing raw information into a new and productive whole, as philosophers tell us it does, then what happens to human intelligence when we let machines do the work of articulation for us? When we delegate our responsibility for making meaning to computer processors and digital networks, do we become less capable of building connections on our own? Will the networks of cells in our brains that help us think atrophy from lack of use? If they do, can they be revived through retraining (through the reading of a good book, perhaps)? Carr offers both scientific evidence and his own book, *The Shallows*, as testament to the possibilities of retraining. To compose his rather dense intellectual history of the man-machine interface, Carr temporarily disconnected from the internet and social media. The result was a revival of his capacity for concentration and contemplative thought. While he fears the lure of "the shallows" will eventually pull him back in, his experiment in disconnection raises a vital point: we do not use technologies in a social vacuum or in isolation from other technologies. The persistence of older media and habits of thoughts can act as a counter-weight to the new pressures, and digital literacy training can help people become smarter users of these tools. In other words, we can develop social protocols to counteract the biases of these new technologies. We can learn to use the tools without being used and abused by them.

So, digital media do not necessarily make us stupid, but is there any evidence that they may be making us smarter? In his book *Everything Bad Is Good for You* (2006), Steven Johnson contends that new media are upgrading the quality of mass culture and, in the process, enhancing our IQs. Digitalization has opened new channels of media distribution, thereby altering the calculus of cultural production in significant ways. Instead of catering to a mass audience using lowest common denominator programming, for example, television producers now court different niche audiences and count on DVRs, DVDs, and internet streaming services to catch viewers up if they get confused. The result is that "the culture is getting more intellectually demanding, not less."[23] Puzzle films like *Run Lola Run* (1998), *Being John Malkovich* (1999), or *Memento* (2000), turn passive spectators into active detectives of meaning, hunting among the narrative clues for the thread that will tie things together. Likewise, complex television narratives like *The Sopranos* (1999–2007), *24* (2001–2010) or *Lost* (2004–2010) require viewers to keep track of dozens of characters across multiple plotlines, all of which promotes what Johnson calls **social intelligence**. Many of these shows immerse viewers in confusing details and offer few clues to orient the audience, thereby encouraging viewers to dig into the texts and meet up online to share information. They go from being passive consumers of meaning to active producers of it. Even reality programs like *Survivor* (2000–), Johnson argues, are "smarter" in that they invite viewers to speculate about how to solve the problems that face the contestants.

Johnson views the rise of the internet as a boon to collective human intelligence, rather than a drain on it. Not only does it make a wealth of information newly available to the masses, it fosters "lean-forward" forms of collaboration and interactivity, which enhance social intelligence and problem-solving skills. It allows individuals to seek, find, edit, and publish information on subjects they care about and to meet like-minded souls with whom to discuss the experience. More than that, it trains users to become intellectually nimble because it is constantly being updated. Each time a new app is released, or Facebook updates its user interface, we must re-learn how to use the medium. The pace of change "forces users to probe and master new environments," thereby "exercising [the] cognitive muscles" associated with problem-solving.[24]

Johnson is particularly sanguine about the possibilities of videogames. He notes that videogames have become increasingly dense in narrative, lush in visuals, and open-ended in their architecture. It is possible to enter a game, like *Fallout 3,* and spend all of your time just exploring the world. The game environment is so comprehensive that literary critic Tom Bissell reports poking around in the most isolated corner of the Wasteland and finding graffiti spray-painted on a rock; in other words, narrative bits are littered throughout the game world, and it is entirely up to the player to find them and put them together. Gamers *must* use their own processors (i.e., brains) to get anything meaningful out the experience. And, if you choose to play the game, instead of just exploring the environment, you must run through a gauntlet of increasingly difficult problems, each of which must be solved before you can move on to the next level. Like novels, then, games immerse you in another world and ask you to speculate about what comes next; they require intense concentration and great commitment from their users; and they are all about delayed gratification. The difference is that passive consumption is not an option in video games. If you do not interact, if you choose to sit back and let the "authors" dictate the story, you will literally go nowhere.

Do the intellectual rewards of gaming parallel the intellectual rewards of reading, though? Do games make users better thinkers, or do they just promote better hand-eye coordination? There is some evidence that gaming and reading build different neural pathways, hence promote different skill sets. Readers are better at abstract, logical thought and retain more of the information they consume, but gamers are better at pattern recognition, visual and spatial analysis, and collaborative learning. They can assess and navigate their environments—including data-rich environments like the internet—more fluidly, avoiding potential dangers and identifying potential assets better than non-gamers. While traditionalists might say this is not a skill set that relates to intelligence, such a claim is only true if we use a stunted definition of intelligence as "book learning." Sociologist Mike Rose's observations of blue-collar workplaces have led him to expand the definition of intelligence to include precisely those skills honed by gaming. "Working smart" for people like waitresses, line workers, or police officers means learning to move efficiently and effectively through an obstacle-laden environment. It involves solving problems on the fly while coordinating your work with others. Thus, an expanded definition of intelligence—one that includes the cognitive demands of everyday life—would require us to recognize spatial analysis, pattern recognition, and social intelligence as valuable intellectual skills.[25]

Does this mean games are outfitting players only for blue-collar work? Not necessarily. According to educational researcher James Paul Gee, games promote precisely those critical thinking and problem-solving skills so highly valued by business leaders and intellectuals. They impart "critical learning" by "teaching kids to think of semiotic domains as design spaces that manipulate . . . us in certain ways and that we can manipulate in certain ways." They also promote reflective learning, which involves a process of acting, assessing our actions, and acting again until our goals are met. In other words, they make players "think like scientists" and intellectuals.[26] This may be why the hottest trend in the business literature is "gamification," or the transformation of work tasks into games.[27] What games do not do, of course, is impart trustworthy information about the world. They do not teach facts (unless they are relevant to the game) and will not lead gamers to be good test-takers, at least when the tests require rote recall of decontextualized information. Games have been shown to inspire information-seeking behaviors, however, and they do make gamers more willing to test ideas through application. As Gee might say, they teach people *how* to learn, not what to learn.

In sum, there is nothing inherent to digital media that suggests they will make us either dumber or smarter. Many forms of digital media are far more intellectually, socially, and emotionally challenging than traditional forms of literature and high culture; other forms may dilute our pool of intellectual resources and derail our efforts to make sense of the world. In the end, the way we engage with our cultural media may prove more decisive than the content or structure of any particular medium, text, or type of text. As literary scholar Gerald Graff puts it, "no necessary connection has ever been established between any text or subject and the educational depth and weight of the discussion it can generate. Real intellectuals turn any subject into grist for their mill through the thoughtful questions they bring to it, whereas a dullard will find a way to drain the interest out of even the richest subject." Graff himself recalls being alienated by schoolwork in his formative years but stimulated by sports fandom. He believes that reading and talking about sports with his buddies after school introduced him to the practices of logical argumentation he would eventually use to build his career. "Sports talk" taught him "how to make arguments, weigh different kinds of evidence, move between particular kinds of generalizations, summarize the views of others, and enter a conversation about ideas." It also enabled him to enter a "public culture of argumentation," which not only valued analytical modes of thought but made the information he possessed relevant, hence memorable. Despite being classified among our amusements, then, sports can promote "intellectualization by other means."[28] The digital media make both information and knowledge communities easier to access. By socializing the pursuit of knowledge, they invite more people to exercise their brains more regularly. This does not necessarily lead to a reinvigorated public sphere of democratic deliberation, however, and the next section takes up the question of whether digital media are ultimately good or bad for democracy.

ARE DIGITAL MEDIA BAD FOR DEMOCRACY?

Democratic societies use representative forms of government to give people a say and a stake in the organization of society. This means we elect officials to stand in for, or represent, us in the halls of power and expect them to be responsive to our needs and desires. In the US, the Bill of Rights guarantees a range of freedoms— namely, freedom of speech, assembly, and the press—which are believed to ensure open lines of communication between the people and their leaders. The people have the right to speak their minds and protest government actions, for example, and the press has the right to expose government malfeasance so that any problems may be identified and corrected. Many people argue that the internet and social media have revived the democratic public sphere by giving ordinary people the means to distribute their views more broadly and connect with like-minded individuals to achieve political goals. Others worry that the growth of digital media will undermine the efficacy of political communications, thereby weakening the basic principles of democracy (representation of, by, and for the people). How should we assess the impact of digital media on political life?

Supporters of the internet as a tool for democracy-building tout its ability to allow more and more people to engage with and contribute to public conversations about the shape of the social order. By expanding access to the public sphere, they claim, the internet will renew popular interest in and access to politics proper. It will empower people to express their views and organize to achieve their goals, thereby heralding a golden age of democratic participation. As proof, they point to online political organizations like MoveOn.org or Townhall.com, both of which offer a platform for partisans in the US (the first is progressive; the second is conservative) to gather information, exchange opinions, and organize in response to developments in the halls of Congress and the White House. Or they mention the role of blogs, Twitter, and Facebook in fomenting the 2012 Arab Spring uprisings. Whether or not activists used Twitter and Facebook to organize the street protests (and there is significant doubt about this), social media still allowed Egyptians, Tunisians, and others to construct and publicize a counter-narrative about life in an autocratic system. Blogs especially gave people a chance to challenge official media depictions of the social order. Finally, supporters point to groups like InvisibleChildren.com, whose "Kony2012" viral video campaign inspired millions of people to spread the word about atrocities in Uganda, especially those committed by Lord's Resistance Army head Joseph Kony. In just seventy-two hours of YouTube exposure, the video was viewed forty-three million times, and it was subsequently shared on Facebook over seven million times. As a result of the campaign, Invisible Children saw a marked increase in funding for its causes (though there is some doubt about what they are doing with that money), and the civil war in Uganda received an enormous, if temporary, boost in mainstream media exposure.

In addition to allowing more people to enter the field of political debate, optimists argue, the internet will make it harder for politicians and economic leaders to hide their misdeeds or ignore the popular will. As citizen journalists gain access to the means of publication, the halls of power will become newly transparent and susceptible to public scrutiny. Social leaders will have to become more responsive to popular concerns because those concerns will no longer be opaque. Supporters of this belief point to operations like Wikileaks, an online whistle-blowing site that has publicized a wealth of inside information about questionable US diplomatic, military, and surveillance practices. Or they tout smaller projects like Ushidi in Kenya, which has collected and mapped citizen reports of ethnic violence in the region as a means of shaming the government into confronting the problem. This argument treats online information sources as equivalent to journalistic institutions and proposes that they will extend the capacity of the people to monitor the government and other power brokers. At the heart of both arguments—the internet will expand political participation, and the internet will make it easier to watch the watchers—lies a belief in the capacity of digital tools to challenge the agenda-setting role of media institutions. As British scholar Stephen Coleman argues, the internet will be a politically progressive force merely because "it shifts control towards the receivers of messages and makes all representations of reality vulnerable to public challenge and disbelief."[29]

Not everyone agrees with this optimistic assessment, however. Skeptics counter that the internet produces a glut of information that dilutes the impact of any particular instance of political speech. According to this view, the fact that more and more people can make their voices heard actually diminishes the impact of any single voice, thereby making political debate nearly impossible to conduct. Instead of a debate, we get everyone talking at once about a range of different issues, and, under those conditions, it can be hard to identify, let alone listen and respond to, any particular argument. Moreover, the cacophony ensures that those with the loudest and most insistent voices will be the most likely to be heard. In that sense, little will change about democratic politics: the power brokers and squeaky wheels will still get all the attention. The only difference is that it will be harder to discern the size of a group from the volume of its communications; even small groups can make a very big noise on the internet.

This brings us to a second concern articulated by skeptics: the internet may actually increase political polarization by allowing like-minded individuals to congregate and to screen out alternative views. Legal scholar Cass Sunstein argues that the mass customization enabled by blogs, newsreaders, and the multichannel television environment allows individuals to selectively control their exposure to information and opinion. We can now create our own customized news feeds, magazines, and TV schedules, and we can use this power to insulate ourselves from other ideas and perspectives. Through a series of experiments, Sunstein has shown that such cocooning actually leads to increased political polarization, as like-minded individuals, unchallenged by alternative perspectives, push each other to increasingly more extreme positions. Rather than reinvigorating the democratic public sphere, then, the internet will promote increased dissension, as different social groups lose their shared reference points and begin to speak past, rather than to, each other.[30]

Finally, skeptics worry that the internet weakens the social ties necessary for true political organization. Rather than reinventing social activism, these critics argue, the internet and social media have allowed us to "[forget] what true activism is."[31] Activism of the sort that has a lasting effect is built on strong social ties. Sociologists who study the phenomenon have determined that what makes an activist stick with the cause over the long term is not his or her passion for the cause. It is the number of close friends and family members who share the same views or also join the cause. Strong relationships empower individuals to defy authority by providing physical and emotional support structures. Without such structures, activists quickly burn out or become bored with the tedious work of day-to-day organizing. Weak ties, of the sort promoted by social media, "seldom lead to high-risk activism." Moreover, activism that takes place via Twitter and Facebook has a low threshold for entry and low expectations for success. Kony2012, for example, required users to do little more than share the video, on the belief that mere exposure would lead to revolutionary change in Uganda. It didn't. Joseph Kony has yet to be apprehended and his rampaging gangs simply moved to other locales (Central African Republic and South Sudan, for example). The Kony2012 campaign has become something of a poster-child for **slacktivism,** or political posturing that does little more than earn the button-pushing slacktivist social approval. As cultural critic Malcolm Gladwell explains, "Facebook activism succeeds not by motivating people to make a real sacrifice but by motivating them to do the things that people do when they are not motivated enough to make a real sacrifice."[32] In that sense, it produces a fantasy of participation that is really a form of political passivity since it makes real activism harder to organize. In the end, internet activism may prevent, rather than encourage, political action.

Perhaps the best we can say is that networked communications, like other technological systems, can be both a boon to political life and a hindrance depending on who is using the tools and how. As Dennis Baron puts it, "these tools can foment revolution, but they can also be used to suppress dissent . . . for every revolutionary manifesto there's an equal and opposite volley of government propaganda. . . . And for every revolutionary Internet site there's a firewall, or in the case of Egypt [or Iran], a switch that shuts it all down."[33] Indeed, for all the celebration of the role of Twitter and Facebook in fueling the Arab Spring rebellions, few citizens in those locales had regular access to the internet or social media and, even those who did, found their access quickly cut off by their governments. What sustained the movements over the long term was good, old-fashioned labor. Young people, in particular, did the hard work of consciousness-raising and organizing necessary to get a critical mass of people into the streets. Far from demonstrating the political efficacy of social media, the Arab Spring seems to have confirmed the lasting importance of old-school methods of political mobilization and confrontation (namely, the grapevine and shoe leather).

In her book *Entertaining the Citizen* (2004), media scholar Liesbet van Zoonen makes a compelling case for a more balanced treatment of the political potential of popular forms. She notes that interest in the realm of official politics—the institutions of government—has declined markedly since World War II, and trust in government is at an all-time low across both the US and Europe. People are simply disengaged from official political life. In such an environment, popular media may serve to impart information and drum up enthusiasm for the work of collective governance. "Politics," she argues, "has to be connected to the everyday culture of its citizens; otherwise it becomes an alien sphere, occupied by strangers no one cares and bothers about." Whatever else popular media do, they do provoke emotion and articulate it to certain causes. By personalizing and dramatizing complex social issues, popular cultural forms "offer a way into politics for people otherwise excluded or bored."[34] And, as John Fiske maintains, popular cultural activity of this low-level sort can "fertilize the growth" of political consciousness, thereby preparing individuals to assume the burdens of activism later on.[35] At any rate, we cannot wish these media away, and they do bring with them some positive affordances—they promote the formation of networks that are resilient and adaptable, for example. Whether this will, as Gladwell claims, "[merely make] the existing social order more efficient," or, as media scholar Clay Shirky argues, make it possible for people to create new ways of ordering society, will depend on how we put these technologies to use.[36]

CONCLUSION

What ties all of these debates together is the basic argument of this book: that popular culture is a terrain of social struggle. Whether amusement is good or bad for us, whether we will become dumber or smarter as a result of a changing media landscape, what form democracy will take under these pressures—these are all examples of how we use the terrain of popular culture to work through problems in our political and social lives. Looked at historically, the cases show how the dominant beliefs, values, and assumptions of society are constructed and may be negotiated and adapted over time. Culture is not a closed body of meanings to be passed on, but an open process of negotiation through which societies test, confirm, adapt, or reject pre-existing social practices.

By focusing our attention on the structures of the media system, media ecology can provide insight into the biases of different technologies, but we should be cautious (as always) about assuming these biases will prevent the emergence of unexpected uses. Biologists know that mutations and variations are common features of all thriving ecosystems. Mutations ensure biodiversity, which, in turn, ensures an ecosystem will be able to resist unexpected threats. New and unanticipated uses of digital media will continue to be discovered, which will require us to shift our theories (or suspicions) accordingly. Meanwhile, just as biodiversity guarantees resilience in a natural ecosystem, the co-presence of multiple forms of mediation in our media ecosystem will help offset the danger posed by any singular media bias. What is bad is monoculture. If we *only* had access to digital delivery platforms or television or print or oral culture—and not all of these at once—then we might be in trouble as a society. In the end, we have to learn to recognize that change and difference are not inherently bad; different ways of doing things are just different, not necessarily deficient or dangerous. "Rather than taking the glass half-empty approach," as Karen Sternheimer suggests, "we might instead look to see what we gain from these changes and how they can [be made to] enhance" the future.[37] Media ecology is a first step in the process. It can help us identify the biases—good and bad—of different systems, but eventually we will need to *do things* to ensure that the positive elements of the new system outweigh the negative ones. We will have to struggle to achieve the vision of the future we want to see. Popular culture, I hope you are now convinced, can be a vehicle to help us to get there.

SUMMARY

- Debates about the impact of new media and cultural forms date back millennia and are "good to think" with because they require us to define, prioritize, and advocate for the values we prefer.

- Many of these debates are really debates about cultural authority—who should have the power to determine what counts as knowledge, intelligence, or taste.

- These debates tend to be staged from the perspective of media ecology, which presumes media have built-in biases that shape the ways we think, feel, and interact.

- Many critics of new media are guilty of both cultural pessimism and technological determinism. In the first case, they assume the effects of new media are all bad, and, in the second, they assume that tools determine their own uses.

- Cultural studies scholars argue that new media have both positive and negative effects, and all of these should be taken into account. They also assume that humans can mitigate the influence of tools using social protocols.

- Rather than assuming our tools will abuse us, we should work to maximize the advantages new tools bring while minimizing the disadvantages.

NOTES

1 Lev Grossman, "Time's Person of the Year: You," December 13, 2006, *Time Magazine*, http://www.time.com/time/magazine/article/0,9171,1569514,00.html (accessed May 31, 2011).

2 Quoted in Robert Mack and Brian Ott, *Critical Media Studies: An Introduction* (Malden, MA: Wiley-Blackwell, 2010), 266.

3 Nicholas Carr, *The Shallows: What the Internet Is Doing to Our Brains* (New York: W.W. Norton & Co., 2010), 17–19. The aphorism is from *Beyond Good and Evil,* which Nietzsche composed under the influence of the typewriter.

4 Ibid., 209.

5 Neil Postman, *Amusing Ourselves to Death: Public Discourse in the Age of Show Business,* 20th anniversary ed. (New York: Penguin Books, 2005), 76–81.

6 Mack and Ott, *Critical Media Studies,* 276.

7 Plato, "The Republic," 2009 [360 B.C.E], http://classics.mit.edu/Plato/republic.html (accessed February 28, 2014).

8 Plato, "Phaedrus," 2009 [360 B.C.E.], http://classics.mit.edu/Plato/phaedrus.html (accessed December 26, 2013).

9 Nicholas Carr, "Is Google Making Us Stupid?," July 1, 2008, *Atlantic,* http://www.theatlantic.com/magazine/archive/2008/07/is-google-making-us-stupid/306868/ (accessed December 1, 2013).

10 Cathy N. Davidson, *Revolution and the Word: The Rise of the Novel in America* (New York: Oxford University Press, 1986), 13, 14.

11 Cited in Davidson, *Revolution and the Word,* 47.

12 Nathaniel A. Rivers and Ryan P. Weber, *Equipment for Living: The Literary Reviews of Kenneth Burke* (Anderson, SC: Parlor Press, 2010).

13 Andrew Solomon, "The Closing of the American Book," July 10, 2004, *New York Times,* http://www.nytimes.com/2004/07/10/opinion/the-closing-of-the-american-book.html (accessed January 1, 2014).

14 Postman, *Amusing Ourselves to Death,* 89, 111.

15 Ibid., 154.

16 Neil Gabler, *Life, the Movie: How Entertainment Conquered Reality* (New York: Vintage Books, 1998), 29–39.

17 Christopher Bodeen, "China to Curb 'Overly Entertaining' Reality TV," October 27, 2011, http://www.huffingtonpost.com/2011/10/26/china-to-curb-overly-ente_n_1032219.html (accessed January 8, 2013).

18 "'Daily Show' Viewers Knowledgeable About Presidential Campaign," (University of Pennsylvania: Annenberg Center for Public Policy, 2004); Matthew Baum, *Soft News Goes to War: Public Opinion and American Foreign Policy in the New Media Age* (Princeton, NJ: Princeton University Press, 2003).

19 Jason Zinser, "The Good, the Bad and *the Daily Show,*" in *They Say, I Say with Readings,* eds. Gerald Graff, Cathy Birkenstein, and Russel Durst (New York: W.W. Norton & Co., 2012), 371.

20 Karen Sternheimer, *Connecting Social Problems and Popular Culture,* 2nd ed. (Boulder, CO: Westview Press, 2013), 75.

21 Mark Bauerlein, *The Dumbest Generation: How the Digital Age Stupefies Young Americans and Jeopardizes Our Future [or, Don't Trust Anyone under 30]* (New York: Penguin Group, 2008).

22 Andrew Keen, *The Cult of the Amateur: How Today's Internet Is Killing Our Culture* (New York: Doubleday, 2007), 15, 60, 186.

23 Steven Johnson, *Everything Bad Is Good for You: How Today's Popular Culture Is Actually Making Us Smarter* (New York: Penguin Group, 2006), 34.

24 Ibid., 110.

25 Mike Rose, "Blue-Collar Brilliance," in *They Say, I Say*

26 James Paul Gee, *What Video Games Have to Teach Us About Learning and Literacy* (New York: Palgrave MacMillan, 2007), 36, 216.

27 For a more critical take on what gamification means—namely, the inculcation of capitalist ideology—see David Golumbia, "Games without Play," *New Literary History* 40, 1 (2009), 179–204.

28 Gerald Graff, "Hidden Intellectualism," in *They Say, I Say*, 381, 383.

29 Stephen Coleman quoted in Mark Andrejevic, *Infoglut: How Too Much Information Is Changing the Way We Think and Know* (New York: Routledge, 2013), 10.

30 Cass Sunstein, *Going to Extremes: How Like Minds Unite and Divide* (New York: Oxford University Press, 2009).

31 Malcolm Gladwell, "Small Change: Why the Revolution Will Not Be Tweeted," in *They Say, I Say*, 317.

32 Ibid., 321.

33 Dennis Baron, "Reforming Egypt in 140 Characters?," in *They Say, I Say*, 331–332.

34 Liesbet Van Zoonen, *Entertaining the Citizen: When Politics and Popular Culture Converge* (Lanham, MD: Rowman & Littlefield Publishers, Inc, 2005), 3.

35 John Fiske, *Understanding Popular Culture* (New York: Routledge, 2011), 126.

36 Clay Shirky, *Cognitive Surplus: How Technology Makes Consumers into Collaborators* (New York: Penguin Books, 2011).

37 Sternheimer, *Connecting Social Problems and Popular Culture*, 95.

REFERENCES

Andrejevic, Mark. *Infoglut: How Too Much Information Is Changing the Way We Think and Know*. New York: Routledge, 2013.

Baron, Dennis. "Reforming Egypt in 140 Characters?" In *They Say, I Say, with Readings,* edited by Gerald Graff, Cathy Birkenstein, and Russel Durst, 329–334. New York: W.W. Norton & Co., 2012.

Bauerlein, Mark. *The Dumbest Generation: How the Digital Age Stupefies Young Americans and Jeopardizes Our Future [or, Don't Trust Anyone under 30]*. New York: Penguin Group, 2008.

Baum, Matthew. *Soft News Goes to War: Public Opinion and American Foreign Policy in the New Media Age*. Princeton, NJ: Princeton University Press, 2003.

Bodeen, Christopher. "China to Curb 'Overly Entertaining' Reality TV." October 27, 2011. http://www.huffingtonpost.com/2011/10/26/china-to-curb-overly-ente_n_1032219.html.

Carr, Nicholas. "Is Google Making Us Stupid?" July 1, 2008. *Atlantic*, http://www.theatlantic.com/magazine/archive/2008/07/is-google-making-us-stupid/306868/.

———. *The Shallows: What the Internet Is Doing to Our Brains*. New York: W.W. Norton & Co., 2010.

"'Daily Show' Viewers Knowledgeable About Presidential Campaign." University of Pennsylvania: Annenberg Center for Public Policy, 2004.

Davidson, Cathy N. *Revolution and the Word: The Rise of the Novel in America*. New York: Oxford University Press, 1986.

Fiske, John. *Understanding Popular Culture*. New York: Routledge, 2011.

Gabler, Neil. *Life, the Movie: How Entertainment Conquered Reality*. New York: Vintage Books, 1998.

Gee, James Paul. *What Video Games Have to Teach Us About Learning and Literacy*. New York: Palgrave MacMillan, 2007.

Gladwell, Malcolm. "Small Change: Why the Revolution Will Not Be Tweeted." In *They Say, I Say, with Readings,* edited by Gerald Graff, Cathy Birkenstein, and Russel Durst, 312–328. New York: W.W. Norton & Co., 2012.

Golumbia, David. "Games without Play," *New Literary History* 40, 1 (2009): 179–204.

Graff, Gerald. "Hidden Intellectualism." In *They Say, I Say, with Readings,* edited by Gerald Graff, Cathy Birkenstein, and Russel Durst, 380–387. New York: W.W. Norton & Co., 2012.

Grossman, Lev. "Time's Person of the Year: You." December 13, 2006. *Time Magazine*, http://www.time.com/time/magazine/article/0,9171,1569514,00.html.

Johnson, Steven. *Everything Bad Is Good for You: How Today's Popular Culture Is Actually Making Us Smarter*. New York: Penguin Group, 2006.

Keen, Andrew. *The Cult of the Amateur: How Today's Internet Is Killing Our Culture*. New York: Doubleday, 2007.

Mack, Robert, and Brian Ott. *Critical Media Studies: An Introduction*. Malden, MA: Wiley-Blackwell, 2010.

Plato. "Phaedrus." 2009 [360 B.C.E.]. http://classics.mit.edu/Plato/phaedrus.html.

———. "The Republic." 2009 [360 B.C.E]. http://classics.mit.edu/Plato/republic.html.

Postman, Neil. *Amusing Ourselves to Death: Public Discourse in the Age of Show Business*. 20th anniversary ed. New York: Penguin Books, 2005.

Rivers, Nathaniel A., and Ryan P. Weber. *Equipment for Living: The Literary Reviews of Kenneth Burke*. Anderson, SC: Parlor Press, 2010.

Rose, Mike "Blue-Collar Brilliance." In *They Say, I Say, with Readings*, edited by Gerald Graff, Cathy Birkenstein, and Russel Durst, 243–255. New York: W.W. Norton & Co., 2012.

Shirky, Clay. *Cognitive Surplus: How Technology Makes Consumers into Collaborators*. New York: Penguin Books, 2011.

Solomon, Andrew. "The Closing of the American Book." July 10, 2004. *New York Times*. http://www.nytimes.com/2004/07/10/opinion/the-closing-of-the-american-book.html.

Sternheimer, Karen. *Connecting Social Problems and Popular Culture*. 2nd ed. Boulder, CO: Westview Press, 2013.

Sunstein, Cass. *Going to Extremes: How Like Minds Unite and Divide*. New York: Oxford University Press, 2009.

Van Zoonen, Liesbet. *Entertaining the Citizen: When Politics and Popular Culture Converge*. Lanham, MD: Rowman & Littlefield Publishers, 2005.

Zinser, Jason. "The Good, the Bad and *the Daily Show*." In *They Say, I Say with Readings*, edited by Gerald Graff, Cathy Birkenstein, and Russel Durst, 363–379. New York: W.W. Norton & Co., 2012.

GLOSSARY

A

Affect: The bodily sensations, feelings, or moods triggered by cultural resources. To study affect is to ask what sensibilities govern relations in a particular text or context.

Affective economics: A strategy utilized by capitalist cultural industries to manage customer relations. The aim is to raise the profile of commercial brands by forging more emotional relationships with customers.

Agency: The power of individuals to choose what to believe or do and to evade, resist, or revise the options society makes available to them.

Agenda-setting: The capacity of media gatekeepers to determine what will be deemed important in society by making some issues more visible than others.

Antagonist: The hero's opponent in a story; often called the villain.

Apparatus: The cluster of technologies and social regulations that govern the operation of a particular cultural medium. In film, this would include the camera, projector, and screen as well as the social protocols that dictate who controls these.

Appropriation: The adoption and adaptation of one group's symbols, artifacts, rituals, or technologies by members of another group. Often involves a subculture adopting elements of the dominant culture and putting them to new, cheeky uses.

Articulation: The notion that meanings are produced through a process of association. The term means both "to express" and "to connect," so the theory implies that what a thing means depends on how it is made to relate to other elements in a cultural system.

Astroturfing: The practice of using fake grassroots websites or pseudo-amateur media productions to promote commercial cultural goods.

Author-function: Associated with Michel Foucault, who suggests we treat the author less as a person and more like a discursive construct, or brand. How does the name of the author help organize the production, circulation, classification, and consumption of texts?

B

Base: The economic foundation of society. Karl Marx believed the economic base determined the content and form of the ideological, political, and legal systems in society, and these systems, in turn, helped legitimize the economic relations. See Superstructure.

C

Canon: In literary theory, the term refers to the "best" books as determined by cultural authorities; in fan practice, it refers to the "best" interpretations based on the source text.

Capitalism: A system of industrial production and exchange based on private property and the pursuit of profit. For Marxists, capitalism is an exploitative social order that divides society into classes and privileges the upper classes over the lower.

Carnival(esque): Carnival is an orchestrated form of transgression that temporarily upends the social order and allows people to blow off steam. Many forms of popular culture allow a similar form of transgression and so may be called "carnivalesque."

Class (or social class): One's socioeconomic status. It is one of the prime determinants of social stratification, or the hierarchical arrangement of groups in society.

Codes: In semiotic terms, a code is a set of rules for naming and classifying things. Different codes may be operative in different social contexts, but codes in general provide a shared interpretive framework that allows people to communicate effectively.

Commutation test: A semiotic exercise that helps one recognize the codes at work in a given representational system. It involves changing out different elements of a sign system (for example, swapping the gender of the hero) to see the assumptions embedded in the text.

Concentration: In economic terms, concentration refers to a situation in which just a few corporations dominate an industry.

Conglomerate: A combination of two or more businesses that do different things but that are folded under one corporate umbrella. For example, the Walt Disney Corporation owns film studios, cable channels, TV stations, publishing houses, and theme parks.

Copy-cat texts: A text that mimics the look and feel of an already successful text or franchise. It is one way cultural producers try to minimize the risks of creation.

Critical theory: An approach to cultural analysis, which views culture as a vehicle for the transmission of ideology and a tool for the reproduction of power relations. The aim (a la Max Horkheimer) is to "liberate human beings from the circumstances that enslave them" by exposing those circumstances to view.

Cross-promotion: The use of one product or service to sell another. For example, the use of a television program, like *Bones* ("The Gamer in the Grease"), to sell a movie, like *Avatar*.

Cultural authorization: The way prestige or legitimacy get attached to certain cultural practices and detached from others. We should ask which gatekeepers and institutions are responsible for assigning legitimacy to a cultural practice in a given context.

Cultural economy: A term coined by John Fiske to describe the circulation and exchange of meanings in a cultural system, as opposed to the exchange of money and goods.

Cultural forum: A term coined by Horace Newcomb and Paul Hirsch to designate a cultural space where social issues are presented and discussed from multiple perspectives. TV is one such space.

Cultural imperialism: The idea that more dominant countries may impose their cultural standards and goods on weaker ones, either wiping out the local culture or assimilating it.

Cultural industries: Those industries charged with making, distributing, and marketing cultural goods, like films, books, or recordings. As industries, they are driven to maximize profits, which affects the form, content, and availability of cultural resources in society.

Cultural studies: An interdisciplinary field of study that focuses on the production and circulation of cultural meanings and pleasures. It assumes that culture is produced by active agents located in specific contexts, and it attempts to delineate the forces that shape their interactions. It is often concerned with race, gender, class, and other power relations.

Culture: The social processes of meaning making and exchange. The cultural systems of a society provide its members with shared resources through which to understand the world and communicate with one another.

D

Diegesis: The world inside a fictional creation; the story-world.

Discourse: The way knowledge is socially constructed and selectively applied to authorize and reinforce power relations. Most commonly associated with Michel Foucault.

Dominant culture: The cultural perspective that is the most powerful, widespread, or influential in a given context. It constitutes the "norms" of the society.

Dominant reading: When the cultural codes of readers or spectators align with those of the author so that the reader takes the preferred message of the text. Generally speaking, the message also reinforces the dominant culture.

E

Elite culture: Culture produced by those with high social status and education. It is often intellectual and/or requires special knowledge or training to decipher.

Emergent (culture): Cultural forms or expressions that anticipate future social developments. They may coexist with and complicate the dominant culture by anticipating its transformation.

Emotion: Emotion refers to the ways we interpret affective states, how we name or voice our feelings. In cultural studies, emotions are assumed to be social, rather than individual. We are socialized to feel in a certain way, and our emotions forge or affirm social connections.

Excorporation: As opposed to incorporation, this term refers to the way people appropriate and use cultural commodities in new and unanticipated ways.

Exnomination: From the Latin, meaning "outside of naming," the term refers to the way a dominant group's perspective may be taken for granted in representation. It is so commonsensical that it goes unnamed. Associated with Roland Barthes.

F

False consciousness: One interpretation of how ideology affects individuals, namely, by lying to them about their real conditions. This view of ideology has been replaced by more sophisticated conceptions. See Ideology and Discourse.

Fan/Fandom: A fan is a person with a strong affinity for a particular cultural object, text, or idol. Fandom refers to the organized groups, subcultures, and practices that emerge from and exist to support the shared affinities of multiple fans.

Feudalism: A way of structuring society around the control of land and the exchange of labor for the use of it. The dominant economic system in the Middle Ages.

Folk culture: The way of life of a local community; emerges organically from within a particular community, rather than being imposed by the state or the cultural industries.

G

Gatekeeping: The power to determine which texts become part of the dominant culture and which do not. May be held by cultural institutions (like museums or media corporations), authorities (like agents), or intermediaries (like critics).

Genre: A system of stylistic and narrative conventions that helps people identify, classify, and interpret texts. As a regulated system, it allows for both predictability and novelty.

Globalization: The way money, goods, people, ideas, and images now flow across geographic and linguistic borders on a routine basis, making distant points seem psychologically near.

H

Hegemony: A term to describe how power works through persuasion and cooptation, rather than confrontation and subordination. Hegemony is achieved when powerful groups are able to make their particular assumptions into the "common sense" of a given society. Such power is unstable and may be regularly challenged, revised, and reaffirmed.

Horizontal integration: When a corporation buys up competing businesses within the same tier of the production chain or acquires holdings across multiple, related industries in the hope of creating mutually beneficial business relations across the holdings. See Synergy.

I

Identification: The process of investing in the social roles and relations available to us in the world or in the world of a text. It involves connecting imaginatively with another person or situation, whether real or fictional.

Identity: The investments individuals make, or refuse to make, in the particular subject positions available to them in a particular social context. Identity is not coherent or stable but subject to constant renegotiation as circumstances and expectations shift. See Subjectivity.

Identity tourism: The temporary trying on of "otherness" especially in the contexts of online play. In that the "tourist" carries social assumptions with him or her, identity tourism often reinforces stereotypes, rather than breaking them down.

Ideology: A socially conditioned way of looking at the world; the beliefs, values, and opinions of a particular group or class in society. In Marxist terms, ideology is imposed by the powerful in an attempt to legitimate their rule.

Ideology critique: An approach to popular culture that seeks to make visible the ideological assumptions embedded in a given work or practice. See Critical theory.

Incorporation: The way individuals get coopted into the reigning social order. It describes how potentially oppositional cultural activities get appropriated by cultural industries and repackaged as "mainstream" commodities or lifestyles.

Inoculation: Associated with Roland Barthes, it refers to the way a modicum of difference or rebellion may be tolerated in the short-term so that the system will be healthier in the long-term; i.e., a small dose of rebellion creates an immunity to revolt.

Intentional approach: An approach to textual analysis that looks to the author as the source of meaning. It assumes representations are the embodiment of the intentions of an author, creator, or speaker who can dictate the "proper" way to read the text.

Interactivity: A relationship between users and media that presupposes the transformation of the latter by the former. The increased ability of users to select, control, and shape their media experiences, either through redaction (editing) or immersive play.

Interpellation: A term coined by the Marxist theorist Louis Althusser to describe the process by which an individual is addressed, or hailed, by his/her cultural discourses and asked to assume a certain identity or subject position. See Ideology and Subjectivity.

Interpretive communities: Localized peer groups that shape the interpretation of a text or practice.

Intertextuality: The way texts incorporate other texts into themselves, either directly (through citation) or indirectly (through referencing and recombination). How texts borrow from a cultural stock of stories and knit these into a new whole.

J

Joint ventures: When two corporations work together either to share the risks and costs associated with production or to increase their control of a particular industry.

M

Mass culture: Culture produced, distributed, and consumed in large quantities. In critical theory, culture produced through such industrial and commercial means is presumed to be formulaic, repetitive, and stupefying.

Materialism: A philosophical orientation that sees the material relations of society as the basis of thought. Assumes different material systems produce different ways of thinking. Associated with Marxism.

McDonaldization: The way the logics associated with the fast food industry (its emphasis on efficiency, calculability, predictability, and control) are being implemented throughout the social. The result is to homogenize and sanitize social experience.

Media bias: A term used to explain how different media possess different characteristics and operate according to different principles. These technological biases produce different sensory balances, which cause us to think and act in different ways.

Media ecology: A term coined by Neil Postman to capture the way media work as environments in themselves and also shape our human environments. The focus is on the ways different media influence our social lives regardless of their messages.

Media literacy: A movement to correct some of the negative impacts of new media by teaching people to question the source, structure, and agenda behind media messages. Practitioners also advocate media training so users can create their own texts.

Micropolitics of everyday life: Small-scale power relations that operate in and through our day-to-day interactions, rather than in and through large-scale social institutions (like the government). How inequality and power work in everyday settings like the family, the workplace, and the classroom.

Moral economy: The informal or tacit rules of engagement that govern otherwise commercial relations; the moral values that ought to govern such exchanges.

Moral panic: A hysterical over-reaction by the public to an issue or group deemed to be a threat to mainstream society. Often fanned by exaggerated media accounts, a moral panic often results in the scapegoating of marginalized social groups (esp. youth and minorities).

N

Narrative: A story or sequence of events that leads from one relatively stable situation to another. Narrative may be fictional or non-fictional and can take many forms (written, recorded, or performed). See Story and Plot.

Negotiated reading: When readers or spectators decode a text in a mixed fashion, accepting some of the intended meanings (or encodings) but not others.

O

Oppositional reading: When readers or spectators bring different codes to bear on a text, decoding it in a way not intended by the encoders.

Othering: When an individual or group defines itself in opposition to another individual or group. Usually this involves projecting fears, biases, or undesirable traits onto the group one is not identified with.

P

Paratexts: Texts or discourses that circulate around and condition our interpretation of a primary text. May include similar texts by the author or in the genre, promotional materials, interviews, "making of" documentaries, gossip, fan production, and so on.

Phatic communication: Trivial or obvious exchanges of information designed primarily to establish contact between people. The contact matters more than the content.

Pleasure principle: A psychoanalytic concept that describes the human compulsion to seek pleasure and avoid pain.

Plot: The way the elements of a narrative are selected and arranged to produce a particular effect. Events usually unfold in a chronological sequence and according to a cause-effect logic, but alterations are possible and may affect the meanings we take. See Narrative and Story.

Political economy: A type of cultural analysis, derived from Marxism, which examines the organization of the systems of cultural production. The aim is to understand how capitalist relations condition political, social, and cultural life.

Polysemy (polysemous): Literally, "many meanings." Contradictions between code systems—the codes of the text, the society, and the reader—enable different interpretations of the text to emerge. Texts with many contradictions are more polysemous (open to more interpretations).

Popular arts: Cultural forms designed for a mass audience and accessible to ordinary people. They are usually simplistic in form and play to audience expectations and beliefs. Scholars who use this term (instead of mass culture) presume even formulaic texts are complex and require thought.

Popular culture: In cultural studies, popular culture refers to what people do with the resources provide by the cultural industries and institutions in their society; how they makes sense of and use those resources.

Post-modernity: A historical period after modernity marked by the centrality of consumption and the move from an industrial economy to a post-industrial, information economy with more flexible labor and market relations.

Pre-sold commodity: A text, genre, franchise, or star with a proven track record and a built-in audience base.

Producerly (texts): A text that is easily accessible yet susceptible to deconstruction and revision by interested readers. It has aspects of both the "readerly" and the "writerly" text in that it is undemanding but full of contradictions or gaps, which open it to interpretation.

Prosumer: A buzz word referring to the way audiences are now consumers *and* producers of culture, who create many of the works hosted by web platforms, like YouTube.

Protagonist: The main character of a narrative, or the character whose actions drive the story forward; commonly referred to as the hero.

Pseudo-individualization: Theodore Adorno's term to describe how mass-produced culture leads to the standardization of individuals. Cultural industries create texts that appear different but are really all the same, so the belief that we have different tastes or preferences is false.

R

Reading formation: An approach to analysis that emphasizes the social and cultural relations that have shaped the creation and interpretation of a text. Focuses on the ways personal interpretations are influenced by a variety of texts, intertexts, paratexts, and ideologies.

Realism: The attempt to represent subject matter truthfully or in an objective fashion. Since this involves processes of representation, however, the result is a coded construction of reality, not the thing itself. The codes of realism change over time and across media.

Reception theory: An approach to analysis that emphasizes the role of the reader, rather than the author or the text, in the creation of meaning. Also known as reader-response criticism.

Redaction: The process of editing. The practices associated with editing—the selection, arrangement, and enhancement of textual elements—are now broadly embraced as forms of creativity. See Remixing.

Relevance: The way popular texts relate to or reference real peoples, events, and ideas. Relevance makes texts usable and applicable to everyday life.

Re-make: A reproduction of a previously successful text or franchise designed to maximize the built-in audience for the new text. See Pre-sold commodity.

Remixing: The selection, editing and recombining of existing cultural forms to create a new text or a new interpretation of the old text. See Redaction.

Representation: A process of mediation, whereby the real is rendered in symbolic form. The processes by which meanings are produced and exchanged through shared sign systems, or texts.

Residual (culture): Cultural forms or expressions that carry past experiences or traditions into the present. They may coexist with and complicate the dominant culture.

Rhetoric: An approach to cultural analysis that examines the way language (including the figural languages of song, film, or art) move or persuade individuals.

S

Semiotics: The study of signs and processes of signification, or meaning-production.

Sequel: A commercial text that continues the story originally told in another such text. For example, *Spider-Man 2* (2004) is the sequel to *Spider-Man* (2002).

Sign/signifier/signified: A sign is a meaningful unit that consists of a signifier (a word, image, or sound) and a signified (the meaning or concept that becomes attached to the signifier). The relationship between the signifier and the signified is relatively unstable and fixed only through social convention.

Slacktivism: Online activism that is casual and requires little real commitment. It is often derided as political posturing.

Social economy: The way cultural technologies, goods and experiences create connections between people; it involves the exchange of social obligations, rather than the exchange of money (financial economy) or meanings (cultural economy).

Social intelligence: The capacity to negotiate complex social relationships and environments in an efficient and effective manner.

Spectacle/spectacular: A visually striking performance or show, often designed to distract attention from more substantive social matters.

Spin-off: A new cultural work derived from an existing text or franchise but which focuses on different characters or explores an element of the story more deeply.

Stars: Actors, performers, authors, directors, or producers who achieve name recognition and fan adoration. Their names may be used to promote new works and attract an audience.

Status: One's place in the social hierarchy, as defined by patterns of consumption or lifestyle choices.

Stereotype: An oversimplified representation of a social group, which serves as a form of shorthand for filmmakers and other creators, but which may produce a negative impression of the group so caricatured. See Othering.

Story: In narrative theory, the story is distinguished from the plot in that it includes everything that happened over the duration of the action. See Narrative and Plot.

Strong ties: Sociological term to describe relationships that are cemented through face-to-face relations of intimacy and trust. Such ties are stronger because they are longer-lasting and built on reciprocity, but their reach is limited. See Weak ties.

Structure of feeling: Raymond Williams coined this phrase to describe the lived experience of a certain social order. The term implies that feelings are socially constructed and that different societies evoke different mixtures of emotions or moods.

Structuring absence: The way a text systematically excludes certain kinds of representations without ever drawing attention to the absence.

Subculture: A marginalized or minoritized group within the larger society that has distinctive cultural practices of its own. Often defined in opposition to mainstream society.

Subjectivity: The subject positions available in a particular social order. These positions are created by the discourses, norms, and values of society and are always limited in range. Individuals are pressured to take up these positions, but they do have some power to resist. See Identity and Agency.

Superstructure: The political, legal, educational, and cultural institutions that shape social consciousness. According to Marxist theory, the superstructure is determined by the economic base of society and helps legitimize existing economic relations.

Symbolic annihilation: The absence or underrepresentation of a group of people in the media. By not representing the group, the media help reinforce social inequality.

Synergy: A way of generating multiple revenue streams at once by selling ancillary merchandise (e.g., novels, soundtracks, videogames, etc.) alongside the primary commodity (e.g., a film or TV show).

T

Taste: A preference for a particular type or style of cultural practice. This preference is socially constructed and positions one within a social hierarchy.

Technological determinism: The assumption that a tool or technology determines its uses and shapes the social structure of society (rather than the other way around).

Themes: The concept or topic that organizes a particular narrative. What we think the work is about and what we think it says about this subject.

Transculturation: A process of cultural appropriation that involves mixing cultural elements into a new whole. Anthropologists insist most cases of cultural contact result in such hybridization, not in domination or homogenization.

Trolling: Often described as combative rhetoric, this is a type of speech on the internet that is designed to offend, provoke, or otherwise derail communication.

V

Vernacular (creativity): Localized idioms, customs, or practices of a people; often used to refer to folk culture. In cultural studies, it refers to practices of creativity enacted on a regular basis by ordinary people (e.g., photography or scrap-booking).

Vertical integration: A corporate strategy to increase one's control in an industry by owning subsidiary operations up and down the value chain. In cultural industries, this entails owning production, distribution, *and* exhibition or retail outlets.

W

Weak ties: Sociological term to describe relationships that are not cemented through face-to-face relations of intimacy and trust. Virtual ties are weaker because they are more contingent, but powerful because they are more flexible and dispersed; they can help connect people across social groups. See Strong ties.

INDEX